MODERN AMERICAN & MODERN BRITISH POETRY

MODERN AMERICAN
&
MODERN BRITISH
Poetry

REVISED, SHORTER EDITION

Edited by Louis Untermeyer

IN CONSULTATION WITH

KARL SHAPIRO AND RICHARD WILBUR

HARCOURT, BRACE & WORLD, INC.
NEW YORK BURLINGAME

Printed in the United States of America

LIST OF COPYRIGHTS

Dial Press—for the selections from *Observations* by Marianne Moore, copyright, 1924 by Dial Press, Inc. For the selections from *Love Poems* by George Barker, copyright 1947, by George Barker and reprinted by permission of Dial Press, Inc. For the selections from *The Espalier* by Sylvia Townsend Warner.

Dodd, Mead & Company—for "Nuns at Eve," reprinted by permission of Dodd, Mead & Company from *The Sorrows of Cold Stone* by John Malcolm Brinnin, copyright 1951 by John Malcolm Brinnin.

Doubleday & Company, Inc.—for "Ajanta," from *Beast in View* by Muriel Rukeyser, copyright 1944 by Muriel Rukeyser. For "My Papa's Waltz," "The Shape of Fire," from *The Lost Son and Other Poems,* by Theodore Roethke; "Elegy for Jane" from *The Waking: Poems 1933-1953,* by Theodore Roethke, copyright 1950 by Theodore Roethke; "Frau Bauman, Frau Schmidt, and Frau Schwartze" from *The Waking: Poems 1933-1953,* by Theodore Roethke, originally published in *The New Yorker*—all of which are reprinted by permission of Doubleday & Company, Inc.

Duckworth & Co.—for the selections from *Bucolic Comedies,* copyright 1923, by Edith Sitwell, and *Troy Park,* copyright 1925, by Edith Sitwell.

Farrar & Rinehart, Inc.—for the selections from *Public Speech* by Archibald MacLeish, copyright 1936. For the selections from *A Draft of XXX Cantos* by Ezra Pound, copyright 1931.

Farrar, Straus & Young, Inc.—for "Invocation of Death," from *The Year One* by Kathleen Raine.

Four Seas Company—for the selections from *The Charnel Rose* by Conrad Aiken, *The Jig of Forslin* by Conrad Aiken, and *The House of Dust* by Conrad Aiken. For the selections from *Sour Grapes* by William Carlos Williams.

Funk & Wagnalls Company—for selections from *Poems: A Selection* by Léonie Adams, copyright, 1954, by Léonie Adams.

Harcourt, Brace and Company, Inc.—for the selections from *Land of the Free* by Archibald MacLeish, copyright 1938; *Smoke and Steel,* copyright 1920, by Carl Sandburg; *Slabs of the Sunburnt West* by Carl Sandburg, copyright, 1922; *Good Morning, America* by Carl Sandburg, copyright, 1928; *The People, Yes* by Carl Sandburg, copyright, 1936; *Person, Place and Thing,* copyright, 1942, by Karl Jay Shapiro; *V-Letter and Other Poems,* copyright, 1944, by Karl Shapiro; *Losses* by Randall Jarrell, copyright, 1948, by Harcourt, Brace and Company, Inc.; *Blood for a Stranger* by Randall Jarrell, copyright, 1942, by Harcourt, Brace and Company, Inc.; *Lord Weary's Castle,* copyright, 1944, 1946, by Robert Lowell; *Collected Poems 1909-1935* by T. S. Eliot, copyright, 1936, by Harcourt, Brace and Company, Inc., *Four Quartets* by T. S. Eliot, copyright, 1943, by T. S. Eliot; *Awake! and Other Wartime Poems,* copyright 1942, by W. R. Rodgers; *The Beautiful Changes and Other Poems,* copyright, 1947, by Richard Wilbur; *Ceremony and Other Poems,* copyright, 1950, by Richard Wilbur; *Collected Poems,* copyright, 1935, 1940, 1949, by William Empson; *A Map of Verona and Other Poems,* copyright, 1947, by Henry Reed—all of these poems reprinted by permission of Harcourt, Brace and Company, Inc.

Harper's Magazine—for "Under Which Lyre" by W. H. Auden.

Harvard Advocate—for "Asides on the Oboe" by Wallace Stevens.

Henry Holt and Company, Inc.—for the selections from *A Boy's Will* (copyright 1915) by Robert Frost; *North of Boston* (copyright 1915) by Robert Frost; *Mountain Interval* (copyright 1916) by Robert Frost; *New Hampshire* (copyright 1923) by Robert Frost; *West-running Brook* (copyright 1928) by Robert Frost; *A Further Range* (copyright 1936) by Robert Frost; *A Witness Tree* (copyright 1942) by Robert Frost; *Steeple Bush* (copyright 1947) by Robert Frost; *The Complete Poems of Robert Frost,* copyright, 1930, 1947, 1949, by Henry Holt and Company, Inc., copyright, 1936, by Robert Frost. All of these poems are copyright by Henry Holt and Company, Inc., and reprinted by their permission. For the selections from *Chicago Poems* (copyright 1916) by Carl Sandburg, and *Cornhuskers* (copyright 1918) by Carl Sandburg, and reprinted by permission. For the selections from *Peacock Pie,* copyright 1914, *The Listeners,* copyright 1916, *The Veil,* copyright 1922, and *Collected Poems,* copyright 1941, by Walter De la Mare. For selections from *A Shropshire Lad* and *Last Poems* by A. E. Housman; *The Collected Poems of A. E. Housman,* copyright, 1922, 1940, by Henry Holt and Company, Inc., copyright, 1950, by Barclays Bank Ltd. For selections from *Poems,* copyright 1917, by Edward Thomas. Reprinted by permission of Henry Holt and Company.

Houghton Mifflin Company—for the selections from *Streets in the Moon* (copyright 1926) by Archibald MacLeish, *New Found Land* (copyright 1930) by Archibald MacLeish, *Poems: 1924-1933* (copyright 1933) by Archibald MacLeish, *Collected Poems 1917-1952* (copyright 1952) by Archibald MacLeish. For the selections from *North & South* (copyright 1946) by Elizabeth Bishop, and from *Poems* by Elizabeth Bishop—all of which are used by permission of and arrangement with Houghton Mifflin Company, the authorized publisher.

ALFRED A. KNOPF, INC.—for the selections from *Punch: The Immortal Liar* (copyright 1921) by Conrad Aiken; *Lustra* (copyright 1917) by Ezra Pound; *Chills and Fever* (copyright 1924) by John Crowe Ransom, *Two Gentlemen in Bonds* (copyright 1927) by John Crowe Ransom, for "Winter Remembered," copyright 1924, 1945 by Alfred A. Knopf, Inc. and "The Equilibrists," copyright 1927, 1945 by Alfred A. Knopf, Inc., from *Selected Poems* by John Crowe Ransom; *Harmonium* (copyright 1923) by Wallace Stevens, *Parts of a World* (copyright 1942) by Wallace Stevens, *Transport to Summer* (copyright 1942, 1947) by Wallace Stevens, from *The Collected Poems of Wallace Stevens,* "Men Made Out of Words" and "Flyer's Fall," (copyright 1947, 1954) by Wallace Stevens, "Le Monocle de Mon Oncle" (copyright 1923, 1931, 1954) by Wallace Stevens, "The World as Meditation" (copyright 1952, 1954) by Wallace Stevens. For selections from *Nets to Catch the Wind* (copyright 1921) by Elinor Wylie; *Black Armour* (copyright 1923) by Elinor Wylie; *Trivial Breath* (copyright 1928) by Elinor Wylie; *Angels and Earthly Creatures* (copyright 1929) by Elinor Wylie; and *Collected Poems of Elinor Wylie* (copyright 1932). "Transfigured Bird," reprinted from *First Poems* by James Merrill, copyright 1949, 1950 by James Merrill. For "Views of the Favorite Colleges," reprinted from *No Arch, No Triumph* by John Malcolm Brinnin, copyright 1945 by Alfred A. Knopf, Inc. For the selections from *Fairies and Fusiliers* by Robert Graves; *Rustic Elegies* by Edith Sitwell, and *The Sleeping Beauty* by Edith Sitwell—all of which are reprinted by permission of and by special arrangement with the publishers.

LITTLE, BROWN & COMPANY—for the selections from *The Poems of Emily Dickinson: Centenary Edition* (copyright 1930) edited by Martha Dickinson Bianchi and Alfred Leete Hampson; *Unpublished Poems of Emily Dickinson* (copyright 1935) edited by Martha Dickinson Bianchi and Alfred Leete Hampson. Reprinted by permission of the publishers.

THE LIVERIGHT CORPORATION—for the selections from *White Buildings* by Hart Crane, copyright 1926 by Boni & Liveright, Inc., and *Collected Poems of Hart Crane,* copyright 1933 by Liveright, Inc. For selections from *Personae* by Ezra Pound, copyright 1926.

THE MACMILLAN COMPANY—for the selections from *Collected Poems* (copyright 1913, 1923) by Vachel Lindsay. For selections from *The Man Against the Sky* (copyright 1916) by Edwin Arlington Robinson; *Collected Poems of Edwin Arlington Robinson* (copyright 1896, 1934 by Edwin Arlington Robinson; copyright 1921, 1935, 1937, and 1944 by The Macmillan Company. *Dionysus in Doubt* (copyright 1925) by Edwin Arlington Robinson. For selections from *Selected Poems* (copyright 1935) by Marianne Moore; *What Are Years* (copyright 1941) by Marianne Moore; *Nevertheless* (copyright 1944) and *Collected Poems* (copyright 1944) by Marianne Moore; *Collected Poems* by Thomas Hardy (copyright 1925 by The Macmillan Company); *The Dynasts* (copyright 1931 by The Macmillan Company); *Poems* by Ralph Hodgson; *Good Friday and Other Poems,* copyright 1916, and *Salt-Water Ballads* by John Masefield; the passage (in this volume entitled "Rounding the Horn") from "Dauber" and two poems from *The Story of a Round-House,* copyright 1913; and *Collected Poems,* copyright 1918, 1925, by John Masefield; *Saturday Market* by Charlotte Mew; *Collected Poems* by James Stephens, copyright 1926; *Poems* by William Butler Yeats, *Later Poems,* copyright 1924, by William Butler Yeats, *The Tower,* copyright 1928, by William Butler Yeats, *Collected Poems,* copyright 1932, 1933, by William Butler Yeats, *Last Poems,* copyright 1940 by Georgina Yeats; *Collected Plays,* copyright 1934 by The Macmillan Company. All of these reprinted by permission of The Macmillan Company.

MACMILLAN AND CO., LIMITED (London)—for the selections from *Collected Poems* by Thomas Hardy and *Late Lyrics and Earlier* by Thomas Hardy.

ROBERT M. MCBRIDE & COMPANY—for the selections from *Those Not Elect* (copyright 1925) by Léonie Adams.

MINTON, BALCH AND COMPANY—for the selections from *Mr. Pope and Other Poems* (copyright 1928) by Allen Tate.

JOHN MURRAY—for the selections from *Poetical Works* by Robert Bridges.

NEW DIRECTIONS—for selections from *In Dreams Begin Responsibilities* by Delmore Schwartz; *The Complete Collected Poems: 1906-1938* of William Carlos Williams; *The Broken Span* by William Carlos Williams; *The Poems of Ezra Pound; The World I Breathe,* copyright 1939, by Dylan Thomas, and *New Poems,* copyright 1943, by Dylan Thomas; *New Directions in Prose and Poetry: 1940; The New British Poets,* edited by Kenneth Rexroth; and *Sacred and Secular Elegies,* copyright 1943, by George Barker; for the selections from *Poems* by Wilfred Owen. Reprinted by permission of New Directions.

THE NEW YORKER—"Little Exercise," by Elizabeth Bishop, copyright 1946 The F-R Pub. Corp.; "The Prodigal," by Elizabeth Bishop, "After the Last Bulletins," and "A Black November Turkey," by Richard Wilbur, copyright 1951, 1953 by The New Yorker Magazine, Inc.

OXFORD UNIVERSITY PRESS—for the selections from *The Poems of Gerard Manley Hopkins,* copyright 1918, 1930. Reprinted by permission of the Oxford University Press and the poet's family. For the selections from *Short Is the Time,* copyright 1940, 1943, by C. Day Lewis; "Proem to 'The Kid,'" from *Collected Poems* by Conrad Aiken, copyright 1953 by Conrad Aiken. Reprinted by permission of Oxford University Press, Inc. Selections from *Undercliff* by Richard Eberhart; *Selected Poems* by Richard Eberhart. Reprinted by permission of Oxford University Press, Inc.

The Poetry Bookshop (London)—for the selections from *The Farmer's Bride* and *The Rambling Sailor* by Charlotte Mew.

Random House—for the selections from *The Selected Poetry of Robinson Jeffers* (copyright 1927, 1928, 1938, by Robinson Jeffers; copyright 1933, 1935, 1937, by Random House, Inc.); *The Double Axe* (copyright 1948) by Robinson Jeffers. *Actfive* (copyright 1948) by Archibald MacLeish. *Poems,* copyright 1934, by W. H. Auden; *On This Island,* copyright 1937, by W. H. Auden, *Another Time,* copyright 1940, by W. H. Auden; *For the Time Being,* copyright 1944, by W. H. Auden; *The Collected Poetry of W. H. Auden,* copyright 1945; *Nones* by W. H. Auden, copyright 1951 by W. H. Auden. *Collected Poems,* copyright 1935, by C. Day Lewis; *Poems: 1935-1940,* copyright 1937, 1940, by Louis MacNeice, *Springboard,* copyright 1945, by Louis MacNeice; *Poems,* copyright 1934, by Stephen Spender; *The Still Centre,* copyright 1939, by Stephen Spender; *Ruins and Visions,* copyright 1942, by Stephen Spender; *Poems of Dedication,* copyright 1947, by Stephen Spender; *The Edge of Being,* copyright 1949 by Stephen Spender; *Person, Place and Thing* by Karl Shapiro, copyright 1940, 1941, by Karl Shapiro, *Trial of a Poet* by Karl Shapiro, copyright 1946 by Karl Shapiro, *Adam and Eve* by Karl Shapiro, copyright 1951 by Karl Shapiro; *The Desert Music* by William Carlos Williams, copyright 1949, 1953, by William Carlos Williams. Reprinted by permission of, and special arrangement with, Random House, Inc.

Routledge & Kegan Paul, Ltd.—for the selections from *Collected Poems* by Sidney Keyes. Published in the United States of America by Henry Holt and Company, Inc.

Muriel Rukeyser—for "Boy with His Hair Cut Short" from *U.S. 1,* published by The Viking Press.

St. Martin's Press, Inc.—for the selections from *A Soul for Sale* by Patrick Kavanagh, Macmillan & Co. Ltd., London, and St. Martin's Press, N. Y.

The Saturday Review of Literature—for "At Rest in the Blast" by Marianne Moore.

Charles Scribner's Sons—for the selections from *Selected Poems* (copyright 1918, 1929) by Conrad Aiken; *Preludes for Memnon* (copyright 1931) by Conrad Aiken; *The Children of the Night* (copyright 1897) and *The Town Down the River* (copyright 1910, by Charles Scribner's Sons, 1938 by Ruth Nivison) by Edwin Arlington Robinson; *Poems: 1928-1931* (copyright 1932) by Allen Tate. *The Toy Fair* by Howard Moss, copyright 1949, 1953, 1954, by Howard Moss—all of which are used by permission of and special arrangement with Charles Scribner's Sons.

The Vanguard Press—for the selections from *The Song of the Cold,* copyright 1948, by Edith Sitwell.

The Viking Press—for the selections from *Amores* by D. H. Lawrence, copyright 1916, by David Herbert Lawrence, 1944 by Frieda Lawrence; *New Poems* by D. H. Lawrence, copyright 1920 by B. W. Huebsch, Inc., 1948 by Frieda Lawrence; *Look! We Have Come Through!* by D. H. Lawrence; *The Espalier* by Sylvia Townsend Warner, and *Time Importuned* by Sylvia Townsend Warner. "Hymn to Priapus" and "Snake" from *Collected Poems of D. H. Lawrence,* copyright 1929 by Jonathan Cape & Harrison Smith, Inc.; "The Ship of Death," from *Last Poems* by D. H. Lawrence, copyright 1933 by Frieda Lawrence. Reprinted by permission of The Viking Press, Inc.

Ann Watkins, Inc.—for "Still Falls the Rain," from *Street Song,* copyright 1942, by Edith Sitwell; "Dirge for the New Sunrise," and "Song: 'Now that Fate is dead and gone'" from *The Song of the Cold,* copyright 1948, by Edith Sitwell.

A. P. Watt & Son—for the selections from *Collected Poems: 1941-1947* by Robert Graves. Reprinted by permission of Robert Graves.

The Yale University Press—for the selection from *Theory of Flight* by Muriel Rukeyser.

Three of the posthumous poems of Thomas Hardy are reprinted by permission of Mrs. Hardy and Mr. Sidney Cockerell, his executors. The poems by Charlotte Mew are reprinted with her consent and her executors'.

The Noonday Press—for "Medusa," "Women," "Decoration," "Statue and Birds," "Simple Autumnal," and "The Dream" by Louise Bogan, copyright 1954 by Louise Bogan. Reprinted by permission of The Noonday Press.

CONTENTS

MODERN BRITISH POETRY

FOREWORD

This Revised, Shorter Edition, undertaken by Louis Untermeyer in consultation with Karl Shapiro and Richard Wilbur, is the fruit of a thorough re-examination of American and English, as well as Irish, poetry during the period commencing with Emily Dickinson in America and Hardy in England and concluding with the young poets of the immediate present.

While the principle of Mr. Untermeyer's earlier collections was a catholic inclusiveness, he and his co-editors have striven in this edition to emphasize the major voices; thus the 133 poets of the Mid-Century (1950) Edition have been reduced to 63. This reduction, however painful and difficult of achievement, has resulted in decided advantages: Most conspicuously it has permitted an increased representation of the more significant poets within the confines of a far more compact volume.

In selecting poets and poems for this volume, the editor and his associates have sought to avoid any narrow criterion of modernity. The poetry of the twentieth century is unusually rich and, to many, bewilderingly diversified. The traditional note, the expression of intense personal feeling which makes a direct appeal to the emotions, is maintained and extended by Hopkins, Housman, and Frost—to name three divergent exemplars—yet there is no mistaking the new idiom and the contemporary tone. More characteristic of modern poetry is the substitution of sensibility for the senses. Such dominant poets as Eliot, Pound, and Dylan Thomas obtain their effects by indirect allusions, by highly suggestive ambiguities and abstractions. They frequently think in terms of myth, and their central characters are symbols. At times, facing a world pervaded by fear, they express what Auden calls the "intellectual disgrace," the disillusion and despair of their society.

But even from the prophets of anxiety there are affirmations—creative answers to the dehumanizing of life and the destruction of the spirit.

This edition preserves the diversity of its predecessors. It reveals the best of the conventions as well as advance-guard experiments; it has room for both Hodgson and Empson, for Robert Bridges as well as Robert Lowell. Nevertheless, it contains nothing which cannot be considered modern, nothing which the editors do not think relevant to contemporary sensibility. Every important development in recent verse is exemplified here, although the poems have been admitted on their own merits, not merely for their illustrative potentialities.

The anthology, moreover, has been brought sharply up to date by the addition of a dozen poets of the latest generation, each represented by enough poems to give an adequate exhibit of his qualities. Included also are several older poets not represented in previous editions—it is particularly pleasant to acknowledge the little-known Irish poets, Austin Clarke and Patrick Kavanagh.

Here, in short, is a rich recapitulation of the finest and, to a great extent, the latest work of 33 American and 30 British poets. The contents of the book are tied to no one school, movement, or tendency. On the contrary, they range widely in subject matter, treatment, and techniques. In their very kaleidoscopic changes, they reflect the complexity, inventiveness, and brilliance of twentieth-century poetry.

MODERN AMERICAN PO

Emily Dickinson

1830-1886

I Never Saw a Moor

I never saw a moor,
I never saw the sea;
Yet know I how the heather looks,
And what a wave must be.

I never spoke with God,
Nor visited in Heaven;
Yet certain am I of the spot
As if the chart were given.

Elysium Is as Far

Elysium is as far as to
The very nearest room,
If in that room a friend await
Felicity or doom.

What fortitude the soul contains,
That it can so endure
The accent of a coming foot,
The opening of a door.

I Never Lost as Much

I never lost as much but twice,
And that was in the sod;
Twice have I stood a beggar
Before the door of God!

Angels, twice descending,
Reimbursed my store.
Burglar, banker, father,
I am poor once more!

I Died for Beauty

I died for beauty, but was scarce
Adjusted in the tomb,
When one who died for truth was lain
In an adjoining room.

He questioned softly why I failed?
"For beauty," I replied.
"And I for truth,—the two are one;
We brethren are," he said.

And so, as kinsmen met a night,
We talked between the rooms,
Until the moss had reached our lips
And covered up our names.

I Like to See It Lap the Miles

I like to see it lap the miles,
And lick the valleys up,
And stop to feed itself at tanks;
And then, prodigious, step

Around a pile of mountains,
And, supercilious, peer
In shanties by the sides of roads;
And then a quarry pare

To fit its sides, and crawl between,
Complaining all the while
In horrid, hooting stanza;
Then chase itself down hill

And neigh like Boanerges;
Then, punctual as a star,
Stop—docile and omnipotent—
At its own stable door.

The Soul Selects

The soul selects her own society,
Then shuts the door;
On her divine majority
Obtrude no more.

Unmoved, she notes the chariots pausing
At her low gate;
Unmoved, an emperor is kneeling
Upon her mat.

I've known her from an ample nation
Choose one;
Then close the valves of her attention
Like stone.

My Life Closed Twice

My life closed twice before its close;
It yet remains to see
If Immortality unveil
A third event to me,

So huge, so hopeless to conceive,
As these that twice befell.
Parting is all we know of heaven,
And all we need of hell.

The Heart Asks Pleasure First

The heart asks pleasure first;
And then, excuse from pain;
And then, those little anodynes
That deaden suffering;

And then, to go to sleep;
And then, if it should be
The will of its Inquisitor,
The liberty to die.

I Cannot Live with You

I cannot live with you.
It would be life,
And life is over there
Behind the shelf

The sexton keeps the key to,
Putting up
Our life, his porcelain,
Like a cup

Discarded of the housewife,
Quaint or broken;
A newer Sèvres pleases,
Old ones crack.

I could not die with you,
For one must wait
To shut the other's gaze down,
You could not.

And I, could I stand by
And see you freeze,
Without my right of frost,
Death's privilege?

Nor could I rise with you,
Because your face
Would put out Jesus',
That new grace

Grow plain and foreign
On my homesick eye,
Except that you, than he
Shone closer by.

They'd judge us—how?
For you served Heaven, you know,
Or sought to;
I could not,

Because you saturated sight,
And I had no more eyes

For sordid excellence
As Paradise.

And were you lost, I would be,
Though my name
Rang loudest
On the heavenly fame.

And were you saved,
And I condemned to be
Where you were not,
That self were hell to me.

So we must keep apart,
You there, I here,
With just the door ajar
That oceans are,
And prayer,
And that pale sustenance,
Despair!

I Heard a Fly Buzz

I heard a fly buzz when I died;
The stillness round my form
Was like the stillness in the air
Between the heaves of storm.

The eyes beside had wrung them dry,
And breaths were gathering sure
For that last onset, when the king
Be witnessed in his power.

I willed my keepsakes, signed away
What portion of me I
Could make assignable,—and then
There interposed a fly,

With blue, uncertain, stumbling buzz,
Between the light and me;
And then the windows failed, and then
I could not see to see.

There's a Certain Slant of Light

There's a certain slant of light,
On winter afternoons,
That oppresses, like the weight
Of cathedral tunes.

Heavenly hurt it gives us;
We can find no scar,
But internal difference
Where the meanings are.

None may teach it anything,
'Tis the seal, despair,—
An imperial affliction
Sent us of the air.

When it comes, the landscape listens,
Shadows hold their breath;
When it goes, 'tis like the distance
On the look of death.

I Measure Every Grief I Meet

I measure every grief I meet
  With analytic eyes;
I wonder if it weighs like mine,
  Or has an easier size.

I wonder if they bore it long,
  Or did it just begin?
I could not tell the date of mine,
  It feels so old a pain.

I wonder if it hurts to live,
  And if they have to try,
And whether, could they choose between,
  They would not rather die.

I wonder if when years have piled—
  Some thousands—on the cause
Of early hurt, if such a lapse
  Could give them any pause;

Or would they go on aching still
  Through centuries above,
Enlightened to a larger pain
  By contrast with the love.

The grieved are many, I am told;
  The reason deeper lies,—
Death is but one and comes but once,
  And only nails the eyes.

There's grief of want, and grief of cold,—
  A sort they call "despair";
There's banishment from native eyes,
  In sight of native air.

And though I may not guess the kind
  Correctly, yet to me
A piercing comfort it affords
  In passing Calvary,

To note the fashions of the cross,
  Of those that stand alone,
Still fascinated to presume
  That some are like my own.

The Brain Is Wider than the Sky

The brain is wider than the sky,
  For, put them side by side,
The one the other will include
  With ease, and you beside.

The brain is deeper than the sea,
  For, hold them, blue to blue,
The one the other will absorb,
  As sponges, buckets do.

The brain is just the weight of God,
  For, lift them, pound for pound,
And they will differ, if they do,
  As syllable from sound.

After Great Pain a Formal Feeling Comes

After great pain a formal feeling comes—
The nerves sit ceremonious like tombs;
The stiff heart questions—was it He that bore?
And yesterday—or centuries before?

The feet mechanical go round
A wooden way,
Of ground or air of Ought,
Regardless grown;
A quartz contentment like a stone.

This is the hour of lead
Remembered if outlived
As freezing persons recollect
The snow—
First chill, then stupor, then
The letting go.

A Cemetery

This quiet Dust was Gentlemen and Ladies,
  And Lads and Girls;
Was laughter and ability and sighing,
  And frocks and curls.

This passive place a Summer's nimble mansion,
  Where Bloom and Bees
Fulfilled their Oriental Circuit,
  Then ceased like these.

Ample Make This Bed

Ample make this bed,
Make this bed with awe;
In it wait till judgment break
Excellent and fair.

Be its mattress straight,
Be its pillow round;

Let no sunrise' yellow noise
Interrupt this ground.

Go Not Too Near a House of Rose

Go not too near a house of rose,
The depredation of a breeze
Or inundation of a dew
Alarm its walls away;
Nor try to tie the butterfly;
Nor climb the bars of ecstasy.
In insecurity to lie
Is joy's insuring quality.

What Soft, Cherubic Creatures

What soft, cherubic creatures
These gentlewomen are!
One would as soon assault a plush
Or violate a star.

Such dimity convictions,
A horror so refined
Of freckled human nature,
Of Deity ashamed,–

It's such a common glory,
A fisherman's degree!
Redemption, brittle lady,
Be so ashamed of thee.

Because I Could Not Stop for Death

Because I could not stop for Death,
He kindly stopped for me;
The carriage held but just ourselves
And Immortality.

We slowly drove, he knew no haste,
And I had put away
My labor, and my leisure too,
For his civility.

We passed the school where children played,
Their lessons scarcely done;
We passed the fields of gazing grain,
We passed the setting sun.

We paused before a house that seemed
A swelling on the ground;
The roof was scarcely visible,
The cornice but a mound.

Since then 'tis centuries; but each
Feels shorter than the day
I first surmised the horses' heads
Were toward eternity.

The Mountains Grow Unnoticed

The mountains grow unnoticed,
Their purple figures rise
Without attempt, exhaustion,
Assistance or applause.

In their eternal faces
The sun with broad delight
Looks long—and last—and golden
For fellowship at night.

Success Is Counted Sweetest

Success is counted sweetest
By those who ne'er succeed.
To comprehend a nectar
Requires sorest need.

Not one of all the purple host
Who took the flag to-day
Can tell the definition,
So clear, of victory,

As he, defeated, dying,
On whose forbidden ear
The distant strains of triumph
Break, agonized and clear.

The Lonely House

I know some lonely houses off the road
A robber'd like the look of,—
Wooden barred,
And windows hanging low,
Inviting to
A portico,
Where two could creep:
One hand the tools,
The other peep
To make sure all's asleep.
Old-fashioned eyes,
Not easy to surprise!

How orderly the kitchen'd look by night,
With just a clock,—
But they could gag the tick,
And mice won't bark;
And so the walls don't tell,
None will.

A pair of spectacles ajar just stir-
An almanac's aware.
Was it the mat winked,
Or a nervous star?
The moon slides down the stair
To see who's there.

There's plunder,—where?
Tankard, or spoon,
Earring, or stone,
A watch, some ancient brooch
To match the grandmamma,
Staid sleeping there.

Day rattles, too,
Stealth's slow;
The sun has got as far
As the third sycamore.
Screams chanticleer,
"Who's there?"

And echoes, trains away,
Sneer—"Where?"
While the old couple, just astir,
Fancy the sunrise left the door ajar!

Pain Has an Element of Blank

Pain has an element of blank;
It cannot recollect
When it began, or if there were
A day when it was not.

It has no future but itself,
Its infinite realms contain
Its past, enlightened to perceive
New periods of pain.

Some Keep the Sabbath

Some keep the Sabbath going to church;
I keep it staying at home,
With a bobolink for a chorister,
And an orchard for a dome.

Some keep the Sabbath in surplice;
I just wear my wings,
And instead of tolling the bell for church,
Our little sexton sings.

God preaches,—a noted clergyman,—
And the sermon is never long;
So instead of getting to heaven at last,
I'm going all along!

The Bee

Like trains of cars on tracks of plush
I hear the level bee:
A jar across the flowers goes,
Their velvet masonry

Withstands until the sweet assault
Their chivalry consumes,
While he, victorious, tilts away
To vanquish other blooms.

His feet are shod with gauze,
His helmet is of gold;
His breast, a single onyx
With chrysoprase, inlaid.

His labor is a chant,
His idleness a tune;
Oh, for a bee's experience
Of clovers and of noon!

Hope Is the Thing with Feathers

Hope is the thing with feathers
That perches in the soul,
And sings the tune without the words,
And never stops at all,

And sweetest in the gale is heard;
And sore must be the storm
That could abash the little bird
That kept so many warm.

I've heard it in the chillest land,
And on the strangest sea;
Yet, never, in extremity,
It asked a crumb of me.

The Wind Tapped Like a Tired Man

The wind tapped like a tired man,
And like a host, "Come in,"
I boldly answered; entered then
My residence within

A rapid, footless guest,
To offer whom a chair
Were as impossible as hand
A sofa to the air.

No bone had he to bind him,
His speech was like the push
Of numerous humming-birds at once
From a superior bush.

His countenance a billow,
His fingers, if he pass,
Let go a music, as of tunes
Blown tremulous in glass.

He visited, still flitting,
Then, like a timid man,
Again he tapped—'twas flurriedly—
And I became alone.

There Came a Wind Like a Bugle

There came a wind like a bugle;
It quivered through the grass,
And a green chill upon the heat
So ominous did pass
We barred the windows and the doors
As from an emerald ghost;
The doom's electric moccasin
That very instant passed.
On a strange mob of panting trees,
And fences fled away,
And rivers where the houses ran
The living looked that day.
The bell within the steeple wild
The flying tidings whirled.
How much can come
And much can go,
And yet abide the world!

The Snake

A narrow fellow in the grass
Occasionally rides;
You may have met him,—did you not?
His notice sudden is.

The grass divides as with a comb,
A spotted shaft is seen;

And then it closes at your feet
And opens further on.

He likes a boggy acre,
A floor too cool for corn.
Yet when a child, and barefoot,
I more than once, at morn,

Have passed, I thought, a whip-lash
Unbraiding in the sun,—
When, stooping to secure it,
It wrinkled and was gone.

Several of nature's people
I know, and they know me;
I feel for them a transport
Of cordiality;

But never met this fellow,
Attended or alone,
Without a tighter breathing,
And zero at the bone.

No Rack Can Torture Me

No rack can torture me,
My soul's at liberty.
Behind this mortal bone
There knits a bolder one

You cannot prick with saw,
Nor rend with scymitar.
Two bodies therefore be;
Bind one, and one will flee.

The eagle of his nest
No easier divest
And gain the sky,
Than mayest thou,

Except thyself may be
Thine enemy.
Captivity is consciousness;
So's liberty.

If I Should Die

If I should die,
And you should live,
And time should gurgle on,
And morn should beam,
And noon should burn,
As it has usual done:
If birds should build as early,
And bees as bustling go,—
One might depart at option
From enterprise below!
'Tis sweet to know that stocks will stand
When we with daisies lie,
That commerce will continue,
And trades as briskly fly.
It makes the parting tranquil
And keeps the soul serene,
That gentlemen so sprightly
Conduct the pleasing scene!

Our Journey Had Advanced

Our journey had advanced;
Our feet were almost come
To that odd fork in Being's road,
Eternity by term.

Our pace took sudden awe,
Our feet reluctant led.
Before were cities, but between,
The forest of the dead.

Retreat was out of hope,—
Behind, a sealed route,
Eternity's white flag before,
And God at every gate.

Edwin Arlington Robinson

1869-1935

Miniver Cheevy

Miniver Cheevy, child of scorn,
Grew lean while he assailed the seasons;
He wept that he was ever born,
And he had reasons.

Miniver loved the days of old
When swords were bright and steeds were prancing;
The vision of a warrior bold
Would set him dancing.

Miniver sighed for what was not,
And dreamed, and rested from his labors;
He dreamed of Thebes and Camelot,
And Priam's neighbors.

Miniver mourned the ripe renown
That made so many a name so fragrant;
He mourned Romance, now on the town,
And Art, a vagrant.

Miniver loved the Medici,
Albeit he had never seen one;
He would have sinned incessantly
Could he have been one.

Miniver cursed the commonplace
And eyed a khaki suit with loathing;
He missed the medieval grace
Of iron clothing.

Miniver scorned the gold he sought,
  But sore annoyed was he without it;
Miniver thought, and thought, and thought,
  And thought about it.

Miniver Cheevy, born too late,
  Scratched his head and kept on thinking;
Miniver coughed, and called it fate,
  And kept on drinking.

Cliff Klingenhagen

Cliff Klingenhagen had me in to dine
With him one day; and after soup and meat,
And all the other things there were to eat,
Cliff took two glasses and filled one with wine
And one with wormwood. Then, without a sign
For me to choose at all, he took the draught
Of bitterness himself, and lightly quaffed
It off, and said the other one was mine.

And when I asked him what the deuce he meant
By doing that, he only looked at me
And grinned, and said it was a way of his.
And though I know the fellow, I have spent
Long time a-wondering when I shall be
As happy as Cliff Klingenhagen is.

Richard Cory

Whenever Richard Cory went down town,
  We people on the pavement looked at him:
He was a gentleman from sole to crown,
  Clean favored, and imperially slim.

And he was always quietly arrayed,
  And he was always human when he talked;
But still he fluttered pulses when he said,
  "Good-morning," and he glittered when he walked.

And he was rich—yes, richer than a king—
  And admirably schooled in every grace:

In fine, we thought that he was everything
  To make us wish that we were in his place.

So on we worked, and waited for the light,
  And went without the meat, and cursed the bread;
And Richard Cory, one calm summer night,
  Went home and put a bullet through his head.

Bewick Finzer

Time was when his half million drew
  The breath of six per cent;
But soon the worm of what-was-not
  Fed hard on his content;
And something crumbled in his brain
  When his half million went.

Time passed, and filled along with his
  The place of many more;
Time came, and hardly one of us
  Had credence to restore,
From what appeared one day, the man
  Whom we had known before.

The broken voice, the withered neck,
  The coat worn out with care,
The cleanliness of indigence,
  The brilliance of despair,
The fond imponderable dreams
  Of affluence,—all were there.

Poor Finzer, with his dreams and schemes,
  Fares hard now in the race,
With heart and eye that have a task
  When he looks in the face
Of one who might so easily
  Have been in Finzer's place.

He comes unfailing for the loan
  We give and then forget;
He comes, and probably for years
  Will he be coming yet,—
Familiar as an old mistake,
  And futile as regret.

Reuben Bright

Because he was a butcher and thereby
Did earn an honest living (and did right)
I would not have you think that Reuben Bright
Was any more a brute than you or I;
For when they told him that his wife must die,
He stared at them and shook with grief and fright,
And cried like a great baby half that night,
And made the women cry to see him cry.

And after she was dead, and he had paid
The singers and the sexton and the rest,
He packed a lot of things that she had made
Most mournfully away in an old chest
Of hers, and put some chopped-up cedar boughs
In with them, and tore down the slaughter-house.

For a Dead Lady

No more with overflowing light
Shall fill the eyes that now are faded,
Nor shall another's fringe with night
Their woman-hidden world as they did.
No more shall quiver down the days
The flowing wonder of her ways,
Whereof no language may requite
The shifting and the many-shaded.

The grace, divine, definitive,
Clings only as a faint forestalling;
The laugh that love could not forgive
Is hushed, and answers to no calling;
The forehead and the little ears
Have gone where Saturn keeps the years;
The breast where roses could not live
Has done with rising and with falling.

The beauty, shattered by the laws
That have creation in their keeping,
No longer trembles at applause,
Or over children that are sleeping;

And we who delve in beauty's lore
Know all that we have known before
Of what inexorable cause
Makes Time so vicious in his reaping.

The Master

(Lincoln. Supposed to have been written not long after the Civil War)

A flying word from here and there
Had sown the name at which we sneered,
But soon the name was everywhere,
To be reviled and then revered:
A presence to be loved and feared,
We cannot hide it, or deny
That we, the gentlemen who jeered,
May be forgotten by and by.

He came when days were perilous
And hearts of men were sore beguiled;
And having made his note of us,
He pondered and was reconciled.
Was ever master yet so mild
As he, and so untamable?
We doubted, even when he smiled,
Not knowing what he knew so well.

He knew that undeceiving fate
Would shame us whom he served unsought;
He knew that he must wince and wait—
The jest of those for whom he fought;
He knew devoutly what he thought
Of us and of our ridicule;
He knew that we must all be taught
Like little children in a school.

We gave a glamour to the task
That he encountered and saw through,
But little of us did he ask,
And little did we ever do.
And what appears if we review
The season when we railed and chaffed?
It is the face of one who knew
That we were learning while we laughed.

The face that in our vision feels
Again the venom that we flung,
Transfigured to the world reveals
The vigilance to which we clung.
Shrewd, hallowed, harassed, and among
The mysteries that are untold,
The face we see was never young,
Nor could it ever have been old.

For he, to whom we had applied
Our shopman's test of age and worth,
Was elemental when he died,
As he was ancient at his birth:
The saddest among kings of earth,
Bowed with a galling crown, this man
Met rancor with a cryptic mirth,
Laconic—and Olympian.

The love, the grandeur, and the fame
Are bounded by the world alone;
The calm, the smoldering, and the flame
Of awful patience were his own:
With him they are forever flown
Past all our fond self-shadowings,
Wherewith we cumber the Unknown
As with inept Icarian wings.

For we were not as other men:
'Twas ours to soar and his to see.
But we are coming down again,
And we shall come down pleasantly;
Nor shall we longer disagree
On what it is to be sublime,
But flourish in our perigee
And have one Titan at a time.

Mr. Flood's Party

Old Eben Flood, climbing alone one night
Over the hill between the town below
And the forsaken upland hermitage
That held as much as he should ever know
On earth again of home, paused warily.

The road was his with not a native near;
And Eben, having leisure, said aloud,
For no man else in Tilbury Town to hear:

"Well, Mr. Flood, we have the harvest moon
Again, and we may not have many more;
The bird is on the wing, the poet says,
And you and I have said it here before.
Drink to the bird." He raised up to the light
The jug that he had gone so far to fill,
And answered huskily: "Well, Mr. Flood,
Since you propose it, I believe I will."

Alone, as if enduring to the end
A valiant armor of scarred hopes outworn,
He stood there in the middle of the road
Like Roland's ghost winding a silent horn.
Below him, in the town among the trees,
Where friends of other days had honored him,
A phantom salutation of the dead
Rang thinly till old Eben's eyes were dim.

Then, as a mother lays her sleeping child
Down tenderly, fearing it may awake,
He set the jug down slowly at his feet
With trembling care, knowing that most things break;
And only when assured that on firm earth
It stood, as the uncertain lives of men
Assuredly did not, he paced away,
And with his hand extended paused again:

"Well, Mr. Flood, we have not met like this
In a long time; and many a change has come
To both of us, I fear, since last it was
We had a drop together. Welcome home!"
Convivially returning with himself,
Again he raised the jug up to the light;
And with an acquiescent quaver said:
"Well, Mr. Flood, if you insist, I might.

"Only a very little, Mr. Flood—
For auld lang syne. No more, sir; that will do."
So, for the time, apparently it did,
And Eben evidently thought so too;
For soon amid the silver loneliness

Of night he lifted up his voice and sang,
Secure, with only two moons listening,
Until the whole harmonious landscape rang—

"For auld lang syne." The weary throat gave out,
The last word wavered; and the song being done,
He raised again the jug regretfully
And shook his head, and was again alone.
There was not much that was ahead of him,
And there was nothing in the town below—
Where strangers would have shut the many doors
That many friends had opened long ago.

George Crabbe

Give him the darkest inch your shelf allows,
Hide him in lonely garrets, if you will,—
But his hard, human pulse is throbbing still
With the sure strength that fearless truth endows.
In spite of all fine science disavows,
Of his plain excellence and stubborn skill
There yet remains what fashion cannot kill,
Though years have thinned the laurel from his brows.

Whether or not we read him, we can feel
From time to time the vigor of his name
Against us like a finger for the shame
And emptiness of what our souls reveal
In books that are as altars where we kneel
To consecrate the flicker, not the flame.

Luke Havergal

Go to the western gate, Luke Havergal,
There where the vines cling crimson on the wall,
And in the twilight wait for what will come.
The leaves will whisper there of her, and some,
Like flying words, will strike you as they fall;
But go, and if you listen, she will call.
Go to the western gate, Luke Havergal—
Luke Havergal.

No, there is not a dawn in eastern skies
To rift the fiery night that's in your eyes;

But there, where western glooms are gathering,
The dark will end the dark, if anything:
God slays himself with every leaf that flies,
And hell is more than half of paradise.
No, there is not a dawn in eastern skies—
In eastern skies.

Out of a grave I come to tell you this,
Out of a grave I come to quench the kiss
That flames upon your forehead with a glow
That blinds you to the way that you must go.
Yes, there is yet one way to where she is,
Bitter, but one that faith may never miss.
Out of a grave I come to tell you this—
To tell you this.

There is the western gate, Luke Havergal,
There are the crimson leaves upon the wall.
Go, for the winds are tearing them away,—
Nor think to riddle the dead words they say,
Nor any more to feel them as they fall;
But go, and if you trust her she will call.
There is the western gate, Luke Havergal—
Luke Havergal.

John Gorham

"Tell me what you're doing over here, John Gorham,
Sighing hard and seeming to be sorry when you're not;
Make me laugh or let me go now, for long faces in the moonlight
Are a sign for me to say again a word that you forgot."—

"I'm over here to tell you what the moon already
May have said or maybe shouted ever since a year ago;
I'm over here to tell you what you are, Jane Wayland,
And to make you rather sorry, I should say, for being so."—

"Tell me what you're saying to me now, John Gorham,
Or you'll never see as much of me as ribbons any more;
I'll vanish in as many ways as I have toes and fingers,
And you'll not follow far for one where flocks have been before."—

"I'm sorry now you never saw the flocks, Jane Wayland,
But you're the one to make of them as many as you need.
And then about the vanishing: It's I who mean to vanish;
And when I'm here no longer you'll be done with me indeed."—

"That's a way to tell me what I am, John Gorham!
How am I to know myself until I make you smile?
Try to look as if the moon were making faces at you,
And a little more as if you meant to stay a little while."—

"You are what it is that over rose-blown gardens
Makes a pretty flutter for a season in the sun;
You are what it is that with a mouse, Jane Wayland,
Catches him and lets him go and eats him up for fun."—

"Sure I never took you for a mouse, John Gorham;
All you say is easy, but so far from being true,
That I wish you wouldn't ever be again the one to think so;
For it isn't cats and butterflies that I would be to you."—

"All your little animals are in one picture—
One I've had before me since a year ago tonight;
And the picture where they live will be of you, Jane Wayland,
Till you find a way to kill them or to keep them out of sight."—

"Won't you ever see me as I am, John Gorham,
Leaving out the foolishness and all I never meant?
Somewhere in me there's a woman, if you know the way to find her.
Will you like me any better if I prove it and repent?"—

"I doubt if I shall ever have the time, Jane Wayland;
And I dare say all this moonlight lying round us might as well
Fall for nothing on the shards of broken urns that are forgotten,
As on two that have no longer much of anything to tell."

How Annandale Went Out

"They called it Annandale—and I was there
To flourish, to find words, and to attend:
Liar, physician, hypocrite, and friend,
I watched him; and the sight was not so fair

As one or two that I have seen elsewhere:
An apparatus not for me to mend—
A wreck, with hell between him and the end,
Remained of Annandale; and I was there.

"I knew the ruin as I knew the man;
So put the two together, if you can,
Remembering the worst you know of me.
Now view yourself as I was, on the spot,
With a slight kind of engine. Do you see?
Like this . . . You wouldn't hang me? I thought not."

The Clerks

I did not think that I should find them there
When I came back again; but there they stood,
As in the days they dreamed of when young blood
Was in their cheeks and women called them fair.
Be sure they met me with an ancient air,—
And yes, there was a shop-worn brotherhood
About them; but the men were just as good,
And just as human as they ever were.

And you that ache so much to be sublime,
And you that feed yourselves with your descent,
What comes of all your visions and your fears?
Poets and kings are but the clerks of Time,
Tiering the same dull webs of discontent,
Clipping the same sad alnage of the years.

The Dark Hills

Dark hills at evening in the west,
Where sunset hovers like a sound
Of golden horns that sang to rest
Old bones of warriors under ground,
Far now from all the bannered ways
Where flash the legions of the sun,
You fade—as if the last of days
Were fading, and all wars were done.

Eros Turannos

She fears him, and will always ask
  What fated her to choose him;
She meets in his engaging mask
  All reasons to refuse him;
But what she meets and what she fears
Are less than are the downward years,
Drawn slowly to the foamless weirs
  Of age, were she to lose him.

Between a blurred sagacity
  That once had power to sound him,
And Love, that will not let him be
  The Judas that she found him,
Her pride assuages her almost,
As if it were alone the cost.
He sees that he will not be lost,
  And waits and looks around him.

A sense of ocean and old trees
  Envelops and allures him;
Tradition, touching all he sees,
  Beguiles and reassures him;
And all her doubts of what he says
Are dimmed with what she knows of days—
Till even prejudice delays
  And fades, and she secures him.

The falling leaf inaugurates
  The reign of her confusion;
The pounding wave reverberates
  The dirge of her illusion;
And home, where passion lived and died,
Becomes a place where she can hide,
While all the town and harbor-side
  Vibrate with her seclusion.

We tell you, tapping on our brows,
  The story as it should be,
As if the story of a house
  Were told, or ever could be;

We'll have no kindly veil between
Her visions and those we have seen,—
As if we guessed what hers have been,
  Or what they are or would be.

Meanwhile we do no harm; for they
  That with a god have striven,
Not hearing much of what we say,
  Take what the god has given;
Though like waves breaking it may be,
Or like a changed familiar tree,
Or like a stairway to the sea
  Where down the blind are driven.

The Sheaves

Where long the shadows of the wind had rolled,
Green wheat was yielding to the change assigned;
And as by some vast magic undivined
The world was turning slowly into gold.
Like nothing that was ever bought or sold
It waited there, the body and the mind;
And with a mighty meaning of a kind
That tells the more the more it is not told.

So in a land where all days are not fair,
Fair days went on till on another day
A thousand golden sheaves were lying there,
Shining and still, but not for long to stay—
As if a thousand girls with golden hair
Might rise from where they slept and go away.

Ben Jonson Entertains a Man from Stratford

You are a friend then, as I make it out,
Of our man Shakespeare, who alone of us
Will put an ass's head in Fairyland
As he would add a shilling to more shillings,
All most harmonious—and out of his
Miraculous inviolable increase
Fills Ilion, Rome, or any town you like
Of olden time with timeless Englishmen;
And I must wonder what you think of him—

Or nonsense anywhere to set him off—
Save only divers and inclement devils
Have made of late his heart their dwelling-place.
A flame half ready to fly out sometimes
At some annoyance may be fanned up in him,
But soon it falls, and when it falls goes out;
He knows how little room there is in there
For crude and futile animosities,
And how much for the joy of being whole,
And how much for long sorrow and old pain.
On our side there are some who may be given
To grow old wondering what he thinks of us
And some above us, who are, in his eyes,
Above himself—and that's quite right and English.
Yet here we smile, or disappoint the gods
Who made it so; the gods have always eyes
To see men scratch; and they see one down here
Who itches, manor-bitten, to the bone,
Albeit he knows himself—yes, yes, he knows—
The lord of more than England and of more
Than all the seas of England in all time
Shall ever wash. D'ye wonder that I laugh?
He sees me, and he doesn't seem to care;
And why the devil should he? I can't tell you.

I'll meet him out alone of a bright Sunday,
Trim, rather spruce, and quite the gentleman.
"What, ho, my lord!" say I. He doesn't hear me;
Wherefore I have to pause and look at him.
He's not enormous, but one looks at him.
A little on the round if you insist,
For now, God save the mark, he's growing old;
He's five and forty, and to hear him talk
These days you'd call him eighty; then you'd add
More years to that. He's old enough to be
The father of a world, and so he is.
"Ben, you're a scholar, what's the time of day?"
Says he; and there shines out of him again
An aged light that has no age or station—
The mystery that's his—a mischievous
Half-mad serenity that laughs at fame
For being won so easy, and at friends
Who laugh at him for what he wants the most,
And for his dukedom down in Warwickshire;—
By which you see we're all a little jealous. . . .

Poor Greene! I fear the color of his name
Was even as that of his ascending soul;
And he was one where there are many others—
Some scrivening to the end against their fate,
Their puppets all in ink and all to die there;
And some with hands that once would shade an eye
That scanned Euripides and Aeschylus
Will reach by this time for a pot-house mop
To slush their first and last of royalties.
Poor devils! and they all play to his hand;
For so it was in Athens and old Rome.
But that's not here or there; I've wandered off.
Greene does it, or I'm careful. Where's that boy?

Yes, he'll go back to Stratford. And we'll miss him?
Dear sir, there'll be no London here without him.
We'll all be riding, one of these fine days,
Down there to see him—and his wife won't like us;
And then we'll think of what he never said
Of women—which, if taken all in all
With what he did say, would buy many horses.
Though nowadays he's not so much for women.
"So few of them," he says, "are worth the guessing."
But there's a worm at work when he says that,
And while he says it one feels in the air
A deal of circumambient hocus-pocus.
They've had him dancing till his toes were tender,
And he can feel 'em now, come chilly rains.
There's no long cry for going into it,
However, and we don't know much about it.
But you in Stratford, like most here in London,
Have more now in the *Sonnets* than you paid for;
He's put one there with all her poison on,
To make a singing fiction of a shadow
That's in his life a fact, and always will be.
But she's no care of ours, though Time, I fear,
Will have a more reverberant ado
About her than about another one
Who seems to have decoyed him, married him,
And sent him scuttling on his way to London—
With much already learned, and more to learn,
And more to follow. Lord! how I see him now,
Pretending, maybe trying, to be like us.
Whatever he may have meant, we never had him;
He failed us, or escaped, or what you will—

And there was that about him (God knows what—
We'd flayed another had he tried it on us)
That made as many of us as had wits
More fond of all his easy distances
Than one another's noise and clap-your-shoulder.
But think you not, my friend, he'd never talk!
Talk? He was eldritch at it; and we listened—
Thereby acquiring much we knew before
About ourselves, and hitherto had held
Irrelevant, or not prime to the purpose.
And there were some, of course, and there be now,
Disordered and reduced amazedly
To resignation by the mystic seal
Of young finality the gods had laid
On everything that made him a young demon;
And one or two shot looks at him already
As he had been their executioner;
And once or twice he was, not knowing it—
Or knowing, being sorry for poor clay
And saying nothing . . . Yet, for all his engines,
You'll meet a thousand of an afternoon
Who strut and sun themselves and see around 'em
A world made out of more that has a reason
Than his, I swear, that he sees here today;
Though he may scarcely give a Fool an exit
But we mark how he sees in everything
A law that, given that we flout it once too often,
Brings fire and iron down on our naked heads.
To me it looks as if the power that made him,
For fear of giving all things to one creature,
Left out the first—faith, innocence, illusion,
Whatever 'tis that keeps us out o' Bedlam—
And thereby, for his too consuming vision,
Empowered him out of nature; though to see him,
You'd never guess what's going on inside him.
He'll break out some day like a keg of ale
With too much independent frenzy in it;
And all for cellaring what he knows won't keep,
And what he'd best forget—but that he can't.
You'll have it, and have more than I'm foretelling;
And there'll be such a roaring at the Globe
As never stunned the bleeding gladiators.
He'll have to change the color of its hair
A bit, for now he calls it Cleopatra.
Black hair would never do for Cleopatra.

But you and I are not yet two old women,
And you're a man of office. What he does
Is more to you than how it is he does it—
And that's what the Lord God has never told him.
They work together, and the Devil helps 'em;
They do it of a morning, or if not,
They do it of a night; in which event
He's peevish of a morning. He seems old;
He's not the proper stomach or the sleep—
And they're two sovran agents to conserve him
Against the fiery art that has no mercy
But what's in that prodigious grand new House.
I gather something happening in his boyhood
Fulfilled him with a boy's determination
To make all Stratford 'ware of him. Well, well,
I hope at last he'll have his joy of it,
And all his pigs and sheep and bellowing beeves,
And frogs and owls and unicorns, moreover,
Be less than hell to his attendant ears.
Oh, past a doubt we'll all go down to see him.

He may be wise. With London two days off,
Down there some wind of heaven may yet revive him,
But there's no quickening breath from anywhere
Shall make of him again the young poised faun
From Warwickshire, who'd made, it seems, already
A legend of himself before I came
To blink before the last of his first lightning.
Whatever there be, there'll be no more of that;
The coming on of his old monster Time
Has made him a still man; and he has dreams
Were fair to think on once, and all found hollow.
He knows how much of what men paint themselves
Would blister in the light of what they are;
He sees how much of what was great now shares
An eminence transformed and ordinary;
He knows too much of what the world has hushed
In others, to be loud now for himself;
He knows now at what height low enemies
May reach his heart, and high friends let him fall;
But what not even such as he may know
Bedevils him the worst: his lark may sing
At heaven's gate how he will, and for as long
As joy may listen, but *he* sees no gate,
Save one whereat the spent clay waits a little

Before the churchyard has it, and the worm.
Not long ago, late in an afternoon,
I came on him unseen down Lambeth way,
And on my life I was afear'd of him:
He gloomed and mumbled like a soul from Tophet,
His hands behind him and his head bent solemn.
"What is it now," said I, "another woman?"
That made him sorry for me, and he smiled.
"No, Ben," he mused; "it's Nothing. It's all Nothing.
We come, we go; and when we're done, we're done;
Spiders and flies—we're mostly one or t'other—
We come, we go; and when we're done, we're done."
"By God, you sing that song as if you knew it!"
Said I, by way of cheering him; "what ails ye?"
"I think I must have come down here to think,"
Says he to that, and pulls his little beard;
"Your fly will serve as well as anybody,
And what's his hour? He flies, and flies, and flies,
And in his fly's mind has a brave appearance;
And then your spider gets him in her net,
And eats him out, and hangs him up to dry.
That's Nature, the kind mother of us all.
And then your slattern housemaid swings her broom,
And where's your spider? And that's Nature, also.
It's Nature, and it's Nothing. It's all Nothing.
It's all a world where bugs and emperors
Go singularly back to the same dust,
Each in his time; and the old, ordered stars
That sang together, Ben, will sing the same
Old stave tomorrow."

When he talks like that,
There's nothing for a human man to do
But lead him to some grateful nook like this
Where we be now, and there to make him drink.
He'll drink, for love of me, and then be sick;
A sad sign always in a man of parts,
And always very ominous. The great
Should be as large in liquor as in love—
And our great friend is not so large in either:
One disaffects him, and the other fails him;
Whatso he drinks that has an antic in it,
He's wondering what's to pay in his insides;
And while his eyes are on the Cyprian
He's fribbling all the time with that damned House.

We laugh here at his thrift, but after all
It may be thrift that saves him from the devil;
God gave it, anyhow—and we'll suppose
He knew the compound of His handiwork.
Today the clouds are with him, but anon
He'll out of 'em enough to shake the tree
Of life itself and bring down fruit unheard-of—
And, throwing in the bruised and whole together,
Prepare a wine to make us drunk with wonder;
And if he live, there'll be a sunset spell
Thrown over him as over a glassed lake
That yesterday was all a black wild water.

God send he live to give us, if no more,
What now's a-rampage in him, and exhibit,
With a decent half-allegiance to the ages
An earnest of at least a casual eye
Turned once on what he owes to Gutenberg,
And to the fealty of more centuries
Than are as yet a picture in our vision.
"There's time enough—I'll do it when I'm old,
And we're immortal men," he says to that;
And then he says to me, "Ben, what's 'immortal'?
Think you by any force of ordination
It may be nothing of a sort more noisy
Than a small oblivion of component ashes
That of a dream-addicted world was once
A moving atomy much like your friend here?"
Nothing will help that man. To make him laugh
I said then he was a mad mountebank—
And by the Lord I nearer made him cry.
I could have eat an eft then, on my knees,
Tails, claws, and all of him; for I had stung
The king of men, who had no sting for me,
And I had hurt him in his memories;
And I say now, as I shall say again,
I love the man this side idolatry.

He'll do it when he's old, he says. I wonder.
He may not be so ancient as all that.
For such as he the thing that is to do
Will do itself—but there's a reckoning;
The sessions that are now too much his own,
The roiling inward of a still outside,
The churning out of all those blood-fed lines,

The nights of many schemes and little sleep,
The full brain hammered hot with too much thinking,
The vexed heart over-worn with too much aching—
This weary jangling of conjoined affairs
Made out of elements that have no end,
And all confused at once, I understand,
Is not what makes a man to live forever.
O, no, not now! He'll not be going now:
There'll be time yet for God knows what explosions
Before he goes. He'll stay awhile. Just wait:
Just wait a year or two for Cleopatra,
For she's to be a balsam and a comfort;
And that's not all a jape of mine now, either.
For granted once the old way of Apollo
Sings in a man, he may then, if he's able,
Strike unafraid whatever strings he will
Upon the last and wildest of new lyres;
Nor out of his new magic, though it hymn
The shrieks of dungeoned hell, shall he create
A madness or a gloom to shut quite out
A cleaving daylight, and a last great calm
Triumphant over shipwreck and all storms.
He might have given Aristotle creeps,
But surely would have given him his *katharsis*.

He'll not be going yet. There's too much yet
Unsung within the man. But when he goes,
I'd stake ye coin o' the realm his only care
For a phantom world he sounded and found wanting
Will be a portion here, a portion there,
Of this or that thing or some other thing
That has a patent and intrinsical
Equivalence in those egregious shillings.
And yet he knows, God help him! Tell me, now,
If ever there was anything let loose
On earth by gods or devils heretofore
Like this mad, careful, proud, indifferent Shakespeare!
Where was it, if it ever was? By heaven,
'Twas never yet in Rhodes or Pergamon—
In Thebes or Nineveh, a thing like this!
No thing like this was ever out of England;
And that he knows. I wonder if he cares.
Perhaps he does. . . . O Lord, that House in Stratford!

New England

Here where the wind is always north-north-east
And children learn to walk on frozen toes,
Wonder begets an envy of all those
Who boil elsewhere with such a lyric yeast
Of love that you will hear them at a feast
Where demons would appeal for some repose,
Still clamoring where the chalice overflows
And crying wildest who have drunk the least.

Passion is here a soilure of the wits,
We're told, and Love a cross for them to bear;
Joy shivers in the corner where she knits
And Conscience always has the rocking-chair,
Cheerful as when she tortured into fits
The first cat that was ever killed by Care.

The Gift of God

Blessed with a joy that only she
Of all alive shall ever know,
She wears a proud humility
For what it was that willed it so,—
That her degree should be so great
Among the favored of the Lord
That she may scarcely bear the weight
Of her bewildering reward.

As one apart, immune, alone,
Or featured for the shining ones,
And like to none that she has known
Of other women's other sons,—
The firm fruition of her need,
He shines anointed; and he blurs
Her vision, till it seems indeed
A sacrilege to call him hers.

She fears a little for so much
Of what is best, and hardly dares
To think of him as one to touch
With aches, indignities, and cares;

She sees him rather at the goal,
Still shining; and her dream foretells
The proper shining of a soul
Where nothing ordinary dwells.

Perchance a canvass of the town
Would find him far from flags and shouts,
And leave him only the renown
Of many smiles and many doubts;
Perchance the crude and common tongue
Would havoc strangely with his worth;
But she, with innocence unwrung,
Would read his name around the earth.

And others, knowing how this youth
Would shine, if love could make him great,
When caught and tortured for the truth
Would only writhe and hesitate;
While she, arranging for his days
What centuries could not fulfill,
Transmutes him with her faith and praise,
And has him shining where she will.

She crowns him with her gratefulness,
And says again that life is good;
And should the gift of God be less
In him than in her motherhood,
His fame, though vague, will not be small,
As upward through her dream he fares,
Half clouded with a crimson fall
Of roses thrown on marble stairs.

Aaron Stark

Withal a meagre man was Aaron Stark—
Cursed and unkempt, shrewd, shrivelled, and morose.
A miser was he, with a miser's nose,
And eyes like little dollars in the dark.
His thin, pinched mouth was nothing but a mark;
And when he spoke there came like sullen blows
Through scattered fangs a few snarled words and close,
As if a cur were chary of its bark.

Glad for the murmur of his hard renown,
Year after year he shambled through the town—

A loveless exile moving with a staff;
And oftentimes there crept into his ears
A sound of alien pity, touched with tears—
And then (and only then) did Aaron laugh.

Karma

Christmas was in the air and all was well
With him, but for a few confusing flaws
In divers of God's images. Because
A friend of his would neither buy nor sell,
Was he to answer for the axe that fell?
He pondered; and the reason for it was,
Partly, a slowly freezing Santa Claus
Upon the corner, with his beard and bell.

Acknowledging an improvident surprise,
He magnified a fancy that he wished
The friend whom he had wrecked were here again.
Not sure of that, he found a compromise;
And from the fullness of his heart he fished
A dime for Jesus who had died for man.

Hillcrest

No sound of any storm that shakes
Old island walls with older seas
Comes here where now September makes
An island in a sea of trees.

Between the sunlight and the shade
A man may learn till he forgets
The roaring of a world remade,
And all his ruins and regrets;

And if he still remembers here
Poor fights he may have won or lost,—
If he be ridden with the fear
Of what some other fight may cost,—

If, eager to confuse too soon
What he has known with what may be,

He reads a planet out of tune
For cause of his jarred harmony,—

If here he venture to unroll
His index of adagios,
And he be given to console
Humanity with what he knows,—

He may by contemplation learn
A little more than what he knew,
And even see great oaks return
To acorns out of which they grew.

He may, if he but listen well,
Through twilight and the silence here,
Be told what there are none may tell
To vanity's impatient ear;

And he may never dare again
Say what awaits him, or be sure
What sunlit labyrinth of pain
He may not enter and endure.

Who knows to-day from yesterday
May learn to count no thing too strange:
Love builds of what Time takes away,
Till Death itself is less than Change.

Who sees enough in his duress
May go as far as dreams have gone;
Who sees a little may do less
Than many who are blind have done;

Who sees unchastened here the soul
Triumphant has no other sight
Than has a child who sees the whole
World radiant with his own delight.

Far journeys and hard wandering
Await him in whose crude surmise
Peace, like a mask, hides everything
That is and has been from his eyes;

And all his wisdom is unfound,
Or like a web that error weaves
On airy looms that have a sound
No louder now than falling leaves.

Robert Frost

1874-

The Pasture

I'm going out to clean the pasture spring;
I'll only stop to rake the leaves away
(And wait to watch the water clear, I may):
I shan't be gone long.—You come too.

I'm going out to fetch the little calf
That's standing by the mother. It's so young,
It totters when she licks it with her tongue.
I shan't be gone long.—You come too.

The Onset

Always the same when on a fated night
At last the gathered snow lets down as white
As may be in dark woods, and with a song
It shall not make again all winter long—
Of hissing on the yet uncovered ground—
I almost stumble looking up and round,
As one, who, overtaken by the end,
Gives up his errand and lets death descend
Upon him where he is, with nothing done
To evil, no important triumph won
More than if life had never been begun.

Yet all the precedent is on my side:
I know that winter-death has never tried
The earth but it has failed; the snow may heap
In long storms an undrifted four feet deep
As measured against maple, birch or oak,
It cannot check the Peeper's silver croak;

And I shall see the snow all go down hill
In water of a slender April rill
That flashes tail through last year's withered brake
And dead weed like a disappearing snake.
Nothing will be left white but here a birch
And there a clump of houses with a church.

The Tuft of Flowers

I went to turn the grass once after one
Who mowed it in the dew before the sun.

The dew was gone that made his blade so keen
Before I came to view the leveled scene.

I looked for him behind an isle of trees;
I listened for his whetstone on the breeze.

But he had gone his way, the grass all mown,
And I must be, as he had been,—alone,

"As all must be," I said within my heart,
"Whether they work together or apart."

But as I said it, swift there passed me by
On noiseless wing a bewildered butterfly,

Seeking with memories grown dim over night
Some resting flower of yesterday's delight.

And once I marked his flight go round and round,
As where some flower lay withering on the ground.

And then he flew as far as eye could see,
And then on tremulous wing came back to me.

I thought of questions that have no reply,
And would have turned to toss the grass to dry;

But he turned first, and led my eye to look
At a tall tuft of flowers beside a brook,

A leaping tongue of bloom the scythe had spared
Beside a reedy brook the scythe had bared.

I left my place to know them by their name,
Finding them butterfly-weed when I came.

The mower in the dew had loved them thus,
By leaving them to flourish, not for us,

Nor yet to draw one thought of ours to him,
But from shèer morning gladness at the brim.

The butterfly and I had lit upon,
Nevertheless, a message from the dawn,

That made me hear the wakening birds around,
And hear his long scythe whispering to the ground,

And feel a spirit kindred to my own;
So that henceforth I worked no more alone;

But glad with him, I worked as with his aid,
And weary, sought at noon with him the shade;

And dreaming, as it were, held brotherly speech
With one whose thought I had not hoped to reach.

"Men work together," I told him from the heart,
"Whether they work together or apart."

Reluctance

Out through the fields and the woods
  And over the walls I have wended;
I have climbed the hills of view
  And looked at the world, and descended;
I have come by the highway home,
  And lo, it is ended.

The leaves are all dead on the ground,
  Save those that the oak is keeping
To ravel them one by one
  And let them go scraping and creeping
Out over the crusted snow,
  When others are sleeping.

And the dead leaves lie huddled and still,
  No longer blown hither and thither;

The last lone aster is gone;
  The flowers of the witch-hazel wither;
The heart is still aching to seek,
  But the feet question "Whither?"

Ah, when to the heart of man
  Was it ever less than a treason
To go with the drift of things
  To yield with a grace to reason,
And bow and accept the end
  Of a love or a season?

Mending Wall

Something there is that doesn't love a wall,
That sends the frozen-ground-swell under it,
And spills the upper bowlders in the sun;
And makes gaps even two can pass abreast.
The work of hunters is another thing:
I have come after them and made repair
Where they have left not one stone on a stone,
But they would have the rabbit out of hiding,
To please the yelping dogs. The gaps I mean,
No one has seen them made or heard them made,
But at spring mending-time we find them there.
I let my neighbor know beyond the hill;
And on a day we meet to walk the line
And set the wall between us once again.
We keep the wall between us as we go.
To each the bowlders that have fallen to each.
And some are loaves and some so nearly balls
We have to use a spell to make them balance:
"Stay where you are until our backs are turned!"
We wear our fingers rough with handling them.
Oh, just another kind of outdoor game,
One on a side. It comes to little more:
There where it is we do not need the wall:
He is all pine and I am apple-orchard.
My apple trees will never get across
And eat the cones under his pines, I tell him.
He only says, "Good fences make good neighbors."
Spring is the mischief in me, and I wonder
If I could put a notion in his head:

"*Why* do they make good neighbors? Isn't it
Where there are cows? But here there are no cows.
Before I built a wall I'd ask to know
What I was walling in or walling out,
And to whom I was like to give offense.
Something there is that doesn't love a wall,
That wants it down!" I could say "elves" to him,
But it's not elves exactly, and I'd rather
He said it for himself. I see him there,
Bringing a stone grasped firmly by the top
In each hand, like an old-stone savage armed.
He moves in darkness, as it seems to me,
Not of woods only and the shade of trees.
He will not go behind his father's saying,
And he likes having thought of it so well
He says again, "Good fences make good neighbors."

The Death of the Hired Man

Mary sat musing on the lamp-flame at the table
Waiting for Warren. When she heard his step,
She ran on tip-toe down the darkened passage
To meet him in the doorway with the news
And put him on his guard. "Silas is back."
She pushed him outward with her through the door
And shut it after her. "Be kind," she said.

She took the market things from Warren's arms
And set them on the porch, then drew him down
To sit beside her on the wooden steps.
"When was I ever anything but kind to him?
But I'll not have the fellow back," he said.
"I told him so last haying, didn't I?
'If he left then,' I said, 'that ended it.'
What good is he? Who else will harbor him
At his age for the little he can do?
What help he is there's no depending on.
Off he goes always when I need him most.
'He thinks he ought to earn a little pay,
Enough at least to buy tobacco with,
So he won't have to beg and be beholden.'
'All right,' I say, 'I can't afford to pay
Any fixed wages, though I wish I could.'
'Someone else can.' 'Then someone else will have to.'

I shouldn't mind his bettering himself
If that was what it was. You can be certain,
When he begins like that, there's someone at him
Trying to coax him off with pocket-money,—
In haying time, when any help is scarce.
In winter he comes back to us. I'm done."

"Sh! not so loud: he'll hear you," Mary said.

"I want him to: he'll have to soon or late."

"He's worn out. He's asleep beside the stove.
When I came up from Rowe's I found him here,
Huddled against the barn-door fast asleep,
A miserable sight, and frightening, too—
You needn't smile—I didn't recognize him—
I wasn't looking for him—and he's changed.
Wait till you see."

"Where did you say he'd been?"

"He didn't say. I dragged him to the house,
And gave him tea and tried to make him smoke.
I tried to make him talk about his travels,
Nothing would do: he just kept nodding off."

"What did he say? Did he say anything?"

"But little."

"Anything? Mary, confess
He said he'd come to ditch the meadow for me."

"Warren!"

"But did he? I just want to know."

"Of course he did. What would you have him say?
Surely you wouldn't grudge the poor old man
Some humble way to save his self-respect.
He added, if you really care to know,
He meant to clear the upper pasture, too.
That sounds like something you have heard before?
Warren, I wish you could have heard the way
He jumbled everything. I stopped to look

Two or three times—he made me feel so queer—
To see if he was talking in his sleep.
He ran on Harold Wilson—you remember—
The boy you had in haying four years since.
He's finished school, and teaching in his college.
Silas declares you'll have to get him back.
He says they two will make a team for work:
Between them they will lay this farm as smooth!
The way he mixed that in with other things.
He thinks young Wilson a likely lad, though daft
On education—you know how they fought
All through July under the blazing sun,
Silas up on the cart to build the load,
Harold along beside to pitch it on."

"Yes, I took care to keep well out of earshot."

"Well, those days trouble Silas like a dream.
You wouldn't think they would. How some things linger!
Harold's young college boy's assurance piqued him.
After so many years he still keeps finding
Good arguments he sees he might have used.
I sympathize. I know just how it feels
To think of the right thing to say too late.
Harold's associated in his mind with Latin.
He asked me what I thought of Harold's saying
He studied Latin like the violin
Because he liked it—that an argument!
He said he couldn't make the boy believe
He could find water with a hazel prong—
Which showed how much good school had ever done him.
He wanted to go over that. But most of all
He thinks if he could have another chance
To teach him how to build a load of hay—"

"I know, that's Silas' one accomplishment.
He bundles every forkful in its place,
And tags and numbers it for future reference,
So he can find and easily dislodge it
In the unloading. Silas does that well.
He takes it out in bunches like birds' nests.
You never see him standing on the hay
He's trying to lift, straining to lift himself."

"He thinks if he could teach him that, he'd be
Some good perhaps to someone in the world.

He hates to see a boy the fool of books.
Poor Silas, so concerned for other folk,
And nothing to look backward to with pride,
And nothing to look forward to with hope,
So now and never any different."

Part of a moon was falling down the west,
Dragging the whole sky with it to the hills.
Its light poured softly in her lap. She saw
And spread her apron to it. She put out her hand
Among the harp-like morning-glory strings,
Taut with the dew from garden bed to eaves,
As if she played unheard some tenderness
That wrought on him beside her in the night.
"Warren," she said, "he has come home to die:
You needn't be afraid he'll leave you this time."

"Home," he mocked gently.

"Yes, what else but home?
It all depends on what you mean by home.
Of course he's nothing to us, any more
Than was the hound that came a stranger to us
Out of the woods, worn out upon the trail."

"Home is the place where, when you have to go there,
They have to take you in."

"I should have called it
Something you somehow haven't to deserve."

Warren leaned out and took a step or two,
Picked up a little stick, and brought it back
And broke it in his hand and tossed it by.
"Silas has better claim on us, you think,
Than on his brother? Thirteen little miles
As the road winds would bring him to his door.
Silas has walked that far no doubt today.
Why didn't he go there? His brother's rich,
A somebody—director in the bank."

"He never told us that."

"We know it though."

"I think his brother ought to help, of course.
I'll see to that if there is need. He ought of right

To take him in, and might be willing to—
He may be better than appearances.
But have some pity on Silas. Do you think
If he'd had any pride in claiming kin
Or anything he looked for from his brother,
He'd keep so still about him all this time?"

"I wonder what's between them."

"I can tell you.
Silas is what he is—we wouldn't mind him—
But just the kind that kinsfolk can't abide.
He never did a thing so very bad.
He don't know why he isn't quite as good
As anyone. He won't be made ashamed
To please his brother, worthless though he is."

"I can't think Si ever hurt anyone."

"No, but he hurt my heart the way he lay
And rolled his old head on that sharp-edged chair-back.
He wouldn't let me put him on the lounge.
You must go in and see what you can do.
I made the bed up for him there tonight.
You'll be surprised at him—how much he's broken.
His working days are done; I'm sure of it."

"I'd not be in a hurry to say that."

"I haven't been. Go, look, see for yourself.
But, Warren, please remember how it is:
He's come to help you ditch the meadow.
He has a plan. You mustn't laugh at him.
He may not speak of it, and then he may.
I'll sit and see if that small sailing cloud
Will hit or miss the moon."

It hit the moon.
Then there were three there, making a dim row,
The moon, the little silver cloud, and she.

Warren returned—too soon, it seemed to her,
Slipped to her side, caught up her hand and waited.

"Warren?" she questioned.

"Dead," was all he answered.

The Road Not Taken

Two roads diverged in a yellow wood,
And sorry I could not travel both
And be one traveler, long I stood
And looked down one as far as I could
To where it bent in the undergrowth;

Then took the other, as just as fair,
And having perhaps the better claim,
Because it was grassy and wanted wear;
Though as for that the passing there
Had worn them really about the same,

And both that morning equally lay
In leaves no step had trodden black.
Oh, I kept the first for another day!
Yet knowing how way leads on to way,
I doubted if I should ever come back.

I shall be telling this with a sigh
Somewhere ages and ages hence:
Two roads diverged in a wood, and I—
I took the one less traveled by,
And that has made all the difference.

The Cow in Apple-Time

Something inspires the only cow of late
To make no more of a wall than an open gate,
And think no more of wall-builders than fools.
Her face is flecked with pomace and she drools
A cider sirup. Having tasted fruit,
She scorns a pasture withering to the root.
She runs from tree to tree where lie and sweeten
The windfalls spiked with stubble and worm-eaten
She leaves them bitten when she has to fly.
She bellows on a knoll against the sky.
Her udder shrivels and the milk goes dry.

After Apple-Picking

My long two-pointed ladder's sticking through a tree
Toward heaven still,
And there's a barrel that I didn't fill
Beside it, and there may be two or three
Apples I didn't pick upon some bough.
But I am done with apple-picking now.
Essence of winter sleep is on the night,
The scent of apples: I am drowsing off.
I cannot rub the strangeness from my sight
I got from looking through a pane of glass
I skimmed this morning from the drinking trough
And held against the world of hoary grass.
It melted, and I let it fall and break.
But I was well
Upon my way to sleep before it fell,
And I could tell
What form my dreaming was about to take.
Magnified apples appear and disappear,
Stem-end and blossom-end,
And every fleck of russet showing clear.
My instep arch not only keeps the ache,
It keeps the pressure of a ladder-round.
I feel the ladder sway as the boughs bend.
And I keep hearing from the cellar bin
The rumbling sound
Of load on load of apples coming in.
For I have had too much
Of apple-picking: I am overtired
Of the great harvest I myself desired.
There were ten thousand thousand fruit to touch,
Cherish in hand, lift down, and not let fall.
For all
That struck the earth,
No matter if not bruised or spiked with stubble,
Went surely to the cider-apple heap
As of no worth.
One can see what will trouble
This sleep of mine, whatever sleep it is.
Were he not gone,
The woodchuck could say whether it's like his

Long sleep, as I describe its coming on,
Or just some human sleep.

An Old Man's Winter Night

All out of doors looked darkly in at him
Through the thin frost, almost in separate stars,
That gathers on the pane in empty rooms.
What kept his eyes from giving back the gaze
Was the lamp tilted near them in his hand.
What kept him from remembering what it was
That brought him to that creaking room was age.
He stood with barrels round him—at a loss.
And having scared the cellar under him
In clomping there, he scared it once again
In clomping off; and scared the outer night,
Which has its sounds, familiar, like the roar
Of trees and crack of branches, common things,
But nothing so like beating on a box.
A light he was to no one but himself
Where now he sat, concerned with he knew what;
A quiet light, and then not even that.
He consigned to the moon, such as she was,
So late-arising, to the broken moon
As better than the sun in any case
For such a charge, his snow upon the roof,
His icicles along the wall to keep;
And slept. The log that shifted with a jolt
Once in the stove, disturbed him and he shifted,
And eased his heavy breathing, but still slept.
One aged man—one man—can't fill a house,
A farm, a countryside, or if he can,
It's thus he does it of a winter night.

Birches

When I see birches bend to left and right
Across the lines of straighter darker trees,
I like to think some boy's been swinging them.
But swinging doesn't bend them down to stay.
Ice-storms do that. Often you must have seen them
Loaded with ice a sunny winter morning

After a rain. They click upon themselves
As the breeze rises, and turn many-colored
As the stir cracks and crazes their enamel.
Soon the sun's warmth makes them shed crystal shells
Shattering and avalanching on the snow-crust—
Such heaps of broken glass to sweep away
You'd think the inner dome of heaven had fallen.
They are dragged to the withered bracken by the load,
And they seem not to break; though once they are bowed
So low for long, they never right themselves:
You may see their trunks arching in the woods
Years afterwards, trailing their leaves on the ground
Like girls on hands and knees that throw their hair
Before them over their heads to dry in the sun.
But I was going to say when Truth broke in
With all her matter-of-fact about the ice-storm
I should prefer to have some boy bend them
As he went out and in to fetch the cows—
Some boy too far from town to learn baseball,
Whose only play was what he found himself,
Summer or winter, and could play alone.
One by one he subdued his father's trees
By riding them down over and over again
Until he took the stiffness out of them,
And not one but hung limp, not one was left
For him to conquer. He learned all there was
To learn about not launching out too soon
And so not carrying the tree away
Clear to the ground. He always kept his poise
To the top branches, climbing carefully
With the same pains you use to fill a cup
Up to the brim, and even above the brim.
Then he flung outward, feet first, with a swish,
Kicking his way down through the air to the ground.

So was I once myself a swinger of birches;
And so I dream of going back to be.
It's when I'm weary of considerations,
And life is too much like a pathless wood
Where your face burns and tickles with the cobwebs
Broken across it, and one eye is weeping
From a twig's having lashed across it open.
I'd like to get away from earth awhile
And then come back to it and begin over.
May no fate willfully misunderstand me

And half grant what I wish and snatch me away
Not to return. Earth's the right place for love:
I don't know where it's likely to go better.
I'd like to go by climbing a birch tree,
And climb black branches up a snow-white trunk
Toward heaven, till the tree could bear no more,
But dipped its top and set me down again.
That would be good both going and coming back.
One could do worse than be a swinger of birches.

The Runaway

Once when the snow of the year was beginning to fall,
We stopped by a mountain pasture to say, "Whose colt?"
A little Morgan had one forefoot on the wall,
The other curled at his breast. He dipped his head
And snorted to us. And then he had to bolt.
We heard the miniature thunder where he fled,
And we saw him, or thought we saw him, dim and gray,
Like a shadow against the curtain of falling flakes.
"I think the little fellow's afraid of the snow.
He isn't winter-broken. It isn't play
With the little fellow at all. He's running away.
I doubt if even his mother could tell him, 'Sakes,
It's only weather.' He'd think she didn't know!
Where is his mother? He can't be out alone."
And now he comes again with a clatter of stone
And mounts the wall again with whited eyes
And all his tail that isn't hair up straight.
He shudders his coat as if to throw off flies.
"Whoever it is that leaves him out so late,
When other creatures have gone to stall and bin,
Ought to be told to come and take him in."

To Earthward

Love at the lips was touch
As sweet as I could bear;
And once that seemed too much;
I lived on air

That crossed me from sweet things,
The flow of—was it musk

From hidden grapevine springs
Down hill at dusk?

I had the swirl and ache
From sprays of honeysuckle
That when they're gathered shake
Dew on the knuckle.

I craved strong sweets, but those
Seemed strong when I was young;
The petal of the rose
It was that stung.

Now no joy but lacks salt
That is not dashed with pain
And weariness and fault;
I crave the stain

Of tears, the aftermark
Of almost too much love,
The sweet of bitter bark
And burning clove.

When stiff and sore and scarred
I take away my hand
From leaning on it hard
In grass and sand,

The hurt is not enough:
I long for weight and strength
To feel the earth as rough
To all my length.

Fire and Ice

Some say the world will end in fire
Some say in ice.
From what I've tasted of desire
I hold with those who favor fire.
But if it had to perish twice,
I think I know enough of hate
To say that for destruction ice
Is also great
And would suffice.

Two Look at Two

Love and forgetting might have carried them
A little further up the mountain side
With night so near, but not much further up.
They must have halted soon in any case
With thoughts of the path back, how rough it was
With rock and washout, and unsafe in darkness;
When they were halted by a tumbled wall
With barbed-wire binding. They stood facing this,
Spending what onward impulse they still had
In one last look the way they must not go,
On up the failing path, where, if a stone
Or earthslide moved at night, it moved itself;
No footstep moved it. "This is all," they sighed,
"Good-night to woods." But not so; there was more.
A doe from round a spruce stood looking at them
Across the wall as near the wall as they.
She saw them in their field, they her in hers.
The difficulty of seeing what stood still,
Like some up-ended bowlder split in two,
Was in her clouded eyes: they saw no fear there.
She seemed to think that two thus they were safe.
Then, as if they were something that, though strange,
She could not trouble her mind with too long,
She sighed and passed unscared along the wall.
"This, then, is all. What more is there to ask?"
But no, not yet. A snort to bid them wait.
A buck from round the spruce stood looking at them
Across the wall, as near the wall as they.
This was an antlered buck of lusty nostril,
Not the same doe come back into her place.
He viewed them quizzically with jerks of head,
As if to ask, "Why don't you make some motion?
Or give some sign of life? Because you can't.
I doubt if you're as living as you look."
Thus till he had them almost feeling dared
To stretch a proffering hand—and a spell-breaking.
Then he too passed unscared along the wall.
Two had seen two, whichever side you spoke from.
"This *must* be all." It was all. Still they stood,
A great wave from it going over them,

As if the earth in one unlooked-for favor
Had made them certain earth returned their love.

The Witch of Coös

(From "Two Witches")

I stayed the night for shelter at a farm
Behind the mountain, with a mother and son,
Two old-believers. They did all the talking.

MOTHER. Folks think a witch who has familiar spirits
She could call up to pass a winter evening,
But won't, should be burned at the stake or something.
Summoning spirits isn't "Button, button,
Who's got the button," I would have them know.

SON. Mother can make a common table rear
And kick with two legs like an army mule.

MOTHER. And when I've done it, what good have I done?
Rather than tip a table for you, let me
Tell you what Ralle the Sioux Control once told me.
He said the dead had souls, but when I asked him
How could that be—I thought the dead were souls,
He broke my trance. Don't that make you suspicious
That there's something the dead are keeping back?
Yes, there's something the dead are keeping back.

SON. You wouldn't want to tell him what we have
Up attic, mother?

MOTHER. Bones—a skeleton.

SON. But the headboard of mother's bed is pushed
Against the attic door: the door is nailed.
It's harmless. Mother hears it in the night
Halting perplexed behind the barrier
Of door and headboard. Where it wants to get
Is back into the cellar where it came from.

MOTHER. We'll never let them, will we, son! We'll never!

SON. It left the cellar forty years ago
And carried itself like a pile of dishes

Up one flight from the cellar to the kitchen,
Another from the kitchen to the bedroom,
Another from the bedroom to the attic,
Right past both father and mother, and neither stopped it.
Father had gone upstairs; mother was downstairs.
I was a baby: I don't know where I was.

MOTHER. The only fault my husband found with me—
I went to sleep before I went to bed,
Especially in winter when the bed
Might just as well be ice and the clothes snow.
The night the bones came up the cellar-stairs
Toffile had gone to bed alone and left me,
But left an open door to cool the room off
So as to sort of turn me out of it.
I was just coming to myself enough
To wonder where the cold was coming from,
When I heard Toffile upstairs in the bedroom
And thought I heard him downstairs in the cellar.
The board we had laid down to walk dry-shod on
When there was water in the cellar in spring
Struck the hard cellar bottom. And then someone
Began the stairs, two footsteps for each step,
The way a man with one leg and a crutch,
Or a little child, comes up. It wasn't Toffile:
It wasn't anyone who could be there.
The bulkhead double-doors were double-locked
And swollen tight and buried under snow.
The cellar windows were banked up with sawdust
And swollen tight and buried under snow.
It was the bones. I knew them—and good reason.
My first impulse was to get to the knob
And hold the door. But the bones didn't try
The door; they halted helpless on the landing,
Waiting for things to happen in their favor.
The faintest restless rustling ran all through them.
I never could have done the thing I did
If the wish hadn't been too strong in me
To see how they were mounted for this walk.
I had a vision of them put together
Not like a man, but like a chandelier.
So suddenly I flung the door wide on him.
A moment he stood balancing with emotion,
And all but lost himself. (A tongue of fire
Flashed out and licked along his upper teeth.

Smoke rolled inside the sockets of his eyes.)
Then he came at me with one hand outstretched,
The way he did in life once; but this time
I struck the hand off brittle on the floor,
And fell back from him on the floor myself.
The finger-pieces slid in all directions.
(Where did I see one of those pieces lately?
Hand me my button-box—it must be there.)
I sat up on the floor and shouted, "Toffile,
It's coming up to you." It had its choice
Of the door to the cellar or the hall.
It took the hall door for the novelty,
And set off briskly for so slow a thing,
Still going every which way in the joints, though,
So that it looked like lightning or a scribble,
From the slap I had just now given its hand.
I listened till it almost climbed the stairs
From the hall to the only finished bedroom,
Before I got up to do anything;
Then ran and shouted, "Shut the bedroom door,
Toffile, for my sake!" "Company?" he said,
"Don't make me get up; I'm too warm in bed."
So lying forward weakly on the handrail
I pushed myself upstairs, and in the light
(The kitchen had been dark) I had to own
I could see nothing. "Toffile, I don't see it.
It's with us in the room though. It's the bones."
"What bones?" "The cellar bones—out of the grave."
That made him throw his bare legs out of bed
And sit up by me and take hold of me.
I wanted to put out the light and see
If I could see it, or else mow the room,
With our arms at the level of our knees,
And bring the chalk-pile down. "I'll tell you what—
It's looking for another door to try.
The uncommonly deep snow has made him think
Of his old song, *The Wild Colonial Boy,*
He always used to sing along the tote road.
He's after an open door to get outdoors.
Let's trap him with an open door up attic."
Toffile agreed to that, and sure enough,
Almost the moment he was given an opening,
The steps began to climb the attic stairs.
I heard them. Toffile didn't seem to hear them.
"Quick!" I slammed to the door and held the knob.

"Toffile, get nails." I made him nail the door shut
And push the headboard of the bed against it.
Then we asked was there anything
Up attic that we'd ever want again.
The attic was less to us than the cellar.
If the bones liked the attic, let them have it.
Let them stay in the attic. When they sometimes
Come down the stairs at night and stand perplexed
Behind the door and headboard of the bed,
Brushing their chalky skull with chalky fingers,
With sounds like the dry rattling of a shutter,
That's what I sit up in the dark to say—
To no one any more since Toffile died.
Let them stay in the attic since they went there.
I promised Toffile to be cruel to them
For helping them be cruel once to him.

SON. We think they had a grave down in the cellar.

MOTHER. We know they had a grave down in the cellar.

SON. We never could find out whose bones they were.

MOTHER. Yes, we could too, son. Tell the truth for once.
They were a man's his father killed for me.
I mean a man he killed instead of me.
The least I could do was to help dig their grave.
We were about it one night in the cellar.
Son knows the story: but 'twas not for him
To tell the truth, suppose the time had come.
Son looks surprised to see me end a lie
We'd kept all these years between ourselves
So as to have it ready for outsiders.
But tonight I don't care enough to lie—
I don't remember why I ever cared.
Toffile, if he were here, I don't believe
Could tell you why he ever cared himself. . . .

She hadn't found the finger-bone she wanted
Among the buttons poured out in her lap.
I verified the name next morning: Toffile.
The rural letter box said Toffile Lajway.

West-running Brook

"Fred, where is north?"
"North? North is there, my love.
The brook runs west."
"West-running Brook then call it."
(West-running Brook men call it to this day.)
"What does it think it's doing running west
When all the other country brooks flow east
To reach the ocean? It must be the brook
Can trust itself to go by contraries
The way I can with you—and you with me—
Because we're—we're—I don't know what we are.
What are we?"
"Young or new?"
"We must be something.
We've said we two. Let's change that to we three.
As you and I are married to each other,
We'll both be married to the brook. We'll build
Our bridge across it, and the bridge shall be
Our arm thrown over it asleep beside it.
Look, look, it's waving to us with a wave
To let us know it hears me."
"Why, my dear,
That wave's been standing off this jut of shore—"
(The black stream, catching on a sunken rock,
Flung backward on itself in one white wave,
And the white water rode the black forever,
Not gaining but not losing, like a bird
White feathers from the struggle of whose breast
Flecked the dark stream and flecked the darker pool
Below the point, and were at last driven wrinkled
In a white scarf against the far shore alders.)
"That wave's been standing off this jut of shore
Ever since rivers, I was going to say,
Were made in heaven. It wasn't waved to us."

"It wasn't, yet it was. If not to you
It was to me—in an annunciation."

"Oh, if you take it off to lady-land,
As 'twere the country of the Amazons
We men must see you to the confines of

And leave you there, ourselves forbid to enter,—
It is your brook! I have no more to say."

"Yes, you have, too. Go on. You thought of something."

"Speaking of contraries, see how the brook
In that white wave runs counter to itself.
It is from that in water we were from
Long, long before we were from any creature.
Here we, in our impatience of the steps,
Get back to the beginning of beginnings,
The stream of everything that runs away.
Some say existence like a Pirouot
And Pirouette, forever in one place,
Stands still and dances, but it runs away,
It seriously, sadly, runs away
To fill the abyss' void with emptiness.
It flows beside us in this water brook,
But it flows over us. It flows between us
To separate us for a panic moment.
It flows between us, over us, and *with* us.
And it is time, strength, tone, light, life and love
And even substance lapsing unsubstantial;
The universal cataract of death
That spends to nothingness—and unresisted,
Save by some strange resistance in itself,
Not just a swerving, but a throwing back,
As if regret were in it and were sacred.
It has this throwing backward on itself
So that the fall of most of it is always
Raising a little, sending up a little.
Our life runs down in sending up the clock.
The brook runs down in sending up our life.
The sun runs down in sending up the brook.
And there is something sending up the sun.
It is this backward motion toward the source,
Against the stream, that most we see ourselves in.
The tribute of the current to the source.
It is from this in nature we are from.
It is most us."

"Today will be the day
You said so."

"No, today will be the day
You said the brook was called West-running Brook."

"Today will be the day of what we both said."

Once by the Pacific

The shattered water made a misty din,
Great waves looked over others coming in,
And thought of doing something to the shore
That water never did to land before.
The clouds were low and hairy in the skies,
Like locks blown forward in the gleam of eyes.
You could not tell, and yet it looked as if
The shore was lucky in being backed by cliff,
The cliff in being backed by continent.
It looked as if a night of dark intent
Was coming, and not only a night, an age.
Someone had better be prepared for rage.
There would be more than ocean water broken
Before God's last *Put out the light* was spoken.

The Bear

The bear puts both arms around the tree above her
And draws it down as if it were a lover
And its choke-cherries lips to kiss good-by,
Then lets it snap back upright in the sky.
Her next step rocks a bowlder on the wall
(She's making her cross-country in the fall.)
Her great weight creaks the barbed-wire in its staples
As she flings over and off down through the maples,
Leaving on one wire tooth a lock of hair.
Such is the uncaged progress of the bear.
The world has room to make a bear feel free;
The universe seems cramped to you and me.
Man acts more like a poor bear in a cage
That all day fights a nervous inward rage,
His mood rejecting all his mind suggests.
He paces back and forth and never rests
The toe-nail click and shuffle of his feet,
The telescope at one end of his beat,
And at the other end the microscope,
Two instruments of nearly equal hope,
And in conjunction giving quite a spread.
Or if he rests from scientific tread,
'Tis only to sit back and sway his head

Through ninety odd degrees of arc, it seems,
Between two metaphysical extremes.
He sits back on his fundamental butt
With lifted snout and eyes (if any) shut,
(He almost looks religious but he's not),
And back and forth he sways from cheek to cheek,
At one extreme agreeing with one Greek,
At the other agreeing with another Greek
Which may be thought, but only so to speak.
A baggy figure, equally pathetic
When sedentary and when peripatetic.

Sand Dunes

Sea waves are green and wet,
But up from where they die
Rise others vaster yet,
And those are brown and dry.

They are the sea made land
To come at the fisher town,
And bury in solid sand
The men she could not drown.

She may know cove and cape,
But she does not know mankind
If by any change of shape
She hopes to cut off mind.

Men left her a ship to sink;
They can leave her a hut as well,
And be but more free to think
For the one more cast-off shell.

The Lovely Shall Be Choosers

The Voice said, "Hurl her down!"

The Voices, "How far down?"

"Seven levels of the world."

"How much time have we?"

"Take twenty years.
She would refuse love safe with wealth and honor.
The Lovely shall be choosers, shall they?
Then let them choose!"

"Then we shall let her choose?"

"Yes, let her choose.
Take up the task beyond her choosing."

Invisible hands crowded on her shoulder
In readiness to weigh upon her.
But she stood straight still,
In broad round ear-rings, gold and jet with pearls,
And broad round suchlike brooch,
Her cheeks high colored,
Proud and the pride of friends.

The Voice asked, "You can let her choose?"

"Yes, we can let her and still triumph."

"Do it by joys. And leave her always blameless.
Be her first joy her wedding,
That though a wedding,
Is yet—well, something *they* know, he and she.
And after that her next joy
That though she grieves, her grief is secret:
Those friends know nothing of her grief to make it shameful.
Her third joy that though now they cannot help but know,
They move in pleasure too far off
To think much or much care.
Give her a child at either knee for fourth joy
To tell once and once only, for them never to forget,
How once she walked in brightness,
And make them see in the winter firelight.
But give her friends, for them she dares not tell
For their foregone incredulousness.
And be her next joy this:
Her never having deigned to tell them.
Make her among the humblest even
Seem to them less than they are.
Hopeless of being known for what she has been,
Failing of being loved for what she is,

Give her the comfort for her sixth of knowing
She fails from strangeness to a way of life
She came to from too high too late to learn.
Then send some *one* with eye to see
And wonder at her where she is
And words to wonder in her hearing how she came there.
But without time to stay and hear her story.
Be her last joy her heart's going out to this one
So that she almost speaks.

You know them—seven in all."

"Trust us," the Voices said.

Stopping by Woods on a Snowy Evening

Whose woods these are I think I know.
His house is in the village though;
He will not see me stopping here
To watch his woods fill up with snow.

My little horse must think it queer
To stop without a farmhouse near
Between the woods and frozen lake
The darkest evening of the year.

He gives his harness bells a shake
To ask if there is some mistake.
The only other sound's the sweep
Of easy wind and downy flake.

The woods are lovely, dark and deep,
But I have promises to keep,
And miles to go before I sleep,
And miles to go before I sleep.

Nothing Gold Can Stay

Nature's first green is gold,
Her hardest hue to hold.
Her early leaf's a flower;
But only so an hour.

Then leaf subsides to leaf.
So Eden sank to grief,
So dawn goes down to day.
Nothing gold can stay.

Tree at My Window

Tree at my window, window tree,
My sash is lowered when night comes on;
But let there never be curtain drawn
Between you and me.

Vague dream-head lifted out of the ground,
And thing next most diffuse to cloud,
Not all your light tongues talking aloud
Could be profound.

But, tree, I have seen you taken and tossed,
And if you have seen me when I slept,
You have seen me when I was taken and swept
And all but lost.

That day she put our heads together,
Fate had her imagination about her,
Your head so much concerned with outer,
Mine with inner, weather.

Spring Pools

These pools that, though in forests, still reflect
The total sky almost without defect,
And like the flowers beside them, chill and shiver,
Will like the flowers beside them soon be gone,
And yet not out by any brook or river,
But up by roots to bring dark foliage on.

The trees that have it in their pent-up buds
To darken nature and be summer woods—
Let them think twice before they use their powers
To blot out and drink up and sweep away
These flowery waters and these watery flowers
From snow that melted only yesterday.

A Sky Pair

CANIS MAJOR

The Great Overdog,
That heavenly beast
With a star in one eye,
Gives a leap in the East.

He dances upright
All the way to the West,
And never once drops
On his forefeet to rest.

I'm a poor Underdog;
But tonight I will bark
With the Great Overdog
That romps through the dark.

THE PEACEFUL SHEPHERD

If heaven were to do again,
And on the pasture bars
I leaned to line the figures in
Between the dotted stars,

I should be tempted to forget,
I think, the Crown of Rule,
The Scales of Trade, the Cross of Faith,
As hardly worth renewal.

For these have governed in our lives,
And see how men have warred!
The Cross, the Crown, the Scales, may all
As well have been the Sword.

Bereft

Where had I heard this wind before
Change like this to a deeper roar?
What would it take my standing there for,
Holding open a restive door,
Looking down hill to a frothy shore?

Summer was past and day was past.
Somber clouds on the West were massed.
Out in the porch's sagging floor
Leaves got up in a coil and hissed,
Blindly struck at my knee and missed.
Something sinister in the tone
Told me my secret must be known:
Word I was in the house alone
Somehow must have gotten abroad;
Word I was in my life alone;
Word I had no one left but God.

Desert Places

Snow falling and night falling fast, oh, fast
In a field I looked into going past,
And the ground almost covered smooth in snow,
But a few weeds and stubble showing last.

The woods around it have it—it is theirs.
All animals are smothered in their lairs.
I am too absent-spirited to count:
The loneliness includes me unawares.

And lonely as it is, that loneliness
Will be more lonely ere it will be less,
A blanker whiteness of benighted snow,
With no expression—nothing to express.

They cannot scare me with their empty spaces
Between stars—on stars void of human races.
I have it in me so much nearer home
To scare myself with my own desert places.

Two Tramps in Mud-Time

Out of the mud two strangers came
And caught me splitting wood in the yard.
And one of them put me off my aim
By hailing cheerily "Hit them hard!"
I knew pretty well why he dropped behind
And let the other go on a way.

I knew pretty well what he had in mind:
He wanted to take my job for pay.

Good blocks of beech it was I split,
As large around as the chopping-block;
And every piece I squarely hit
Fell splinterless as a cloven rock.
The blows that a life of self-control
Spares to strike for the common good
That day, giving a loose to my soul,
I spent on the unimportant wood.

The sun was warm but the wind was chill.
You know how it is with an April day:
When the sun is out and the wind is still,
You're one month on in the middle of May.
But if you so much as dare to speak,
A cloud comes over the sunlit arch,
A wind comes off a frozen peak,
And you're two months back in the middle of March.

A bluebird comes tenderly up to alight
And fronts the wind to unruffle a plume,
His song so pitched as not to excite
A single flower as yet to bloom.
It is snowing a flake: and he half knew
Winter was only playing possum.
Except in color he isn't blue,
But he wouldn't advise a thing to blossom.

The water for which we may have to look
In summertime with a witching-wand,
In every wheelrut's now a brook,
In every print of a hoof a pond.
Be glad of water, but don't forget
The lurking frost in the earth beneath
That will steal forth after the sun is set
And show on the water its crystal teeth.

The time when most I loved my task
These two must make me love it more
By coming with what they came to ask.
You'd think I never had felt before
The weight of an ax head poised aloft,
The grip on earth of outspread feet,

The life of muscles rocking soft
And smooth and moist in vernal heat.

Out of the woods two hulking tramps
(From sleeping God knows where last night
But not long since in the lumber camps).
They thought all chopping was theirs of right.
Men of the woods and lumber-jacks,
They judged me by their appropriate tool.
Except as a fellow handled an ax,
They had no way of knowing a fool.

Nothing on either side was said.
They knew they had but to stay their stay
And all their logic would fill my head:
As that I had no right to play
With what was another man's work for gain.
My right might be love but theirs was need.
And where the two exist in twain
Theirs was the better right—agreed.

But yield who will to their separation,
My object in life is to unite
My avocation and my vocation
As my two eyes make one in sight.
Only where love and need are one,
And the work is play for mortal stakes,
Is the deed ever really done
For Heaven and the future's sakes.

Departmental

OR, MY ANT JERRY

An ant on the table-cloth
Ran into a dormant moth
Of many times her size.
He showed not the least surprise.
His business wasn't with such.
He gave it scarcely a touch,
And was off on his duty run.
Yet if he encountered one
Of the hive's enquiry squad
Whose work is to find out God

And the nature of time and space,
He would put him onto the case.
Ants are a curious race;
One crossing with hurried tread
The body of one of their dead
Isn't given a moment's arrest—
Seems not even impressed.
But he no doubt reports to any
With whom he crosses antennae,
And they no doubt report
To the higher up at court.
Then word goes forth in Formic:
"Death's come to Jerry McCormic,
Our selfless forager Jerry.
Will the special Janizary
Whose office it is to bury
The dead of the commissary
Go bring him home to his people.
Lay him in state on a sepal.
Wrap him for shroud in a petal.
Embalm him with ichor of nettle.
This is the word of your Queen."
And presently on the scene
Appears a solemn mortician;
And taking formal position
With feelers calmly atwiddle,
Seizes the dead by the middle,
And heaving him high in air,
Carries him out of there.
No one stands round to stare.
It is nobody else's affair.

It couldn't be called ungentle.
But how thoroughly departmental.

A Considerable Speck

A speck that would have been beneath my sight
On any but a paper sheet so white
Set off across what I had written there,
And I had idly poised my pen in air
To stop it with a period of ink,
When something strange about it made me think

This was no dust speck by my breathing blown,
But unmistakably a living mite
With inclinations it could call its own.
It paused as with suspicion of my pen,
And then came racing wildly on again
To where my manuscript was not yet dry,
Then paused again and either drank or smelt—
With horror, for again it turned to fly.
Plainly with an intelligence I dealt.
It seemed too tiny to have room for feet,
Yet must have had a set of them complete
To express how much it didn't want to die.
It ran with terror and with cunning crept.
It faltered! I could see it hesitate—
Then in the middle of the open sheet
Cower down in desperation to accept
Whatever I accorded it of fate.
I have none of the tenderer-than-thou
Political collectivistic love
With which the modern world is being swept—
But this poor microscopic item now!
Since it was nothing I knew evil of
I let it lie there till I hope it slept.
I have a mind myself, and recognize
Mind where I meet with it in any guise.
No one can know how glad I am to find
On any sheet the least display of mind.

Happiness Makes Up in Height for What It Lacks in Length

Oh stormy, stormy world,
The days you were not swirled
Around with mist and cloud,
Or wrapped as in a shroud,
And the sun's brilliant ball
Was not in part or all
Obscured from mortal view,
Were days so very few
I can but wonder whence
I get the lasting sense
Of so much warmth and light.
If my mistrust is right

It may be altogether
From one day's perfect weather
When starting clear at dawn
The day went clearly on
To finish clear at eve.
I verily believe
My fair impression may
Be all from that one day
No shadow crossed but ours,
As through the blazing flowers
We went from house to wood
For change of solitude.

Come In

As I came to the edge of the woods,
Thrush music—hark!
Now if it was dusk outside,
Inside it was dark.

Too dark in the woods for a bird
By sleight of wing
To better its perch for the night,
Though it still could sing.

The last of the light of the sun
That had died in the west
Still lived for one song more
In a thrush's breast.

Far in the pillared dark
Thrush music went—
Almost like a call to come in
To the dark and lament.

But no, I was out for stars:
I would not come in.
I meant not even if asked;
And I hadn't been.

Directive

Back out of all this now too much for us,
Back in a time made simple by the loss
Of detail, burned, dissolved, and broken off
Like graveyard marble sculpture in the weather,
There is a house that is no more a house
Upon a farm that is no more a farm
And in a town that is no more a town.
The road there, if you'll let a guide direct you
Who only has at heart your getting lost,
May seem as if it should have been a quarry—
Great monolithic knees the former town
Long since gave up pretense of keeping covered.
And there's a story in a book about it:
Besides the wear of iron wagon wheels
The ledges show lines ruled southeast northwest,
The chisel work of an enormous Glacier
That braced his feet against the Arctic Pole.
You must not mind a certain coolness from him
Still said to haunt this side of Panther Mountain.
Nor need you mind the serial ordeal
Of being watched from forty cellar holes
As if by eye pairs out of forty firkins.
As for the woods' excitement over you
That sends light rustle rushes to their leaves,
Charge that to upstart inexperience.
Where were they all not twenty years ago?
They think too much of having shaded out
A few old pecker-fretted apple trees.
Make yourself up a cheering song of how
Someone's road home from work this once was,
Who may be just ahead of you on foot
Or creaking with a buggy load of grain.
The height of the adventure is the height
Of country where two village cultures faded
Into each other. Both of them are lost.
And if you're lost enough to find yourself
By now, pull in your ladder road behind you
And put a sign up CLOSED to all but me.
Then make yourself at home. The only field
Now left's no bigger than a harness gall.

First there's the children's house of make believe,
Some shattered dishes underneath a pine,
The playthings in the playhouse of the children.
Weep for what little things could make them glad.
Then for the house that is no more a house,
But only a belilaced cellar hole,
Now slowly closing like a dent in dough.
This was no playhouse but a house in earnest.
Your destination and your destiny's
A brook that was the water of the house,
Cold as a spring as yet so near its source,
Too lofty and original to rage.
(We know the valley streams that when aroused
Will leave their tatters hung on barb and thorn.)
I have kept hidden in the instep arch
Of an old cedar at the waterside
A broken drinking goblet like the Grail
Under a spell so the wrong ones can't find it,
So can't get saved, as Saint Mark says they mustn't.
(I stole the goblet from the children's playhouse.)
Here are your waters and your watering place.
Drink and be whole again beyond confusion.

Neither Out Far Nor In Deep

The people along the sand
All turn and look one way.
They turn their back on the land.
They look at the sea all day.

As long as it takes to pass
A ship keeps raising its hull;
The wetter ground like glass
Reflects a standing gull.

The land may vary more;
But wherever the truth may be—
The water comes ashore,
And the people look at the sea.

They cannot look out far.
They cannot look in deep.
But when was that ever a bar
To any watch they keep?

Provide, Provide

The witch that came (the withered hag)
To wash the steps with pail and rag,
Was once the beauty Abishag,

The picture pride of Hollywood.
Too many fall from great and good
For you to doubt the likelihood.

Die early and avoid the fate.
Or if predestined to die late,
Make up your mind to die in state.

Make the whole stock exchange your own!
If need be occupy a throne,
Where nobody can call *you* crone.

Some have relied on what they knew;
Others on being simply true.
What worked for them might work for you.

No memory of having starred
Atones for later disregard,
Or keeps the end from being hard.

Better to go down dignified
With boughten friendship at your side
Than none at all. Provide, provide!

The Gift Outright

The land was ours before we were the land's.
She was our land more than a hundred years
Before we were her people. She was ours
In Massachusetts, in Virginia;
But we were England's, still colonials,
Possessing what we still were unpossessed by,
Possessed by what we now no more possessed.
Something we were withholding made us weak
Until we found out that it was ourselves
We were withholding from our land of living,

And forthwith found salvation in surrender.
Such as we were we gave ourselves outright
(The deed of gift was many deeds of war)
To the land vaguely realizing westward,
But still unstoried, artless, unenhanced,
Such as she was, such as she would become.

Choose Something Like a Star

O Star (the fairest one in sight),
We grant your loftiness the right
To some obscurity of cloud—
It will not do to say of night,
Since dark is what brings out your light.
Some mystery becomes the proud.
But to be wholly taciturn
In your reserve is not allowed.
Say something to us we can learn
By heart and when alone repeat.
Say something! And it says "I burn."
But say with what degree of heat.
Talk Fahrenheit, talk Centigrade.
Use language we can comprehend.
Tell us what elements you blend.
It gives us strangely little aid,
But does tell something in the end.
And steadfast as Keats' Eremite,
Not even stooping from its sphere,
It asks a little of us here.
It asks of us a certain height,
So when at times the mob is swayed
To carry praise or blame too far,
We may choose something like a star
To stay our minds on and be staid.

Carl Sandburg

1878-

Chicago

Hog Butcher for the World,
Tool Maker, Stacker of Wheat,
Player with Railroads and the Nation's Freight Handler;
Stormy, husky, brawling,
City of the Big Shoulders:
They tell me you are wicked and I believe them, for I have seen your painted women under the gas lamps luring the farm boys.
And they tell me you are crooked and I answer: Yes, it is true I have seen the gunman kill and go free to kill again.
And they tell me you are brutal and my reply is: On the faces of women and children I have seen the marks of wanton hunger.
And having answered so I turn once more to those who sneer at this my city, and I give them back the sneer and say to them:
Come and show me another city with lifted head singing so proud to be alive and coarse and strong and cunning.
Flinging magnetic curses amid the toil of piling job on job, here is a tall bold slugger set vivid against the little soft cities;
Fierce as a dog with tongue lapping for action, cunning as a savage pitted against the wilderness,
Bareheaded,
Shoveling,
Wrecking,
Planning,
Building, breaking, rebuilding.
Under the smoke, dust all over his mouth, laughing with white teeth,
Under the terrible burden of destiny laughing as a young man laughs,

Laughing even as an ignorant fighter laughs who has never lost a battle,
Bragging and laughing that under his wrist is the pulse, and under his ribs the heart of the people,
Laughing!
Laughing the stormy, husky, brawling laughter of Youth, half-naked, sweating, proud to be Hog Butcher, Tool Maker, Stacker of Wheat, Player with Railroads and Freight Handler to the Nation.

Fog

The fog comes
on little cat feet.
It sits looking
over harbor and city
on silent haunches
and then moves on.

Grass

Pile the bodies high at Austerlitz and Waterloo.
Shovel them under and let me work—
I am the grass; I cover all.

And pile them high at Gettysburg
And pile them high at Ypres and Verdun.
Shovel them under and let me work.
Two years, ten years, and passengers ask the conductor:
What place is this?
Where are we now?

I am the grass.
Let me work.

Cool Tombs

When Abraham Lincoln was shoveled into the tombs, he forgot the copperheads and the assassin . . . in the dust, in the cool tombs.

And Ulysses Grant lost all thought of con men and Wall Street, cash and collateral turned ashes . . . in the dust, in the cool tombs.

Pocahontas' body, lovely as a poplar, sweet as a red haw in November or a pawpaw in May, did she wonder? does she remember? . . . in the dust, in the cool tombs?

Take any streetful of people buying clothes and groceries, cheering a hero or throwing confetti and blowing tin horns . . . tell me if the lovers are losers . . . tell me if any get more than the lovers . . . in the dust . . . in the cool tombs.

Limited

I am riding on a limited express, one of the crack trains of the nation.
Hurtling across the prairie into blue haze and dark air go fifteen all-steel coaches holding a thousand people.
(All the coaches shall be scrap and rust and all the men and women laughing in the diners and sleepers shall pass to ashes.)
I ask a man in the smoker where he is going and he answers: "Omaha."

Four Preludes on Playthings of the Wind

"The Past Is a Bucket of Ashes."

I

The woman named Tomorrow
sits with a hairpin in her teeth
and takes her time
and does her hair the way she wants it
and fastens at last the last braid and coil
and puts the hairpin where it belongs
and turns and drawls: Well, what of it?
My grandmother, Yesterday, is gone.
What of it? Let the dead be dead.

II

The doors were cedar
and the panel strips of gold

and the girls were golden girls
and the panels read and the girls chanted:
    We are the greatest city,
    and the greatest nation:
    nothing like us ever was.

The doors are twisted on broken hinges,
Sheets of rain swish through on the wind
    where the golden girls ran and the panels read:
    We are the greatest city,
    the greatest nation,
    nothing like us ever was.

III

It has happened before.
Strong men put up a city and got
    a nation together,
And paid singers to sing and women
    to warble: We are the greatest city,
        the greatest nation,
        nothing like us ever was.

And while the singers sang
and the strong men listened
and paid the singers well,
  there were rats and lizards who listened
  . . . and the only listeners left now
  . . . are . . . the rats . . . and the lizards.

And there are black crows
crying, "Caw, caw,"
bringing mud and sticks
building a nest
  over the words carved
  on the doors where the panels were cedar
  and the strips on the panels were gold
  and the golden girls came singing:
    We are the greatest city,
    the greatest nation:
    nothing like us ever was.

The only singers now are crows crying, "Caw, caw,"
And the sheets of rain whine in the wind and doorways.
And the only listeners now are . . . the rats . . . and the lizards.

IV

The feet of the rats
scribble on the doorsills;
the hieroglyphs of the rat footprints
chatter the pedigrees of the rats
and babble of the blood
and gabble of the breed
of the grandfathers and the great-grandfathers
of the rats.

And the wind shifts
and the dust on a doorsill shifts
and even the writing of the rat footprints
tells us nothing, nothing at all
about the greatest city, the greatest nation
where the strong men listened
and the women warbled: Nothing like us ever was.

Jazz Fantasia

Drum on your drums, batter on your banjos, sob on the long cool winding saxophones. Go to it, O jazzmen.

Sling your knuckles on the bottoms of the happy tin pans, let your trombones ooze, and go husha-husha-hush with the slippery sandpaper.

Moan like an autumn wind high in the lonesome treetops, moan soft like you wanted somebody terrible, cry like a racing car slipping away from a motorcycle-cop, bang-bang! you jazzmen, bang altogether drums, traps, banjos, horns, tin cans—make two people fight on the top of a stairway and scratch each other's eyes in a clinch tumbling down the stairs.

Can the rough stuff . . . Now a Mississippi steamboat pushes up the night river with a hoo-hoo-hoo-oo . . . and the green lanterns calling to the high soft stars . . . a red moon rides on the humps of the low river hills. . . . Go to it, O jazzmen.

A.E.F.

There will be a rusty gun on the wall, sweetheart,
The rifle grooves curling with flakes of rust.
A spider will make a silver string nest in the darkest, warmest
corner of it.
The trigger and the range-finder, they too will be rusty.
And no hands will polish the gun, and it will hang on the wall.
Forefingers and thumbs will point absently and casually toward
it.
It will be spoken among half-forgotten, wished-to-be-forgotten
things.
They will tell the spider: Go on, you're doing good work.

Losers

If I should pass the tomb of Jonah
I would stop there and sit for a while;
Because I was swallowed one time deep in the dark
And came out alive after all.

If I pass the burial spot of Nero
I shall say to the wind, "Well, well!"—
I who have fiddled in a world on fire,
I who have done so many stunts not worth the doing.

I am looking for the grave of Sinbad too.
I want to shake his ghost-hand and say,
"Neither of us died very early, did we?"

And the last sleeping-place of Nebuchadnezzar—
When I arrive there I shall tell the wind:
"You ate grass; I have eaten crow—
Who is better off now or next year?"

Jack Cade, John Brown, Jesse James,
There too I could sit down and stop for a while.
I think I could tell their headstones:
"God, let me remember all good losers."

I could ask people to throw ashes on their heads
In the name of that sergeant at Belleau Woods,
Walking into the drumfires, calling his men,
"Come on, you . . . Do you want to live forever?"

Wind Song

Long ago I learned how to sleep,
In an old apple orchard where the wind swept by counting its money and throwing it away,
In a wind-gaunt orchard where the limbs forked out and listened or never listened at all,
In a passel of trees where the branches trapped the wind into whistling, "Who, who are you?"
I slept with my head in an elbow on a summer afternoon and there I took a sleep lesson.
There I went away saying: I know why they sleep, I know how they trap the tricky winds.
Long ago I learned how to listen to the singing wind and how to forget and how to hear the deep whine,
Slapping and lapsing under the day blue and the night stars:
Who, who are you?

Who can ever forget
listening to the wind go by
counting its money
and throwing it away?

Upstream

The strong men keep coming on,
They go down shot, hanged, sick, broken.
They live on fighting, singing, lucky as plungers.
The strong mothers pulling them on . . .
The strong mothers pulling them from a dark sea, a great prairie, a long mountain.
Call hallelujah, call amen, call deep thanks.
The strong men keep coming on.

The People Will Live On

(From "The People, Yes")

The people will live on.
The learning and blundering people will live on.
They will be tricked and sold and again sold
And go back to the nourishing earth for rootholds,
The people so peculiar in renewal and comeback,
You can't laugh off their capacity to take it.
The mammoth rests between his cyclonic dramas.

The people so often sleepy, weary, enigmatic,
is a vast huddle with many units saying:
"I earn my living.
I make enough to get by
and it takes all my time.
If I had more time
I could do more for myself
and maybe for others.
I could read and study
and talk things over
and find out about things.
It takes time.
I wish I had the time."

The people is a tragic and comic two-face:
hero and hoodlum: phantom and gorilla twisting to moan with a gargoyle mouth: "They
buy me and sell me . . . it's a game . . .
sometime I'll break loose . . ."

Once having marched
Over the margins of animal necessity,
Over the grim line of sheer subsistence
Then man came
To the deeper rituals of his bones,
To the lights lighter than any bones,
To the time for thinking things over,
To the dance, the song, the story,
Or the hours given over to dreaming,
Once having so marched.

Between the finite limitations of the five senses
and the endless yearnings of man for the beyond
the people hold to the humdrum bidding of work and food
while reaching out when it comes their way
for lights beyond the prison of the five senses,
for keepsakes lasting beyond any hunger or death.
    This reaching is alive.
The panderers and liars have violated and smutted it.
    Yet this reaching is alive yet
    for lights and keepsakes.

The people know the salt of the sea
and the strength of the winds
lashing the corners of the earth.
The people take the earth
as a tomb of rest and a cradle of hope.
Who else speaks for the Family of Man?
They are in tune and step
with constellations of universal law.

The people is a polychrome,
a spectrum and a prism
held in a moving monolith,
a console organ of changing themes,
a clavilux of color poems
wherein the sea offers fog
and the fog moves off in rain
and the labrador sunset shortens
to a nocturne of clear stars
serene over the shot spray
of northern lights.

The steel mill sky is alive.
The fire breaks white and zigzag
shot on a gun-metal gloaming.
Man is a long time coming.
Man will yet win.
Brother may yet line up with brother:

This old anvil laughs at many broken hammers.
    There are men who can't be bought.
    The fireborn are at home in fire.
    The stars make no noise.
    You can't hinder the wind from blowing.

Time is a great teacher.
Who can live without hope?

In the darkness with a great bundle of grief
the people march.
In the night, and overhead a shovel of stars for
keeps, the people march:
"Where to? what next?"

Vachel Lindsay

1879-1931

The Congo

(A Study of the Negro Race)

I. THEIR BASIC SAVAGERY

Fat black bucks in a wine-barrel room,
Barrel-house kings, with feet unstable,
Sagged and reeled and pounded on the table,
Pounded on the table,
Beat an empty barrel with the handle of a
broom,
Hard as they were able,
Boom, boom, BOOM,
With a silk umbrella and the handle of a broom,
Boomlay, boomlay, boomlay, BOOM.

A deep rolling bass.

THEN I had religion, THEN I had a vision.
I could not turn from their revel in derision.
THEN I SAW THE CONGO, CREEPING THROUGH THE
BLACK,
CUTTING THROUGH THE JUNGLE WITH A GOLDEN
TRACK.

More deliberate. Solemnly chanted.

Then along that riverbank
A thousand miles

Tattooed cannibals danced in files;
Then I heard the boom of the blood-lust song
And a thigh-bone beating on a tin-pan gong.
And "Blood" screamed the whistles and the fifes
 of the warriors,
"Blood" screamed the skull-faced, lean witch-
 doctors,
"Whirl ye the deadly voo-doo rattle,
Harry the uplands,
Steal all the cattle,
Rattle-rattle, rattle-rattle,
Bing!
Boomlay, boomlay, boomlay, Boom,"
A roaring, epic, rag-time tune
From the mouth of the Congo
To the Mountains of the Moon.
Death is an Elephant,
Torch-eyed and horrible,
Foam-flanked and terrible.
Boom, steal the pygmies,
Boom, kill the Arabs,
Boom, kill the white men,
Hoo, Hoo, Hoo.
Listen to the yell of Leopold's ghost
Burning in Hell for his hand-maimed host.
Hear how the demons chuckle and yell
Cutting his hands off, down in Hell.
Listen to the creepy proclamation,
Blown through the lairs of the forest-nation,
Blown past the white-ants' hill of clay,
Blown past the marsh where the butterflies
 play:—
"Be careful what you do,
Or Mumbo-Jumbo, God of the Congo,
And all of the other
Gods of the Congo,
Mumbo-Jumbo will hoo-doo you,
Mumbo-Jumbo will hoo-doo you,
Mumbo-Jumbo will hoo-doo you."

A rapidly piling climax of speed and racket.

With a philosophic pause.

Shrilly and with a heavily accented meter.

Like the wind in the chimney.

All the o sounds very golden. Heavy accents very heavy. Light accents very light. Last line whispered.

II. THEIR IRREPRESSIBLE HIGH SPIRITS

Wild crap-shooters with a whoop and a call
Danced the juba in their gambling-hall

Rather shrill and high.

And laughed fit to kill, and shook the town,
And guyed the policemen and laughed them down
With a boomlay, boomlay, boomlay, BOOM. . . .
THEN I SAW THE CONGO, CREEPING THROUGH THE BLACK,
CUTTING THROUGH THE JUNGLE WITH A GOLDEN TRACK.

Read exactly as in first section.

A Negro fairyland swung into view,
A minstrel river
Where dreams come true.
The ebony palace soared on high
Through the blossoming trees to the evening sky,
The inlaid porches and casements shone
With gold and ivory and elephant-bone.
And the black crowd laughed till their sides were sore
At the baboon butler in the agate door,
And the well-known tunes of the parrot band
That trilled on the bushes of that magic land.

Lay emphasis on the delicate ideas. Keep as light-footed as possible.

A troupe of skull-faced witch-men came
Through the agate doorway in suits of flame,
Yes, long-tailed coats with a gold-leaf crust
And hats that were covered with diamond-dust.
And the crowd in the court gave a whoop and a call
And danced the juba from wall to wall.

With pomposity.

But the witch-men suddenly stilled the throng
With a stern cold glare, and a stern old song:—
"Mumbo-Jumbo will hoo-doo you." . . .

With a great deliberation and ghostliness.

Just then from the doorway, as fat as shotes,
Came the cake-walk princes in their long red coats,
Shoes with a patent leather shine,
And tall silk hats that were red as wine.

With overwhelming assurance, good cheer, and pomp.

And they pranced with their butterfly partners there,
Coal-black maidens with pearls in their hair,
Knee-skirts trimmed with the jessamine sweet,
And bells on their ankles and little black feet.
And the couples railed at the chant and the frown
Of the witch-men lean, and laughed them down

With growing speed and sharply marked dance-rhythm.

(O rare was the revel, and well worth while
That made those glowering witch-men smile.)

The cake-walk royalty then began
To walk for a cake that was tall as a man
To the tune of "Boomlay, boomlay, BOOM,"
While the witch-men laughed, with a sinister air,
And sang with the scalawags prancing there:—
"Walk with care, walk with care,
Or Mumbo-Jumbo, God of the Congo,
And all of the other
Gods of the Congo,
Mumbo-Jumbo will hoo-doo you.
Beware, beware, walk with care,
Boomlay, boomlay, boomlay, boom.
Boomlay, boomlay, boomlay, boom,
Boomlay, boomlay, boomlay, boom,
Boomlay, boomlay, boomlay,
BOOM."

With a touch of Negro dialect, and as rapidly as possible toward the end.

O rare was the revel, and well worth while
That made those glowering witch-men smile.

Slow philosophic calm.

III. THE HOPE OF THEIR RELIGION

A good old Negro in the slums of the town
Preached at a sister for her velvet gown.
Howled at a brother for his low-down ways,
His prowling, guzzling, sneak-thief days.
Beat on the Bible till he wore it out,
Starting the jubilee revival shout.
And some had visions, as they stood on chairs,
And sang of Jacob, and the golden stairs.
And they all repented, a thousand strong,
From their stupor and savagery and sin and wrong
And slammed their hymn books till they shook the room
With "Glory, glory, glory,"
And "Boom, boom, BOOM."

Heavy bass. With a literal imitation of camp-meeting racket, and trance.

THEN I SAW THE CONGO, CREEPING THROUGH THE BLACK,
CUTTING THROUGH THE JUNGLE WITH A GOLDEN TRACK.

Exactly as in the first section.

And the gray sky opened like a new-rent veil
And showed the Apostles with their coats of
mail.
In bright white steel they were seated round
And their fire-eyes watched where the Congo
wound.
And the twelve Apostles, from their thrones on
high,
Thrilled all the forest with their heavenly cry:—
"Mumbo-Jumbo will die in the jungle;
Never again will he hoo-doo you,
Never again will he hoo-doo you."

Sung to the tune of "Hark, ten thousand harps and voices."

Then along that river, a thousand miles
The vine-snared trees fell down in files.
Pioneer angels cleared the way
For a Congo paradise, for babes at play,
For sacred capitals, for temples clean.
Gone were the skull-faced witch-men lean.
There, where the wild ghost-gods had wailed
A million boats of the angels sailed
With oars of silver, and prows of blue
And silken pennants that the sun shone through.
'Twas a land transfigured, 'twas a new creation.
Oh, a singing wind swept the Negro nation
And on through the backwoods clearing flew:—
"Mumbo-Jumbo is dead in the jungle.
Never again will he hoo-doo you.
Never again will he hoo-doo you."

With growing deliberation and joy.

In a rather high key—as delicately as possible.

To the tune of "Hark, ten thousand harps and voices."

Redeemed were the forests, the beasts and the
men,
And only the vulture dared again
By the far, lone mountains of the moon
To cry, in the silence, the Congo tune:—
"Mumbo-Jumbo will hoo-doo you,
Mumbo . . . Jumbo . . . will . . . hoo-doo . . .
you."

Dying off into a penetrating, terrified whisper.

General William Booth Enters into Heaven

(To be sung to the tune of "The Blood of the Lamb" with indicated instruments)

I

(Bass drum beaten loudly.)
Booth led boldly with his big bass drum—
(Are you washed in the blood of the Lamb?)
The Saints smiled gravely and they said: "He's come."
(Are you washed in the blood of the Lamb?)
Walking lepers followed, rank on rank,
Lurching bravos from the ditches dank,
Drabs from the alleyways and drug fiends pale—
Minds still passion-ridden, soul-powers frail:—
Vermin-eaten saints with moldy breath,
Unwashed legions with the ways of Death—
(Are you washed in the blood of the Lamb?)

(Banjos.)
Every slum had sent its half-a-score
The round world over. (Booth had groaned for more.)
Every banner that the wide world flies
Bloomed with glory and transcendent dyes.
Big-voiced lasses made their banjos bang,
Tranced, fanatical they shrieked and sang:—
"Are you washed in the blood of the Lamb?"
Hallelujah! It was queer to see
Bull-necked convicts with that land make free.
Loons with trumpets blowed a blare, blare, blare
On, on upward thro' the golden air!
(Are you washed in the blood of the Lamb?)

II

(Bass drum slower and softer.)
Booth died blind and still by faith he trod,
Eyes still dazzled by the ways of God.
Booth led boldly, and he looked the chief,
Eagle countenance in sharp relief,
Beard a-flying, air of high command
Unabated in that holy land.

(Sweet flute music.)
Jesus came from out the court-house door,
Stretched his hands above the passing poor.
Booth saw not, but led his queer ones there
Round and round the mighty court-house square.
Yet in an instant all that blear review
Marched on spotless, clad in raiment new.
The lame were straightened, withered limbs uncurled
And blind eyes opened on a new, sweet world.

(Bass drum louder.)
Drabs and vixens in a flash made whole!
Gone was the weasel-head, the snout, the jowl!
Sages and sibyls now, and athletes clean,
Rulers of empires, and of forests green!

(Grand chorus of all instruments. Tambourines to the foreground.)
The hosts were sandaled, and their wings were fire!
(Are you washed in the blood of the Lamb?)
But their noise played havoc with the angel-choir.
(Are you washed in the blood of the Lamb?)
Oh, shout Salvation! It was good to see
Kings and Princes by the Lamb set free.
The banjos rattled and the tambourines
Jing-jing-jingled in the hands of Queens.

(Reverently sung, no instruments.)
And when Booth halted by the curb for prayer
He saw his Master thro' the flag-filled air.
Christ came gently with a robe and crown
For Booth the soldier, while the throng knelt down.
He saw King Jesus. They were face to face,
And he knelt a-weeping in that holy place.
Are you washed in the blood of the Lamb?

The Eagle That Is Forgotten

(John P. Altgeld. Born December 30, 1847;
died March 12, 1902)

Sleep softly . . . eagle forgotten . . . under the stone.
Time has its way with you there, and the clay has its own.
"We have buried him now," thought your foes, and in secret rejoiced.
They made a brave show of their mourning, their hatred unvoiced,

They had snarled at you, barked at you, foamed at you, day after day,
Now you were ended. They praised you, . . . and laid you away.

The others that mourned you in silence and terror and truth,
The widow bereft of her pittance, the boy without youth,
The mocked and the scorned and the wounded, the lame and the poor
That should have remembered forever, . . . remember no more.

Where are those lovers of yours, on what name do they call,
The lost, that in armies wept over your funeral pall?
They call on the names of a hundred high-valiant ones,
A hundred white eagles have risen, the sons of your sons,
The zeal in their wings is a zeal that your dreaming began,
The valor that wore out your soul in the service of man.

Sleep softly, . . . eagle forgotten, . . . under the stone.
Time has its way with you there, and the clay has its own.
Sleep on, O brave-hearted, O wise man, that kindled the flame—
To live in mankind is far more than to live in a name,
To live in mankind, far, far more . . . than to live in a name

Wallace Stevens

1879-1955

Anecdote of the Jar

I placed a jar in Tennessee,
And round it was, upon a hill.
It made the slovenly wilderness
Surround that hill.

The wilderness rose up to it,
And sprawled around, no longer wild.

The jar was round upon the ground
And tall and of a port in air.

It took dominion everywhere.
The jar was gray and bare.
It did not give of bird or bush,
Like nothing else in Tennessee.

Peter Quince at the Clavier

I

Just as my fingers on these keys
Make music, so the self-same sounds
On my spirit make a music, too.

Music is feeling, then, not sound;
And thus it is that what I feel,
Here in this room, desiring you,

Thinking of your blue-shadowed silk,
Is music. It is like the strain
Waked in the elders by Susanna:

Of a green evening, clear and warm,
She bathed in her still garden, while
The red-eyed elders, watching, felt

The basses of their beings throb
In witching chords, and their thin blood
Pulse pizzicati of Hosanna.

II

In the green water, clear and warm,
Susanna lay,
She searched
The touch of springs,
And found
Concealed imaginings.
She sighed,
For so much melody.

Upon the bank, she stood
In the cool

Of spent emotions.
She felt, among the leaves,
The dew
Of old devotions.

She walked upon the grass,
Still quavering.
The winds were like her maids,
On timid feet,
Fetching her woven scarves,
Yet wavering.

A breath upon her hand
Muted the night.
She turned—
A cymbal crashed,
And roaring horns.

III

Soon, with a noise like tambourines,
Came her attendant Byzantines.

They wondered why Susanna cried
Against the elders by her side;

And as they whispered, the refrain
Was like a willow swept by rain.

Anon, their lamps' uplifted flame
Revealed Susanna and her shame.

And then, the simpering Byzantines
Fled, with a noise like tambourines.

IV

Beauty is momentary in the mind—
The fitful tracing of a portal;
But in the flesh it is immortal.

The body dies; the body's beauty lives.
So evenings die, in their green going,
A wave, interminably flowing.
So gardens die, their meek breath scenting
The cowl of Winter, done repenting.

So maidens die, to the auroral
Celebration of a maiden's choral.

Susanna's music touched the bawdy strings
Of those white elders; but, escaping,
Left only Death's ironic scraping.
Now, in its immortality, it plays
On the clear viol of her memory,
And makes a constant sacrament of praise.

To the One of Fictive Music

Sister and mother and diviner love,
And of the sisterhood of the living dead
Most near, most clear, and of the clearest bloom,
And of the fragrant mothers the most dear
And queen, and of diviner love the day
And flame and summer and sweet fire, no thread
Of cloudy silver sprinkles in your gown
Its venom of renown, and on your head
No crown is simpler than the simple hair.

Now, of the music summoned by the birth
That separates us from the wind and sea,
Yet leaves us in them, until earth becomes,
By being so much of the things we are,
Gross effigy and simulacrum, none
Gives motion to perfection more serene
Than yours, out of our imperfections wrought,
Most rare, or ever of more kindred air
In the laborious weaving that you wear.

For so retentive of themselves are men
That music is intensest which proclaims
The near, the clear, and vaunts the clearest bloom,
And of all vigils musing the obscure,
That apprehends the most which sees and names,
As in your name, an image that is sure,
Among the arrant spices of the sun,
O bough and bush and scented vine, in whom
We give ourselves our likest issuance.

Yet not too like, yet not so like to be
Too near, too clear, saving a little to endow

Our feigning with the strange unlike, whence springs
The difference that heavenly pity brings.
For this, musician, in your girdle fixed
Bear other perfumes. On your pale head wear
A band entwining, set with fatal stones.
Unreal, give back to us what once you gave:
The imagination that we spurned and crave.

Sunday Morning

I

Complacencies of the peignoir, and late
Coffee and oranges in a sunny chair,
And the green freedom of a cockatoo
Upon a rug mingle to dissipate
The holy hush of ancient sacrifice.
She dreams a little, and she feels the dark
Encroachment of that old catastrophe,
As a calm darkens among water-lights.
The pungent oranges and bright, green wings
Seem things in some procession of the dead,
Winding across wide water, without sound.
The day is like wide water, without sound,
Stilled for the passing of her dreaming feet
Over the seas, to silent Palestine,
Dominion of the blood and sepulchre.

II

Why should she give her bounty to the dead?
What is divinity if it can come
Only in silent shadows and in dreams?
Shall she not find in comforts of the sun,
In pungent fruit and bright, green wings, or else
In any balm or beauty of the earth,
Things to be cherished like the thought of heaven?
Divinity must live within herself:
Passions of rain, or moods in falling snow;
Grievings in loneliness, or unsubdued
Elations when the forest blooms; gusty
Emotions on wet roads on autumn nights;
All pleasures and all pains, remembering
The bough of summer and the winter branch.
These are the measures destined for her soul.

III

Jove in the clouds had his inhuman birth.
No mother suckled him, no sweet land gave
Large-mannered motions to his mythy mind.
He moved among us, as a muttering king,
Magnificent, would move among his hinds,
Until our blood, commingling, virginal,
With heaven, brought such requital to desire
The very hinds discerned it, in a star.
Shall our blood fail? Or shall it come to be
The blood of paradise? And shall the earth
Seem all of paradise that we shall know?
The sky will be much friendlier then than now,
A part of labor and a part of pain,
And next in glory to enduring love,
Not this dividing and indifferent blue.

IV

She says, "I am content when wakened birds,
Before they fly, test the reality
Of misty fields, by their sweet questionings;
But when the birds are gone, and their warm fields
Return no more, where, then, is paradise?"
There is not any haunt of prophecy,
Nor any old chimera of the grave,
Neither the golden underground, nor isle
Melodious, where spirits gat them home,
Nor visionary south, nor cloudy palm
Remote on heaven's hill, that has endured
As April's green endures; or will endure
Like her remembrance of awakened birds,
Or her desire for June and evening, tipped
By the consummation of the swallow's wings.

V

She says, "But in contentment I still feel
The need of some imperishable bliss."
Death is the mother of beauty; hence from her,
Alone, shall come fulfilment to our dreams
And our desires. Although she strews the leaves
Of sure obliteration on our paths,
The path sick sorrow took, the many paths
Where triumph rang its brassy phrase, or love

Whispered a little out of tenderness,
She makes the willow shiver in the sun
For maidens who were wont to sit and gaze
Upon the grass, relinquished to their feet.
She causes boys to pile new plums and pears
On disregarded plate. The maidens taste
And stray impassioned in the littering leaves.

VI

Is there no change of death in paradise?
Does ripe fruit never fall? Or do the boughs
Hang always heavy in that perfect sky,
Unchanging, yet so like our perishing earth,
With rivers like our own that seek for seas
They never find, the same receding shores
That never touch with inarticulate pang?
Why set the pear upon those river-banks
Or spice the shores with odors of the plum?
Alas, that they should wear our colors there,
The silken weavings of our afternoons,
And pick the strings of our insipid lutes!
Death is the mother of beauty, mystical,
Within whose burning bosom we devise
Our earthly mothers waiting, sleeplessly.

VII

Supple and turbulent, a ring of men
Shall chant in orgy on a summer morn
Their boisterous devotion to the sun,
Not as a god, but as a god might be,
Naked among them, like a savage source.
Their chant shall be a chant of paradise,
Out of their blood, returning to the sky;
And in their chant shall enter, voice by voice,
The windy lake wherein their lord delights,
The trees, like serafim, and echoing hills,
That choir among themselves long afterward.
They shall know well the heavenly fellowship
Of men that perish and of summer morn.
And whence they came and whither they shall go
The dew upon their feet shall manifest.

VIII

She hears, upon that water without sound,
A voice that cries, "The tomb in Palestine
Is not the porch of spirits lingering.
It is the grave of Jesus, where he lay."
We live in an old chaos of the sun,
Or old dependency of day and night,
Or island solitude, unsponsored, free,
Of that wide water, inescapable.
Deer walk upon our mountains, and the quail
Whistle about us their spontaneous cries;
Sweet berries ripen in the wilderness;
And, in the isolation of the sky,
At evening, casual flocks of pigeons make
Ambiguous undulations as they sink,
Downward to darkness, on extended wings.

Domination of Black

At night, by the fire,
The colors of the bushes
And of the fallen leaves,
Repeating themselves,
Turned in the room,
Like the leaves themselves
Turning in the wind.
Yes: but the color of the heavy hemlocks
Came striding.
And I remembered the cry of the peacocks.

The colors of their tails
Were like the leaves themselves
Turning in the wind,
In the twilight wind.
They swept over the room,
Just as they flew from the boughs of the hemlocks
Down to the ground.
I heard them cry—the peacocks.
Was it a cry against the twilight
Or against the leaves themselves
Turning in the wind,
Turning as the flames
Turned in the fire,

Turning as the tails of the peacocks
Turned in the loud fire,
Loud as the hemlocks
Full of the cry of the peacocks?
Or was it a cry against the hemlocks?

Out of the window,
I saw how the planets gathered
Like the leaves themselves
Turning in the wind.
I saw how the night came,
Came striding like the color of the heavy hemlocks.
I felt afraid.
And I remembered the cry of the peacocks.

Sea Surface Full of Clouds

I

In that November off Tehuantepec,
The slopping of the sea grew still one night
And in the morning summer hued the deck

And made one think of rosy chocolate
And gilt umbrellas. Paradisal green
Gave suavity to the perplexed machine

Of ocean, which like limpid water lay.
Who, then, in that ambrosial latitude
Out of the light evolved the moving blooms,

Who, then, evolved the sea-blooms from the clouds
Diffusing balm in that Pacific calm?
C'était mon enfant, mon bijou, mon âme.

The sea-clouds whitened far below the calm
And moved, as blooms move, in the swimming green
And in its watery radiance, while the hue

Of heaven in an antique reflection rolled
Round those flotillas. And sometimes the sea
Poured brilliant iris on the glistening blue.

II

In that November off Tehuantepec
The slopping of the sea grew still one night.
At breakfast jelly yellow streaked the deck

And made one think of chop-house chocolate
And sham umbrellas. And a sham-like green
Capped summer-seeming on the tense machine

Of ocean, which in sinister flatness lay.
Who, then, beheld the rising of the clouds
That strode submerged in that malevolent sheen,

Who saw the mortal massives of the blooms
Of water moving on the water-floor?
C'était mon frère du ciel, ma vie, mon or.

The gongs rang loudly as the windy blooms
Hoo-hooed it in the darkened ocean-blooms.
The gongs grew still. And then blue heaven spread

Its crystalline pendentives on the sea
And the macabre of the water-glooms.
In an enormous undulation fled.

III

In that November off Tehuantepec,
The slopping of the sea grew still one night,
And a pale silver patterned on the deck

Made one think of porcelain chocolate
And pied umbrellas. An uncertain green,
Piano-polished, held the tranced machine

Of ocean, as a prelude holds and holds.
Who, seeing silver petals of white blooms
Unfolding in the water, feeling sure

Of the milk within the saltiest spurge, heard, then,
The sea unfolding in the sunken clouds?
Oh! C'était mon extase et mon amour.

So deeply sunken were they that the shrouds,
The shrouding shadows, made the petals black
Until the rolling heaven made them blue,

A blue beyond the rainy hyacinth,
And smiting the crevasses of the leaves
Deluged the ocean with a sapphire hue.

IV

In that November off Tehuantepec
The night-long slopping of the sea grew still.
A mallow morning dozed upon the deck

And made one think of musky chocolate
And frail umbrellas. A too-fluent green
Suggested malice in the dry machine

Of ocean, pondering dank stratagem.
Who then beheld the figures of the clouds,
Like blooms secluded in the thick marine?

Like blooms? Like damasks that were shaken off
From the loosed girdles in the spangling must.
C'était ma foi, la nonchalance divine.

The nakedness would rise and suddenly turn
Salt masks of beard and mouths of bellowing,
Would— But more suddenly the heaven rolled

Its bluest sea-clouds in the thinking green
And the nakedness became the broadest blooms,
Mile-mallows that a mallow sun cajoled.

V

In that November off Tehuantepec
Night stilled the slopping of the sea. The day
Came, bowing and voluble, upon the deck,

Good clown. . . . One thought of Chinese chocolate
And large umbrellas. And a motley green
Followed the drift of the obese machine

Of ocean, perfected in indolence.
What pistache one, ingenious and droll,
Beheld the sovereign clouds as jugglery

And the sea as turquoise-turbaned Sambo, neat
At tossing saucers—cloudy-conjuring sea?
C'était mon esprit batard, l'ignominie.

The sovereign clouds came clustering. The conch
Of loyal conjuration trumped. The wind
Of green blooms turning crisped the motley hue

To clearing opalescence. Then the sea
And heaven rolled as one and from the two
Came fresh transfigurings of freshest blue.

Annual Gaiety

In the morning in the blue snow
The catholic sun, its majesty,
Pinks and pinks the ice-hard melanchole.

Wherefore those prayers to the moon?
Or is it that alligators lie
Along the edges of your eye
Basking in desert Florida?

Père Guzz, in heaven, thumb your lyre
And chant the January fire
And joy of snow and snow.

Homunculus et la Belle Étoile

In the sea, Biscayne, there prinks
The young emerald, evening star,
Good light for drunkards, poets, widows,
And ladies soon to be married.

By this light the salty fishes
Arch in the sea like tree-branches,
Going in many directions
Up and down.

This light conducts
The thoughts of drunkards, the feelings
Of widows and trembling ladies,
The movements of fishes.

How pleasant an existence it is
That this emerald charms philosophers,
Until they become thoughtlessly willing
To bathe their hearts in later moonlight,

Knowing that they can bring back thought
In the night that is still to be silent,
Reflecting this thing and that,
Before they sleep!

It is better that, as scholars,
They should think hard in the dark cuffs
Of voluminous cloaks,
And shave their heads and bodies.

It might well be that their mistress
Is no gaunt fugitive phantom.
She might, after all, be a wanton,
Abundantly beautiful, eager,

Fecund,
From whose being by starlight, on sea-coast,
The innermost good of their seeking
Might come in the simplest of speech.

It is a good light, then, for those
That know the ultimate Plato,
Tranquilizing with this jewel
The torments of confusion.

Two Figures in Dense Violet Light

I had as lief be embraced by the porter at the hotel
As to get no more from the moonlight
Than your moist hand.

Be the voice of night and Florida in my ear.
Use dusky words and dusky images.
Darken your speech.

Speak, even, as if I did not hear you speaking,
But spoke for you perfectly in my thoughts,
Conceiving words,

As the night conceives the sea-sounds in silence,
And out of their droning sibilants makes
A serenade.

Say, puerile, that the buzzards crouch on the ridge-pole
And sleep with one eye watching the stars fall
Below Key West.

Say that the palms are clear in a total blue,
Are clear and are obscure; that it is night;
That the moon shines.

Bouquet of Belle Scavoir

It is she alone that matters.
She made it. It is easy to say
The figures of speech, as why she chose
This dark, particular rose.

Everything in it is herself.
Yet the freshness of the leaves, the burn
Of the colors, are tinsel changes,
Out of the changes of both light and dew.

How often had he walked
Beneath summer and the sky
To receive her shadow into his mind . . .
Miserable that it was not she.

The sky is too blue, the earth too wide.
The thought of her takes her away.
The form of her in something else
Is not enough.

The reflection of her here, and then there,
Is another shadow, another evasion,
Another denial. If she is everywhere,
She is nowhere, to him.

But this she has made. If it is
Another image, it is one she has made.
It is she that he wants, to look at directly,
Someone before him to see and to know.

Le Monocle de Mon Oncle

I

"Mother of heaven, regina of the clouds,
O sceptre of the sun, crown of the moon,
There is not nothing, no, no, never nothing,
Like the clashed edges of two words that kill."
And so I mocked her in magnificent measure.
Or was it that I mocked myself alone?
I wish that I might be a thinking stone.
The sea of spuming thought foists up again
The radiant bubble that she was. And then
A deep up-pouring from some saltier well
Within me, bursts its watery syllable.

II

A red bird flies across the golden floor.
It is a red bird that seeks out his choir
Among the choirs of wind and wet and wing.
A torrent will fall from him when he finds.
Shall I uncrumple this much-crumpled thing?
I am a man of fortune greeting heirs;
For it has come that thus I greet the spring.
These choirs of welcome choir for me farewell.
No spring can follow past meridian.
Yet you persist with anecdotal bliss
To make believe a starry *connaissance*.

III

Is it for nothing, then, that old Chinese
Sat tittivating by their mountain pools
Or in the Yangtse studied out their beards?
I shall not play the flat historic scale.
You know how Utamaro's beauties sought
The end of love in their all-speaking braids.
You know the mountainous coiffures of Bath.
Alas! Have all the barbers lived in vain
That not one curl in nature has survived?
Why, without pity on these studious ghosts,
Do you come dripping in your hair from sleep?

IV

This luscious and impeccable fruit of life
Falls, it appears, of its own weight to earth.
When you were Eve, its acrid juice was sweet,
Untasted, in its heavenly, orchard air.
An apple serves as well as any skull
To be the book in which to read a round,
And is as excellent, in that it is composed
Of what, like skulls, comes rotting back to ground.
But it excels in this that as the fruit
Of love, it is a book too mad to read
Before one merely reads to pass the time.

V

In the high west there burns a furious star.
It is for fiery boys that star was set
And for sweet-smelling virgins close to them.
The measure of the intensity of love
Is measure, also, of the verve of earth.
For me, the firefly's quick, electric stroke
Ticks tediously the time of one more year.
And you? Remember how the crickets came
Out of their mother grass, like little kin,
In the pale nights, when your first imagery
Found inklings of your bond to all that dust.

VI

If men at forty will be painting lakes
The ephemeral blues must merge for them in one,
The basic slate, the universal hue.
There is a substance in us that prevails.
But in our amours amorists discern
Such fluctuations that their scrivening
Is breathless to attend each quirky turn.
When amorists grow bald, then amours shrink
Into the compass and curriculum
Of introspective exiles, lecturing.
It is a theme for Hyacinth alone.

VII

The mules that angels ride come slowly down
The blazing passes, from beyond the sun.
Descensions of their tinkling bells arrive.

These muleteers are dainty of their way.
Meantime centurions guffaw and beat
Their shrilling tankards on the table-boards.
This parable, in sense, amounts to this:
The honey of heaven may or may not come,
But that of earth both comes and goes at once.
Suppose these couriers brought amid their train
A damsel heightened by eternal bloom. . . .

VIII

Like a dull scholar, I behold, in love,
An ancient aspect touching a new mind.
It comes, it blooms, it bears its fruit and dies.
This trivial trope reveals a way of truth.
Our bloom is gone. We are the fruit thereof.
Two golden gourds distended on our vines,
Into the autumn weather, splashed with frost,
Distorted by hale fatness, turned grotesque.
We hang like warty squashes, streaked and rayed,
The laughing sky will see the two of us
Washed into rinds by rotting winter rains.

IX

In verses wild with motion, full of din,
Loudened by cries, by clashes, quick and sure
As the deadly thought of men accomplishing
Their curious fates in war, come, celebrate
The faith of forty, ward of Cupido.
Most venerable heart, the lustiest conceit
Is not too lusty for your broadening.
I quiz all sounds, all thoughts, all everything
For the music and manner of the paladins
To make oblation fit. Where shall I find
Bravura adequate to this great hymn?

X

The fops of fancy in their poems leave
Memorabilia of the mystic spouts,
Spontaneously watering their gritty soils.
I am a yeoman, as such fellows go.
I know no magic trees, no balmy boughs,
No silver-ruddy, gold-vermilion fruits.
But, after all, I know a tree that bears
A semblance to the thing I have in mind.

It stands gigantic, with a certain tip
To which all birds come sometime in their time.
But when they go that tip still tips the tree.

XI

If sex were all, then every trembling hand
Could make us squeak, like dolls, the wished-for words.
But note the unconscionable treachery of fate,
That makes us weep, laugh, grunt and groan, and shout
Doleful heroics, pinching gestures forth
From madness or delight, without regard
To that first foremost law. Anguishing hour!
Last night, we sat beside a pool of pink,
Clippered with lilies scudding the bright chromes,
Keen to the point of starlight, while a frog
Boomed from his very belly odious chords.

XII

A blue pigeon it is, that circles the blue sky,
On side-long wing, around and round and round.
A white pigeon it is, that flutters to the ground,
Grown tired of flight. Like a dark rabbi, I
Observed, when young, the nature of mankind,
In lordly study. Every day, I found
Man proved a gobbet in my mincing world.
Like a rose rabbi, later, I pursued,
And still pursue, the origin and course
Of love, but until now I never knew
That fluttering things have so distinct a shade.

Gallant Château

Is it bad to have come here
And to have found the bed empty?

One might have found tragic hair,
Bitter eyes, hands hostile and cold.

There might have been a light on a book
Lighting a pitiless verse or two.

There might have been the immense solitude
Of the wind upon the curtains.

Pitiless verse? A few words tuned
And tuned and tuned and tuned.

It is good. The bed is empty,
The curtains are stiff and prim and still.

The Idea of Order at Key West

She sang beyond the genius of the sea.
The water never formed to mind or voice,
Like a body wholly body, fluttering
Its empty sleeves; and yet its mimic motion
Made constant cry, caused constantly a cry,
That was not ours although we understood,
Inhuman, of the veritable ocean.

The sea was not a mask. No more was she.
The song and water were not medleyed sound,
Even if what she sang was what she heard,
Since what she sang she uttered word by word.
It may be that in all her phrases stirred
The grinding water and the gasping wind;
But it was she and not the sea we heard.

For she was the maker of the song she sang.
The ever-hooded, tragic-gestured sea
Was merely a place by which she walked to sing.
Whose spirit is this? we said, because we knew
It was the spirit that we sought and knew
That we should ask this often as she sang.

If it was only the dark voice of the sea
That rose, or even colored by many waves;
If it was only the outer voice of sky
And cloud, of the sunken coral water-walled,
However clear, it would have been deep air,
The heaving speech of air, a summer sound
Repeated in a summer without end
And sound alone. But it was more than that,
More even than her voice, and ours, among
The meaningless plungings of water and the wind,
Theatrical distances, bronze shadows heaped
On high horizons, mountainous atmospheres
Of sky and sea.

It was her voice that made
The sky acutest at its vanishing.
She measured to the hour its solitude.
She was the single artificer of the world
In which she sang. And when she sang, the sea,
Whatever self it had, became the self
That was her song, for she was maker. Then we,
As we beheld her striding there alone,
Knew that there never was a world for her
Except the one she sang and, singing, made.

Ramon Fernandez, tell me, if you know,
Why, when the singing ended and we turned
Toward the town, tell why the glassy lights,
The lights in the fishing boats at anchor there,
As the night descended, tilting in the air,
Mastered the night and portioned out the sea,
Fixing emblazoned zones and fiery poles,
Arranging, deepening, enchanting night.

Oh! Blessed rage for order, pale Ramon,
The maker's rage to order words of the sea,
Words of the fragrant portals, dimly-starred,
And of ourselves and of our origins,
In ghostlier demarcations, keener sounds.

Asides on the Oboe

The prologues are over. It is question, now,
Of final belief. So, say that final belief
Must be in a fiction. It is time to choose.

I

That obsolete fiction of the wide river in
An empty land; the gods that Boucher killed;
And the metal heroes that time granulates—
The philosophers' man alone still walks in dew,
Still by the sea-side mutters milky lines
Concerning an immaculate imagery.
If you say on the hautboy man is not enough
Can never stand as god, is ever wrong
In the end, however naked, tall, there is still
The impossible possible philosophers' man,

The man who has had the time to think enough,
The central man, the human globe, responsive
As a mirror with a voice, the man of glass,
Who in a million diamonds sums us up.

II

He is the transparence of the place in which
He is, and in his poems we find peace.
He sets this peddler's pie and cries in summer,
The glass man, cold and numbered, dewily cries,
"Thou art not August unless I make thee so."
Clandestine steps upon imagined stairs
Climb through the night, because his cuckoos call.

III

One year, death and war prevented the jasmine scent
And the jasmine islands were bloody martyrdoms.
How was it then with the central man? Did we
Find peace? We found the sum of men. We found,
If we found the central evil, the central good.
We buried the fallen without jasmine crowns.
There was nothing he did not suffer, no; nor we.

It was not as if the jasmine ever returned.
But we and the diamond globe at last were one.
We had always been partly one. It was as we came
To see him, that we were wholly one, as we heard
Him chanting for those buried in their blood,
In the forests that had been jasmine, that we knew
The glass man, without external reference.

The Glass of Water

That the glass would melt in heat,
That the water would freeze in cold,
Shows that this object is merely a state,
One of many, between two poles. So,
In the metaphysical, there are these poles.

Here in the centre stands the glass. Light
Is the lion that comes down to drink. There
And in that state, the glass is a pool.

Ruddy are his eyes and ruddy are his claws
When light comes down to wet his frothy jaws

And in the water winding weeds move round.
And there and in another state—the refractions,
The *metaphysica,* the plastic parts of poems
Crash in the mind— But, fat Jocundus, worrying
About what stands here in the centre, not in the glass,

But in the centre of our lives, this time, this day,
It is a state, this spring among the politicians
Playing cards. In a village of the indigenes,
One would have still to discover. Among the dogs and dung,
One would continue to contend with one's ideas.

The Sense of the Sleight-of-Hand Man

One's grand flights, one's Sunday baths,
One's tootings at the weddings of the soul
Occur as they occur. So bluish clouds
Occurred above the empty house and the leaves
Of the rhododendrons rattled their gold,
As if someone lived there. Such floods of white
Came bursting from the clouds. So the wind
Threw its contorted strength around the sky.

Could you have said the bluejay suddenly
Would swoop to earth? It is a wheel, the rays
Around the sun. The wheel survives the myths.
The fire eye in the clouds survives the gods.
To think of a dove with an eye of grenadine
And pines that are cornets, so it occurs,
And a little island full of geese and stars:
It may be that the ignorant man, alone,
Has any chance to mate his life with life
That is the sensual, pearly spouse, the life
That is fluent in even the wintriest bronze.

The Motive for Metaphor

You like it under the trees in autumn,
Because everything is half dead.
The wind moves like a cripple among the leaves
And repeats words without meaning.

In the same way, you were happy in spring,
With the half colors of quarter-things,
The slightly brighter sky, the melting clouds,
The single bird, the obscure moon—

The obscure moon lighting an obscure world
Of things that would never be quite expressed,
Where you yourself were never quite yourself
And did not want nor have to be,

Desiring the exhilarations of changes:
The motive for metaphor, shrinking from
The weight of primary noon,
The A B C of being,

The ruddy temper, the hammer
Of red and blue, the hard sound—
Steel against intimation—the sharp flash,
The vital, arrogant, fatal, dominant X.

Men Made Out of Words

What should we be without the sexual myth,
The human reverie or poem of death?

Castratos of moon-mash— Life consists
Of propositions about life. The human

Reverie is a solitude in which
We compose these propositions, torn by dreams,

By the terrible incantations of defeats
And by the fear that defeats and dreams are one.

The whole race is a poet that writes down
The eccentric propositions of its fate.

Flyer's Fall

This man escaped the dirty fates,
Knowing that he died nobly, as he died.

Darkness, nothingness of human after-death,
Receive and keep him in the deepnesses of space—

Profundum, physical thunder, dimension in which
We believe without belief, beyond belief.

The World as Meditation

J'ai passé trop de temps à travailler mon violon, à voyager. Mais l'exercice essentiel du compositeur—la méditation—rien ne l'a jamais suspendu en moi. Je vis un rêve permanent, qui ne s'arrête ni nuit ni jour.

GEORGES ENESCO

Is it Ulysses that approaches from the east,
The interminable adventurer? The trees are mended.
That winter is washed away. Someone is moving

On the horizon and lifting himself up above it.
A form of fire approaches the cretonnes of Penelope,
Whose mere savage presence awakens the world in which she
dwells.

She has composed, so long, a self with which to welcome him,
Companion to his self for her, which she imagined,
Two in a deep-founded sheltering, friend and dear friend.

The trees had been mended, as an essential exercise
In an inhuman meditation, larger than her own.
No winds like dogs watched over her at night.

She wanted nothing he could not bring her by coming alone.
She wanted no fetchings. His arms would be her necklace.
And her belt, the final fortune of their desire.

But was it Ulysses? Or was it only the warmth of the sun
On her pillow? The thought kept beating in her like her heart.
The two kept beating together. It was only day.

It was Ulysses and it was not. Yet they had met,
Friend and dear friend and a planet's encouragement.
The barbarous strength within her would never fail.

She would talk a little to herself as she combed her hair,
Repeating his name with its patient syllables,
Never forgetting him that kept coming constantly so near.

William Carlos Williams

1883-

Metric Figure

There is a bird in the poplars—
It is the sun!
The leaves are little yellow fish
Swimming in the river;
The bird skims above them—
Day is on his wings.
Phoenix!
It is he that is making
The great gleam among the poplars.
It is his singing
Outshines the noise
Of leaves clashing in the wind.

Love Song

Sweep the house clean,
hang fresh curtains
in the windows
put on a new dress
and come with me!

The elm is scattering
its little loaves
of sweet smells
from a white sky!

Who shall hear of us
in the time to come?

Let him say there was
a burst of fragrance
from black branches.

Dawn

Ecstatic bird songs pound
the hollow vastness of the sky
with metallic clinkings—
beating color up into it
at a far edge,—beating it, beating it
with rising, triumphant ardor,—
stirring it into warmth,
quickening in it a spreading change,—
bursting wildly against it as
dividing the horizon, a heavy sun
lifts himself—is lifted—
bit by bit above the edge
of things,—runs free at last
out into the open—! lumbering
glorified in full release upward—
songs cease.

Poem

By the road to the contagious hospital,
under the surge of the blue
mottled clouds driven from the
northeast—cold wind. Beyond, the
waste of broad, muddy fields,
brown with dried weeds, standing and fallen,

patches of standing water,
the scattering of tall trees.

All along the road the reddish,
purplish, forked, upstanding, twiggy
stuff of brushes and small trees
with dead, brown leaves under them
leafless vines—

Lifeless in appearance, sluggish,
dazed spring approaches—

They enter the new world naked,
cold, uncertain of all
save that they enter. All about them
the cold, familiar wind—

Now the grass, tomorrow
the stiff curl of wild-carrot leaf.

One by one objects are defined—
It quickens: clarity, outline of leaf,

But now the stark dignity of
entrance— Still, the profound change
has come upon them; rooted, they
grip down and begin to awaken.

January

Again I reply to the triple winds
running chromatic fifths of derision
outside my window:
Play louder.
You will not succeed. I am
bound more to my sentences
the more you batter at me
to follow you.
And the wind,
as before, fingers perfectly
its derisive music.

Queen-Ann's-Lace

Her body is not so white as
anemone petals nor so smooth—nor
so remote a thing. It is a field
of the wild carrot taking
the field by force; the grass
does not raise above it.
Here is no question of whiteness,
white as can be, with a purple mole
at the center of each flower.
Each flower is a hand's span

of her whiteness. Wherever
his hand has lain there is
a tiny purple blemish. Each part
is a blossom under his touch
to which the fibers of her being
stem one by one, each to its end,
until the whole field is a
white desire, empty, a single stem,
a cluster, flower by flower,
a pious wish to whiteness gone over—
or nothing.

Daisy

The dayseye hugging the earth
in August, ha! Spring is
gone down in purple,
weeds stand high in the corn,
the rainbeaten furrow
is clotted with sorrel
and crabgrass, the
branch is black under
the heavy mass of the leaves—
The sun is upon a
slender green stem
ribbed lengthwise.
He lies on his back—
it is a woman also—
he regards his former
majesty and
round the yellow center,
split and creviced and done into
minute flowerheads, he sends out
his twenty rays—a little
and the wind is among them
to grow cool there!

One turns the thing over
in his hand and looks
at it from the rear: brownedged,
green and pointed scales
armor his yellow.
But turn and turn,

the crisp petals remain
brief, translucent, greenfastened,
barely touching at the edges:
blades of limpid seashell.

On Gay Wallpaper

The green-blue ground
is ruled with silver lines
to say the sun is shining

And on this mural sea
of grass or dreams lie flowers
or baskets of desires

Heaven knows what they are
between cerulean shapes
laid regularly round

Mat roses and tridentate
leaves of gold
threes, threes and threes

Three roses and three stems
the basket floating
standing in the horns of blue

Repeated to the ceiling
to the windows
where the day

Blows in
the scalloped curtains to
the sound of rain.

Tract

I will teach you my townspeople
how to perform a funeral—
for you have it over a troop
of artists—
unless one should scour the world—
you have the ground sense necessary.

See! the hearse leads.
I begin with a design for a hearse.
For Christ's sake not black–
nor white either–and not polished!
Let it be weathered–like a farm wagon–
with gilt wheels (this could be
applied fresh at small expense)
or no wheels at all:
a rough dray to drag over the ground.

Knock the glass out!
My God!–glass, my townspeople!
For what purpose? Is it for the dead
to look out or for us to see
how well he is housed or to see
the flowers or the lack of them–
or what?
To keep the rain and snow from him?
He will have a heavier rain soon:
pebbles and dirt and what not.
Let there be no glass–
and no upholstery! phew!
and no little brass rollers
and small easy wheels on the bottom–
my townspeople what are you thinking of!

A rough plain hearse then
with gilt wheels and no top at all.
On this the coffin lies
by its own weight.

No wreaths please–
especially no hot-house flowers.
Some common memento is better,
something he prized and is known by:
his old clothes–a few books perhaps–
God knows what! You realize
how we are about these things,
my townspeople–
something will be found–anything–
even flowers if he had come to that.
So much for the hearse.

For heaven's sake though see to the driver!
Take off the silk hat! In fact

that's no place at all for him
up there unceremoniously
dragging our friend out to his own dignity!
Bring him down—bring him down!
Low and inconspicuous! I'd not have him ride
on the wagon at all—damn him—
the undertaker's understrapper!
Let him hold the reins
and walk at the side
and inconspicuously too!

Then briefly as to yourselves:
Walk behind—as they do in France,
seventh class, or if you ride
Hell take curtains! Go with some show
of inconvenience; sit openly—
to the weather as to grief.
Or do you think you can shut grief in?
What—from us? We who have perhaps
nothing to lose? Share with us
share with us—it will be money
in your pockets.
Go now
I think you are ready.

Smell

Oh strong ridged and deeply hollowed
nose of mine! what will you not be smelling?
What tactless asses we are, you and I, boney nose,
always indiscriminate, always unashamed,
and now it is the souring flowers of the bedraggled
poplars: a festering pulp on the wet earth
beneath them. With what deep thirst
we quicken our desires
to that rank odor of a passing springtime!
Can you not be decent? Can you not reserve your ardors
for something less unlovely? What girl will care
for us, do you think, if we continue in these ways?
Must you taste everything? Must you know everything?
Must you have a part in everything?

A Goodnight

Go to sleep—though of course you will not—
to tideless waves thundering slantwise against
strong embankments, rattle and swish of spray
dashed thirty feet high, caught by the lake wind,
scattered and strewn broadcast in over the steady
car rails! Sleep, sleep! Gulls' cries in a wind-gust
broken by the wind; calculating wings set above
the field of waves breaking.
Go to sleep to the lunge between foam-crests,
refuse churned in the recoil. Food! Food!
Offal! Offal! that holds them in the air, wave-white
for the one purpose, feather upon feather, the wild
chill in their eyes, the hoarseness in their voices—
sleep, sleep . . .

Gentlefooted crowds are treading out your lullaby.
Their arms nudge, they brush shoulders,
hitch this way, then that, mass and surge at the crossings—
lullaby, lullaby! The wild-fowl police whistles,
the enraged roar of the traffic, machine shrieks:
it is all to put you to sleep,
to soften your limbs in relaxed postures,
and that your head slip sidewise, and your hair loosen
and fall over your eyes and over your mouth,
brushing your lips wistfully that you may dream,
sleep and dream—

A black fungus springs out about lonely church doors—
sleep, sleep. The Night, coming down upon
the wet boulevard, would start you awake with his
message, to have in at your window. Pay no
heed to him. He storms at your sill with
cooings, with gesticulations, curses!
You will not let him in. He would keep you from sleeping.
He would have you sit under your desk lamp
brooding, pondering; he would have you
slide out the drawer, take up the ornamented dagger
and handle it. It is late, it is nineteen-nineteen—
go to sleep, his cries are a lullaby;
his jabbering is a sleep-well-my-baby; he is
a crackbrained messenger.

The maid waking you in the morning
when you are up and dressing,
the rustle of your clothes as you raise them—
it is the same tune.
At table the cold, greenish, split grapefruit, its juice
on the tongue, the clink of the spoon in
your coffee, the toast odors say it over and over.

The open street-door lets in the breath of
the morning wind from over the lake.
The bus coming to a halt grinds from its sullen brakes—
lullaby, lullaby. The crackle of a newspaper,
the movement of the troubled coat beside you—
sleep, sleep, sleep, sleep . . .
It is the sting of snow, the burning liquor of
the moonlight, the rush of rain in the gutters packed
with dead leaves: go to sleep, go to sleep.
And the night passes—and never passes—

The Red Wheelbarrow

so much depends
upon

a red wheel
barrow

glazed with rain
water

beside the white
chickens

Flowers by the Sea

When over the flowery, sharp pasture's
edge, unseen, the salt ocean

lifts its form—chicory and daisies
tied, released, seem hardly flowers alone

but color and the movement—or the shape
perhaps—of restlessness, whereas

the sea is circled and sways
peacefully upon its plantlike stem

The Poor

It's the anarchy of poverty
delights me, the old
yellow wooden house indented
among the new brick tenements

Or a cast iron balcony
with panels showing oak branches
in full leaf. It fits
the dress of the children

reflecting every stage and
custom of necessity—
Chimneys, roofs, fences of
wood and metal in an unfenced

age and enclosing next to
nothing at all: the old man
in a sweater and soft black
hat who sweeps the sidewalk—

his own ten feet of it—
in a wind that fitfully
turning his corner has
overwhelmed the entire city

These

are the desolate, dark weeks
when nature in its barrenness
equals the stupidity of man.

The year plunges into night
and the heart plunges
lower than night

to an empty, windswept place
without sun, stars or moon
but a peculiar light as of thought

that spins a dark fire—
whirling upon itself until,
in the cold, it kindles

to make a man aware of nothing
that he knows, not loneliness
itself— Not a ghost but

would be embraced—emptiness,
despair— (They
whine and whistle) among

the flashes and booms of war;
houses of whose rooms
the cold is greater than can be thought,

the people gone that we loved,
the beds lying empty, the couches
damp, the chairs unused—

Hide it away somewhere
out of the mind, let it get roots
and grow, unrelated to jealous

ears and eyes—for itself.
In this mine they come to dig—all.
Is this the counterfoil to sweetest

music? The source of poetry that
seeing the clock stopped, says,
The clock has stopped

that ticked yesterday so well?
and hears the sound of lakewater
splashing—that is now stone.

Illegitimate Things

Water still flows—
The thrush still sings

though in
the skirts of the sky

at the bottom of
the distance

huddle . . .
. . . echoing cannon!

Whose silence revives
valley after

valley to peace
as poems still conserve

the language
of old ecstasies.

The Yachts

contend in a sea which the land partly encloses
shielding them from the too heavy blows
of an ungoverned ocean which when it chooses

tortures the biggest hulls, the best man knows
to pit against its beating, and sinks them pitilessly.
Mothlike in mists, scintillant in the minute

brilliance of cloudless days, with broad bellying sails
they glide to the wind tossing green water
from their sharp prows while over them the crew crawls

ant-like, solicitously grooming them, releasing,
making fast as they turn, lean far over and having
caught the wind again, side by side, head for the mark.

In a well guarded arena of open water surrounded by
lesser and greater craft which, sycophant, lumbering
and flittering follow them, they appear youthful, rare

as the light of a happy eye, live with the grace
of all that in the mind is feckless, free and
naturally to be desired. Now the sea which holds them

is moody, lapping their glossy sides, as if feeling
for some slightest flaw but fails completely.
Today no race. Then the wind comes again. The yachts

move, jockeying for a start, the signal is set and they
are off. Now the waves strike at them but they are too
well made, they slip through, though they take in canvas.

Arms with hands grasping seek to clutch at the prows.
Bodies thrown recklessly in the way are cut aside.
It is a sea of faces about them in agony, in despair

until the horror of the race dawns staggering the mind,
the whole sea become an entanglement of watery bodies
lost to the world bearing what they cannot hold. Broken,

beaten, desolate, reaching from the dead to be taken up
they cry out, failing, failing! their cries rising
in waves still as the skillful yachts pass over.

The Yellow Season

The black, long-tailed
one then, unexpectedly, another
glide easily on a curtain
of yellow leaves, upward—

The season wakens! loveliness
chirping and barking stands
among the branches, its
narrow-clawed toes and furry
hands moving in the leaves—

Round white eyes dotted with
jet live still, alert—in
all gentleness! unabated
beyond the crackle
of death's stinking certainty.

To a Dog Injured in the Street

IT IS MYSELF,
not the poor beast lying there
yelping with pain
that brings me to myself with a start—
as at the explosion
of a bomb, a bomb that has laid
all the world waste.

I can do nothing
but sing about it
and so I am assuaged
from my pain.

A DROWSY NUMBNESS drowns my sense
as if of hemlock
I had drunk. I think
of the poetry
of René Char
and all he must have seen
and suffered
that has brought him
to speak only of
sedgy rivers,
of daffodils and tulips
whose roots they water,
even to the freeflowing river
that laves the rootlets
of those sweet scented flowers
that people the
milky
way.

I REMEMBER *Norma*
our English setter of my childhood
her silky ears
and expressive eyes.
She had a litter
of pups one night
in our pantry and I kicked
one of them
thinking, in my alarm,
that they
were biting her breasts
to destroy her.

I REMEMBER also
a dead rabbit
lying harmlessly
on the outspread palm
of a hunter's hand.
As I stood by
watching

he took a hunting knife
and with a laugh
thrust it
up into the animal's private parts.
I almost fainted.

WHY SHOULD I think of that now?
the cries of a dying dog
are to be blotted out
as best I can.
René Char,
you are a poet who believes
in the power of beauty
to right all wrongs.
I believe it also.
With invention and courage
we shall surpass
the pitiful dumb beasts,
let all men believe it,
as you have taught me also
to believe it.

The Descent

The descent beckons
as the ascent beckoned.
Memory is a kind
of accomplishment,
a sort of renewal
even
an initiation, since the spaces it opens are new places
inhabited by hordes
heretofore unrealized,
of new kinds—
since their movements
are towards new objectives
(even though formerly they were abandoned).

NO DEFEAT is made up entirely of defeat—since
the world it opens is always a place
formerly
unsuspected. A
world lost,

a world unsuspected,
beckons to new places
and no whiteness (lost) is so white as the memory
of whiteness .

WITH EVENING, love wakens
though its shadows
which are alive by reason
of the sun shining—
grow sleepy now and drop away
from desire

LOVE WITHOUT shadows stirs now
beginning to awaken
as night
advances.

THE DESCENT
made up of despairs
and without accomplishment
realizes a new awakening:
which is a reversal
of despair.
For what we cannot accomplish, what
is denied to love,
what we have lost in the anticipation—
a descent follows,
endless and indestructible .

Elinor Wylie

1885-1928

The Eagle and the Mole

Avoid the reeking herd,
Shun the polluted flock,
Live like that stoic bird,
The eagle of the rock.

The huddled warmth of crowds
Begets and fosters hate;
He keeps, above the clouds,
His cliff inviolate.

When flocks are folded warm,
And herds to shelter run,
He sails above the storm,
He stares into the sun.

If in the eagle's track
Your sinews cannot leap,
Avoid the lathered pack,
Turn from the steaming sheep.

If you would keep your soul
From spotted sight or sound,
Live like the velvet mole;
Go burrow underground.

And there hold intercourse
With roots of trees and stones,
With rivers at their source,
And disembodied bones.

Madman's Song

Better to see your cheek grown hollow,
Better to see your temple worn,
Than to forget to follow, follow,
After the sound of a silver horn.

Better to bind your brow with willow
And follow, follow until you die,
Than to sleep with your head on a golden pillow,
Nor lift it up when the hunt goes by.

Better to see your cheek grown sallow
And your hair grown gray, so soon, so soon,
Than to forget to hallo, hallo,
After the milk-white hounds of the moon.

Sanctuary

This is the bricklayer; hear the thud
Of his heavy load dumped down on stone.
His lustrous bricks are brighter than blood,
His smoking mortar whiter than bone.

Set each sharp-edged, fire-bitten brick
Straight by the plumb-line's shivering length;
Make my marvelous wall so thick
Dead nor living may shake its strength.

Full as a crystal cup with drink
Is my cell with dreams, and quiet, and cool.
Stop, old man! You must leave a chink;
How can I breathe? *You can't, you fool!*

Velvet Shoes

Let us walk in the white snow
  In a soundless space;
With footsteps quiet and slow,
  At a tranquil pace,
  Under veils of white lace.

I shall go shod in silk,
  And you in wool,
White as a white cow's milk,
  More beautiful
  Than the breast of a gull.

We shall walk through the still town
  In a windless peace;
We shall step upon white down,
  Upon silver fleece,
  Upon softer than these.

We shall walk in velvet shoes:
  Wherever we go
Silence will fall like dews
  On white silence below.
  We shall walk in the snow.

August

Why should this Negro insolently stride
Down the red noonday on such noiseless feet?
Piled in his barrow, tawnier than wheat,
Lie heaps of smoldering daisies, somber-eyed,
Their copper petals shriveled up with pride,
Hot with a superfluity of heat,
Like a great brazier borne alone the street
By captive leopards, black and burning pied.

Are there no water-lilies, smooth as cream,
With long stems dripping crystal? Are there none
Like those white lilies, luminous and cool,
Plucked from some hemlock-darkened northern stream
By fair-haired swimmers, diving where the sun
Scarce warms the surface of the deepest pool?

Puritan Sonnet

Down to the Puritan marrow of my bones
There's something in this richness that I hate.
I love the look, austere, immaculate,
Of landscapes drawn in pearly monotones.
There's something in my very blood that owns
Bare hills, cold silver on a sky of slate,
A thread of water, churned to milky spate
Streaming through slanted pastures fenced with stones.

I love those skies, thin blue or snowy gray,
Those fields sparse-planted, rendering meager sheaves;
That spring, briefer than apple-blossom's breath,
Summer, so much too beautiful to stay,
Swift autumn, like a bonfire of leaves,
And sleepy winter, like the sleep of death.

Let No Charitable Hope

Now let no charitable hope
Confuse my mind with images
Of eagle and of antelope;
I am in nature none of these.

I was, being human, born alone;
I am, being woman, hard beset;
I live by squeezing from a stone
The little nourishment I get.

In masks outrageous and austere
The years go by in single file;
But none has merited my fear,
And none has quite escaped my smile.

Peter and John

Twelve good friends
Walked under the leaves
Binding the ends
Of the barley sheaves.

Peter and John
Lay down to sleep
Pillowed upon
A haymaker's heap.

John and Peter
Lay down to dream.
The air was sweeter
Than honey and cream.

Peter was bred
In the salty cold.
His hair was red
And his eyes were gold.

John had a mouth
Like a wing bent down.
His brow was smooth
And his eyes were brown.

Peter to slumber
Sank like a stone,
Of all their number
The bravest one.

John more slowly
Composed himself,

Young and holy
Among the Twelve.

John as he slept
Cried out in grief,
Turned and wept
On the golden leaf:

"Peter, Peter,
Stretch me your hand
Across the glitter
Of the harvest land!

"Peter, Peter,
Give me a sign!
This was a bitter
Dream of mine,—

"Bitter as aloes
It parched my tongue.
Upon the gallows
My life was hung.

"Sharp it seemed
As a bloody sword.
Peter, I dreamed
I was Christ the Lord!"

Peter turned
To holy Saint John:
His body burned
In the falling sun.

In the falling sun
He burned like flame:
"John, Saint John,
I have dreamed the same!

"My bones were hung
On an elder tree;
Bells were rung
Over Galilee.

"A silver penny
Sealed each of my eyes.
Many and many
A cock crew thrice."

When Peter's word
Was spoken and done,
"Were you Christ the Lord
In your dream?" said John.

"No," said the other,
"That I was not.
I was our brother
Iscariot."

Full Moon

My bands of silk and miniver
Momently grew heavier;
The black gauze was beggarly thin;
The ermine muffled mouth and chin;
I could not suck the moonlight in.

Harlequin in lozenges
Of love and hate, I walked in these
Striped and ragged rigmaroles;
Along the pavement my footsoles
Trod warily on living coals.

Shouldering the thoughts I loathed,
In their corrupt disguises clothed,
Mortality I could not tear
From my ribs, to leave them bare
Ivory in silver air.

There I walked and there I raged;
The spiritual savage caged
Within my skeleton, raged afresh
To feel, behind a carnal mesh,
The clean bones crying in the flesh.

Birthday Sonnet

Take home Thy prodigal child, O Lord of Hosts!
Protect the sacred from the secular danger;
Advise her, that Thou never needst avenge her;
Marry her mind neither to man's nor ghost's

Nor holier domination's, if the costs
Of such commingling should transport or change her;
Defend her from familiar and stranger,
And earth's and air's contagions and rusts.

Instruct her strictly to preserve Thy gift
And alter not its grain in atom sort;
Angels may wed her to their ultimate hurt
And men embrace a specter in a shift
So that no drop of the pure spirit fall
Into the dust: defend Thy prodigal.

O Virtuous Light

A private madness has prevailed
Over the pure and valiant mind;
The instrument of reason failed
And the star-gazing eyes struck blind.

Sudden excess of light has wrought
Confusion in the secret place
Where the slow miracles of thought
Take shape through patience into grace.

Mysterious as steel and flint
The birth of this destructive spark
Whose inward growth has power to print
Strange suns upon the natural dark.

O break the walls of sense in half
And make the spirit fugitive!
This light begotten of itself
Is not a light by which to live!

The fire of farthing tallow dips
Dispels the menace of the skies
So it illuminate the lips
And enter the discerning eyes.

O virtuous light, if thou be man's
Or matter of the meteor stone,
Prevail against this radiance
Which is engendered of its own!

Sonnet from "One Person"

I hereby swear that to uphold your house
I would lay my bones in quick destroying lime
Or turn my flesh to timber for all time;
Cut down my womanhood; lop off the boughs
Of that perpetual ecstasy that grows
From the heart's core; condemn it as a crime
If it be broader than a beam, or climb
Above the stature that your roof allows.

I am not the heartstone nor the cornerstone
Within this noble fabric you have builded;
Not by my beauty was its cornice gilded;
Not on my courage were its arches thrown:
My lord, adjudge my strength, and set me where
I bear a little more than I can bear.

This Corruptible

The Body, long oppressed
And pierced, then prayed for rest
(Being but apprenticed to the other Powers);
And kneeling in that place
Implored the thrust of grace
Which makes the dust lie level with the flowers.

Then did that fellowship
Of three, the Body strip;
Beheld his wounds, and none among them mortal;
The Mind severe and cool;
The Heart still half a fool;
The fine-spun Soul, a beam of sun can startle.

These three, a thousand years
Had made adventurers
Amid all villainies the earth can offer,
Applied them to resolve
From the universal gulph
What pangs the poor material flesh may suffer.

"This is a pretty pass;
To hear the growing grass
Complain; the clay cry out to be translated;
Will not this grosser stuff
Receive reward enough
If stabled after laboring, and baited?"

Thus spoke the Mind in scorn.
The Heart, which had outworn
The Body, and was weary of its fashion,
Preferring to be dressed
In skin of bird or beast,
Replied more softly, in a feigned compassion.

"Anatomy most strange
Crying to chop and change;
Inferior copy of a higher image;
While I, the noble guest,
Sick of your second-best
Sigh for embroidered archangelic plumage:

"For shame, thou fustian cloak!"
And then the Spirit spoke;
Within the void it swung securely tethered
By strings composed of cloud;
It spoke both low and loud
Above a storm no lesser star had weathered.

"O lodging for the night!
O house of my delight!
O lovely hovel builded for my pleasure!
Dear tenement of clay
Endure another day
As coffin sweetly fitted to my measure.

"Take Heart and call to Mind
Although we are unkind;
Although we steal your shelter, strength, and clothing;
'Tis you who shall escape
In some enchanting shape
Or be dissolved to elemental nothing.

"You, the unlucky slave,
Are the lily on the grave;
The wave that runs above the bones a-whitening;
You are the new-mown grass;

And the wheaten bread of the Mass;
And the fabric of the rain, and the lightning.

"If one of us elect
To leave the poor suspect
Imperfect bosom of the earth our parent;
And from the world avert
The Spirit of the Heart
Upon a further and essential errand;

"His chain he cannot slough
Nor cast his substance off;
He bears himself upon his flying shoulder;
The Heart, infirm and dull;
The Mind, in any skull;
Are captive still, and wearier and colder.

" 'Tis you who are the ghost,
Disintegrated, lost;
The burden shed; the dead who need not bear it;
O grain of God in power,
Endure another hour!
It is but for an hour," said the Spirit.

Hymn to Earth

Farewell, incomparable element,
Whence man arose, where he shall not return;
And hail, imperfect urn
Of his last ashes, and his firstborn fruit;
Farewell, the long pursuit,
And all the adventures of his discontent;
The voyages which sent
His heart averse from home:
Metal of clay, permit him that he come
To thy slow-burning fire as to a hearth;
Accept him as a particle of earth.

Fire, being divided from the other three,
It lives removed, or secret at the core;
Most subtle of the four,
When air flies not, nor water flows,
It disembodied goes,

Being light, elixir of the first decree,
More volatile than he;
With strength and power to pass
Through space, where never his least atom was:
He has no part in it, save as his eyes
Have drawn its emanation from the skies.

A wingless creature heavier than air,
He is rejected of its quintessence;
Coming and going hence,
In the twin minutes of his birth and death,
He may inhale as breath,
As breath relinquish heaven's atmosphere,
Yet in it have no share,
Nor can survive therein
Where its outer edge is filtered pure and thin:
It doth but lend its crystal to his lungs
For his early crying, and his final songs.

The element of water has denied
Its child; it is no more his element;
It never will relent;
Its silver harvests are more sparsely given
Than the rewards of heaven,
And he shall drink cold comfort at its side:
The water is too wide:
The seamew and the gull
Feather a nest made soft and pitiful
Upon its foam; he has not any part
In the long swell of sorrow at its heart.

Hail and farewell, beloved element,
Whence he departed, and his parent once;
See where thy spirit runs
Which for so long hath had the moon to wife;
Shall this support his life
Until the arches of the waves be bent
And grow shallow and spent?
Wisely it cast him forth
With his dead weight of burdens nothing worth,
Leaving him, for the universal years,
A little seawater to make his tears.

Hail, element of earth, receive thy own,
And cherish, at thy charitable breast,
This man, this mongrel beast:

He plows the sand, and, at his hardest need,
He sows himself for seed;
He plows the furrow, and in this lies down
Before the corn is grown;
Between the apple bloom
And the ripe apple is sufficient room
In time, and matter, to consume his love
And make him parcel of a cypress grove.

Receive him as thy lover for an hour
Who will not weary, by a longer stay,
The kind embrace of clay;
Even within thine arms he is dispersed
To nothing, as at first;
The air flings downward from its four-quartered tower
Him whom the flames devour;
At the full tide, at the flood,
The sea is mingled with his salty blood:
The traveler dust, although the dust be vile,
Sleeps as thy lover for a little while.

Ezra Pound

1885-

Salutation

O Generation of the thoroughly smug
        and thoroughly uncomfortable,
I have seen fishermen picnicking in the sun,
I have seen them with untidy families,
I have seen their smiles full of teeth
        and heard ungainly laughter.
And I am happier than you are,
And they were happier than I am;
And the fish swim in the lake
        and do not even own clothing.

The Garden

En robe de parade.
SAMAIN

Like a skein of loose silk blown against a wall
She walks by the railing of a path in Kensington Gardens,
And she is dying piece-meal
        of a sort of emotional anaemia.

And round about there is a rabble
Of the filthy, sturdy, unkillable infants of the very poor.
They shall inherit the earth.

In her is the end of breeding.
Her boredom is exquisite and excessive.
She would like some one to speak to her,
And is almost afraid that I
        will commit that indiscretion.

Sestina: Altaforte

Loquitur: En *Bertrans de Born.*
  Dante Alighieri put this man in hell for that he was a stirrer up of strife. Eccovi! Judge ye!
  Have I dug him up again?
The scene is at his castle, Altaforte. "Papiols" is his jongleur.
"The Leopard," the device of Richard Cœur de Lion.

Damn it all! all this our South stinks peace.
You whoreson dog, Papiols, come! Let's to music!
I have no life save when the swords clash.
But ah! when I see the standards gold, vair, purple, opposing
And the broad fields beneath them turn crimson,
Then howl I my heart nigh mad with rejoicing.

In hot summer have I great rejoicing
When the tempests kill the earth's foul peace,
And the lightnings from black heav'n flash crimson,
And the fierce thunders roar me their music
And the winds shriek through the clouds mad, opposing,
And through all the riven skies God's swords clash.

Hell grant soon we hear again the swords clash!
And the shrill neighs of destriers in battle rejoicing,
Spiked breast to spiked breast opposing!
Better one hour's stour than a year's peace
With fat boards, bawds, wine and frail music!
Bah! there's no wine like the blood's crimson!

And I love to see the sun rise blood-crimson.
And I watch his spears through the dark clash
And it fills all my heart with rejoicing
And pries wide my mouth with fast music
When I see him so scorn and defy peace,
His lone might 'gainst all darkness opposing.

The man who fears war and squats opposing
My words for stour, hath no blood of crimson,
But is fit only to rot in womanish peace
Far from where worth's won and the swords clash
For the death of such sluts I go rejoicing;
Yea, I fill all the air with my music.

Papiols, Papiols, to the music!
There's no sound like to swords swords opposing,
No cry like the battle's rejoicing
When our elbows and swords drip the crimson
And our charges 'gainst "The Leopard's" rush clash.
May God damn for ever all who cry "Peace!"

And let the music of the swords make them crimson!
Hell grant soon we hear again the swords clash!
Hell blot black for alway the thought "Peace"!

The River-Merchant's Wife: a Letter

(After Rihaku)

While my hair was still cut straight across my forehead
I played about the front gate, pulling flowers.
You came by on bamboo stilts, playing horse,
You walked about my seat, playing with blue plums.
And we went on living in the village of Chokan:
Two small people, without dislike or suspicion.

At fourteen I married My Lord you.
I never laughed, being bashful.

Lowering my head, I looked at the wall.
Called to, a thousand times, I never looked back.

At fifteen I stopped scowling,
I desired my dust to be mingled with yours
Forever and forever and forever.
Why should I climb the look out?

At sixteen you departed,
You went into far Ku-to-yen, by the river of swirling eddies,
And you have been gone five months.
The monkeys make sorrowful noise overhead.

You dragged your feet when you went out.
By the gate now, the moss is grown, the different mosses,
Too deep to clear them away!
The leaves fall early this autumn, in wind.
The paired butterflies are already yellow with August
Over the grass in the West garden;
They hurt me. I grow older.
If you are coming down through the narrows of the river Kiang,
Please let me know beforehand,
And I will come out to meet you
        As far as Cho-fu-Sa.

An Immorality

Sing we for love and idleness,
Naught else is worth the having.

Though I have been in many a land,
There is naught else in living.

And I would rather have my sweet,
Though rose-leaves die of grieving,

Than do high deeds in Hungary
To pass all men's believing.

A Virginal

No, no! Go from me. I have left her lately.
I will not spoil my sheath with lesser brightness,
For my surrounding air hath a new lightness;
Slight are her arms, yet they have bound me straitly
And left me cloaked as with a gauze of æther;
As with sweet leaves; as with a subtle clearness.
Oh, I have picked up magic in her nearness
To sheathe me half in half the things that sheathe her.
No, no! Go from me. I have still the flavour,
Soft as spring wind that's come from birchen bowers.
Green come the shoots, aye April in the branches,
As winter's wound with her sleight hand she staunches,
Hath of the trees a likeness of the savour:
As white their bark, so white this lady's hours.

Greek Epigram

Day and night are never weary,
Nor yet is God of creating
For day and night their torch-bearers
The aube and the crepuscule.

So, when I weary of praising the dawn and the sunset,
Let me be no more counted among the immortals;
But number me amid the wearying ones,
Let me be a man as the herd,
And as the slave that is given in barter.

Dance Figure

(For the Marriage in Cana of Galilee)

Dark eyed,
O woman of my dreams,
Ivory sandalled,
There is none like thee among the dancers,
None with swift feet.

I have not found thee in the tents,
In the broken darkness.

I have not found thee at the well-head
Among the women with pitchers.

Thine arms are as a young sapling under the bark;
Thy face as a river with lights.

White as an almond are thy shoulders;
As new almonds stripped from the husk.
They guard thee not with eunuchs;
Not with bars of copper.

Gilt turquoise and silver are in the place of thy rest.
A brown robe with threads of gold woven in patterns hast thou
gathered about thee,
O Nathat-Ikanaie, "Tree-at-the-river."

As a rillet among the sedge are thy hands upon me;
Thy fingers a frosted stream.

Thy maidens are white like pebbles;
Their music about thee!

There is none like thee among the dancers;
None with swift feet.

Ballad of the Goodly Fere

(Simon Zelotes speaketh it somewhile after
the Crucifixion)

Ha' we lost the goodliest fere [1] o' all
For the priests and the gallows tree?
Aye, lover he was of brawny men,
O' ships and the open sea.

When they came wi' a host to take Our Man
His smile was good to see,
"First let these go!" quo' our Goodly Fere,
"Or I'll see ye damned," says he.

Aye, he sent us out through the crossed high spears,
And the scorn of his laugh rang free,

[1] Fere: mate, companion.

"Why took ye not me when I walked about
Alone in the town?" says he.

Oh we drank his "Hale" in the good red wine
When we last made company,
No capon priest was the Goodly Fere
But a man o' men was he.

I ha' seen him drive a hundred men
Wi' a bundle o' cords swung free,
When they took the high and holy house
For their pawn and treasury.

They'll no get him a' in a book I think
Though they write it cunningly;
No mouse of the scrolls was the Goodly Fere
But aye loved the open sea.

If they think they ha' snared our Goodly Fere
They are fools to the last degree.
"I'll go to the feast," quo' our Goodly Fere,
"Though I go to the gallows tree."

"Ye ha' seen me heal the lame and the blind,
And wake the dead," says he,
"Ye shall see one thing to master all:
'Tis how a brave man dies on the tree."

A son of God was the Goodly Fere
That bade us his brothers be.
I ha' seen him cow a thousand men.
I ha' seen him upon the tree.

He cried no cry when they drave the nails
And the blood gushed hot and free,
The hounds of the crimson sky gave tongue
But never a cry cried he.

I ha' seen him cow a thousand men
On the hills o' Galilee,
They whined as he walked out calm between,
Wi' his eyes like the gray o' the sea.

Like the sea that brooks no voyaging
With the winds unleashed and free,

Like the sea that he cowed at Gennesaret
Wi' twey words spoke' suddenly.

A master of men was the Goodly Fere,
A mate of the wind and sea,
If they think they ha' slain our Goodly Fere
They are fools eternally.

I ha' seen him eat o' the honey-comb
Sin' they nailed him to the tree.

A Girl

The tree has entered my hands,
The sap has ascended my arms,
The tree has grown in my breast—
Downward,
The branches grow out of me, like arms.

Tree you are,
Moss you are,
You are violets with wind above them.
A child—so high—you are;
And all this is folly to the world.

In a Station of the Metro

The apparition of these faces in the crowd;
Petals on a wet, black bough.

Fan-Piece, for Her Imperial Lord

O fan of white silk,
        clear as frost on the grass-blade,
You also are laid aside.

Δώρια

Be in me as the eternal moods
        of the bleak wind, and not
As transient things are—
        gayety of flowers.

Have me in the strong loneliness
            of sunless cliffs
And of grey waters.
            Let the gods speak softly of us
In days hereafter,
            the shadowy flowers of Orcus
Remember thee.

Piere Vidal Old

It is of Piere Vidal, the fool par excellence *of all Provence, of whom the tale tells how he ran mad, as a wolf, because of his love for Loba of Penautier, and how men hunted him with dogs through the mountains of Cabaret and brought him for dead to the dwelling of this Loba (she-wolf) of Penautier, and how she and her Lord had him healed and made welcome, and he stayed some time at that court. He speaks:*

When I but think upon the great dead days
And turn my mind upon that splendid madness,
Lo! I do curse my strength
And blame the sun his gladness;
For that the one is dead
And the red sun mocks my sadness.

Behold me, Vidal, that was fool of fools!
Swift as the king wolf was I and as strong
When tall stags fled me through the alder brakes,
And every jongleur knew me in his song,
And the hounds fled and the deer fled
And none fled over long.

Even the grey pack knew me and knew fear.
God! how the swiftest hind's blood spurted hot
Over the sharpened teeth and purpling lips!
Hot was that hind's blood yet it scorched me not
As did first scorn, then lips of the Penautier!
Aye ye are fools, if ye think time can blot

From Piere Vidal's remembrance that blue night.
God! but the purple of the sky was deep!
Clear, deep, translucent, so the stars me seemed
Set deep in crystal; and because my sleep
—Rare visitor—came not,—the Saints I guerdon
For that restlessness—Piere set to keep

One more fool's vigil with the hollyhocks.
Swift came the Loba, as a branch that's caught,
Torn, green and silent in the swollen Rhone,
Green was her mantle, close, and wrought
Of some thin silk stuff that's scarce stuff at all,
But like a mist wherethrough her white form fought.

And conquered! Ah God! conquered!
Silent my mate came as the night was still.
Speech? Words? Faugh! Who talks of words and love?!
Hot is such love and silent,
Silent as fate is, and as strong until
It faints in taking and in giving all.

Stark, keen, triumphant, till it plays at death.
God! she was white then, splendid as some tomb
High wrought of marble, and the panting breath
Ceased utterly. Well, then I waited, drew,
Half-sheathed, then naked from its saffron sheath
Drew full this dagger that doth tremble here.

Just then she woke and mocked the less keen blade.
Ah God, the Loba! and my only mate!
Was there such flesh made ever and unmade!
God curse the years that turn such women grey!
Behold here Vidal, that was hunted, flayed,
Shamed and yet bowed not and that won at last.

And yet I curse the sun for his red gladness,
I that have known strath, garth, brake, dale,
And every run-away of the wood through that great madness,
Behold me shrivelled as an old oak's trunk
And made men's mock'ry in my rotten sadness!

No man hath heard the glory of my days:
No man hath dared and won his dare as I:
One night, one body and one welding flame!
What do ye own, ye niggards! that can buy
Such glory of the earth? Or who will win
Such battle-guerdon with his "prowesse high"?

O Age gone lax! O stunted followers,
That mask at passions and desire desires,
Behold me shrivelled, and your mock of mocks;

And yet I mock you by the mighty fires
That burnt me to this ash.

. . . .

Ah! Cabaret! Ah Cabaret, thy hills again!

. . . .

Take your hands off me! . . . *Sniffing the air.*
Ha! this scent is hot!

Silet

When I behold how black, immortal ink
Drips from my deathless pen—ah, well-away!
Why should we stop at all for what I think?
There is enough in what I chance to say.

It is enough that we once came together;
What is the use of setting it to rime?
When it is autumn do we get spring weather,
Or gather may of harsh northwindish time?

It is enough that we once came together;
What if the wind have turned against the rain?
It is enough that we once came together;
Time has seen this, and will not turn again.

And who are we, who know that last intent,
To plague tomorrow with a testament!

Portrait d'une Femme

Your mind and you are our Sargasso Sea,
London has swept about you this score years
And bright ships left you this or that in fee:
Ideas, old gossip, oddments of all things,
Strange spars of knowledge and dimmed wares of price.
Great minds have sought you—lacking someone else.
You have been second always. Tragical?
No. You preferred it to the usual thing:
One dull man, dulling and uxorious,
One average mind—with one thought less, each year.
Oh, you are patient. I have seen you sit
Hours, where something might have floated up.

And now you pay one. Yes, you richly pay.
You are a person of some interest, one comes to you
And takes strange gain away:
Trophies fished up; some curious suggestion;
Fact that leads nowhere; and a tale for two,
Pregnant with mandrakes, or with something else
That might prove useful and yet never proves,
That never fits a corner or shows use,
Or finds its hour upon the loom of days:
The tarnished, gaudy, wonderful old work;
Idols, and ambergris and rare inlays.
These are your riches, your great store; and yet
For all this sea-hoard of deciduous things,
Strange woods half sodden, and new brighter stuff:
In the slow float of differing light and deep,
No! there is nothing! In the whole and all,
Nothing that's quite your own.
Yet this is you.

The Return

See, they return; ah, see the tentative
Movements, and the slow feet,
The trouble in the pace and the uncertain
Wavering!

See, they return, one, and by one,
With fear, as half-awakened;
As if the snow should hesitate
And murmur in the wind,
and half turn back;
These were the "Wing'd-with-Awe,"
Inviolable.

Gods of the wingèd shoe!
With them the silver hounds,
sniffing the trace of air!

Haie! Haie!
These were the swift to harry;
These were the keen-scented;
These were the souls of blood.

Slow on the leash,
pallid the leash-men!

Envoi

(From "Hugh Selwyn Mauberley")

Go, dumb-born book,
Tell her that sang me once that song of Lawes:
Hadst thou but song
As thou hast subjects known,
Then were there cause in thee that should condone
Even my faults that heavy upon me lie,
And build her glories their longevity.

Tell her that sheds
Such treasure in the air,
Recking naught else but that her graces give
Life to the moment,
I would bid them live
As roses might, in magic amber laid,
Red overwrought with orange and all made
One substance and one colour
Braving time.

Tell her that goes
With song upon her lips
But sings not out the song, nor knows
The maker of it, some other mouth,
May be as fair as hers,
Might, in new ages, gain her worshippers,
When our two dusts with Waller's shall be laid,
Siftings on siftings in oblivion,
Till change hath broken down
All things save Beauty alone.

The Rest

O helpless few in my country,
O remnant enslaved!

Artists broken against her,
Astray, lost in the villages,
Mistrusted, spoken-against,

Lovers of beauty, starved,
Thwarted with systems,
Helpless against the control;

You who cannot wear yourselves out
By persisting to successes,
You who can only speak,
Who cannot steel yourselves into reiteration;

You of the finer sense,
Broken against false knowledge,
You who can know at first hand,
Hated, shut in, mistrusted:

Take thought:
I have weathered the storm,
I have beaten out my exile.

Ité

Go, my songs, seek your praise from the young and from the
intolerant,
Move among the lovers of perfection alone.
Seek ever to stand in the hard Sophoclean light
And take your wounds from it gladly.

From "Impressions of François-Marie Arouet (de Voltaire)"

To Madame du Châtelet

If you'd have me go on loving you
Give me back the time of the thing.

Will you give me dawn light at evening?
Time has driven me out from the fine plaisaunces,
The parks with the swards all over dew,
And grass going glassy with the light on it,
The green stretches where love is and the grapes
Hang in yellow-white and dark clusters ready for pressing.
And if now we can't fit with our time of life
There is not much but its evil left us.

Life gives us two minutes, two seasons—
One to be dull in;
Two deaths—and to stop loving and being lovable,
That is the real death,
The other is little beside it.

Crying after the follies gone by me,
Quiet talking is all that is left us—
Gentle talking, not like the first talking, less lively;
And to follow after friendship, as they call it,
Weeping that we can follow naught else.

From "Homage to Sextus Propertius"

I

Shades of Callimachus, Coan ghosts of Philetas
It is in your grove I would walk,
I who come first from the clear font
Bringing the Grecian orgies into Italy,
and the dance into Italy.
Who hath taught you so subtle a measure,
in what hall have you heard it;
What foot beat out your time-bar,
what water has mellowed your whistles?

Out-weariers of Apollo will, as we know, continue their Martian generalities,
We have kept our erasers in order.
A new-fangled chariot follows the flower-hung horses;
A young Muse with young loves clustered about her
ascends with me into the æther, . . .
And there is no high-road to the Muses.

Annalists will continue to record Roman reputations,
Celebrities from the Trans-Caucasus will belaud Roman celebrities
And expound the distentions of Empire,
But for something to read in normal circumstances?
For a few pages brought down from the forked hill unsullied?
I ask a wreath which will not crush my head.
And there is no hurry about it;
I shall have, doubtless, a boom after my funeral,
Seeing that long standing increases all things
regardless of quality.

And who would have known the towers
pulled down by a deal-wood horse;
Or of Achilles withstaying waters by Simois
Or of Hector spattering wheel-rims,
Or of Polydmantus, by Scamander, or Helenus and Deiphoibos?
Their door-yards would scarcely know them, or Paris.
Small talk O Ilion, and O Troad
twice taken by Oetian gods,
If Homer had not stated your case!

And I also among the later nephews of this city
shall have my dog's day,
With no stone upon my contemptible sepulchre;
My vote coming from the temple of Phoebus in Lycia, at Patara,
And in the meantime my songs will travel,
And the devirginated young ladies will enjoy them
when they have got over the strangeness,
For Orpheus tamed the wild beasts—
and held up the Threician river;
And Citharaon shook up the rocks by Thebes
and danced them into a bulwark at his pleasure,
And you, O Polyphemus? Did harsh Galatea almost
Turn to your dripping horses, because of a tune, under Aetna?
We must look into the matter.
Bacchus and Apollo in favour of it,
There will be a crowd of young women doing homage to my palaver,
Though my house is not propped up by Taenarian columns from Laconia (associated with Neptune and Cerberus),
Though it is not stretched upon gilded beams;
My orchards do not lie level and wide
as the forests of Phaecia,
the luxurious and Ionian,
Nor are my caverns stuffed stiff with a Marcian vintage,
My cellar does not date from Numa Pompilius,
Nor bristle with wine jars,
Nor is it equipped with a frigidaire patent;
Yet the companions of the Muses
will keep their collective nose in my books,
And weary with historical data, they will turn to my dance tune.

Happy who are mentioned in my pamphlets,
the songs shall be a fine tomb-stone over their beauty.
But against this?
Neither expensive pyramids scraping the stars in their route,

Nor houses modelled upon that of Jove in East Elis,
Nor the monumental effigies of Mausolus,
are a complete elucidation of death.

Flame burns, rain sinks into the cracks
And they all go to rack ruin beneath the thud of the years.
Stands genius a deathless adornment,
a name not to be worn out with the years.

VI

When, when, and whenever death closes our eyelids,
Moving naked over Acheron
Upon the one raft, victor and conqueror together,
Marius and Jugurtha together,
one tangle of shadows.

Caesar plots against India,
Tigris and Euphrates shall, from now on, flow at his bidding,
Tibet shall be full of Roman policemen,
The Parthians shall get used to our statuary
and acquire a Roman religion;
One raft on the veiled flood of Acheron,
Marius and Jugurtha together.

Nor at my funeral either will there be any long trail,
bearing ancestral lares and images;
No trumpets filled with my emptiness,
Nor shall it be on an Atalic bed;
The perfumed cloths will be absent.
A small plebeian procession.
Enough, enough and in plenty
There will be three books at my obsequies
Which I take, my not unworthy gift, to Persephone.

You will follow the bare scarified breast
Nor will you be weary of calling my name, nor too weary
To place the last kiss on my lips
When the Syrian onyx is broken.

"He who is now vacant dust
"Was once the slave of one passion:"
Give that much inscription
"Death why tardily come?"

You, sometimes, will lament a lost friend,
        For it is a custom:
This care for past men,

Since Adonis was gored in Idalia, and the Cytharean
Ran crying with out-spread hair,
        In vain, you call back the shade,
In vain, Cynthia. Vain call to unanswering shadow,
        Small talk comes from small bones.

Canto I

And then went down to the ship,
Set keel to breakers, forth on the godly sea, and
We set up mast and sail on that swart ship,
Bore sheep aboard her, and our bodies also
Heavy with weeping, and winds from sternward
Bore us out onward with bellying canvas,
Circe's this craft, the trim-coifed goddess.
Then sat we amidships, wind jamming the tiller,
Thus with stretched sail, we went over sea till day's end.
Sun to his slumber, shadows o'er all the ocean,
Came we then to the bounds of deepest water,
To the Kimmerian lands, and peopled cities
Covered with close-webbed mist, unpierced ever
With glitter of sun-ray
Nor with stars stretched, nor looking back from heaven
Swartest night stretched over wretched men there.
The ocean flowing backward, came we then to the place
Aforesaid by Circe.
Here did they rites, Perimedes and Eurylochus,
And drawing sword from my hip
I dug the ell-square pitkin;
Poured we libations unto each the dead,
First mead and then sweet wine, water mixed with white flour.
Then prayed I many a prayer to the sickly death's-heads;
As set in Ithaca, sterile bulls of the best
For sacrifice, heaping the pyre with goods,
A sheep to Tiresias only, black and a bell-sheep.
Dark blood flowed in the fosse,
Souls out of Erebus, cadaverous dead, of brides
Of youths and of the old who had borne much;
Souls stained with recent tears, girls tender,

Men many, mauled with bronze lance heads,
Battle spoil, bearing yet dreory [1] arms,
These many crowded about me; with shouting,
Pallor upon me, cried to my men for more beasts;
Slaughtered the herds, sheep slain of bronze;
Poured ointment, cried to the gods,
To Pluto the strong, and praised Proserpine;
Unsheathed the narrow sword,
I sat to keep off the impetuous impotent dead,
Till I should hear Tiresias.
But first Elpenor came, our friend Elpenor,
Unburied, cast on the wide earth,
Limbs that we left in the house of Circe,
Unwept, unwrapped in sepulchre, since toils urged other.
Pitiful spirit. And I cried in hurried speech:
"Elpenor, how art thou come to this dark coast?
"Cam'st thou afoot, outstripping seamen?"
And he in heavy speech:
"Ill fate and abundant wine. I slept in Circe's ingle.
"Going down the long ladder unguarded,
"I fell against the buttress,
"Shattered the nape-nerve, the soul sought Avernus.
"But thou, O King, I bid remember me, unwept, unburied,
"Heap up mine arms, be tomb by sea-board, and inscribed:
" '*A man of no fortune and with a name to come.*'
"And set my oar up, that I swung mid fellows."

And Anticlea came, whom I beat off, and then Tiresias Theban,
Holding his golden wand, knew me, and spoke first:
"A second time? why? man of ill star,
"Facing the sunless dead and this joyless region?
"Stand from the fosse, leave me my bloody bever
"For soothsay."
And I stepped back,
And he strong with the blood, said then: "Odysseus
"Shalt return through spiteful Neptune, over dark seas,
"Lose all companions." And then Anticlea came.
Lie quiet Divus. I mean that is Andreas Divus,
In officina Wecheli, 1538, out of Homer.
And he sailed, by Sirens and thence outward and away
And unto Circe.
Venerandam,
In the Cretan's phrase, with the golden crown, Aphrodite,

1 Dreory: Anglo-Saxon for "bloody."

Cypri munimenta sortita est, mirthful, oricalchi, with golden
Girdles and breast bands, thou with dark eyelids
Bearing the golden bough of Argicida. So that:

Canto II

Hang it all, Robert Browning,
there can be but the one "Sordello."
But Sordello, and my Sordello?
Lo Sordels si fo di Mantovana.
So-shu churned in the sea.
Seal sports in the spray-whited circles of cliff-wash,
Sleek head, daughter of Lir,
        eyes of Picasso
Under black fur-hood, lithe daughter of Ocean;
And the wave runs in the beach-groove:
"Eleanor, ἑλέναυς and ἑλέπτολις!"
        And poor old Homer blind, blind, as a bat,
Ear, ear for the sea-surge, murmur of old men's voices:
"Let her go back to the ships,
"Back among Grecian faces, lest evil come on our own,
"Evil and further evil, and a curse cursed on our children,
"Moves, yes she moves like a goddess
"And has the face of a god
        and the voice of Schoeney's daughters,
"And doom goes with her in walking,
"Let her go back to the ships,
        back among Grecian voices."
And by the beach-run, Tyro,
        Twisted arms of the sea-god,
Lithe sinews of water, gripping her, cross-hold,
And the blue-gray glass of the wave tents them,
Glare azure of water, cold-welter, close cover.
Quiet sun-tawny sand-stretch,
The gulls broad out their wings,
        nipping between the splay feathers;
Snipe come for their bath,
        bend out their wing-joints,
Spread wet wings to the sun-film,
And by Scios,
        to left of the Naxos passage,
Naviform rock overgrown,
        algæ cling to its edge,

There is a wine-red glow in the shallows,
a tin flash in the sun-dazzle.

The ship landed in Scios,
men wanting spring-water,
And by the rock-pool a young boy loggy with vine-must,
"To Naxos? Yes, we'll take you to Naxos,
Cum' along lad." "Not that way!"
"Aye, that way is Naxos."
And I said: "It's a straight ship."
And an ex-convict out of Italy
knocked me into the fore-stays,
(He was wanted for manslaughter in Tuscany)
And the whole twenty against me,
Mad for a little slave money.
And they took her out of Scios
And off her course . . .
And the boy came to, again, with the racket,
And looked out over the bows,
and to eastward, and to the Naxos passage.
God-sleight then, god-sleight:
Ship stock fast in sea-swirl,
Ivy upon the oars, King Pentheus,
grapes with no seed but sea-foam,
Ivy in scupper-hole.
Aye, I, Acœtes, stood there,
and the god stood by me,
Water cutting under the keel,
Sea-break from stern forrards,
wake running off from the bow,
And where was gunwhale, there now was vine-trunk,
And tenthril where cordage had been,
grape-leaves on the rowlocks,
Heavy vine on the oarshafts,
And, out of nothing, a breathing,
hot breath on my ankles,
Beasts like shadows in glass,
a furred tail upon nothingness.
Lynx-purr, and heathery smell of beasts,
where tar smell had been,
Sniff and pad-foot of beasts,
eye-glitter out of black air.
The sky overshot, dry, with no tempest,
Sniff and pad-foot of beasts,
fur brushing my knee-skin,

Rustle of airy sheaths,
        dry forms in the *æther*.
And the ship like a keel in ship-yard,
        slung like an ox in smith's sling,
Ribs stuck fast in the ways,
        grape-cluster over pin-rack,
        void air taking pelt.
Lifeless air become sinewed,
        feline leisure of panthers,
Leopards sniffing the grape shoots by scupper-hole,
Crouched panthers by fore-hatch,
And the sea blue-deep about us,
        green-ruddy in shadows.
And Lyæus: "From now, Acœtes, my altars,
Fearing no bondage,
        fearing no cat of the wood,
Safe with my lynxes,
        feeding grapes to my leopards,
Olibanum is my incense,
        the vines grow in my homage."

The back-swell now smooth in the rudder-chains,
Black snout of a porpoise
        where Lycabs had been,
Fish-scales on the oarsmen.
        And I worship.
I have seen what I have seen.
        When they brought the boy I said:
"He has a god in him,
        though I do not know which god."
And they kicked me into the fore-stays.
I have seen what I have seen:
        Medon's face like the face of a dory,
Arms shrunk into fins. And you, Pentheus,
Had as well listen to Tiresias, and to Cadmus,
        or your luck will go out of you.
Fish-scales over groin muscles,
        lynx-purr amid sea . . .
And of a later year,
        pale in the wine-red algæ,
If you will lean over the rock,
        the coral face under wave-tinge,
Rose-paleness under water-shift,
        Ileuthyeria, fair Dafne of sea-bords,
The swimmer's arms turned to branches,

Who will say in what year,
        fleeing what band of tritons,
The smooth brows, seen, and half seen,
        now ivory stillness.

And So-shu churned in the sea, So-shu also,
        using the long moon for a churn-stick . . .
Lithe turning of water,
        sinews of Poseidon,
Black azure and hyaline,
        glass wave over Tyro,
Close cover, unstillness,
        bright welter of wave-cords,
Then quiet water,
        quiet in the buff sands,
Sea-fowl stretching wing-joints,
        splashing in rock-hollows and sand-hollows
In the wave-runs by the half-dune;
Glass-glint of wave in the tide-rips against sunlight,
        pallor of Hesperus,
Grey peak of the wave,
        wave, colour of grape's pulp,

Olive grey in the near,
        far, smoke grey of the rock-slide,
Salmon-pink wings of the fish-hawk
        cast grey shadows in water,
The tower like a one-eyed great goose
        cranes up out of the olive-grove,

And we have heard the fauns chiding Proteus
        in the smell of hay under the olive-trees,
And the frogs singing against the fauns
        in the half-light.
And . . .

From "Canto LXXXI"

What thou lovest well remains,
                                the rest is dross
What thou lov'st well shall not be reft from thee
What thou lov'st well is thy true heritage
Whose world, or mine or theirs
                                or is it of none?

First came the seen, then thus the palpable
        Elysium, though it were in the halls of hell,
What thou lovest well is thy true heritage

The ant's a centaur in his dragon world.
Pull down thy vanity, it is not man
Made courage, or made order, or made grace,
        Pull down thy vanity, I say pull down.
Learn of the green world what can be thy place
In scaled invention or true artistry,
Pull down thy vanity,
                                        Paquin pull down!
The green casque has outdone your elegance.

"Master thyself, then others shall thee beare"
        Pull down thy vanity
Thou art a beaten dog beneath the hail,
A swollen magpie in a fitful sun,
Half black half white
Nor knowst'ou wing from tail
Pull down thy vanity
                                How mean thy hates
Fostered in falsity,
                                Pull down thy vanity,
Rathe to destroy, niggard in charity,
Pull down thy vanity,
                                I say pull down.

But to have done instead of not doing
                                this is not vanity
To have, with decency, knocked
That a Blunt should open
                    To have gathered from the air a live tradition
or from a fine old eye the unconquered flame
This is not vanity.
        Here error is all in the not done,
all in the diffidence that faltered.

Marianne Moore

1887-

A Talisman

Under a splintered mast,
torn from the ship and cast
near her hull,

a stumbling shepherd found,
embedded in the ground,
a sea-gull

of lapis lazuli,
a scarab of the sea,
with wings spread–

curling its coral feet,
parting its beak to greet
men long dead.

That Harp You Play so Well

O David, if I had
Your power, I should be glad–
In harping, with the sling,
In patient reasoning!

Blake, Homer, Job, and you,
Have made old wine-skins new.
Your energies have wrought
Stout continents of thought.

But, David, if the heart
Be brass, what boots the art
Of exorcising wrong,
Of harping to a song?

The scepter and the ring
And every royal thing
    Will fail. Grief's lustiness
    Must cure the harp's distress.

To a Steam Roller

The illustration
is nothing to you without the application.
  You lack half wit. You crush all the particles down
    into close conformity, and then walk back and forth on
      them.

Sparkling chips of rock
are crushed down to the level of the parent block.
  Were not "impersonal judgment in esthetic
    matters, a metaphysical impossibility," you

might fairly achieve
it. As for butterflies, I can hardly conceive
  of one's attending upon you; but to question
    the congruence of the complement is vain, if it exists.

England

with its baby rivers and little towns, each with its abbey or its
    cathedral,
with voices—one voice perhaps, echoing through the transept—
    the
criterion of suitability and convenience: and Italy with its equal
shores—contriving an epicureanism from which the grossness
    has been

extracted: and Greece with its goats and its gourds, the nest of
    modified illusions:
and France, the "chrysalis of the nocturnal butterfly," in
whose products mystery of construction diverts one from what
    was originally one's
object—substance at the core: and the East with its snails, its
    emotional

shorthand and jade cockroaches, its rock crystal and its imper-
    turbability,
all of museum quality: and America where there

is the little old ramshackle victoria in the south, where cigars
are smoked on the
street in the north; where there are no proof readers, no silk-
worms, no digressions;

the wild man's land; grass-less, linksless, languageless country—
in which letters are written
not in Spanish, not in Greek, not in Latin, not in shorthand,
but in plain American which cats and dogs can read! The letter
a in psalm and calm when
pronounced with the sound of *a* in candle, is very noticeable
but

why should continents of misapprehension have to be accounted
for by the
fact? Does it follow that because there are poisonous toadstools
which resemble mushrooms, both are dangerous? In the case of
mettlesomeness which may be
mistaken for appetite, of heat which may appear to be haste,
no con-

clusions may be drawn. To have misapprehended the matter,
is to have confessed
that one has not looked far enough. The sublimated wisdom
of China, Egyptian discernment, the cataclysmic torrent of
emotion compressed
in the verbs of the Hebrew language, the books of the man
who is able

to say, "I envy nobody but him and him only, who catches
more fish than
I do,"—the flower and fruit of all that noted superi-
ority—should one not have stumbled upon it in America, must
one imagine
that it is not there? It has never been confined to one locality.

The Fish

Wade
through black jade.
Of the crow-blue mussel-shells, one keeps
adjusting the ash-heaps;
opening and shutting itself like

an
injured fan.
  The barnacles which encrust the side
  of the wave, cannot hide
    there for the submerged shafts of the

sun,
split like spun
  glass, move themselves with spotlight swiftness
  into the crevices—
    in and out, illuminating

the
turquoise sea
  of bodies. The water drives a wedge
  of iron through the iron edge
    of the cliff, whereupon the stars,

pink
rice grains, ink-
  bespattered jelly-fish, crabs like green
  lilies, and submarine
    toadstools, slide each on the other.

All
external
  marks of abuse are present on this
  defiant edifice—
    all the physical features of

ac-
cident—lack
  of cornice, dynamite grooves, burns and
  hatchet strokes, these things stand
    out on it; the chasm-side is

dead.
Repeated
  evidence has proved that it can live
  on what can not revive
    its youth. The sea grows old in it.

Poetry

I, too, dislike it: there are things that are important beyond all
this fiddle.
Reading it, however, with a perfect contempt for it, one discovers in
it, after all, a place for the genuine.
Hands that can grasp, eyes
that can dilate, hair that can rise
if it must, these things are important not because a

high-sounding interpretation can be put upon them but because they are
useful. When they become so derivative as to become un-
intelligible,
the same thing may be said for all of us, that we
do not admire what
we cannot understand: the bat
holding on upside down or in quest of something to

eat, elephants pushing, a wild horse taking a roll, a tireless
wolf under
a tree, the immovable critic twitching his skin like a horse
that feels a flea, the base-
ball fan, the statistician—
nor is it valid
to discriminate against "business documents and

school-books"; all these phenomena are important. One must
make a distinction
however: when dragged into prominence by half poets, the
result is not poetry,
nor till the poets among us can be
"literalists of
the imagination"—above
insolence and triviality and can present

for inspection, "imaginary gardens with real toads in them,"
shall we have
it. In the meantime, if you demand on the one hand,
the raw material of poetry in
all its rawness and
that which is on the other hand
genuine, then you are interested in poetry.

Nevertheless

you've seen a strawberry
    that's had a struggle; yet
    was, where the fragments met,

a hedgehog or a star-
    fish for the multitude
    of seeds. What better food

than apple-seeds—the fruit
    within the fruit—locked in
    like counter-curved twin

hazel-nuts? Frost that kills
    the little rubber-plant-
    leaves of *kok-saghyz*-stalks, can't

harm the roots; they still grow
    in frozen ground. Once where
    there was a prickly-pear-

leaf clinging to barbed wire,
    a root shot down to grow
    in earth two feet below;

as carrots form mandrakes
    or a ram's-horn root some-
    times. Victory won't come

to me unless I go
    to it; a grape-tendril
    ties a knot in knots till

knotted thirty times,—so
    the bound twig that's under-
    gone and over-gone, can't stir.

The weak overcomes its
    menace, the strong over-
    comes itself. What is there

like fortitude! What sap
    went through that little thread
    to make the cherry red!

A Carriage from Sweden

They say there is a sweeter air
    where it was made, than we have here;
    a Hamlet's castle atmosphere.
At all events there is in Brooklyn
something that makes me feel at home.

No one may see this put-away
    museum-piece, this country cart
    that inner happiness made art;
and yet, in this city of freckled
integrity it is a vein

of resined straightness from north-wind
    hardened Sweden's once-opposed-to-
    compromise archipelago
of rocks. Washington and Gustavus
Adolphus, forgive our decay.

Seats, dashboard and sides of smooth gourd-
    rind texture, a flowered step, swan-
    dart brake, and swirling crustacean-
tailed equine amphibious creatures
that garnish the axle-tree! What

a fine thing! What unannoying
    romance! And how beautiful, she
    with the natural stoop of the
snowy egret, gray-eyed and straight-haired,
for whom it should come to the door,—

of whom it reminds me. The split
    pine fair hair, steady gannet-clear
    eyes and the pine-needled-path deer-
swift step; that is Sweden, land of the
free and the soil for a spruce-tree—

vertical though a seedling—all
    needles: from a green trunk, green shelf
    on shelf fanning out by itself.
The deft white-stockinged dance in thick-soled
shoes! Denmark's sanctuaried Jews!

The puzzle-jugs and hand-spun rugs,
  the root-legged kracken shaped like dogs,
  the hanging buttons and the frogs
that edge the Sunday jackets! Sweden,
you have a runner called the Deer, who

when he's run a race, likes to run
    more; you have the sun-right gable-
    ends due east and west, the table
spread as for a banquet; and the put-
in twin vest-pleats with a fish-fin

effect when you need none. Sweden,
    what makes the people dress that way
    and those who see you wish to stay?
The runner, not too tired to run more
at the end of the race? And that

cart, dolphin-graceful? A Dalgrén
    light-house, self-lit?—responsive and
    responsible. I understand;
it's not pine-needle-paths that give spring
when they're run on, it's a Sweden

of moated white castles,—the bed
    of densely grown flowers in an S,
    meaning Sweden and stalwartness,
skill, and a surface that says
Made in Sweden: carts are my trade.

See in the Midst of Fair Leaves

and much fruit, the swan—
  one line of the mathematician's
sign greater-than drawn
  to an apex where the lake is
met by the weight on it; or an angel
standing in the sun; how well
  armed, how manly;

and promenading
  in sloughs of despond, a monster,
man when human nothing
  more, grown to immaturity,

punishing debtors, seeking his due as
an arrow turned inward has
no chance of peace.

What Are Years?

What is our innocence,
what is our guilt? All are
naked, none is safe. And whence
is courage: the unanswered question,
the resolute doubt—
dumbly calling, deafly listening—that
in misfortune, even death,
encourages others
and in its defeat, stirs

the soul to be strong? He
sees deep and is glad, who
accedes to mortality
and in his imprisonment, rises
upon himself as
the sea in a chasm, struggling to be
free and unable to be,
in its surrendering
finds its continuing.

So he who strongly feels,
behaves. The very bird,
grown taller as he sings, steels
his form straight up. Though he is captive,
his mighty singing
says, satisfaction is a lowly
thing, how pure a thing is joy.
This is mortality,
this is eternity.

The Mind Is an Enchanting Thing

is an enchanted thing
like the glaze on a
katydid-wing
subdivided by sun
till the nettings are legion.
Like Gieseking playing Scarlatti;

like the apteryx-awl
as a beak, or the
kiwi's rain-shawl
of haired feathers, the mind
feeling its way as though blind,
walks along with its eyes on the ground.

It has memory's ear
that can hear without
having to hear.
Like the gyroscope's fall,
truly unequivocal
because trued by regnant certainty,

it is a power of
strong enchantment. It
is like the dove-
neck animated by
sun; it is memory's eye;
it's conscientious inconsistency.

It tears off the veil; tears
the temptation, the
mist the heart wears,
from its eyes,—if the heart
has a face; it takes apart
dejection. It's fire in the dove-neck's

iridescence; in the
inconsistencies
of Scarlatti.
Unconfusion submits
its confusion to proof; it's
not a Herod's oath that cannot change.

In Distrust of Merits

Strengthened to live, strengthened to die for
medals and positioned victories?
They're fighting, fighting, fighting the blind
man who thinks he sees,—
who cannot see that the enslaver is

enslaved; the hater, harmed. O shining O
firm star, O tumultuous
ocean lashed till small things go
as they will, the mountainous
wave makes us who look, know

depth. Lost at sea before they fought! O
star of David, star of Bethlehem,
O black imperial lion
of the Lord—emblem
of a risen world—be joined at last, be
joined. There is hate's crown beneath which all is
death; there's love's without which none
is king; the blessed deeds bless
the halo. As contagion
of sickness makes sickness,

contagion of trust can make trust. They're
fighting in deserts and caves, one by
one, in battalions and squadrons;
they're fighting that I
may yet recover from the disease, *my*
self; some have it lightly, some will die. "Man's
wolf to man?" And we devour
ourselves? The enemy could not
have made a greater breach in our
defenses. One pilot-

ing a blind man can escape him, but
Job disheartened by false comfort knew,
that nothing is so defeating
as a blind man who
can see. O alive who are dead, who are
proud not to see, O small dust of the earth
that walks so arrogantly,
trust begets power and faith is
an affectionate thing. We
vow, we make this promise

to the fighting—it's a promise—"We'll
never hate black, white, red, yellow, Jew,
Gentile, Untouchable." We are
not competent to
make our vows. With set jaw they are fighting,

fighting, fighting,—some we love whom we know,
some we love but know not—that
hearts may feel and not be numb.
It cures me; or am I what
I can't believe in? Some

in snow, some on crags, some in quicksands,
little by little, much by much, they
are fighting fighting fighting that where
there was death there may
be life. "When a man is prey to anger,
he is moved by outside things; when he holds
his ground in patience patience
patience, that is action or
beauty," the soldier's defense
and hardest armor for

the fight. The world's an orphan's home. Shall
we never have peace without sorrow?
without pleas of the dying for
help that won't come? O
quiet form upon the dust, I cannot
look and yet I must. If these great patient
dyings—all these agonies
and woundbearings and blood shed—
can teach us how to live, these
dyings were not wasted.

Hate-hardened heart, O heart of iron,
iron is iron till it is rust.
There never was a war that was
not inward; I must
fight till I have conquered in myself what
causes war, but I would not believe it.
I inwardly did nothing.
O Iscariotlike crime!
Beauty is everlasting
and dust is for a time.

At Rest in the Blast

Like a bulwark against fate,
By the thrust of the blast
Lead-saluted;
Saluted by lead?
As though flying
Old Glory full mast.

Pent by power that holds it fast—
A paradox. . . . Hard-pressed,
You take the blame
And are inviolate—
Down-cast but not cast

Down. Some would bind by promises,
But not the tempest-tossed—
Borne by the might
Of the storm to a height,
From destruction—
At rest in the blast.

Robinson Jeffers

1887-

Compensation

Solitude that unmakes me one of men
In snow-white hands brings singular recompense,
Evening me with kindlier natures when
On the needled pinewood the cold dews condense
About the hour of Rigel fallen from heaven
In wintertime, or when the long night tides
Sigh blindly from the sand-dune backward driven,
Or when on stormwings of the northwind rides

The foamscud with the cormorants, or when passes
A horse or dog with brown affectionate eyes,
Or autumn frosts are pricked by earliest grasses,
Or whirring from her covert a quail flies.
Why, even in humanity, beauty and good
Show from the mountainside of solitude.

Age in Prospect

Praise youth's hot blood if you will, I think that happiness
Rather consists in having lived clear through
Youth and hot blood, on to the wintrier hemisphere
Where one has time to wait and to remember.

Youth and hot blood are beautiful, so is peacefulness.
Youth had some islands in it, but age is indeed
An island and a peak; age has infirmities,
Not few, but youth is all one fever.

To look around and to love in his appearances,
Though a little calmly, the universal God's
Beauty is better I think than to lip eagerly
The mother's breast or another woman's.

And there is no possession more sure than memory's;
But if I reach that gray island, that peak,
My hope is still to possess with eyes the homeliness
Of ancient loves, ocean and mountains,

And meditate the sea-mouth of mortality
And the fountain six feet down with a quieter thirst
Than now I feel for old age; a creature progressively
Thirsty for life will be for death too.

Clouds of Evening

Enormous cloud-mountains that form over Point Lobos and
 into the sunset,
Figures of fire on the walls of tonight's storm,
Foam of gold in gorges of fire, and the great file of warrior
 angels:
Dreams gathering in the curdled brain of the earth—

The sky the brain-vault—on the threshold of sleep: poor earth, you, like your children
By inordinate desires tortured, make dreams?
Storms more enormous, wars nobler, more toppling mountains, more jeweled waters, more free
Fires on impossible headlands . . . as a poor girl
Wishing her lover taller and more desirous, and herself maned with gold,
Dreams the world right, in the cold bed, about dawn.
Dreams are beautiful; the slaves of form are beautiful also; I have grown to believe
A stone is a better pillow than many visions.

To the Stone-Cutters

Stone-cutters fighting time with marble, you foredefeated
Challengers of oblivion,
Eat cynical earnings, knowing rock splits, records fall down,
The square-limbed Roman letters
Scale in the thaws, wear in the rain. The poet as well
Builds his monument mockingly;
For man will be blotted out, the blithe earth die, the brave sun
Die blind, his heart blackening:
Yet stones have stood for a thousand years, and pained thoughts found
The honey of peace in old poems.

Gale in April

Intense and terrible beauty, how has our race with the frail naked nerves,
So little a craft swum down from its far launching?
Why now, only because the northwest blows and the headed grass billows,
Great seas jagging the west and on the granite
Blanching, the vessel is brimmed, this dancing play of the world is too much passion.
A gale in April so overfilling the spirit,
Though his ribs were thick as the earth's, arches of mountain, how shall one dare to live,
Though his blood were like the earth's rivers and his flesh iron,
How shall one dare to live? One is born strong, how do the weak endure it?

The strong lean upon death as on a rock,
After eighty years there is shelter and the naked nerves shall be covered with deep quietness.
O beauty of things, go on, go on, O torture
Of intense joy, I have lasted out my time, I have thanked God and finished,
Roots of millennial trees fold me in the darkness,
Northwest winds shake their tops, not to the root, not to the root, I have passed
From beauty to the other beauty, peace, the night splendor.

Apology for Bad Dreams

I

In the purple light, heavy with redwood, the slopes drop seaward,
Headlong convexities of forest, drawn in together to the steep ravine. Below, on the sea-cliff,
A lonely clearing; a little field of corn by the streamside; a roof under spared trees. Then the ocean
Like a great stone someone has cut to a sharp edge and polished to shining. Beyond it, the fountain
And furnace of incredible light flowing up from the sunk sun. In the little clearing a woman
Was punishing a horse; she had tied the halter to a sapling at the edge of the wood; but when the great whip
Clung to the flanks the creature kicked so hard she feared he would snap the halter; she called from the house
The young man her son; who fetched a chain tie-rope, they working together
Noosed the small rusty links round the horse's tongue
And tied him by the swollen tongue to the tree.
Seen from this height they are shrunk to insect size,
Out of all human relation. You cannot distinguish
The blood dripping from where the chain is fastened,
The beast shuddering; but the thrust neck and the legs
Far apart. You can see the whip fall on the flanks. . . .
The gesture of the arm. You cannot see the face of the woman.
The enormous light beats up out of the west across the cloud-bars of the trade-wind. The ocean
Darkens, the high clouds brighten, the hills darken together.
Unbridled and unbelievable beauty

Covers the evening world . . . not covers, grows apparent out of it, as Venus down there grows out
From the lit sky. What said the prophet? "I create good: and I create evil: I am the Lord."

II

This coast crying out for tragedy like all beautiful places,
(The quiet ones ask for quieter suffering; but here the granite cliff the gaunt cypresses' crown
Demands what victim? The dykes of red lava and black what Titan? The hills like pointed flames
Beyond Soberanes, the terrible peaks of the bare hills under the sun, what immolation?)
This coast crying out for tragedy like all beautiful places: and like the passionate spirit of humanity
Pain for its bread: God's, many victims', the painful deaths, the horrible transfigurements: I said in my heart,
"Better invent than suffer: imagine victims
Lest your own flesh be chosen the agonist, or you
Martyr some creature to the beauty of the place." And I said,
"Burn sacrifices once a year to magic
Horror away from the house, this little house here
You have built over the ocean with your own hands
Beside the standing bowlders: for what are we,
The beast that walks upright, with speaking lips
And little hair, to think we should always be fed,
Sheltered, intact, and self-controlled? We sooner more liable
Than the other animals. Pain and terror, the insanities of desire; not accidents, but essential,
And crowd up from the core." I imagined victims for those wolves, I made the phantoms to follow.
They have hunted the phantoms and missed the house. It is not good to forget over what gulfs the spirit
Of the beauty of humanity, the petal of a lost flower blown seaward by the night-wind, floats to its quietness.

III

Bowlders blunted like an old bear's teeth break up from the headland; below them
All the soil is thick with shells, the tide-rock feasts of a dead people.
Here the granite flanks are scarred with ancient fire, the ghosts of the tribe

Crouch in the nights beside the ghost of a fire, they try to remember the sunlight,
Light has died out of their skies. These have paid something for the future
Luck of the country, while we living keep old griefs in memory: though God's
Envy is not a likely fountain of ruin, to forget evil calls down
Sudden reminders from the cloud: remembered deaths be our redeemers;
Imagined victims our salvation: white as the half moon at midnight
Someone flamelike passed me, saying, "I am Tamar Cauldwell, I have my desire,"
Then the voice of the sea returned, when she had gone by, the stars to their towers.
. . . Beautiful country, burn again, Point Pinos down to the Sur Rivers
Burn as before with bitter wonders, land and ocean and the Carmel water.

IV

He brays humanity in a mortar to bring the savor
From the bruised root: a man having bad dreams, who invents victims, is only the ape of that God.
He washes it out with tears and many waters, calcines it with fire in the red crucible,
Deforms it, makes it horrible to itself: the spirit flies out and stands naked, he sees the spirit.
He takes it in the naked ecstasy; it breaks in his hand, the atom is broken, the power that massed it
Cries to the power that moves the stars, "I have come home to myself, behold me.
I bruised myself in the flint mortar and burnt me
In the red shell, I tortured myself, I flew forth,
Stood naked of myself and broke me in fragments,
And here am I moving the stars that are me."
I have seen these ways of God: I know of no reason
For fire and change and torture and the old returnings.
He being sufficient might be still. I think they admit no reason; they are the ways of my love.
Unmeasured power, incredible passion, enormous craft: no thought apparent but burns darkly
Smothered with its own smoke in the human brain-vault: no thought outside: a certain measure in phenomena:
The fountains of the boiling stars, the flowers on the foreland, the ever-returning roses of dawn.

Promise of Peace

The heads of strong old age are beautiful
Beyond all grace of youth. They have strange quiet,
Integrity, health, soundness, to the full
They've dealt with life and been attempered by it.
A young man must not sleep; his years are war
Civil and foreign but the former's worse;
But the old can breathe in safety now that they are
Forgetting what youth meant, the being perverse,
Running the fool's gauntlet and being cut
By the whips of the five senses. As for me,
If I should wish to live long it were but
To trade those fevers for tranquillity,
Thinking though that's entire and sweet in the grave
How shall the dead taste the deep treasure they have?

Birth-Dues

Joy is a trick in the air; pleasure is merely contemptible, the
dangled
Carrot the ass follows to market or precipice;
But limitary pain—the rock under the tower and the hewn
coping
That takes thunder at the head of the turret—
Terrible and real. Therefore a mindless dervish carving himself
With knives will seem to have conquered the world.

The world's God is treacherous and full of unreason; a tor-
turer, but also
The only foundation and the only fountain.
Who fights him eats his own flesh and perishes of hunger; who
hides in the grave
To escape him is dead; who enters the Indian
Recession to escape him is dead; who falls in love with the
God is washed clean
Of death desired and of death dreaded.

He has joy, but joy is a trick in the air; and pleasure, but
pleasure is contemptible;
And peace; and is based on solider than pain.

He has broken boundaries a little and that will estrange him;
he is monstrous, but not
To the measure of the God. . . . But I having told you—
However I suppose that few in the world have energy to hear
effectively—
Have paid my birth-dues; am quits with the people.

Credo

My friend from Asia has powers and magic, he plucks a blue
leaf from the young blue-gum
And gazing upon it, gathering and quieting
The God in his mind, creates an ocean more real than the
ocean, the salt, the actual
Appalling presence, the power of the waters.
He believes that nothing is real except as we make it.
I humbler have found in my blood
Bred west of Caucasus a harder mysticism.
Multitude stands in my mind but I think that the ocean in
the bone vault is only
The bone vault's ocean: out there is the ocean's;
The water is the water, the cliff is the rock, come shocks and
flashes of reality. The mind
Passes, the eye closes, the spirit is a passage;
The beauty of things was born before eyes and sufficient to
itself; the heart-breaking beauty
Will remain when there is no heart to break for it.

Love the Wild Swan

"I hate my verses, every line, every word,
Oh pale and brittle pencils ever to try
One grass-blade's curve, or the throat of one bird
That clings to twig, ruffled against white sky.
Oh cracked and twilight mirrors ever to catch
One color, one glinting flash, of the splendor of things.
Unlucky hunter, Oh bullets of wax,
The lion beauty, the wild-swan wings, the storm of the wings."
—This wild swan of a world is no hunter's game.
Better bullets than yours would miss the white breast,
Better mirrors than yours would crack in the flame.
Does it matter whether you hate your . . . self? At least

Love your eyes that can see, your mind that can
Hear the music, the thunder of the wings. Love the wild swan.

Shine, Perishing Republic

While this America settles in the mold of its vulgarity, heavily thickening to empire,
And protest, only a bubble in the molten mass, pops and sighs out, and the mass hardens,

I sadly smiling remember that the flower fades to make fruit, the fruit rots to make earth.
Out of the mother; and through the spring exultances, ripeness and decadence; and home to the mother.

You making haste, haste on decay: not blameworthy; life is good, be it stubbornly long or suddenly
A mortal splendor: meteors are not needed less than mountains: shine, perishing republic.

But for my children, I would have them keep their distance from the thickening center; corruption
Never has been compulsory, when the cities lie at the monster's feet there are left the mountains.

And boys, be in nothing so moderate as in love of man, a clever servant, insufferable master.
There is the trap that catches noblest spirits, that caught—they say—God, when he walked on earth.

Hurt Hawks

The broken pillar of the wing jags from the clotted shoulder,
The wing trails like a banner in defeat,
No more to use the sky forever but live with famine
And pain a few days: cat nor coyote
Will shorten the week of waiting for death, there is game without talons.

He stands under the oak-bush and waits
The lame feet of salvation; at night he remembers freedom
And flies in a dream, the dawns ruin it.
He is strong and pain is worse to the strong, incapacity is worse.

The curs of the day come and torment him
At distance, no one but death the redeemer will humble that
head,
The intrepid readiness, the terrible eyes.
The wild God of the world is sometimes merciful to those
That ask mercy, not often to the arrogant.
You do not know him, you communal people, or you have
forgotten him;
Intemperate and savage, the hawk remembers him;
Beautiful and wild, the hawks, and men that are dying re-
member him.

I'd sooner, except the penalties, kill a man than a hawk; but
the great redtail
Had nothing left but unable misery
From the bone too shattered for mending, the wing that trailed
under his talons when he moved.
We had fed him six weeks, I gave him freedom,
He wandered over the foreland hill and returned in the eve-
ning, asking for death,
Not like a beggar, still eyed with the old
Implacable arrogance. I gave him the lead gift in the twilight.
What fell was relaxed,
Owl-downy, soft feminine feathers; but what
Soared: the fierce rush: the night-herons by the flooded river
cried fear at its rising
Before it was quite unsheathed from reality.

Prescription of Painful Ends

Lucretius felt the change of the world in his time, the great
republic coming to the height
Whence no way leads but downward, Plato in his time watched
Athens
Dance the down path. The future is ever a misted landscape,
no man foreknows it, but at cyclical turns
There is a change felt in the rhythm of events: as when an
exhausted horse
Falters and recovers, then the rhythm of the running hoofbeats
is altered, he will run miles yet,
But he must fall: we have felt it again in our own lifetime,
slip, shift and speed-up

In the gallop of the world, and now suspect that, come peace
or war, the progress of America and Europe
Becomes a long process of deterioration—starred with famous
Byzantiums and Alexandrias,
Surely,—but downward. One desires at such times
To gather the insights of the age summit against future loss,
against the narrowing mind and the tyrants,
The pedants, the mystagogues, the swarms of barbarians: time-
conscious poems, poems for treasuries: Lucretius
Sings his great theory of natural origins and of wise conduct;
Plato smiling carves dreams, bright cells
Of incorruptible wax to hive the Greek honey.

Our own time, much greater
and far less fortunate,
Has acids for honey and for fine dreams
The immense vulgarities of misapplied science and decaying
Christianity: therefore one christens each poem, in dutiful
Hope of burning off at least the top crust of the time's un-
cleanness, from the acid bottles.

May-June, 1940

Foreseen for so many years: these evils, this monstrous violence,
these massive agonies: no easier to bear.
We saw them with slow stone strides approach, everyone saw
them; we closed our eyes against them, we looked
And they had come nearer. We ate and drank and slept, they
came nearer. Sometimes we laughed, they were nearer.
Now
They are here. And now a blind man foresees what follows
them: degradation, famine, recovery and so forth, and the
Epidemic manias: but not enough death to serve us, not
enough death. It would be better for men
To be few and live far apart, where none could infect another;
then slowly the sanity of field and mountain
And the cold ocean and glittering stars might enter their minds.

Another
dream, another dream.
We shall have to accept certain limitations
In future, and abandon some humane dreams; only hard-
minded, sleepless and realist. can ride this rock-slide

To new fields down the dark mountain; and we shall have to
perceive that these insanities are normal;
We shall have to perceive that battle is a burning flower or
like a huge music, and the dive-bomber's screaming orgasm
As beautiful as other passions; and that death and life are not
serious alternatives. One has known all these things
For many years: there is greater and darker to know
In the next hundred.

And why do you cry, my dear, why do you cry?
It is all in the whirling circles of time.
If millions are born millions must die,
If England goes down and Germany up
The stronger dog will still be on top,
All in the turning of time.
If civilization goes down, that
Would be an event to contemplate.
It will not be in our time, alas, my dear,
It will not be in our time.

Original Sin

The man-brained and man-handed ground-ape, physically
The most repulsive of all hot-blooded animals
Up to that time of the world: they had dug a pitfall
And caught a mammoth, but how could their sticks and stones
Reach the life in that hide? They danced around the pit,
shrieking
With ape excitement, flinging sharp flints in vain, and the
stench of their bodies
Stained the white air of dawn; but presently one of them
Remembered the yellow dancer, wood-eating fire
That guards the cave-mouth: he ran and fetched him, and
others
Gathered sticks at the wood's edge; they made a blaze
And pushed it into the pit, and they fed it high, around the
mired sides
Of their huge prey. They watched the long hairy trunk
Waver over the stifle-trumpeting pain,
And they were happy.

Meanwhile the intense color and nobility of sunrise,
Rose and gold and amber, flowed up the sky. Wet rocks were
shining, a little wind

Stirred the leaves of the forest and the marsh flag-flowers; the
soft valley between the low hills
Became as beautiful as the sky; while in its midst, hour after
hour, the happy hunters
Roasted their living meat slowly to death.

These are the people.
This is the human dawn. As for me, I would rather
Be a worm in a wild apple than a son of man.
But we are what we are, and we might remember
Not to hate any person, for all are vicious;
And not to be astonished at any evil, all are deserved;
And not fear death; it is the only way to be cleansed.

T. S. Eliot

1888-

The Love Song of J. Alfred Prufrock

S'io credesse che mia risposta fosse
A persona che mai tornasse al mondo,
Questa fiamma staria senza piu scosse.
Ma perciocche giammai di questo fondo
Non torno vivo alcun, s'i'odo il vero,
Senza tema d'infamia ti rispondo.

Let us go then, you and I,
When the evening is spread out against the sky
Like a patient etherized upon a table;
Let us go, through certain half-deserted streets,
The muttering retreats
Of restless nights in one-night cheap hotels
And sawdust restaurants with oyster-shells:
Streets that follow like a tedious argument
Of insidious intent
To lead you to an overwhelming question . . .

Oh, do not ask, "What is it?"
Let us go and make our visit.

In the room the women come and go
Talking of Michelangelo.

The yellow fog that rubs its back upon the window-panes,
The yellow smoke that rubs its muzzle on the window-panes
Licked its tongue into the corners of the evening,
Lingered upon the pools that stand in drains,
Let fall upon its back the soot that falls from chimneys,
Slipped by the terrace, made a sudden leap,
And seeing that it was a soft October night,
Curled once about the house, and fell asleep.

And indeed there will be time
For the yellow smoke that slides along the street,
Rubbing its back upon the window-panes;
There will be time, there will be time
To prepare a face to meet the faces that you meet;
There will be time to murder and create,
And time for all the works and days of hands
That lift and drop a question on your plate;
Time for you and time for me,
And time yet for a hundred indecisions,
And for a hundred visions and revisions,
Before the taking of a toast and tea.

In the room the women come and go
Talking of Michelangelo.

And indeed there will be time
To wonder, "Do I dare?" and, "Do I dare?"
Time to turn back and descend the stair,
With a bald spot in the middle of my hair—
[They will say: "How his hair is growing thin!"]
My morning coat, my collar mounting firmly to the chin,
My necktie rich and modest, but asserted by a simple pin—
[They will say: "But how his arms and legs are thin!"]
Do I dare
Disturb the universe?
In a minute there is time
For decisions and revisions which a minute will reverse.

For I have known them all already, known them all:—
Have known the evenings, mornings, afternoons,
I have measured out my life with coffee spoons;
I know the voices dying with a dying fall

Beneath the music from a farther room.
So how should I presume?

And I have known the eyes already, known them all—
The eyes that fix you in a formulated phrase,
And when I am formulated, sprawling on a pin,
When I am pinned and wriggling on the wall,
Then how should I begin
To spit out all the butt-ends of my days and ways?
And how should I presume?

And I have known the arms already, known them all—
Arms that are braceleted and white and bare
[But in the lamplight, downed with light brown hair!]
Is it perfume from a dress
That makes me so digress?
Arms that lie along a table, or wrap about a shawl.
And should I then presume?
And how should I begin?

Shall I say, I have gone at dusk through narrow streets
And watched the smoke that rises from the pipes
Of lonely men in shirt-sleeves, leaning out of windows? . . .

I should have been a pair of ragged claws
Scuttling across the floors of silent seas.

And the afternoon, the evening, sleeps so peacefully!
Smoothed by long fingers,
Asleep . . . tired . . . or it malingers,
Stretched on the floor, here beside you and me.
Should I, after tea and cakes and ices,
Have the strength to force the moment to its crisis?
But though I have wept and fasted, wept and prayed,
Though I have seen my head [grown slightly bald] brought in upon a platter,
I am no prophet—and here's no great matter;
I have seen the moment of my greatness flicker,
And I have seen the eternal Footman hold my coat, and snicker,
And in short, I was afraid.

And would it have been worth it, after all,
After the cups, the marmalade, the tea,

Among the porcelain, among some talk of you and me,
Would it have been worth while,
To have bitten off the matter with a smile,
To have squeezed the universe into a ball
To roll it toward some overwhelming question,
To say: "I am Lazarus, come from the dead,
Come back to tell you all, I shall tell you all"—
If one, settling a pillow by her head,
    Should say: "That is not what I meant at all.
    That is not it, at all."

And would it have been worth it, after all,
Would it have been worth while,
After the sunsets and the dooryards and the sprinkled streets,
After the novels, after the teacups, after the skirts that trail
    along the floor—
And this, and so much more?—
It is impossible to say just what I mean!
But as if a magic lantern threw the nerves in patterns on a
    screen:
Would it have been worth while
If one, settling a pillow or throwing off a shawl,
And turning toward the window, should say:
    "That is not it at all,
    That is not what I meant, at all."

No! I am not Prince Hamlet, nor was meant to be;
Am an attendant lord, one that will do
To swell a progress, start a scene or two,
Advise the prince; no doubt, an easy tool,
Deferential, glad to be of use,
Politic, cautious, and meticulous;
Full of high sentence, but a bit obtuse;
At times, indeed, almost ridiculous—
Almost, at times, the Fool.

I grow old. . . . I grow old. . . .
I shall wear the bottoms of my trousers rolled.

Shall I part my hair behind? Do I dare to eat a peach?
I shall wear white flannel trousers, and walk upon the beach.
I have heard the mermaids singing, each to each.

I do not think that they will sing to me.

I have seen them riding seaward on the waves
Combing the white hair of the waves blown back
When the wind blows the water white and black.

We have lingered in the chambers of the sea
By sea-girls wreathed with seaweed red and brown
Till human voices wake us, and we drown.

The Waste Land

"Nam Sibyllam quidem Cumis ego ipse oculis meis vidi in ampulla pendere, et cum illi pueri dicerent: Σιβυλλα τί θέλεις; *respondebat illa:* ἀποθανεῖν θέλω."

For Ezra Pound
il miglior fabbro

I. THE BURIAL OF THE DEAD

April is the cruellest month, breeding
Lilacs out of the dead land, mixing
Memory and desire, stirring
Dull roots with spring rain.
Winter kept us warm, covering
Earth in forgetful snow, feeding
A little life with dried tubers.
Summer surprised us, coming over the Starnbergersee
With a shower of rain; we stopped in the colonnade,
And went on in sunlight, into the Hofgarten, 10
And drank coffee, and talked for an hour.
Bin gar keine Russin, stamm' aus Litauen, echt deutsch.
And when we were children, staying at the archduke's,
My cousin's, he took me out on a sled,
And I was frightened. He said, Marie,
Marie, hold on tight. And down we went.
In the mountains, there you feel free.
I read, much of the night, and go south in the winter.

What are the roots that clutch, what branches grow
Out of this stony rubbish? Son of man, 20
You cannot say, or guess, for you know only
A heap of broken images, where the sun beats,
And the dead tree gives no shelter, the cricket no relief,
And the dry stone no sound of water. Only
There is shadow under this red rock,
(Come in under the shadow of this red rock),

And I will show you something different from either
Your shadow at morning striding behind you
Or your shadow at evening rising to meet you;
I will show you fear in a handful of dust. 30
Frisch weht der Wind
Der Heimat zu,
Mein Irisch Kind,
Wo weilest du?
"You gave me hyacinths first a year ago;
"They called me the hyacinth girl."
—Yet when we came back, late, from the Hyacinth garden,
Your arms full, and your hair wet, I could not
Speak, and my eyes failed, I was neither
Living nor dead, and I knew nothing, 40
Looking into the heart of light, the silence.
Oed' und leer das Meer.

Madame Sosostris, famous clairvoyante,
Had a bad cold, nevertheless
Is known to be the wisest woman in Europe,
With a wicked pack of cards. Here, said she,
Is your card, the drowned Phoenician Sailor,
(Those are pearls that were his eyes. Look!)
Here is Belladonna, the Lady of the Rocks,
The lady of situations. 50
Here is the man with three staves, and here the Wheel,
And here is the one-eyed merchant, and this card,
Which is blank, is something he carries on his back,
Which I am forbidden to see. I do not find
The Hanged Man. Fear death by water.
I see crowds of people, walking round in a ring.
Thank you. If you see dear Mrs. Equitone,
Tell her I bring the horoscope myself:
One must be so careful these days.

Unreal City, 60
Under the brown fog of a winter dawn,
A crowd flowed over London Bridge, so many,
I had not thought death had undone so many.
Sighs, short and infrequent, were exhaled,
And each man fixed his eyes before his feet.
Flowed up the hill and down King William Street,
To where Saint Mary Woolnoth kept the hours
With a dead sound on the final stroke of nine.

There I saw one I knew, and stopped him, crying: "Stetson!
"You who were with me in the ships at Mylae! 70
"That corpse you planted last year in your garden,
"Has it begun to sprout? Will it bloom this year?
"Or has the sudden frost disturbed its bed?
"Oh keep the Dog far hence, that's friend to men,
"Or with his nails he'll dig it up again!
"You! hypocrite lecteur!—mon semblable,—mon frère!"

II. A GAME OF CHESS

The Chair she sat in, like a burnished throne,
Glowed on the marble, where the glass
Held up by standards wrought with fruited vines
From which a golden Cupidon peeped out 80
(Another hid his eyes behind his wing)
Doubled the flames of sevenbranched candelabra
Reflecting light upon the table as
The glitter of her jewels rose to meet it,
From satin cases poured in rich profusion;
In vials of ivory and coloured glass
Unstoppered, lurked her strange synthetic perfumes,
Unguent, powdered, or liquid—troubled, confused
And drowned the sense in odours; stirred by the air
That freshened from the window, these ascended 90
In fattening the prolonged candle-flames,
Flung their smoke into the laquearia,
Stirring the pattern on the coffered ceiling.
Huge sea-wood fed with copper
Burned green and orange, framed by the coloured stone,
In which sad light a carvèd dolphin swam.
Above the antique mantel was displayed
As though a window gave upon the sylvan scene
The change of Philomel, by the barbarous king
So rudely forced; yet there the nightingale 100
Filled all the desert with inviolable voice
And still she cried, and still the world pursues,
"Jug Jug" to dirty ears.
And other withered stumps of time
Were told upon the walls; staring forms
Leaned out, leaning, hushing the room enclosed.
Footsteps shuffled on the stair.
Under the firelight, under the brush, her hair
Spread out in fiery points
Glowed into words, then would be savagely still. 110

"My nerves are bad to-night. Yes, bad. Stay with me.
"Speak to me. Why do you never speak. Speak.
"What are you thinking of? What thinking? What?
"I never know what you are thinking. Think."

I think we are in rats' alley
Where the dead men lost their bones.

"What is that noise?"
The wind under the door.
"What is that noise now? What is the wind doing?"
Nothing again nothing. 120
"Do
"You know nothing? Do you see nothing? Do you remember
"Nothing?"
I remember
Those are pearls that were his eyes.
"Are you alive, or not? Is there nothing in your head?"
But

O O O O that Shakespeherian Rag—
It's so elegant
So intelligent 130
"What shall I do now? What shall I do?"
"I shall rush out as I am, and walk the street
"With my hair down, so. What shall we do tomorrow?
"What shall we ever do?"
The hot water at ten.
And if it rains, a closed car at four.
And we shall play a game of chess,
Pressing lidless eyes and waiting for a knock upon the door.

When Lil's husband got demobbed, I said—
I didn't mince my words, I said to her myself, 140
HURRY UP PLEASE ITS TIME
Now Albert's coming back, make yourself a bit smart.
He'll want to know what you done with that money he
gave you
To get yourself some teeth. He did, I was there.
You have them all out, Lil, and get a nice set,
He said, I swear, I can't bear to look at you.
And no more can't I, I said, and think of poor Albert,
He's been in the army four years, he wants a good time,
And if you don't give it him, there's others will, I said.
Oh is there, she said. Something o' that, I said. 150

Then I'll know who to thank, she said, and give me a
straight look.
HURRY UP PLEASE ITS TIME
If you don't like it you can get on with it, I said.
Others can pick and choose if you can't.
But if Albert makes off, it won't be for lack of telling.
You ought to be ashamed, I said, to look so antique.
(And her only thirty-one.)
I can't help it, she said, pulling a long face,
It's them pills I took, to bring it off, she said.
(She's had five already, and nearly died of young George.) 160
The chemist said it would be all right, but I've never been
the same.
You are a proper fool, I said.
Well, if Albert won't leave you alone, there it is, I said,
What you get married for if you don't want children?
HURRY UP PLEASE ITS TIME
Well, that Sunday Albert was home, they had a hot
gammon,
And they asked me in to dinner, to get the beauty of it
hot—
HURRY UP PLEASE ITS TIME
HURRY UP PLEASE ITS TIME
Goonight Bill. Goonight Lou. Goonight May. Goonight. 170
Ta ta. Goonight. Goonight.
Good night, ladies, good night, sweet ladies, good night, good
night.

III. THE FIRE SERMON

The river's tent is broken: the last fingers of leaf
Clutch and sink into the wet bank. The wind
Crosses the brown land, unheard. The nymphs are departed.
Sweet Thames, run softly, till I end my song.
The river bears no empty bottles, sandwich papers,
Silk handkerchiefs, cardboard boxes, cigarette ends
Or other testimony of summer nights. The nymphs are
departed.
And their friends, the loitering heirs of city directors; 180
Departed, have left no addresses.
By the waters of Leman I sat down and wept . . .
Sweet Thames, run softly till I end my song,
Sweet Thames, run softly, for I speak not loud or long.
But at my back in a cold blast I hear
The rattle of the bones, and chuckle spread from ear to ear.
A rat crept softly through the vegetation

Dragging its slimy belly on the bank
While I was fishing in the dull canal
On a winter evening round behind the gashouse 190
Musing upon the king my brother's wreck
And on the king my father's death before him.
White bodies naked on the low damp ground
And bones cast in a little low dry garret,
Rattled by the rat's foot only, year to year.
But at my back from time to time I hear
The sound of horns and motors, which shall bring
Sweeney to Mrs. Porter in the spring.
O the moon shone bright on Mrs. Porter
And on her daughter 200
They wash their feet in soda water
Et O ces voix d'enfants, chantant dans la coupole!

Twit twit twit
Jug jug jug jug jug jug
So rudely forc'd.
Tereu

Unreal City
Under the brown fog of a winter noon
Mr. Eugenides, the Smyrna merchant
Unshaven, with a pocket full of currants 210
C.i.f. London: documents at sight,
Asked me in demotic French
To luncheon at the Cannon Street Hotel
Followed by a weekend at the Metropole.

At the violet hour, when the eyes and back
Turn upward from the desk, when the human engine waits
Like a taxi throbbing waiting,
I Tiresias, though blind, throbbing between two lives,
Old man with wrinkled female breasts, can see
At the violet hour, the evening hour that strives 220
Homeward, and brings the sailor home from sea,
The typist home at teatime, clears her breakfast, lights
Her stove, and lays out food in tins.
Out of the window perilously spread
Her drying combinations touched by the sun's last rays,
On the divan are piled (at night her bed)
Stockings, slippers, camisoles, and stays.
I Tiresias, old man with wrinkled dugs

Perceived the scene, and foretold the rest—
I too awaited the expected guest. 230
He the young man carbuncular, arrives,
A small house agent's clerk, with one bold stare,
One of the low on whom assurance sits
As a silk hat on a Bradford millionaire.
The time is now propitious, as he guesses,
The meal is ended, she is bored and tired,
Endeavours to engage her in caresses
Which still are unreproved, if undesired.
Flushed and decided, he assaults at once;
Exploring hands encounter no defence; 240
His vanity requires no response,
And makes a welcome of indifference.
(And I Tiresias have foresuffered all
Enacted on this same divan or bed;
I who have sat by Thebes below the wall
And walked among the lowest of the dead.)
Bestows one final patronising kiss,
And gropes his way, finding the stairs unlit . . .

She turns and looks a moment in the glass,
Hardly aware of her departed lover; 250
Her brain allows one half-formed thought to pass:
"Well now that's done: and I'm glad it's over."
When lovely woman stoops to folly and
Paces about her room again, alone,
She smoothes her hair with automatic hand,
And puts a record on the gramophone.

"This music crept by me upon the waters"
And along the Strand, up Queen Victoria Street.
O City city, I can sometimes hear
Beside a public bar in Lower Thames Street, 260
The pleasant whining of a mandoline
And a clatter and a chatter from within
Where fishmen lounge at noon: where the walls
Of Magnus Martyr hold
Inexplicable splendour of Ionian white and gold.

The river sweats
Oil and tar
The barges drift
With the turning tide
Red sails 270

Wide
To leeward, swing on the heavy spar.
The barges wash
Drifting logs
Down Greenwich reach
Past the Isle of Dogs.
                    Weialala leia
                    Wallala leialala

Elizabeth and Leicester
Beating oars 280
The stern was formed
A gilded shell
Red and gold
The brisk swell
Rippled both shores
Southwest wind
Carried down stream
The peal of bells
White towers
                    Weialala leia 290
                    Wallala leialala

"Trams and dusty trees.
Highbury bore me. Richmond and Kew
Undid me. By Richmond I raised my knees
Supine on the floor of a narrow canoe."

"My feet are at Moorgate, and my heart
Under my feet. After the event
He wept. He promised 'a new start.'
I made no comment. What should I resent?"

"On Margate Sands. 300
I can connect
Nothing with nothing.
The broken fingernails of dirty hands.
My people humble people who expect
Nothing."
                    la la

To Carthage then I came

Burning burning burning burning
O Lord Thou pluckest me out
O Lord Thou pluckest 310

burning

IV. DEATH BY WATER

Phlebas the Phoenician, a fortnight dead,
Forgot the cry of gulls, and the deep sea swell
And the profit and loss.
A current under sea
Picked his bones in whispers. As he rose and fell
He passed the stages of his age and youth
Entering the whirlpool.
Gentile or Jew
O you who turn the wheel and look to windward, 320
Consider Phlebas, who was once handsome and tall as you.

V. WHAT THE THUNDER SAID

After the torchlight red on sweaty faces
After the frosty silence in the gardens
After the agony in stony places
The shouting and the crying
Prison and palace and reverberation
Of thunder of spring over distant mountains
He who was living is now dead
We who were living are now dying
With a little patience 330

Here is no water but only rock
Rock and no water and the sandy road
The road winding above among the mountains
Which are mountains of rock without water
If there were water we should stop and drink
Amongst the rock one cannot stop or think
Sweat is dry and feet are in the sand
If there were only water amongst the rock
Dead mountain mouth of carious teeth that cannot spit
Here one can neither stand nor lie nor sit 340
There is not even silence in the mountains
But dry sterile thunder without rain
There is not even solitude in the mountains
But red sullen faces sneer and snarl
From doors of mudcracked houses
If there were water
And no rock
If there were rock
And also water
And water 350
A spring

A pool among the rock
If there were the sound of water only
Not the cicada
And dry grass singing
But sound of water over a rock
Where the hermit-thrush sings in the pine trees
Drip drop drip drop drop drop drop
But there is no water

Who is the third who walks always beside you?
When I count, there are only you and I together 360
But when I look ahead up the white road
There is always another one walking beside you
Gliding wrapt in a brown mantle, hooded
I do not know whether a man or a woman
—But who is that on the other side of you?

What is that sound high in the air
Murmur of maternal lamentation
Who are those hooded hordes swarming
Over endless plains, stumbling in cracked earth
Ringed by the flat horizon only 370
What is the city over the mountains
Cracks and reforms and bursts in the violet air
Falling towers
Jerusalem Athens Alexandria
Vienna London
Unreal

A woman drew her long black hair out tight
And fiddled whisper music on those strings
And bats with baby faces in the violet light
Whistled, and beat their wings 380
And crawled head downward down a blackened wall
And upside down in air were towers
Tolling reminiscent bells, that kept the hours
And voices singing out of empty cisterns and exhausted
wells.

In this decayed hole among the mountains
In the faint moonlight, the grass is singing
Over the tumbled graves, about the chapel
There is the empty chapel, only the wind's home.

It has no windows, and the door swings,
Dry bones can harm no one. 390
Only a cock stood on the rooftree
Co co rico co co rico
In a flash of lightning. Then a damp gust
Bringing rain

Ganga was sunken, and the limp leaves
Waited for rain, while the black clouds
Gathered far distant, over Himavant.
The jungle crouched, humped in silence.
Then spoke the thunder
DA 400
Datta: what have we given?
My friend, blood shaking my heart
The awful daring of a moment's surrender
Which an age of prudence can never retract
By this, and this only, we have existed
Which is not to be found in our obituaries
Or in memories draped by the beneficent spider
Or under seals broken by the lean solicitor
In our empty rooms
DA 410
Dayadhvam: I have heard the key
Turn in the door once and turn once only
We think of the key, each in his prison
Thinking of the key, each confirms a prison
Only at nightfall, aethereal rumours
Revive for a moment a broken Coriolanus
DA
Damyata: The boat responded
Gaily, to the hand expert with sail and oar
The sea was calm, your heart would have responded 420
Gaily, when invited, beating obedient
To controlling hands

I sat upon the shore
Fishing, with the arid plain behind me
Shall I at least set my lands in order?
London Bridge is falling down falling down falling down
Poi s'ascose nel foco che gli affina
Quando fiam uti chelidon—O swallow swallow
Le Prince d'Aquitaine à la tour abolie
These fragments I have shored against my ruins 430

Why then Ile fit you. Hieronymo's mad againe.
Datta. Dayadhvam. Damyata.
Shantih shantih shantih

Notes by T. S. Eliot on "The Waste Land"

Not only the title, but the plan and a good deal of the incidental symbolism of the poem were suggested by Miss Jessie L. Weston's book on the Grail legend: *From Ritual to Romance* (Cambridge). Indeed, so deeply am I indebted, Miss Weston's book will elucidate the difficulties of the poem much better than my notes can do; and I recommend it (apart from the great interest of the book itself) to any who think such elucidation of the poem worth the trouble. To another work of anthropology I am indebted in general, one which has influenced our generation profoundly; I mean *The Golden Bough;* I have used especially the two volumes *Adonis, Attis, Osiris.* Anyone who is acquainted with these works will immediately recognise in the poem certain references to vegetation ceremonies.

I. THE BURIAL OF THE DEAD

Line 20. Cf. Ezekiel II, i.
23. Cf. Ecclesiastes XII, v.
31. V. Tristan und Isolde, I, verses 5-8.
42. Id. III, verse 24.
46. I am not familiar with the exact constitution of the Tarot pack of cards, from which I have obviously departed to suit my own convenience. The Hanged Man, a member of the traditional pack, fits my purpose in two ways: because he is associated in my mind with the Hanged God of Frazer, and because I associate him with the hooded figure in the passage of the disciples to Emmaus in Part V. The Phoenician Sailor and the Merchant appear later; also the "crowds of people," and Death by Water is executed in Part IV. The Man with Three Staves (an authentic member of the Tarot pack) I associate, quite arbitrarily, with the Fisher King himself.
60. Cf. Baudelaire:
"Fourmillante cité, cité pleine de rêves,
"Où le spectre en plein jour raccroche le passant."
63. Cf. Inferno III, 55-57:
"si lunga tratta
di gente, ch'io non avrei mai creduto
che morte tanta n'avesse disfatta."

64. Cf. Inferno IV, 25-27:

"Quivi, secondo che per ascoltare,
"non avea pianto, ma' che di sospiri,
"che l'aura eterna facevan tremare."

68. A phenomenon which I have often noticed.

74. Cf. the Dirge in Webster's *White Devil.*

76. V. Baudelaire, Preface to *Fleurs du Mal.*

II. A GAME OF CHESS

77. Cf. *Antony and Cleopatra,* II, ii, l. 190.

92. Laquearia. V. *Aeneid,* I, 726:
dependent lychni laquearibus aureis incensi, et noctem flammis funalia vincunt.

98. Sylvan scene. V. Milton, *Paradise Lost,* IV, 140.

99. V. Ovid, *Metamorphoses,* VI, Philomela.

100. Cf. Part III, l. 204.

115. Cf. Part III, l. 195.

118. Cf. Webster: "Is the wind in that door still?"

126. Cf. Part I, l. 37, 48.

138. Cf. the game of chess in Middleton's *Women beware Women.*

III. THE FIRE SERMON

176. V. Spenser, *Prothalamion.*

192. Cf. *The Tempest,* I, ii.

196. Cf. Marvell, *To His Coy Mistress.*

197. Cf. Day, *Parliament of Bees:*

"When of the sudden, listening, you shall hear,
"A noise of horns and hunting, which shall bring
"Actaeon to Diana in the spring,
"Where all shall see her naked skin . . ."

199. I do not know the origin of the ballad from which these lines are taken: it was reported to me from Sydney, Australia.

202. V. Verlaine, *Parsifal.*

210. The currants were quoted at a price "carriage and insurance free to London"; and the Bill of Lading etc. were to be handed to the buyer upon payment of the sight draft.

218. Tiresias, although a mere spectator and not indeed a "character," is yet the most important personage in the poem, uniting all the rest. Just as the one-eyed merchant, seller of currants, melts into the Phoenician Sailor, and the latter is not wholly distinct from Ferdinand Prince of Naples, so all the women are one woman, and the two sexes meet in Tiresias. What Tiresias *sees,* in fact, is the substance of the poem. The whole passage from Ovid is of great anthropological interest:

'. . . Cum Iunone iocos et maior vestra profecto est
Quam, quae contingit maribus,' dixisse, 'voluptas.'
Illa negat; placuit quae sit sententia docti
Quaerere Tiresiae: venus huic erat utraque nota.
Nam duo magnorum viridi coeuntia silva
Corpora serpentum baculi violaverat ictu
Deque viro factus, mirabile, femina septem
Egerat autumnos; octavo rursus eosdem
Videt et 'est vestrae si tanta potentia plagae,'
Dixit 'ut auctoris sortem in contraria mutet,
Nunc quoque vos feriam!' percussis anguibus isdem
Forma prior rediit genetivaque venit imago.
Arbiter hic igitur sumptus de lite iocosa
Dicta Iovis firmat; gravius Saturnia iusto
Nec pro materia fertur doluisse suique
Iudicis aeterna damnavit lumina nocte,
At pater omnipotens (neque enim licet inrita cuiquam
Facta dei fecisse deo) pro lumine adempto
Scire futura dedit poenamque levavit honore.

221. This may not appear as exact as Sappho's lines, but I had in mind the "longshore" or "dory" fisherman, who returns at nightfall.

253. V. Goldsmith, the song of *The Vicar of Wakefield.*

257. V. *The Tempest,* as above.

264. The interior of St. Magnus Martyr is to my mind one of the finest among Wren's interiors. See *The Proposed Demolition of Nineteen City Churches:* (P. S. King & Son, Ltd.).

266. The Song of the (three) Thames-daughters begins here. From line 292 to 306 inclusive they speak in turn. V. *Götterdämmerung* III, i: the Rhine-daughters.

279. V. Froude, *Elizabeth,* Vol. I, ch. iv, letter of De Quadra to Philip of Spain:

"In the afternoon we were in a barge, watching the games on the river. (The queen) was alone with Lord Robert and myself on the poop, when they began to talk nonsense, and went so far that Lord Robert at last said, as I was on the spot there was no reason why they should not be married if the queen pleased."

293. Cf. *Purgatorio,* V, 133:

"Ricorditi di me, che son la Pia;
"Siena mi fe', disfecemi Maremma."

307. V. St. Augustine's *Confessions:* "to Carthage then I came, where a cauldron of unholy loves sang all about mine ears."

308. The complete text of the Buddha's Fire Sermon (which corresponds in importance to the Sermon on the Mount) from which these words are taken, will be found translated in the late Henry Clarke Warren's *Buddhism in Translation* (Harvard Oriental Series). Mr. Warren was one of the great pioneers of Buddhist studies in the Occident.

309. From St. Augustine's *Confessions* again. The collocation of these two representatives of eastern and western asceticism, as the culmination of this part of the poem, is not an accident.

V. WHAT THE THUNDER SAID

In the first part of Part V three themes are employed: the journey to Emmaus, the approach to the Chapel Perilous (see Miss Weston's book) and the present decay of eastern Europe.

357. This is *Turdus aonalaschkae pallasii,* the hermit-thrush which I have heard in Quebec Province. Chapman says (*Handbook of Birds of Eastern North America*) "it is most at home in secluded woodland and thickety retreats. . . . Its notes are not remarkable for variety or volume, but in purity and sweetness of tone and exquisite modulation they are unequalled." Its "water-dripping song" is justly celebrated.

360. The following lines were stimulated by the account of one of the Antarctic expeditions (I forget which, but I think one of Shackleton's): it was related that the party of explorers, at the extremity of their strength, had the constant delusion that there was *one more member* than could actually be counted.

366-76. Cf. Hermann Hesse, *Blick ins Chaos:* "Schon ist halb Europa, schon ist zumindest der halbe Osten Europas auf dem Wege zum Chaos, fährt betrunken im heiligen Wahn am Abgrund entlang und singt dazu, singt betrunken und hymnisch wie Dmitri Karamasoff sang. Ueber diese Lieder lacht der Bürger beleidigt, der Heilige und Seher hört sie mit Tränen."

401. "Datta, dayadhvam, damyata" (Give, sympathize, control). The fable of the meaning of the Thunder is found in the *Brihadaranyaka—Upanishad,* 5, 1. A translation is found in Deussen's *Sechzig Upanishads des Veda,* p. 489.

407. Cf. Webster, *The White Devil,* V, vi:

"... they'll remarry
Ere the worm pierce your winding-sheet, ere the spider
Make a thin curtain for your epitaphs."

411. Cf. *Inferno,* XXXIII, 46:

"ed io sentii chiavar l'uscio di sotto
all'orribile torre."

Also F. H. Bradley, *Appearance and Reality,* p. 346.

"My external sensations are no less private to myself than are my thoughts or my feelings. In either case my experience falls within my own circle, a circle closed on the outside; and, with all its elements alike, every sphere is opaque to the others which surround it. . . . In brief, regarded as an existence which appears in a soul, the whole world for each is peculiar and private to that soul."

424. V. Weston: *From Ritual to Romance;* chapter on the Fisher King.

427. V. *Purgatorio,* XXVI, 148.

> "'Ara vos prec per aquella valor
> 'que vos guida al som de l'escalina,
> 'sovegna vos a temps de ma dolor.'
> Poi s'ascose nel foco che gli affina."

428. V. *Pervigilium Veneris.* Cf. Philomela in Parts II and III.

429. V. Gerard de Nerval, Sonnet *El Desdichado.*

431. V. Kyd's *Spanish Tragedy.*

433. Shantih. Repeated as here, a formal ending to an Upanishad. "The Peace which passeth understanding" is our equivalent to this word.

The Hollow Men

Mistah Kurtz—he dead.
A penny for the Old Guy.

I

We are the hollow men
We are the stuffed men
Leaning together
Headpiece filled with straw. Alas!
Our dried voices, when
We whisper together
Are quiet and meaningless
As wind in dry grass
Or rats' feet over broken glass
In our dry cellar

Shape without form, shade without colour,
Paralyzed force, gesture without motion;

Those who have crossed
With direct eyes, to death's other Kingdom

Remember us—if at all—not as lost
Violent souls, but only
As the hollow men
The stuffed men.

II

Eyes I dare not meet in dreams
In death's dream kingdom
These do not appear:
There, the eyes are
Sunlight on a broken column
There, is a tree swinging
And voices are
In the wind's singing
More distant and more solemn
Than a fading star.

Let me be no nearer
In death's dream kingdom
Let me also wear
Such deliberate disguises
Rat's coat, crowskin, crossed staves
In a field
Behaving as the wind behaves
No nearer—

Not that final meeting
In the twilight kingdom

III

This is the dead land
This is cactus land
Here the stone images
Are raised, here they receive
The supplication of a dead man's hand
Under the twinkle of a fading star.

Is it like this
In death's other kingdom
Waking alone
At the hour when we are
Trembling with tenderness
Lips that would kiss
Form prayers to broken stone.

IV

The eyes are not here
There are no eyes here
In this valley of dying stars
In this hollow valley
This broken jaw of our lost kingdoms

In this last of meeting places
We grope together
And avoid speech
Gathered on this beach of the tumid river

Sightless, unless
The eyes reappear
As the perpetual star
Multifoliate rose
Of death's twilight kingdom
The hope only
Of empty men.

V

Here we go round the prickly pear
Prickly pear prickly pear
Here we go round the prickly pear
At five o'clock in the morning.

Between the idea
And the reality
Between the motion
And the act
Falls the Shadow
For Thine is the Kingdom

Between the conception
And the creation
Between the emotion
And the response
Falls the Shadow
Life is very long

Between the desire
And the spasm
Between the potency

And the existence
Between the essence
And the descent
Falls the Shadow
For Thine is the Kingdom

For Thine is
Life is
For Thine is the

This is the way the world ends
This is the way the world ends
This is the way the world ends
Not with a bang but a whimper.

Journey of the Magi

"A cold coming we had of it,
Just the worst time of the year
For a journey, and such a long journey:
The ways deep and the weather sharp,
The very dead of winter."
And the camels galled, sore-footed, refractory,
Lying down in the melting snow.
There were times we regretted
The summer palaces on slopes, the terraces,
And the silken girls bringing sherbet.
Then the camel men cursing and grumbling
And running away, and wanting their liquor and women,
And the night-fires going out, and the lack of shelters,
And the cities hostile and the towns unfriendly
And the villages dirty and charging high prices:
A hard time we had of it.
At the end we preferred to travel all night,
Sleeping in snatches,
With the voices singing in our ears, saying
That this was all folly.

Then at dawn we came down to a temperate valley,
Wet, below the snow line, smelling of vegetation;
With a running stream and a water-mill beating the darkness,
And three trees on the low sky,
And an old white horse galloped away in the meadow.
Then we came to a tavern with vine-leaves over the lintel,

Six hands at an open door dicing for pieces of silver,
And feet kicking the empty wine-skins.
But there was no information, and so we continued
And arriving at evening, not a moment too soon
Finding the place; it was (you may say) satisfactory.

All this was a long time ago, I remember,
And I would do it again, but set down
This set down
This: were we led all that way for
Birth or Death? There was a Birth, certainly,
We had evidence and no doubt. I had seen birth and death,
But had thought they were different; this Birth was
Hard and bitter agony for us, like Death, our death.
We returned to our places, these Kingdoms,
But no longer at ease here, in the old dispensation,
With an alien people clutching their gods.
I should be glad of another death.

Ash-Wednesday

I

Because I do not hope to turn again
Because I do not hope
Because I do not hope to turn
Desiring this man's gift and that man's scope
I no longer strive to strive towards such things
(Why should the agèd eagle stretch its wings?)
Why should I mourn
The vanished power of the usual reign?

Because I do not hope to know again
The infirm glory of the positive hour
Because I do not think
Because I know I shall not know
The one veritable transitory power
Because I cannot drink
There, where trees flower, and springs flow, for there is nothing
again

Because I know that time is always time
And place is always and only place
And what is actual is actual only for one time
And only for one place

I rejoice that things are as they are and
I renounce the blessèd face
And renounce the voice.
Because I cannot hope to turn again
Consequently I rejoice, having to construct something
Upon which to rejoice.

And pray to God to have mercy upon us
And I pray that I may forget
These matters that with myself I too much discuss
Too much explain
Because I do not hope to turn again
Let these words answer
For what is done, not to be done again
May the judgment not be too heavy upon us

Because these wings are no longer wings to fly
But merely vans to beat the air
The air which is now thoroughly small and dry
Smaller and dryer than the will
Teach us to care and not to care
Teach us to sit still.

Pray for us sinners now and at the hour of our death
Pray for us now and at the hour of our death.

II

Lady, three white leopards sat under a juniper-tree
In the cool of the day, having fed to satiety
On my legs my heart my liver and that which had been contained
In the hollow round of my skull. And God said
Shall these bones live? shall these
Bones live? And that which had been contained
In the bones (which were already dry) said chirping:
Because of the goodness of this Lady
And because of her loveliness, and because
She honors the Virgin in meditation,
We shine with brightness. And I who am here dissembled
Proffer my deeds to oblivion, and my love
To the posterity of the desert and the fruit of the gourd.
It is this which recovers
My guts the strings of my eyes and the indigestible portions
Which the leopards reject. The Lady is withdrawn

In a white gown, to contemplation, in a white gown.
Let the whiteness of bones atone to forgetfulness.
There is no life in them. As I am forgotten
And would be forgotten, so I would forget
Thus devoted, concentrated in purpose. And God said
Prophesy to the wind, to the wind only, for only
The wind will listen. And the bones sang chirping
With the burden of the grasshopper, saying

Lady of silences
Calm and distressed
Torn and most whole
Rose of memory
Rose of forgetfulness
Exhausted and life-giving
Worried reposeful
The single Rose
Is now the Garden
Where all loves end
Terminate torment
Of love unsatisfied
The greater torment
Of love satisfied
End of the endless
Journey to no end
Conclusion of all that
Is inconclusible
Speech without word and
Word of no speech
Grace to the Mother
For the Garden
Where all love ends.

Under a juniper-tree the bones sang, scattered and shining
We are glad to be scattered, we did little good to each other,
Under a tree in the cool of the day, with the blessing of sand,
Forgetting themselves and each other, united
In the quiet of the desert. This is the land which ye
Shall divide by lot. And neither division nor unity
Matters. This is the land. We have our inheritance.

III

At the first turning of the second stair
I turned and saw below

The same shape twisted on the banister
Under the vapor in the fetid air
Struggling with the devil of the stairs who wears
The deceitful face of hope and of despair.

At the second turning of the second stair
I left them twisting, turning below;
There were no more faces and the stair was dark,
Damp, jaggèd, like an old man's mouth drivelling, beyond repair,
Or the toothed gullet of an agèd shark.

At the first turning of the third stair
Was a slotted window bellied like the fig's fruit
And beyond the hawthorn blossom and a pasture scene
The broadbacked figure drest in blue and green
Enchanted the maytime with an antique flute.
Blown hair is sweet, brown hair over the mouth blown,
Lilac and brown hair;
Distraction, music of the flute, stops and steps of the mind over the third stair,
Fading, fading; strength beyond hope and despair
Climbing the third stair.

Lord, I am not worthy
Lord, I am not worthy

but speak the word only.

IV

Who walked between the violet and the violet
Who walked between
The various ranks of varied green
Going in white and blue, in Mary's colour,
Talking of trivial things
In ignorance and in knowledge of eternal dolour
Who moved among the others as they walked,
Who then made strong the fountains and made fresh the springs

Made cool the dry rock and made firm the sand
In blue of larkspur, blue of Mary's colour,
Sovegna vos

Here are the years that walk between, bearing
Away the fiddles and the flutes, restoring
One who moves in the time between sleep and waking, wearing

White light folded, sheathed about her, folded.
The new years walk, restoring
Through a bright cloud of tears, the years, restoring
With a new verse the ancient rhyme. Redeem
The time. Redeem
The unread vision in the higher dream
While jewelled unicorns draw by the gilded hearse.

The silent sister veiled in white and blue
Between the yews, behind the garden god,
Whose flute is breathless, bent her head and sighed but spoke
    no word

But the fountain sprang up and the bird sang down
Redeem the time, redeem the dream
The token of the word unheard, unspoken

Till the wind shake a thousand whispers from the yew

And after this our exile

V

If the lost word is lost, if the spent word is spent
If the unheard, unspoken
Word is unspoken, unheard;
Still is the unspoken word, the Word unheard,
The Word without a word, the Word within
The world and for the world;
And the light shone in darkness and
Against the Word the unstilled world still whirled
About the center of the silent Word.

O my people, what have I done unto thee.

Where shall the word be found, where will the word
Resound? Not here, there is not enough silence,
Not on the sea or on the islands, not
On the mainland, in the desert or the rain land,
For those who walk in darkness
Both in the day time and in the night time

The right time and the right place are not here
No place of grace for those who avoid the face
No time to rejoice for those who walk among noise and deny
    the voice

Will the veiled sister pray for
Those who walk in darkness, who chose thee and oppose thee,
Those who are torn on the horn between season and season,
    time and time, between
Hour and hour, word and word, power and power, those who
    wait
In darkness? Will the veiled sister pray
For children at the gate
Who will not go away and cannot pray:
Pray for those who chose and oppose

O my people, what have I done unto thee.

Will the veiled sister between the slender
Yew trees pray for those who offend her
And are terrified and cannot surrender
And affirm before the world and deny between the rocks
In the last desert between the last blue rocks
The desert in the garden the garden in the desert
Of drouth, spitting from the mouth the withered apple-seed.

O my people.

VI

Although I do not hope to turn again
Although I do not hope
Although I do not hope to turn

Wavering between the profit and the loss
In this brief transit where the dreams cross
The dreamcrossed twilight between birth and dying
(Bless me father) though I do not wish to wish these things
From the wide window towards the granite shore
The white sails still fly seaward, seaward flying
Unbroken wings

And the lost heart stiffens and rejoices
In the lost lilac and the lost sea voices
And the weak spirit quickens to rebel
For the bent golden-rod and the lost sea smell

Quickens to recover
The cry of quail and the whirling plover
And the blind eye creates
The empty forms between the ivory gates
And smell renews the salt savour of the sandy earth

This is the time of tension between dying and birth
The place of solitude where three dreams cross
Between blue rocks
But when the voices shaken from the yew-tree drift away
Let the other yew be shaken and reply.

Blessèd sister, holy mother, spirit of the fountain, spirit of the
    garden,
Suffer us not to mock ourselves with falsehood
Teach us to care and not to care
Teach us to sit still
Even among these rocks,
Our peace in His will
And even among these rocks
Sister, mother
And spirit of the river, spirit of the sea,
Suffer me not to be separated

And let my cry come unto Thee.

course of the poem moves from despair to hope – nature IS regenerated & harmonized

Burnt Norton

(From "Four Quartets")

I

Time present and time past
Are both perhaps present in time future,
And time future contained in time past.
If all time is eternally present
All time is unredeemable.
What might have been is an abstraction
Remaining a perpetual possibility
Only in a world of speculation.
What might have been and what has been
Point to one end, which is always present.
Footfalls echo in the memory
Down the passage which we did not take
Towards the door we never opened

Into the rose-garden. My words echo
Thus, in your mind.
                                        But to what purpose
Disturbing the dust on a bowl of rose-leaves
I do not know.
                              Other echoes
Inhabit the garden. Shall we follow?
Quick, said the bird, find them, find them,
Round the corner. Through the first gate,
Into our first world, shall we follow
The deception of the thrush? Into our first world.
There they were, dignified, invisible,
Moving without pressure, over the dead leaves,
In the autumn heat, through the vibrant air,
And the bird called, in response to
The unheard music hidden in the shrubbery,
And the unseen eyebeam crossed, for the roses
Had the look of flowers that are looked at.
There they were as our guests, accepted and accepting.
So we moved, and they, in a formal pattern,
Along the empty alley, into the box circle,
To look down into the drained pool.
Dry the pool, dry concrete, brown edged,
And the pool was filled with water out of sunlight,
And the lotos rose, quietly, quietly,
The surface glittered out of heart of light,
And they were behind us, reflected in the pool.
Then a cloud passed, and the pool was empty.
Go, said the bird, for the leaves were full of children,
Hidden excitedly, containing laughter.
Go, go, go, said the bird: human kind
Cannot bear very much reality.
Time past and time future
What might have been and what has been
Point to one end, which is always present.

II

Garlic and sapphires in the mud
Clot the bedded axle-tree.
The trilling wire in the blood
Sings below inveterate scars
And reconciles forgotten wars.
The dance along the artery
The circulation of the lymph

Are figured in the drift of stars
Ascend to summer in the tree
We move above the moving tree
In light upon the figured leaf
And hear upon the sodden floor
Below, the boarhound and the boar
Pursue their pattern as before
But reconciled among the stars.

At the still point of the turning world. Neither flesh nor flesh-
less;
Neither from nor towards; at the still point, there the dance is,
But neither arrest nor movement. And do not call it fixity,
Where past and future are gathered. Neither movement from
nor towards,
Neither ascent nor decline. Except for the point, the still point,
There would be no dance, and there is only the dance.
I can only say, *there* we have been: but I cannot say where.
And I cannot say, how long, for that is to place it in time.

The inner freedom from the practical desire,
The release from action and suffering, release from the inner
And the outer compulsion, yet surrounded
By a grace of sense, a white light still and moving,
Erhebung without motion, concentration
Without elimination, both a new world
And the old made explicit, understood
In the completion of its partial ecstasy,
The resolution of its partial horror.
Yet the enchainment of past and future
Woven in the weakness of the changing body,
Protects mankind from heaven and damnation
Which flesh cannot endure
Time past and time future
Allow but a little consciousness.
To be conscious is not to be in time
But only in time can the moment in the rose-garden,
The moment in the arbour where the rain beat,
The moment in the draughty church at smokefall
Be remembered; involved with past and future.
Only through time time is conquered.

III

Here is a place of disaffection
Time before and time after

In a dim light: neither daylight
Investing form with lucid stillness
Turning shadow into transient beauty
With slow rotation suggesting permanence
Nor darkness to purify the soul
Emptying the sensual with deprivation
Cleansing affection from the temporal.
Neither plenitude nor vacancy. Only a flicker
Over the strained time-ridden faces
Distracted from distraction by distraction
Filled with fancies and empty of meaning
Tumid apathy with no concentration
Men and bits of paper, whirled by the cold wind
That blows before and after time,
Wind in and out of unwholesome lungs
Time before and time after.
Eructation of unhealthy souls
Into the faded air, the torpid
Driven on the wind that sweeps the gloomy hills of London,
Hampstead and Clerkenwell, Campden and Putney,
Highgate, Primrose and Ludgate. Not here
Not here the darkness, in this twittering world.

Descend lower, descend only
Into the world of perpetual solitude,
World not world, but that which is not world,
Internal darkness, deprivation
And destitution of all property,
Desiccation of the world of sense,
Evacuation of the world of fancy,
Inoperancy of the world of spirit;
This is the one way, and the other
Is the same, not in movement
But abstention from movement; while the world moves
In appetency, on its metalled ways
Of time past and time future.

IV

Time and the bell have buried the day,
The black cloud carries the sun away.
Will the sunflower turn to us, will the clematis
Stray down, bend to us; tendril and spray
Clutch and cling?
Chill
Fingers of yew be curled

Down on us? After the kingfisher's wing
Has answered light to light, and is silent, the light is still
At the still point of the turning world.

V

Words move, music moves
Only in time; but that which is only living
Can only die. Words, after speech, reach
Into the silence. Only by the form, the pattern,
Can words or music reach
The stillness, as a Chinese jar still
Moves perpetually in its stillness.
Not the stillness of the violin, while the note lasts,
Not that only, but the co-existence,
Or say that the end precedes the beginning,
And the end and the beginning were always there
Before the beginning and after the end.
And all is always now. Words strain,
Crack and sometimes break, under the burden,
Under the tension, slip, slide, perish,
Decay with imprecision, will not stay in place,
Will not stay still. Shrieking voices
Scolding, mocking, or merely chattering,
Always assail them. The Word in the desert
Is most attacked by voices of temptation,
The crying shadow in the funeral dance,
The loud lament of the disconsolate chimera.

The detail of the pattern is movement,
As in the figure of the ten stairs.
Desire itself is movement
Not in itself desirable;
Love is itself unmoving,
Only the cause and end of movement,
Timeless, and undesiring
Except in the aspect of time
Caught in the form of limitation
Between un-being and being.
Sudden in a shaft of sunlight
Even while the dust moves
There rises the hidden laughter
Of children in the foliage
Quick now, here, now, always—
Ridiculous the waste sad time
Stretching before and after.

John Crowe Ransom

1888-

Bells for John Whiteside's Daughter

There was such speed in her little body,
And such lightness in her footfall,
It is no wonder that her brown study
Astonishes us all.

Her wars were bruited in our high window.
We looked among orchard trees and beyond,
Where she took arms against her shadow,
Or harried unto the pond

The lazy geese, like a snow cloud
Dripping their snow on the green grass,
Tricking and stopping, sleepy and proud,
Who cried in goose, Alas,

For the tireless heart within the little
Lady with rod that made them rise
From their noon apple-dreams, and scuttle
Goose-fashion under the skies!

But now go the bells, and we are ready;
In one house we are sternly stopped
To say we are vexed at her brown study,
Lying so primly propped.

fables of the existence of the human condition

Blue Girls

Twirling your blue skirts, traveling the sward
Under the towers of your seminary,
Go listen to your teachers old and contrary
Without believing a word.

reads like a child's limmerick

Tie the white fillets then about your lustrous hair
And think no more of what will come to pass
Than bluebirds that go walking on the grass
And chattering on the air.

Practice your beauty, blue girls, before it fail;
And I will cry with my loud lips and publish
Beauty which all our power shall never establish,
It is so frail.

For I could tell you a story which is true:
I know a lady with a terrible tongue,
Blear eyes fallen from blue,
All her perfections tarnished—and yet it is not long
Since she was lovelier than any of you.

Lady Lost

This morning, there flew up the lane
A timid lady-bird to our bird-bath
And eyed her image dolefully as death;
This afternoon, knocked on our windowpane
To be let in from the rain.

And when I caught her eye
She looked aside, but at the clapping thunder
And sight of the whole earth blazing up like tinder
Looked in on us again most miserably,
Indeed as if she would cry.

So I will go out into the park and say,
"Who has lost a delicate brown-eyed lady
In the West End Section? Or has anybody
Injured some fine woman in some dark way,
Last night or yesterday?

"Let the owner come and claim possession,
No questions will be asked. But stroke her gently
With loving words, and she will evidently
Resume her full soft-haired white-breasted fashion,
And her right home and her right passion."

Here Lies a Lady

Here lies a lady of beauty and high degree.
Of chills and fever she died, of fever and chills,
The delight of her husband, her aunts, an infant of three,
And of medicos marveling sweetly on her ills.

For either she burned, and her confident eyes would blaze,
And her fingers fly in a manner to puzzle their heads—
What was she making? Why, nothing; she sat in a maze
Of old scraps of laces, snipped into curious shreds—

Or this would pass, and the light of her fire decline
Till she lay discouraged and cold as a thin stalk white and
blown,
And would not open her eyes, to kisses, to wine.
The sixth of these states was her last; the cold settled down.

Sweet ladies, long may ye bloom, and toughly I hope ye may
thole,
But was she not lucky? In flowers and lace and mourning,
In love and great honor we bade God rest her soul
After six little spaces of chill, and six of burning.

Janet Waking

Beautifully Janet slept
Till it was deeply morning. She woke then
And thought about her dainty-feathered hen,
To see how it had kept.

One kiss she gave her mother,
Only a small one gave she to her daddy
Who would have kissed each curl of his shining baby;
No kiss at all for her brother.

"Old Chucky, Old Chucky!" she cried,
Running on little pink feet upon the grass
To Chucky's house, and listening. But alas,
Her Chucky had died.

It was a transmogrifying bee
Came droning down on Chucky's old bald head

And sat and put the poison. It scarcely bled,
But how exceedingly

And purply did the knot
Swell with the venom and communicate
Its rigor! Now the poor comb stood up straight
But Chucky did not.

So there was Janet
Kneeling on the wet grass, crying her brown hen
(Translated far beyond the daughters of men)
To rise and walk upon it.

And weeping fast as she had breath
Janet implored us, "Wake her from her sleep!"
And would not be instructed in how deep
Was the forgetful kingdom of death.

Spiel of the Three Mountebanks

THE SWARTHY ONE—
Villagers who gather round,
This is Fides, my lean hound.
Bring your bristled village curs
To try his fang and tooth, sweet sirs:
He will rend them, he is savage,
Thinking nothing but to ravage,
Nor with cudgel, fire, rope,
May ye control my misanthrope;
He would tear the moon in the sky
And fly at Heaven, could he fly.
And for his ravening without cease
I have had of him no peace.
Only once I bared the knife
To quit my devil of his life,
But listen, how I heard him say,
"Think you I shall die today?
Since your mother cursed and died,
I am keeping at your side,
We are firmly knit together,
Two ends tugging at one tether,
And you shall see when I shall die
That you are mortal even as I."

Bring your stoutest-hearted curs
If ye would risk him, gentle sirs.

THE THICK ONE—
Countrymen, here's a noble frame,
Humphrey is my elephant's name.
When my father's back was bent
Under steep impediment,
Humphrey came to my possession,
With patient strength for all his passion.
Have ye a mountain to remove?
It is Humphrey's dearest love.
Pile his burden to the skies,
Loose a pestilence of flies,
Foot him in the quick morass
Where no laden beast can pass:
He will staunch his weariless back
And march unswerving on the track.
Have ye seen a back so wide,
Such impenetrable hide?
Nor think ye by this Humphrey hill
Prince Hamlet bare his fardels ill?
Myself I like it not for us
To wear beneath an incubus;
I take offense, but in no rage
May I dispose my heritage;
Though in good time the vast and tough
Shall sink and totter soon enough.
So pile your population up:
They are a drop in Humphrey's cup;
Add all your curses to his pack
To make one straw for Humphrey's back.

THE PALE ONE—
If ye remark how poor I am,
Come, citizens, behold my lamb!
Have ye a lion, ounce, or scourge,
Or any beast of dainty gorge?
Agnus lays his tender youth
Between the very enemy's mouth,
And though he sniff his delicate meat,
He may not bruise that flesh nor eat,
He may not rend him limb from limb,
If Agnus do but bleat on him.

Fierce was my youth, but like a dream
I saw a temple, and a stream,
And where I knelt and washed my sore
This infant lamb stood on the shore,
He mounted with me from the river.
And still he cries, as brave as ever,
"Lay me down by the lion's side
To match my frailty with his pride;
Fain would I welter in my blood
To teach these lions true lionhood."
So daily Agnus would be slain
But daily is denied again,
And still the hungry lions range
While Agnus waits upon a change;
Only the coursing lions die
And in their deserts mortify.
So bring us lion, leopard, bear,
To try of Agnus without fear,
And ye less gentle than I am,
Come, be instructed of my Lamb.

Antique Harvesters

(Scene: Of the Mississippi the bank sinister, and of the Ohio the bank sinister)

Tawny are the leaves turned, but they still hold.
It is the harvest; what shall this land produce?
A meager hill of kernels, a runnel of juice.
Declension looks from our land, it is old.
Therefore let us assemble, dry, gray, spare,
And mild as yellow air.

"I hear the creak of a raven's funeral wing."
The young men would be joying in the song
Of passionate birds; their memories are not long.
What is it thus rehearsed in sable? "Nothing."
Trust not but the old endure, and shall be older
Than the scornful beholder.

We pluck the spindling ears and gather the corn.
One spot has special yield? "On this spot stood
Heroes and drenched it with their only blood."
And talk meets talk, as echoes from the horn

Of the hunter—echoes are the old men's arts,
Ample are the chambers of their hearts.

Here come the hunters, keepers of a rite.
The horn, the hounds, the lank mares coursing by
Under quaint archetypes of chivalry;
And the fox, lovely ritualist, in flight
Offering his unearthly ghost to quarry;
And the fields, themselves to harry.

Resume, harvesters. The treasure is full bronze
Which you will garner for the Lady, and the moon
Could tinge it no yellower than does this noon;
But the gray will quench it shortly—the fields, men, stones.
Pluck fast, dreamers; prove as you rumble slowly
Not less than men, not wholly.

Bare the arm too, dainty youths, bend the knees
Under bronze burdens. And by an autumn tone
As by a gray, as by a green, you will have known
Your famous Lady's image; for so have these.
And if one say that easily will your hands
More prosper in other lands,

Angry as wasp-music be your cry then:
"Forsake the Proud Lady, of the heart of fire,
The look of snow, to the praise of a dwindled choir,
Song of degenerate specters that were men?
The sons of the fathers shall keep her, worthy of
What these have done in love."

True, it is said of our Lady, she ageth.
But see, if you peep shrewdly, she hath not stooped;
Take no thought of her servitors that have drooped,
For we are nothing; and if one talk of death—
Why, the ribs of the earth subsist frail as a breath
If but God wearieth.

Piazza Piece

—I am a gentleman in a dustcoat trying
To make you hear. Your ears are soft and small
And listen to an old man not at all;
They want the young men's whispering and sighing.

But see the roses on your trellis dying
And hear the spectral singing of the moon—
For I must have my lovely lady soon.
I am a gentleman in a dustcoat trying.

—I am a lady young in beauty waiting
Until my truelove comes, and then we kiss.
But what gray man among the vines is this
Whose words are dry and faint as in a dream?
Back from my trellis, sir, before I scream!
I am a lady young in beauty waiting.

Captain Carpenter

Captain Carpenter rose up in his prime
Put on his pistols and went riding out
But had got wellnigh nowhere at that time
Till he fell in with ladies in a rout.

It was a pretty lady and all her train
That played with him so sweetly but before
An hour she'd taken a sword with all her main
And twined him of his nose for evermore.

Captain Carpenter mounted up one day
And rode straightway into a stranger rogue
That looked unchristian but be that as it may
The Captain did not wait upon prologue.

But drew upon him out of his great heart
The other swung against him with a club
And cracked his two legs at the shinny part
And let him roll and stick like any tub.

Captain Carpenter rode many a time
From male and female took he sundry harms
He met the wife of Satan crying "I'm
The she-wolf bids you shall bear no more arms."

Their strokes and counters whistled in the wind
I wish he had delivered half his blows
But where she should have made off like a hind
The bitch bit off his arms at the elbows.

And Captain Carpenter parted with his ears
To a black devil that used him in this wise
O Jesus ere his threescore and ten years
Another had plucked out his sweet blue eyes.

Captain Carpenter got up on his roan
And sallied from the gate in hell's despite
I heard him asking in the grimmest tone
If any enemy yet there was to fight?

"To any adversary it is fame
If he risk to be wounded by my tongue
Or burnt in two beneath my red heart's flame
Such are the perils he is cast among.

"But if he can he has a pretty choice
From an anatomy with little to lose
Whether he cut my tongue and take my voice
Or whether it be my round red heart he choose."

It was the neatest knave that ever was seen
Stepping in perfume from his lady's bower
Who at this word put in his merry mien
And fell on Captain Carpenter like a tower.

I would not knock old fellows in the dust
But there lay Captain Carpenter on his back
His weapons were the old heart in his bust
And a blade shook between rotten teeth alack.

The rogue in scarlet and gray soon knew his mind
He wished to get his trophy and depart;
With gentle apology and touch refined
He pierced him and produced the Captain's heart.

God's mercy rest on Captain Carpenter now
I thought him Sirs an honest gentleman
Citizen husband soldier and scholar enow
Let jangling kites eat of him if they can.

But God's deep curses follow after those
That shore him of his goodly nose and ears
His legs and strong arms at the two elbows
And eyes that had not watered seventy years.

The curse of hell upon the sleek upstart
Who got the Captain finally on his back
And took the red red vitals of his heart
And made the kites to whet their beaks clack clack.

Parting, Without a Sequel

She has finished and sealed the letter
At last, which he so richly has deserved,
With characters venomous and hatefully curved,
And nothing could be better.

But even as she gave it,
Saying to the blue-capped functioner of doom,
"Into his hands," she hoped the leering groom
Might somewhere lose and leave it.

Then all the blood
Forsook the face. She was too pale for tears,
Observing the ruin of her younger years.
She went and stood

Under her father's vaunting oak
Who kept his peace in wind and sun, and glistened
Stoical in the rain; to whom she listened
If he spoke.

And now the agitation of the rain
Rasped his sere leaves, and he talked low and gentle,
Reproaching the wan daughter by the lintel;
Ceasing, and beginning again.

Away went the messenger's bicycle,
His serpent's track went up the hill forever.
And all the time she stood there hot as fever
And cold as any icicle.

Vision by Sweetwater

Go and ask Robin to bring the girls over
To Sweetwater, said my Aunt; and that was why
It was like a dream of ladies sweeping by
The willows, clouds, deep meadowgrass, and the river.

Robin's sisters and my Aunt's lily daughter
Laughed and talked, and tinkled light as wrens
If there were a little colony all hens
To go walking by the steep turn of Sweetwater.

Let them alone, dear Aunt, just for one minute
Till I go fishing in the dark of my mind:
Where have I seen before, against the wind,
These bright virgins, robed and bare of bonnet,

Flowing with music of their strange quick tongue
And adventuring with delicate paces by the stream,—
Myself a child, old suddenly at the scream
From one of the white throats which it hid among?

Winter Remembered

Two evils, monstrous either one apart,
Possessed me, and were long and loath at going:
A cry of Absence, Absence, in the heart,
And in the wood the furious winter blowing.

Think not, when fire was bright upon my bricks,
And past the tight boards hardly a wind could enter,
I glowed like them, the simple burning sticks,
Far from my cause, my proper heat and centre.

Better to walk forth in the murderous air
And wash my wound in the snows; that would be healing;
Because my heart would throb less painful there,
Being caked with cold, and past the smart of feeling.

And where I went, the hugest winter blast
Would have this body bowed, these eyeballs streaming,
And though I think this heart's blood froze not fast,
It ran too small to spare one drop for dreaming.

Dear love, these fingers that had known your touch,
And tied our separate forces first together,
Were ten poor idiot fingers not worth much,
Ten frozen parsnips hanging in the weather.

The Equilibrists

Full of her long white arms and milky skin
He had a thousand times remembered sin.
Alone in the press of people travelled he,
Minding her jacinth, and myrrh, and ivory.

Mouth he remembered: the quaint orifice
From which came heat that flamed upon the kiss,
Till cold words came down spiral from the head,
Grey doves from the officious tower illsped.

Body: it was a white field ready for love,
On her body's field, with the gaunt tower above,
The lilies grew, beseeching him to take,
If he would pluck and wear them, bruise and break.

Eyes talking: Never mind the cruel words,
Embrace my flowers, but not embrace the swords.
But what they said, the doves came straightway flying
And unsaid: Honor, Honor, they came crying.

Importunate her doves. Too pure, too wise,
Clambering on his shoulder, saying, Arise,
Leave me now, and never let us meet,
Eternal distance now command thy feet.

Predicament indeed, which thus discovers
Honor among thieves, Honor between lovers.
O such a little word is Honor, they feel!
But the grey word is between them cold as steel.

At length I saw these lovers fully were come
Into their torture of equilibrium;
Dreadfully had forsworn each other, and yet
They were bound each to each, and they did not forget.

And rigid as two painful stars, and twirled
About the clustered night their prison world,
They burned with fierce love always to come near,
But Honor beat them back and kept them clear.

Ah, the strict lovers, they are ruined now!
I cried in anger. But with puddled brow

Devising for those gibbeted and brave
Came I descanting: Man, what would you have?

For spin your period out, and draw your breath,
A kinder saeculum begins with Death.
Would you ascend to Heaven and bodiless dwell?
Or take your bodies honorless to Hell?

In Heaven you have heard no marriage is,
No white flesh tinder to your lecheries,
Your male and female tissue sweetly shaped
Sublimed away, and furious blood escaped.

Great lovers lie in Hell, the stubborn ones
Infatuate of the flesh upon the bones;
Stuprate, they rend each other when they kiss,
The pieces kiss again, no end to this.

But still I watched them spinning, orbited nice.
Their flames were not more radiant than their ice.
I dug in the quiet earth and wrought the tomb
And made these lines to memorize their doom:—

Epitaph

Equilibrists lie here; stranger, tread light;
Close, but untouching in each other's sight;
Mouldered the lips and ashy the tall skull,
Let them lie perilous and beautiful.

Prelude to an Evening

Do not enforce the tired wolf
Dragging his infected wound homeward
To sit tonight with the warm children
Naming the pretty kings of France.

The images of the invaded mind
Being as monsters in the dreams
Of your most brief enchanted headful,
Suppose a miracle of confusion:

That dreamed and undreamt become each other
And mix the night and day of your mind;

And it does not matter your twice crying
From mouth unbeautied against the pillow

To avert the gun of the same old soldier;
For cry, cock-crow, or the iron bell
Can crack the sleep-sense of outrage,
Annihilate phantoms who were nothing.

But now, by our perverse supposal,
There is a drift of fog on your mornings;
You in your peignoir, dainty at your orange cup,
Feel poising round the sunny room

Invisible evil, deprived and bold.
All day the clock will metronome
Your gallant fear; the needles clicking,
The heels detonating the stair's cavern.

Freshening the water in the blue bowls
For the buckberries, with not all your love,
You shall be listening for the low wind,
The warning sibilance of pines.

You like a waning moon, and I accusing
Our too banded Eumenides,
While you pronounce Noes wanderingly
And smooth the heads of the hungry children.

Painting: A Head

By dark severance the apparition head
Smiles from the air a capital on no
Column or a Platonic perhaps head
On a canvas sky depending from nothing;

Stirs up an old illusion of grandeur
By tickling the instinct of heads to be
Absolute and to try decapitation
And to play truant from the body bush;

But too happy and beautiful for those sorts
Of head (homekeeping heads are happiest)
Discovers maybe thirty unwidowed years
Of not dishonoring the faithful stem;

Is nameless and has authored for the evil
Historian headhunters neither book
Nor state and is therefore distinct from tart
Heads with crowns and guilty gallery heads;

So that the extravagant device of art
Unhousing by abstraction this once head
Was capital irony by a loving hand
That knew the no treason of a head like this;

Makes repentance in an unlovely head
For vinegar disparagement of flesh
Till, the hurt flesh recusing, the hard egg
Is shrunken to its own deathlike surface;

And an image thus: the body bears the head
(So hardly one they terribly are two)
Feeds and obeys and unto please what end?
Not to the glory of tyrant head but to

The increase of body. Beauty is of body.
The flesh contouring shallowly on a head
Is a rock-garden needing body's love
And best bodiness to colorify

The big blue birds sitting and sea-shell flats
And caves and on the iron acropolis
To spread the hyacinthine hair and rear
The olive garden for the nightingales.

Conrad Aiken

1889-

Bread and Music

Music I heard with you was more than music,
And bread I broke with you was more than bread;
Now that I am without you, all is desolate;
All that was once so beautiful is dead.

Your hands once touched this table and this silver,
And I have seen your fingers hold this glass.
These things do not remember you, belovèd,
And yet your touch upon them will not pass.

For it was in my heart you moved among them,
And blessed them with your hands and with your eyes;
And in my heart they will remember always,—
They knew you once, O beautiful and wise.

Morning Song from "Senlin"

It is morning, Senlin says, and in the morning
When the light drips through the shutters like the dew,
I arise, I face the sunrise,
And do the things my fathers learned to do.
Stars in the purple dusk above the rooftops
Pale in a saffron mist and seem to die,
And I myself on a swiftly tilting planet
Stand before a glass and tie my tie.

Vine-leaves tap my window,
Dew-drops sing to the garden stones,
The robin chirps in the chinaberry tree
Repeating three clear tones.

It is morning. I stand by the mirror
And tie my tie once more.
While waves far off in a pale rose twilight
Crash on a white sand shore.
I stand by a mirror and comb my hair:
How small and white my face!—
The green earth tilts through a sphere of air
And bathes in a flame of space.
There are houses hanging above the stars
And stars hung under a sea . . .
And a sun far off in a shell of silence
Dapples my walls for me. . . .

It is morning, Senlin says, and in the morning
Should I not pause in the light to remember God?
Upright and firm I stand on a star unstable,
He is immense and lonely as a cloud.

I will dedicate this moment before my mirror
To him alone, for him I will comb my hair.
Accept these humble offerings, clouds of silence!
I will think of you as I descend the stair.

Vine-leaves tap my window,
The snail-track shines on the stones;
Dew-drops flash from the chinaberry tree
Repeating two clear tones.

It is morning, I awake from a bed of silence,
Shining I rise from the starless waters of sleep.
The walls are about me still as in the evening,
I am the same, and the same name still I keep.
The earth revolves with me, yet makes no motion,
The stars pale silently in a coral sky.
In a whistling void I stand before my mirror,
Unconcerned, and tie my tie.

There are horses neighing on far-off hills
Tossing their long white manes,
And mountains flash in the rose-white dusk,
Their shoulders black with rains. . . .

It is morning, I stand by the mirror
And surprise my soul once more;
The blue air rushes above my ceiling,
There are suns beneath my floor. . . .

. . . It is morning, Senlin says, I ascend from darkness
And depart on the winds of space for I know not where;
My watch is wound, a key is in my pocket,
And the sky is darkened as I descend the stair.
There are shadows across the windows, clouds in heaven,
And a god among the stars; and I will go
Thinking of him as I might think of daybreak
And humming a tune I know. . . .

Vine-leaves tap at the window,
Dew-drops sing to the garden stones,
The robin chirps in the chinaberry tree
Repeating three clear tones.

Portrait of a Girl

This is the shape of the leaf, and this of the flower,
And this the pale bole of the tree
Which watches its bough in a pool of unwavering water
In a land we never shall see.

The thrush on the bough is silent, the dew falls softly,
In the evening is hardly a sound. . . .
And the three beautiful pilgrims who come here together
Touch lightly the dust of the ground.

Touch it with feet that trouble the dust but as wings do,
Come shyly together, are still,
Like dancers who wait in a pause of the music, for music
The exquisite silence to fill . . .

This is the thought of the first, and this of the second,
And this the grave thought of the third:
"Linger we thus for a moment, palely expectant,
And silence will end, and the bird

"Sing the pure phrase, sweet phrase, clear phrase in the twilight
To fill the blue bell of the world;
And we, who on music so leaflike have drifted together,
Leaflike apart shall be whirled

"Into what but the beauty of silence, silence forever? . . ."
. . . This is the shape of the tree,
And the flower and the leaf, and the three pale beautiful pilgrims:
This is what you are to me.

And in the Hanging Gardens—

And in the hanging gardens there is rain
From midnight until one, striking the leaves
And bells of flowers, and stroking boles of planes,
And drawing slow arpeggios over pools
And stretching strings of sound from eaves to ferns.

The princess reads. The knave of diamonds sleeps.
The king is drunk, and flings a golden goblet
Down from the turret window (curtained with rain)
Into the lilacs.
And at one o'clock
The vulcan under the garden wakes and beats
The gong upon his anvil. Then the rain
Ceases, but gently ceases, dripping still,
And sound of falling water fills the dark
As leaves grow bold and upright, and as eaves
Part with water. The princess turns the page
Beside the candle, and between two braids
Of golden hair. And reads: "From there I went
Northward a journey of four days, and came
To a wild village in the hills, where none
Was living save the vulture and the rat
And one old man who laughed but could not speak.
The roofs were fallen in, the well grown over
With weed. And it was here my father died.
Then eight days further, bearing slightly west,
The cold wind blowing sand against our faces,
The food tasting of sand. And as we stood
By the dry rock that marks the highest point
My brother said: 'Not too late is it yet
To turn, remembering home.' And we were silent
Thinking of home." The princess shuts her eyes
And feels the tears forming beneath her eyelids
And opens them, and tears fall on the page.
The knave of diamonds in the darkened room
Throws off his covers, sleeps, and snores again.
The king goes slowly down the turret stairs
To find the goblet.
And at two o'clock
The vulcan in his smithy underground
Under the hanging gardens, where the drip
Of rain among the clematis and ivy
Still falls from sipping flower to purple flower,
Smites twice his anvil, and the murmur comes
Among the roots and vines. The princess reads:
"As I am sick, and cannot write you more,
And have not long to live, I give this letter
To him, my brother, who will bear it south
And tell you how I died. Ask how it was,
There in the northern desert, where the grass
Was withered, and the horses, all but one,

Perished . . ." The princess drops her golden head
Upon the page between her two white arms
And golden braids. The knave of diamonds wakes
And at his window in the darkened room
Watches the lilacs tossing, where the king
Seeks for the goblet.
And at three o'clock
The moon inflames the lilac heads, and thrice
The vulcan, in his root-bound smithy, clangs
His anvil; and the sounds creep softly up
Among the vines and walls. The moon is round,
Round as a shield above the turret top.
The princess blows her candle out, and weeps
In the pale room, where scent of lilacs comes,
Weeping, with hands across her eyelids, thinking
Of withered grass, withered by sandy wind.
The knave of diamonds, in his darkened room,
Holds in his hands a key, and softly steps
Along the corridor, and slides the key
Into the door that guards her. Meanwhile, slowly,
The king, with raindrops on his beard and hands,
And dripping sleeves, climbs up the turret stairs,
Holding the goblet upright in one hand;
And pauses on the midmost step to taste
One drop of wine wherewith wild rain has mixed.

Annihilation

While the blue noon above us arches
And the poplar sheds disconsolate leaves,
Tell me again why love bewitches
And what love gives.

Is it the trembling finger that traces
The eyebrow's curve, the curve of the cheek?
The mouth that quivers, while the hand caresses,
But cannot speak?

No, not these, not in these is hidden
The secret, more than in other things:
Not only the touch of a hand can gladden
Till the blood sings.

It is the leaf that falls between us,
The bell that murmurs, the shadows that move,

The autumnal sunlight that fades upon us,
These things are love.

It is the "No, let us sit here longer,"
The "Wait till tomorrow," the "Once I knew"—
These trifles, said as you touch my finger
And the clock strikes two.

The world is intricate, and we are nothing.
It is the complex world of grass,
The twig on the path, a look of loathing,
Feelings that pass—

These are the secret; and I could hate you
When, as I lean for another kiss,
I see in your eyes that I do not meet you,
And that love is this.

Rock meeting rock can know love better
Than eyes that stare or lips that touch.
All that we know in love is bitter,
And it is not much.

The Quarrel

Suddenly, after the quarrel, while we waited,
Disheartened, silent, with downcast looks, nor stirred
Eyelid nor finger, hopeless both, yet hoping
Against all hope to unsay the sundering word:

While all the room's stillness deepened, deepened about us,
And each of us crept his thought's way to discover
How, with as little sound as the fall of a leaf,
The shadow had fallen, and lover quarreled with lover;

And while, in the quiet, I marveled—alas, alas—
At your deep beauty, your tragic beauty, torn
As the pale flower is torn by the wanton sparrow—
This beauty, pitied and loved, and now forsworn;

It was then, when the instant darkened to its darkest,—
When faith was lost with hope, and the rain conspired
To strike its gray arpeggios against our heartstrings,—
When love no longer dared, and scarcely desired:

It was then that suddenly, in the neighbor's room,
The music started: that brave quartette of strings
Breaking out of the stillness, as out of our stillness,
Like the indomitable heart of life that sings

When all is lost; and startled from our sorrow,
Tranced from our grief by that diviner grief,
We raised remembering eyes, each looked at other,
Blinded with tears of joy; and another leaf

Fell silently as that first; and in the instant
The shadow had gone, our quarrel became absurd;
And we rose, to the angelic voices of the music,
And I touched your hand, and we kissed, without a word.

At a Concert of Music

Be still, while the music rises about us: the deep enchantment
Towers, like a forest of singing leaves and birds,
Built for an instant by the heart's troubled beating,
Beyond all power of words.

And while you are silent, listening, I escape you,
And I run, by a secret path, through that bright wood
To another time, forgotten, and another woman,
And another mood.

Then, too, the music's pure algebra of enchantment
Wrought all about us a bird-voice-haunted grove.
Then, too, I escaped, as now, to an earlier moment
And a brighter love.

Alas! Can I never have peace in the shining instant?
The hard bright crystal of being, in time and space?
Must I always touch, in the moment, a remembered moment,
A remembered face?

Absolve me: I would adore you, had I the secret,
With all this music's power, for yourself alone:
I would try to answer, in the world's chaotic symphony,
Your one clear tone:

But alas, alas, being everything you are nothing;
The history of all my life is in your face;
And all I can grasp is an earlier, more haunted moment,
And a happier place.

Tetélestai

I

How shall we praise the magnificence of the dead,
The great man humbled, the haughty brought to dust?
Is there a horn we should not blow as proudly
For the meanest of us all, who creeps his days,
Guarding his heart from blows, to die obscurely?
I am no king, have laid no kingdoms waste,
Taken no princes captive, led no triumphs
Of weeping women through long walls of trumpets;
Say rather, I am no one, or an atom;
Say rather, two great gods, in a vault of starlight,
Play ponderingly at chess, and at the game's end
One of the pieces, shaken, falls to the floor
And runs to the darkest corner; and that piece
Forgotten there, left motionless, is I. . . .
Say that I have no name, no gifts, no power,
Am only one of millions, mostly silent;
One who came with eyes and hands and a heart,
Looked on beauty, and loved it, and left it.
Say that the fates of time and space obscured me,
Led me a thousand ways to pain, bemused me,
Wrapped me in ugliness; and like great spiders
Dispatched me at their leisure. . . . Well, what then?
Should I not hear, as I lie down in dust,
The horns of glory blowing above my burial?

II

Morning and evening opened and closed above me:
Houses were built above me; trees let fall
Yellowing leaves upon me, hands of ghosts;
Rain has showered its arrows of silver upon me
Seeking my heart; winds have roared and tossed me;
Music in long blue waves of sound has borne me
A helpless weed to shores of unthought silence;
Time, above me, within me, crashed its gongs
Of terrible warning, sifting the dust of death;
And here I lie. Blow now your horns of glory
Harshly over my flesh, you trees, you waters!
You stars and suns, Canopus, Deneb, Rigel,
Let me, as I lie down, here in this dust,

Hear, far off, your whispered salutation!
Roar now above my decaying flesh, you winds,
Whirl out your earth-scents over this body, tell me
Of ferns and stagnant pools, wild roses, hillsides!
Anoint me, rain, let crash your silver arrows
On this hard flesh! I am the one who named you,
I lived in you, and now I die in you.
I your son, your daughter, treader of music,
Lie, broken, conquered. . . . Let me not fall in silence.

III

I, the restless one; the circler of circles;
Herdsman and roper of stars, who could not capture
The secret of self; I who was tyrant to weaklings,
Striker of children; destroyer of women; corrupter
Of innocent dreamers, and laugher at beauty; I,
Too easily brought to tears and weakness by music,
Baffled and broken by love, the helpless beholder
Of the war in my heart, of desire with desire, the struggle
Of hatred with love, terror with hunger; I
Who laughed without knowing the cause of my laughter, who
grew
Without wishing to grow, a servant to my own body;
Loved without reason the laughter and flesh of a woman,
Enduring such torments to find her! I who at last
Grow weaker, struggle more feebly, relent in my purpose,
Choose for my triumph an easier end, look backward
At earlier conquests; or, caught in the web, cry out
In a sudden and empty despair, "Tetélestai!"
Pity me, now! I, who was arrogant, beg you!
Tell me, as I lie down, that I was courageous.
Blow horns of victory now, as I reel and am vanquished.
Shatter the sky with trumpets above my grave.

IV

. . . Look! this flesh how it crumbles to dust and is blown!
These bones, how they grind in the granite of frost and are
nothing!
This skull, how it yawns for a flicker of time in the darkness,
Yet laughs not and sees not! It is crushed by a hammer of
sunlight,
And the hands are destroyed. . . Press down through the
leaves of the jasmine,

Dig through the interlaced roots—nevermore will you find me;
I was no better than dust, yet you cannot replace me. . . .
Take the soft dust in your hand—does it stir: does it sing?
Has it lips and a heart? Does it open its eyes to the sun?
Does it run, does it dream, does it burn with a secret, or
tremble
In terror of death? Or ache with tremendous decisions? . . .
Listen! . . . It says: "I lean by the river. The willows
Are yellowed with bud. White clouds roar up from the south
And darken the ripples; but they cannot darken my heart,
Nor the face like a star in my heart! . . . Rain falls on the
water
And pelts it, and rings it with silver. The willow trees glisten,
The sparrow chirps under the eaves; but the face in my heart
Is a secret of music. . . . I wait in the rain and am silent."
Listen again! . . . It says: "I have worked, I am tired,
The pencil dulls in my hand; I see through the window
Walls upon walls of windows with faces behind them,
Smoke floating up to the sky, an ascension of sea-gulls.
I am tired. I have struggled in vain, my decision was fruitless,
Why then do I wait? with darkness, so easy, at hand! . . .
But tomorrow, perhaps. . . . I will wait and endure till to-
morrow!" . . .
Or again: "It is dark. The decision is made. I am vanquished
By terror of life. The walls mount slowly about me
In coldness. I had not the courage. I was forsaken.
I cried out, was answered by silence . . . Tetélestai! . . ."

V

Hear how it babbles!—Blow the dust out of your hand,
With its voices and visions, tread on it, forget it, turn home-
ward
With dreams in your brain. . . . This, then, is the humble, the
nameless,—
The lover, the husband and father, the struggler with shadows,
The one who went down under shoutings of chaos, the
weakling
Who cried his "forsaken!" like Christ on the darkening hill-
top! . . .
This, then, is the one who implores, as he dwindles to silence,
A fanfare of glory. . . . And which of us dares to deny him?

But How It Came from Earth

But how it came from earth this little white
this waxen edge this that is sharp and white
this that is mortal and bright the petals bent
and all so curved as if for lovers meant
and why the earth unfolded in this shape
as coldly as words from the warm mouth escape

Or what it is that made the blood so speak
or what it was it wanted that made this
breath of curled air this hyacinth this word
this that is deeply seen profoundly heard
miracle of quick device
from fire and ice

Or why the snail puts out a horn to see
or the brave heart puts up a hand to take
or why the mind, as if to agonize,
will close, a century ahead, its eyes—
a hundred years put on the clock
its own mortality to mock—

Christ come, Confucius come, and tell us why
the mind delights before its death to die
embracing nothing as a lover might
in a terrific ecstasy of night—
and tell us why the hyacinth is sprung
from the world's dull tongue.

Did death so dream of life, is this its dream?
Does the rock think of flowers in its sleep?
Then words and flowers are only thoughts of stone
unconscious of the joy it thinks upon;
and we ourselves are only the rock's words
stammered in a dark dream of men and birds.

Prelude VI

This is not you? These phrases are not you?
That pomegranate of verses was not you?
The green bright leaf not you, nor the gold fruit
Burning amongst the leaves,—hot fruit of gold,—
Nor bird, nor bough, nor bole, nor heaven's blue? . . .
Alas, dear woman, I have sung in vain.

Let me dishevel then once more the leaves
Of Cupid's bright thesaurus, and there find
The word of words, the crimson seed of seeds,
The aureate sound of sounds; and out of this
Conceive once more your beauty, and in terms
Your feminine keen eye will not disdain.

For this is you: on April page it is,
Again on June, and once more on December;
On August page I find it twice; and March
Chronicles it in footnote; and July
Asserts it roundly. Thus, from page to page,
I find you many times in many terms.

It is a snowflake, which is like a star,
And melts upon the hand; it is a cobweb,
Shot with silver, that from the golden lip
Of April's dandelion hangs to the grass;
It is a raindrop,—of tremendous worth,—
Which slides the whole length of a lilac leaf. . . .

This is not you? These symbols are not you?
Not snowflake, cobweb, raindrop? . . . Woman, woman,
You are too literal, too strict with me.
What would you have? Some simple copper coin—
I love you, you are lovely, I adore you?
Or (better still) dumb silence, and a look?

No, no, this will not do; I am not one
For whom these silences are sovereign;
The pauses in the music are not music,
Although they make the music what it is.
Therefore I thumb once more the god's thesaurus,
For phrase and praise, and find it all for you.

It is a star which might be thought a snowflake,
Lost in a twinkling; it is a dandelion
Shrouded with silver brightness; it is a leaf
Which lets the raindrop go, but keeps its light. . . .
It is the purple veining in the white
That makes the pure throat of the iris pure. . . .

Yet you would have me say your hair is Helen's,—
Your gait angelic; while I turn from these
To the vast pages of that manuscript
On which the stars are stars, the world a world;
And there I find you written down, between
Arcturus and a primrose and the sea.

Cloister

So, in the evening, to the simple cloister:
This place of boughs, where sounds of water, softly,
Lap on the stones. And this is what you are:
Here, in this dusty room, to which you climb
By four steep flights of stairs. The door is closed:
The furies of the city howl behind you:
The last bell plunges rock-like to the sea:
The horns of taxis wail in vain. You come
Once more, at evening, to this simple cloister;
Hushed by the quiet walls, you stand at peace.

What ferns of thought are these, the cool and green,
Dripping with moisture, that festoon these walls?
What water-lights are these, whose pallid rings
Dance with the leaves, or speckle the pale stones?
What spring is this, that bubbles the cold sand,
Urging the sluggish grains of white and gold? . . .
Peace. The delicious silence throngs with ghosts
Of wingèd sound and shadow. These are you.

Now in the evening, in the simple cloister,
You stand and wait; you stand and listen, waiting
For wingèd sounds, and wingèd silences,
And long-remembered shadows. Here the rock
Lets down its vine of many-colored flowers:
Waiting for you, or waiting for the lizard
To move his lifted claw, or shift his eye

Quick as a jewel. Here the lizard waits
For the slow snake to slide among cold leaves.
And, on the bough that arches the deep pool,
Lapped in a sound of water, the brown thrush
Waits, too, and listens, till his silence makes
Silence as deep as song. And time becomes
A timeless crystal, an eternity,
In which the gone and coming are at peace.

What bird is this, whose silence fills the trees
With rich delight? What leaves and boughs are these,
What lizard, and what snake? . . . The bird is gone:
And while you wait, another comes and goes,—
Another and another; yet your eye,
Although it has not moved, can scarcely say
If birds have come and gone,—so quick, so brief,—
Or if the thrush who waits there is the same. . . .
The snake and lizard change, yet are the same:
The flowers, many-colored, on the vine,
Open and close their multitude of stars,—
Yet are the same. . . . And all these things are you.

Thus, in the evening, in the simple cloister,
Eternity adds ring to ring, the darker
Beyond the brighter; and your silence fills
With such a world of worlds,—so still, so deep,—
As never voice could speak, whether it were
The ocean's or the bird's. The night comes on:
You wait and listen, in the darkened room,
To all these ghosts of change. And they are you.

Proem to "The Kid"

(William Blackstone—Died 1675)

Where now he roves, by wood or swamp whatever,
the always restless, always moving on,
his books burned, and his own book lost forever,
under the cold stars of New England, gone,

scholar who loved, and therefor left, the most,
secret and solitary, no Indian-giver,
who to his own cost played the generous host
and asked adventurers across his river:

what would he make of us, if he could see,
after so many tides have ringed this coast,
what manner of men his children's children be
to welcome home his still inquisitive ghost?

He, more than all, of individual grace,
the pilgrim innocence, self-knowledge sure,
stepped like an angel in this savage place,
and, in all nature, found no evil-doer.

A summer's freedom on a bramble shore
whose wild rose the Lords Bishop could not blight,
then the Lords Brethren saw him close his door,
bidding his orchards, and his house, good-night.

Now by the lamplit wall his friendly nod
salutes the late wayfarer on that hill
where wych-elms ward some semblance of the sod
he knew by Cam's side, and he measures still

the common field he found and kept aright,
setting his rose-trees and his fruit-trees out:
these, and his books, and truth, all his delight,
and the locked heart of man his only doubt.

Edna St. Vincent Millay

1892-1950

Renascence

All I could see from where I stood
Was three long mountains and a wood;
I turned and looked another way,
And saw three islands in a bay.

So with my eyes I traced the line
Of the horizon, thin and fine,
Straight around till I was come
Back to where I'd started from;
And all I saw from where I stood
Was three long mountains and a wood.
Over these things I could not see;
These were the things that bounded me;
And I could touch them with my hand,
Almost, I thought, from where I stand.

And all at once things seemed so small
My breath came short, and scarce at all.
But, sure, the sky is big, I said;
Miles and miles above my head;
So here upon my back I'll lie
And look my fill into the sky.
And so I looked, and, after all,
The sky was not so very tall.
The sky, I said, must somewhere stop,
And—sure enough!—I see the top!
The sky, I thought, is not so grand;
I 'most could touch it with my hand!
And, reaching up my hand to try,
I screamed to feel it touch the sky.

I screamed, and—lo!—Infinity
Came down and settled over me;
Forced back my scream into my chest,
Bent back my arm upon my breast,
And, pressing of the Undefined
The definition on my mind,
Held up before my eyes a glass
Through which my shrinking sight did pass
Until it seemed I must behold
Immensity made manifold;
Whispered to me a word whose sound
Deafened the air for worlds around,
And brought unmuffled to my ears
The gossiping of friendly spheres,
The creaking of the tented sky,
The ticking of Eternity.

I saw and heard, and knew at last
The How and Why of all things, past,

And present, and forevermore.
The universe, cleft to the core,
Lay open to my probing sense
That, sickening, I would fain pluck thence
But could not,—nay! But needs must suck
At the great wound, and could not pluck
My lips away till I had drawn
All venom out.—Ah, fearful pawn!
For my omniscience I paid toll
In infinite remorse of soul.
All sin was of my sinning, all
Atoning mine, and mine the gall
Of all regret. Mine was the weight
Of every brooded wrong, the hate
That stood behind each envious thrust,
Mine every greed, mine every lust.
And all the while for every grief,
Each suffering, I craved relief
With individual desire,—
Craved all in vain! And felt fierce fire
About a thousand people crawl;
Perished with each,—then mourned for all!
A man was starving in Capri;
He moved his eyes and looked at me;
I felt his gaze, I heard his moan,
And knew his hunger as my own.
I saw at sea a great fog-bank
Between two ships that struck and sank;
A thousand screams the heavens smote;
And every scream tore through my throat;
No hurt I did not feel, no death
That was not mine; mine each last breath
That, crying, met an answering cry
From the compassion that was I.
All suffering mine, and mine its rod;
Mine, pity like the pity of God.
Ah, awful weight! Infinity
Pressed down upon the finite me!
My anguished spirit, like a bird,
Beating against my lips I heard;
Yet lay the weight so close about
There was no room for it without.
And so beneath the weight lay I
And suffered death, but could not die.

Long had I lain thus, craving death,
When quietly the earth beneath
Gave way, and inch by inch, so great
At last had grown the crushing weight,
Into the earth I sank till I
Full six feet under ground did lie,
And sank no more,—there is no weight
Can follow here, however great.
From off my breast I felt it roll,
And as it went my tortured soul
Burst forth and fled in such a gust
That all about me swirled the dust.

Deep in the earth I rested now;
Cool is its hand upon the brow
And soft its breast beneath the head
Of one who is so gladly dead.
And all at once, and over all,
The pitying rain began to fall.
I lay and heard each pattering hoof
Upon my lowly, thatchèd roof.
And seemed to love the sound far more
Than ever I had done before.
For rain it hath a friendly sound
To one who's six feet underground;
And scarce the friendly voice or face:
A grave is such a quiet place.

The rain, I said, is kind to come
And speak to me in my new home.
I would I were alive again
To kiss the fingers of the rain,
To drink into my eyes the shine
Of every slanting silver line,
To catch the freshened, fragrant breeze
From drenched and dripping apple-trees.
For soon the shower will be done,
And then the broad face of the sun
Will laugh above the rain-soaked earth
Until the world with answering mirth
Shakes joyously, and each round drop
Rolls, twinkling, from its grass-blade top.
How can I bear it; buried here,
While overhead the sky grows clear

And blue again after the storm?
O, multi-colored, multiform,
Belovèd beauty over me,
That I shall never, never see
Again! Spring-silver, autumn-gold,
That I shall never more behold!
Sleeping your myriad magics through,
Close-sepulchered away from you!
O God, I cried, give me new birth,
And put me back upon the earth!
Upset each cloud's gigantic gourd
And let the heavy rain, down-poured
In one big torrent, set me free,
Washing my grave away from me!

I ceased; and, through the breathless hush
That answered me, the far-off rush
Of herald wings came whispering
Like music down the vibrant string
Of my ascending prayer, and—crash!
Before the wild wind's whistling lash
The startled storm-clouds reared on high
And plunged in terror down the sky,
And the big rain in one black wave
Fell from the sky and struck my grave.

I know not how such things can be,
I only know there came to me
A fragrance such as never clings
To aught save happy living things;
A sound as of some joyous elf
Singing sweet songs to please himself,
And, through and over everything,
A sense of glad awakening.
The grass, a tip-toe at my ear,
Whispering to me I could hear;
I felt the rain's cool finger-tips
Brushed tenderly across my lips,
Laid gently on my sealèd sight,
And all at once the heavy night
Fell from my eyes and I could see,—
A drenched and dripping apple-tree,
A last long line of silver rain,
A sky grown clear and blue again.

And as I looked a quickening gust
Of wind blew up to me and thrust
Into my face a miracle
Of orchard-breath, and with the smell,—
I know not how such things can be!—
I breathed my soul back into me.

Ah! Up then from the ground sprang I
And hailed the earth with such a cry
As is not heard save from a man
Who has been dead and lives again.
About the trees my arms I wound;
Like one gone mad I hugged the ground;
I raised my quivering arms on high;
I laughed and laughed into the sky,
Till at my throat a strangling sob
Caught fiercely, and a great heart-throb
Sent instant tears into my eyes;
O God, I cried, no dark disguise
Can e'er hereafter hide from me
Thy radiant identity!
Thou canst not move across the grass
But my quick eyes will see Thee pass,
Nor speak, however silently,
But my hushed voice will answer Thee.
I know the path that tells Thy way
Through the cool eve of every day;
God, I can push the grass apart
And lay my finger on Thy heart!

The world stands out on either side
No wider than the heart is wide;
Above the world is stretched the sky,—
No higher than the soul is high.
The heart can push the sea and land
Farther away on either hand;
The soul can split the sky in two,
And let the face of God shine through.
But East and West will pinch the heart
That cannot keep them pushed apart;
And he whose soul is flat—the sky
Will cave in on him by and by.

Spring

To what purpose, April, do you return again?
Beauty is not enough.
You can no longer quiet me with the redness
Of little leaves opening stickily.
I know what I know.
The sun is hot on my neck as I observe
The spikes of the crocus.
The smell of the earth is good.
It is apparent that there is no death.
But what does that signify?
Not only under ground are the brains of men
Eaten by maggots.
Life in itself
Is nothing,
An empty cup, a flight of uncarpeted stairs,
It is not enough that yearly, down this hill,
April
Comes like an idiot, babbling and strewing flowers.

What Lips My Lips Have Kissed

What lips my lips have kissed, and where, and why,
I have forgotten, and what arms have lain
Under my head till morning; but the rain
Is full of ghosts tonight, that tap and sigh
Upon the glass and listen for reply;
And in my heart there stirs a quiet pain
For unremembered lads that not again
Will turn to me at midnight with a cry.

Thus in the winter stands the lonely tree,
Nor knows what birds have vanished one by one,
Yet knows its boughs more silent than before:
I cannot say what loves have come and gone;
I only know that summer sang in me
A little while, that in me sings no more.

Pity Me Not

Pity me not because the light of day
At close of day no longer walks the sky;
Pity me not for beauties passed away
From field and thicket as the year goes by;
Pity me not the waning of the moon,
Nor that the ebbing tide goes out to sea,
Nor that a man's desire is hushed so soon,
And you no longer look with love on me.

This have I known always: love is no more
Than the wide blossom which the wind assails;
Than the great tide that treads the shifting shore,
Strewing fresh wreckage gathered in the gales.
Pity me that the heart is slow to learn
What the swift mind beholds at every turn.

Elegy

Let them bury your big eyes
In the secret earth securely,
Your thin fingers, and your fair,
Soft, indefinite-colored hair,—
All of these in some way, surely,
From the secret earth shall rise.
Not for these I sit and stare,
Broken and bereft completely;
Your young flesh that sat so neatly
On your little bones will sweetly
Blossom in the air.

But your voice,—never the rushing
Of a river underground,
Not the rising of the wind
In the trees before the rain,
Not the woodcock's watery call,
Not the note the white-throat utters,
Not the feet of children pushing
Yellow leaves along the gutters
In the blue and bitter fall,
Shall content my musing mind

For the beauty of that sound
That in no new way at all
Ever will be heard again.

Sweetly through the sappy stalk
Of the vigorous weed,
Holding all it held before,
Cherished by the faithful sun,
On and on eternally
Shall your altered fluid run,
Bud and bloom and go to seed;
But your singing days are done;
But the music of your talk
Never shall the chemistry
Of the secret earth restore.
All your lovely words are spoken.
Once the ivory box is broken,
Beats the golden bird no more.

Euclid Alone Has Looked on Beauty Bare

Euclid alone has looked on Beauty bare.
Let all who prate of Beauty hold their peace,
And lay them prone upon the earth and cease
To ponder on themselves, the while they stare
At nothing, intricately drawn nowhere
In shapes of shifting lineage; let geese
Gabble and hiss, but heroes seek release
From dusty bondage into luminous air.

O blinding hour, O holy, terrible day,
When first the shaft into his vision shone
Of light anatomized! Euclid alone
Has looked on Beauty bare. Fortunate they
Who, though once only and then but far away,
Have heard her massive sandal set on stone.

On Hearing a Symphony of Beethoven

Sweet sounds, oh, beautiful music, do not cease!
Reject me not into the world again.
With you alone is excellence and peace,
Mankind made plausible, his purpose plain.

Enchanted in your air benign and shrewd,
With limbs a-sprawl and empty faces pale,
The spiteful and the stingy and the rude
Sleep like the scullions in the fairy-tale.
This moment is the best the world can give:
The tranquil blossom on the tortured stem.
Reject me not, sweet sounds! oh, let me live,
Till Doom espy my towers and scatter them,
A city spell-bound under the aging sun.
Music my rampart, and my only one.

Sonnet to Gath

Country of hunchbacks!—where the strong, straight spine
Jeered at by crooked children, makes his way
Through by-streets at the kindest hour of day,
Till he deplore his stature, and incline
To measure manhood with a gibbous line;
Till out of loneliness, being flawed with clay,
He stoop into his neighbor's house and say,
"Your roof is low for me—the fault is mine."

Dust in an urn long since, dispersed and dead
Is great Apollo; and the happier he;
Since who amongst you all would lift a head
At a god's radiance on the mean door-tree,
Saving to run and hide your dates and bread,
And cluck your children in about your knee?

See Where Capella with Her Golden Kids

See where Capella with her golden kids
Grazes the slope between the east and north?
Thus when the builders of the pyramids
Flung down their tools at nightfall and poured forth
Homeward to supper and a poor man's bed,
Shortening the road with friendly jest and slur,
The risen She-Goat showing blue and red
Climbed the clear dusk, and three stars followed her.
Safe in their linen and their spices lie
The kings of Egypt; even as long ago

Under these constellations, with long eye
And scented limbs they slept, and feared no foe.
Their will was law; their will was not to die.
And so they had their way; or nearly so.

The Return

Earth does not understand her child,
  Who from the loud gregarious town
Returns, depleted and defiled,
  To the still woods, to fling him down.

Earth cannot count the sons she bore:
  The wounded lynx, the wounded man
Come trailing blood unto her door;
  She shelters both as best she can.

But she is early up and out,
  To trim the year or strip its bones;
She has no time to stand about
  Talking of him in undertones

Who has no aim but to forget,
  Be left in peace, be lying thus
For days, for years, for centuries yet,
  Unshaven and anonymous;

Who, marked for failure, dulled by grief,
  Has traded in his wife and friend
For this warm ledge, this alder leaf:
  Comfort that does not comprehend.

Archibald MacLeish

1892-

Ars Poetica

A poem should be palpable and mute
As a globed fruit

Dumb
As old medallions to the thumb

Silent as the sleeve-worn stone
Of casement ledges where the moss has grown—

A poem should be wordless
As the flight of birds

A poem should be motionless in time
As the moon climbs

Leaving, as the moon releases
Twig by twig the night-entangled trees,

Leaving, as the moon behind the winter leaves,
Memory by memory the mind—

A poem should be motionless in time
As the moon climbs

A poem should be equal to:
Not true

For all the history of grief
An empty doorway and a maple leaf

For love
The leaning grasses and two lights above the sea—

A poem should not mean
But be.

Memorial Rain

Ambassador Puser the ambassador
Reminds himself in French, felicitous tongue,
What these (young men no longer) lie here for
In rows that once, and somewhere else, were young—

All night in Brussels the wind had tugged at my door:
I had heard the wind at my door and the trees strung
Taut, and to me who had never been before
In that country it was a strange wind blowing
Steadily, stiffening the walls, the floor,
The roof of my room. I had not slept for knowing
He too, dead, was a stranger in that land
And felt beneath the earth in the wind's flowing
A tightening of roots and would not understand,
Remembering lake winds in Illinois,
That strange wind. I had felt his bones in the sand
Listening.

—Reflects that these enjoy
Their country's gratitude, that deep repose,
That peace no pain can break, no hurt destroy,
That rest, that sleep—

At Ghent the wind rose.
There was a smell of rain and a heavy drag
Of wind in the hedges but not as the wind blows
Over fresh water when the waves lag
Foaming and the willows huddle and it will rain:
I felt him waiting.

—Indicates the flag
Which (may he say) enisles in Flanders' plain
This little field these happy, happy dead
Have made America—

In the ripe grain
The wind coiled glistening, darted, fled,
Dragging its heavy body: at Waereghem
The wind coiled in the grass above his head:
Waiting—listening—

—Dedicates to them
This earth their bones have hallowed, this last gift
A grateful country—

Under the dry grass stem
The words are blurred, are thickened, the words sift
Confused by the rasp of the wind, by the thin grating
Of ants under the grass, the minute shift
And tumble of dusty sand separating
From dusty sand. The roots of the grass strain,
Tighten, the earth is rigid, waits—he is waiting—

And suddenly, and all at once, the rain!

The people scatter, they run into houses, the wind
Is trampled under the rain, shakes free, is again
Trampled. The rain gathers, running in thinned
Spurts of water that ravel in the dry sand
Seeping into the sand under the grass roots, seeping
Between cracked boards to the bones of a clenched hand:
The earth relaxes, loosens; he is sleeping,
He rests, he is quiet, he sleeps in a strange land.

Immortal Autumn

I speak this poem now with grave and level voice
In praise of autumn of the far-horn-winding fall
I praise the flower-barren fields the clouds the tall
Unanswering branches where the wind makes sullen noise

I praise the fall it is the human season now
No more the foreign sun does meddle at our earth
Enforce the green and thaw the frozen soil to birth
Nor winter yet weigh all with silence the pine bough

But now in autumn with the black and outcast crows
Share we the spacious world the whispering year is gone

There is more room to live now the once secret dawn
Comes late by daylight and the dark unguarded goes

Between the mutinous brave burning of the leaves
And winter's covering of our hearts with his deep snow
We are alone there are no evening birds we know
The naked moon the tame stars circle at our eaves

It is the human season on this sterile air
Do words outcarry breath the sound goes on and on
I hear a dead man's cry from autumn long since gone

I cry to you beyond this bitter air.

You, Andrew Marvell

And here face down beneath the sun
And here upon earth's noonward height
To feel the always coming on
The always rising of the night:

To feel creep up the curving east
The earthy chill of dusk and slow
Upon those under lands the vast
And ever-climbing shadow grow

And strange at Ecbatan the trees
Take leaf by leaf the evening strange
The flooding dark about their knees
The mountains over Persia change

And now at Kermanshah the gate
Dark empty and the withered grass
And through the twilight now the late
Few travelers in the westward pass

And Baghdad darken and the bridge
Across the silent river gone
And through Arabia the edge
Of evening widen and steal on

And deepen on Palmyra's street
The wheel rut in the ruined stone
And Lebanon fade out and Crete
High through the clouds and overblown

And over Sicily the air
Still flashing with the landward gulls
And loom and slowly disappear
The sails above the shadowy hulls

And Spain go under and the shore
Of Africa the gilded sand
And evening vanish and no more
The low pale light across that land

Nor now the long light on the sea:

And here face downward in the sun
To feel how swift how secretly
The shadow of the night comes on . . .

The End of the World

Quite unexpectedly as Vasserot
The armless ambidextrian was lighting
A match between his great and second toe
And Ralph the lion was engaged in biting
The neck of Madame Sossman while the drum
Pointed, and Teeny was about to cough
In waltz-time swinging Jocko by the thumb—
Quite unexpectedly the top blew off:

And there, there overhead, there, there, hung over
Those thousands of white faces, those dazed eyes,
There in the starless dark, the poise, the hover,
There with vast wings across the canceled skies,
There in the sudden blackness, the black pall
Of nothing, nothing, nothing—nothing at all.

The Too-Late Born

We too, we too, descending once again
The hills of our own land, we too have heard
Far off— Ah, que ce cor a longue haleine—
The horn of Roland in the passages of Spain,
The first, the second blast, the failing third,

And with the third turned back and climbed once more
The steep road southward, and heard faint the sound
Of swords, of horses, the disastrous war,
And crossed the dark defile at last, and found
At Roncevaux upon the darkening plain
The dead against the dead and on the silent ground
The silent slain—

Epistle to Be Left in the Earth

. . . It is colder now
there are many stars
we are drifting
North by the Great Bear
the leaves are falling
The water is stone in the scooped rocks
to southward
Red sun gray air
the crows are
Slow on their crooked wings
the jays have left us
Long since we passed the flares of Orion
Each man believes in his heart he will die
Many have written last thoughts and last letters
None know if our deaths are now or forever
None know if this wandering earth will be found

We lie down and the snow covers our garments
I pray you
you (if any open this writing)
Make in your mouths the words that were our names
I will tell you all we have learned
I will tell you everything
The earth is round
there are springs under the orchards
The loam cuts with a blunt knife
beware of
Elms in thunder
the lights in the sky are stars
We think they do not see
we think also
The trees do not know nor the leaves of the grasses
hear us

The birds too are ignorant
Do not listen
Do not stand at dark in the open windows
We before you have heard this
they are voices
They are not words at all but the wind rising
Also none among us has seen God
(. . . We have thought often
The flaws of sun in the late and driving weather
Pointed to one tree but it was not so)
As for the nights I warn you the nights are dangerous
The wind changes at night and the dreams come

It is very cold
there are strange stars near Arcturus

Voices are crying an unknown name in the sky

Speech to a Crowd

Tell me, my patient friends—awaiters of messages—
From what other shore: from what stranger:
Whence was the word to come? Who was to lesson you?

Listeners under a child's crib in a manger—
Listeners once by the oracles: now by the transoms—
Whom are you waiting for? Who do you think will explain?

Listeners thousands of years and still no answer—
Writers at night to Miss Lonely-Hearts: awkward spellers—
Open your eyes! There is only earth and the man!

There is only you: there is no one else on the telephone
No one else is on the air to whisper:
No one else but you will push the bell.

No one knows if you don't: neither ships
Nor landing-fields decode the dark between:
You have your eyes and what your eyes see *is*.

The earth you see is really the earth you are seeing:
The sun is truly excellent: truly warm:
Women are beautiful as you have seen them—

Their breasts (believe it) like cooing of doves in a portico:
They bear at their breasts tenderness softly. Look at them!
Look at yourselves. You are strong. You are well formed.

Look at the world—the world you never took!
It is really true you may live in the world heedlessly:
Why do you wait to read it in a book then?

Write it yourselves! Write to yourselves if you need to!
Tell yourselves there is sun and the sun will rise:
Tell yourselves the earth has food to feed you:—

Let the dead men say that men must die!
Who better than you can know what death is?
How can a bone or a broken body surmise it?

Let the dead shriek with their whispering breath:
Laugh at them! Say the murdered gods may wake
But we who work have end of work together:

Tell yourselves the earth is yours to take!

Waiting for messages out of the dark you were poor.
The world was always yours: you will not take it.

Land of the Free

(Conclusion of the Sound Track)

We wonder whether the dream of American liberty
Was two hundred years of pine and hardwood
And three generations of the grass

And the generations are up: the years over

We don't know

It was two hundred years from the smell of the tidewater
Up through the Piedmont: on through the piney woods:
Till we came out
With our led calves and our lean women
In the oak openings of Illinois

It was three generations from the oak trees—
From the islands of elm and the islands of oak in the prairie...

Till we heeled out with our plows and our steel harrows
On the grass-drowned reef bones of the Plains

"Four score and seven years" said the Orator

We remember it differently: we remember it
Kansas: Illinois: Ohio: Connecticut.
We remember it Council Bluffs: St. Louis:
Wills Creek: the Cumberland: Shenandoah—

The long harangues of the grass in the wind are our histories

We tell our freedom backward by the land
We tell our past by the gravestones and the apple trees

We wonder whether the great American dream
Was the singing of locusts out of the grass to the west and the
West is behind us now:
The west wind's away from us:

We wonder if the liberty is done:
The dreaming is finished

We can't say

We aren't sure

Or if there's something different men can dream
Or if there's something different men can mean by
Liberty

Or if there's liberty a man can mean that's
Men: not land

We wonder

We don't know

We're asking

The Learned Men

Whose minds like horse or ox,
Dispassionate in the stall,
Grow great in girth and wax
Beyond the animal,

While mine, like country hog,
Grows leaner as I age,
Chivvied by flea and dog,
Baited by love and rage.

If mind by God was meant
To grow and gain in girth,
Swelling in sweet content,
I cease, I have no worth:

But if it was God's will
That mind, no wish refused,
Should waste by wanting still
By God I am well used!

"Not Marble nor the Gilded Monuments"

for Adele

The praisers of women in their proud and beautiful poems,
Naming the grave mouth and the hair and the eyes,
Boasted those they loved should be forever remembered:
These were lies.

The words sound but the face in the Istrian sun is forgotten.
The poet speaks but to her dead ears no more.
The sleek throat is gone—and the breast that was troubled to
listen:
Shadow from door.

Therefore I will not praise your knees nor your fine walking
Telling you men shall remember your name as long
As lips move or breath is spent or the iron of English
Rings from a tongue.

I shall say you were young, and your arms straight, and your
mouth scarlet:
I shall say you will die and none will remember you:
Your arms change, and none remember the swish of your
garments,
Nor the click of your shoe.

Not with my hand's strength, not with difficult labor
Springing the obstinate words to the bones of your breast

And the stubborn line to your young stride and the breath to
your breathing
And the beat to your haste
Shall I prevail on the hearts of unborn men to remember.

(What is a dead girl but a shadowy ghost
Or a dead man's voice but a distant and vain affirmation
Like dream words most)

Therefore I will not speak of the undying glory of women.
I will say you were young and straight and your skin fair
And you stood in the door and the sun was a shadow of leaves
on your shoulders
And a leaf in your hair—

I will not speak of the famous beauty of dead women:
I will say the shape of a leaf lay once on your hair.
Till the world ends and the eyes are out and the mouths
broken,
Look! It is there!

Men

(on a phrase of Apollinaire)

Our history is grave noble and tragic.
We trusted the look of the sun on the green leaves.
We built our towns of stone with enduring ornaments.
We worked the hard flint for basins of water.

We believed in the feel of the earth under us.
We planted corn grapes apple trees rhubarb.
Nevertheless we knew others had died.
Everything we have done has been faithful and dangerous.

We believed in the promises made by the brows of women.
We begot children at night in the warm wool.
We comforted those who wept in fear on our shoulders.
Those who comforted us had themselves vanished.

We fought at the dikes in the bright sun for the pride of it.
We beat drums and marched with music and laughter.
We were drunk and lay with our fine dreams in the straw.
We saw the stars through the hair of lewd women.

Our history is grave noble and tragic.
Many of us have died and are not remembered.
Many cities are gone and their channels broken.
We have lived a long time in this land and with honor.

Calypso's Island

I know very well, goddess, she is not beautiful
As you are: could not be. She is a woman,
Mortal, subject to the chances: duty of

Childbed, sorrow that changes cheeks, the tomb—
For unlike you she will grow grey, grow older,
Grey and older, sleep in that small room.

She is not beautiful as you, O golden!
You are immortal and will never change
And can make me immortal also, fold

Your garment round me, make me whole and strange
As those who live forever, not the while
That we live; keep me from those dogging dangers—

Ships and the wars—in this green, far-off island,
Silent of all but sea's eternal sound
Or sea-pine's when the lull of surf is silent.

Goddess, I know how excellent this ground,
What charmed contentment of the removed heart
The bees make in the lavender where pounding

Surf sounds far off, and the bird that darts
Darts through its own eternity of light,
Motionless in motion, and the startled

Hare is startled into stone, the fly
Forever golden in the flickering glance
Of leafy sunlight that still holds it. I

Know you, goddess, and your caves that answer
Ocean's confused voices with a voice:
Your poplars where the storms are turned to dances;

Arms where the heart is turned. You give the choice
To hold forever what forever passes,
To hide from what will pass, forever. Moist,

Moist are your well-stones, goddess, cool your grasses!
And she—she is a woman with that fault
Of change that will be death in her at last!

Nevertheless I long for the cold, salt,
Restless, contending sea and for the island
Where the grass dies and the seasons alter:

Where that one wears the sunlight for a while.

E. E. Cummings

1894-

when god lets my body be

when god lets my body be

From each brave eye shall sprout a tree
fruit that dangles therefrom

the purpled world will dance upon
Between my lips which did sing

a rose shall beget the spring
that maidens whom passion wastes

will lay between their little breasts
My strong fingers beneath the snow

Into strenuous birds shall go
my love walking in the grass

their wings will touch with her face
and all the while shall my heart be

With the bulge and nuzzle of the sea

Impression

stinging
gold swarms
upon the spires
silver

chants the litanies the
great bells are ringing with rose
the lewd fat bells
and a tall

wind
is dragging
the
sea

with

dream

-S

La Guerre

I

the bigness of cannon
is skilful,

but i have seen
death's clever enormous voice
which hides in a fragility
of poppies . . . .

i say that sometimes
on these long talkative animals
are laid fists of huger silence

I have seen all the silence
filled with vivid noiseless boys

at Roupy
i have seen
between barrages,

the night utter ripe unspeaking girls.

II

O sweet spontaneous
earth how often have
the
doting

fingers of
prurient philosophers pinched
and
poked

thee
, has the naughty thumb
of science prodded
thy

beauty . how
often have religions taken
thee upon their scraggy knees
squeezing and

buffeting thee that thou mightest conceive
gods
(but
true

to the incomparable
couch of death thy
rhythmic
lover

thou answerest

them only with

spring)

Chanson Innocente

in Just-
spring   when the world is mud-
luscious the little
lame balloonman

whistles   far   and wee

and eddieandbill come
running from marbles and
piracies and it's
spring

when the world is puddle-wonderful

the queer
old balloonman whistles
far   and   wee
and bettyandisbel come dancing

from hop-scotch and jump-rope and

it's
spring
and
        the

                goat-footed

balloonMan   whistles
far
and
wee

Portrait

Buffalo Bill's
defunct
        who used to
        ride a watersmooth-silver
                                                stallion
and break onetwothreefourfive pigeonsjustlikethat
                                                                Jesus

he was a handsome man
and what i want to know is
how do you like your blueeyed boy
Mister Death

Sonnet

a wind has blown the rain away and blown
the sky away and all the leaves away,
and the trees stand. I think i too have known
autumn too long

(and what have you to say,
wind wind wind—did you love somebody
and have you the petal of somewhere in your heart
pinched from dumb summer?
O crazy daddy
of death dance cruelly for us and start

the last leaf whirling in the final brain
of air!) Let us as we have seen see
doom's integration . . . . a wind has blown the rain

away and the leaves and the sky and the
trees stand:
the trees stand. The trees,
suddenly wait against the moon's face.

Sonnet

this is the garden: colours come and go,
frail azures fluttering from night's outer wing
strong silent greens serenely lingering,
absolute lights like baths of golden snow.
This is the garden: pursed lips do blow
upon cool flutes within wide glooms, and sing
(of harps celestial to the quivering string)
invisible faces hauntingly and slow.

This is the garden. Time shall surely reap
and on Death's blade lie many a flower curled,
in other lands where other songs be sung;
yet stand They here enraptured, as among
the slow deep trees perpetual of sleep
some silver-fingered fountain steals the world.

POEM, OR BEAUTY HURTS MR. VINAL

take it from me kiddo
believe me
my country, 'tis of

you, land of the Cluett
Shirt Boston Garter and Spearmint
Girl With The Wrigley Eyes (of you
land of the Arrow Ide
and Earl &
Wilson
Collars) of you i
sing: land of Abraham Lincoln and Lydia E. Pinkham,
land above all of Just Add Hot Water And Serve—
from every B. V. D.

let freedom ring

amen. i do however protest, anent the un
-spontaneous and otherwise scented merde which
greets one (Everywhere Why) as divine poesy per
that and this radically defunct periodical. i would

suggest that certain ideas gestures
rhymes, like Gillette Razor Blades
having been used and reused
to the mystical moment of dullness, emphatically are
Not To Be Resharpened. (Case in point

if we are to believe these gently O sweetly
melancholy trillers amid the thrillers
these crepuscular violinists among my and your
skyscrapers— Helen & Cleopatra were Just Too Lovely,
The Snail's On The Thorn enter Morn and God's
In His andsoforth

do you get me?) according
to such supposedly indigenous
throstles Art is O World O Life
a formula: example, Turn Your Shirttails Into
Drawers and If It Isn't An Eastman It Isn't A

Kodak therefore my friends let
us now sing each and all fortissimo A-
mer
i

ca, I
love,
You. And there're a
hun-dred-mil-lion-oth-ers, like
all of you successfully if
delicately gelded (or spaded)
gentlemen (and ladies)– pretty

littleliverpill-
hearted-Nujolneeding-There's-A-Reason
americans (who tensetendoned and with
upward vacant eyes, painfully
perpetually crouched, quivering, upon the
sternly allotted sandpile
–how silently
emit a tiny violetflavored nuisance: Odor?

ono.
comes out like a ribbon lies flat on the brush

ITEM

this man is o so
Waiter
this;woman is

please shut that
the pout And affectionate leer
interminable pyramidal,napkins
(this man is oh so tired of this
a door opens by itself
woman.) they so to speak were in

Love once?
now
her mouth opens too far
and:she attacks her Lobster without
feet mingle under the
mercy.
(exit the hors d'oeuvres)

since feeling is first

since feeling is first
who pays any attention
to the syntax of things
will never wholly kiss you;

wholly to be a fool
while Spring is in the world

my blood approves,
and kisses are a better fate
than wisdom
lady i swear by all flowers. Don't cry
—the best gesture of my brain is less than
your eyelids' flutter which says

we are for each other: then
laugh, leaning back in my arms
for life's not a paragraph

And death i think is no parenthesis

somewhere i have never travelled

somewhere i have never travelled,gladly beyond
any experience,your eyes have their silence:
in your most frail gesture are things which enclose me,
or which i cannot touch because they are too near

your slightest look easily will unclose me
though i have closed myself as fingers,
you open always petal by petal myself as Spring opens
(touching skilfully,mysteriously)her first rose

or if your wish be to close me,i and
my life will shut very beautifully,suddenly,
as when the heart of this flower imagines
the snow carefully everywhere descending;

nothing which we are to perceive in this world equals
the power of your intense fragility:whose texture

compels me with the colour of its countries,
rendering death and forever with each breathing

(i do not know what it is about you that closes
and opens;only something in me understands
the voice of your eyes is deeper than all roses)
nobody,not even the rain,has such small hands

if there are any heavens

if there are any heavens my mother will(all by herself)have
one. It will not be a pansy heaven nor
a fragile heaven of lilies-of-the-valley but
it will be a heaven of blackred roses

my father will be(deep like a rose
tall like a rose)

standing near my

(swaying over her
silent)
with eyes which are really petals and see

nothing with the face of a poet really which
is a flower and not a face with
hands
which whisper
This is my beloved my

(suddenly in sunlight
he will bow,

& the whole garden will bow)

i thank You God for most this amazing

i thank You God for most this amazing
day:for the leaping greenly spirits of trees
and a blue true dream of sky;and for everything
which is natural which is infinite which is yes

(i who have died am alive again today,
and this is the sun's birthday;this is the birth
day of life and of love and wings:and of the gay
great happening illimitably earth)

how should tasting touching hearing seeing
breathing any—lifted from the no
of all nothing—human merely being
doubt unimaginable You?

(now the ears of my ears awake and
now the eyes of my eyes are opened)

anyone lived in a pretty how town

anyone lived in a pretty how town
(with up so floating many bells down)
spring summer autumn winter
he sang his didn't he danced his did.

Women and men(both little and small)
cared for anyone not at all
they sowed their isn't they reaped their same
sun moon stars rain

children guessed(but only a few
and down they forgot as up they grew
autumn winter spring summer)
that noone loved him more by more

when by now and tree by leaf
she laughed his joy she cried his grief
bird by snow and stir by still
anyone's any was all to her

someones married their everyones
laughed their cryings and did their dance
(sleep wake hope and then)they
said their nevers they slept their dream

stars rain sun moon
(and only the snow can begin to explain
how children are apt to forget to remember
with up so floating many bells down)

one day anyone died i guess
(and noone stooped to kiss his face)
busy folk buried them side by side
little by little and was by was

all by all and deep by deep
and more by more they dream their sleep
noone and anyone earth by april
wish by spirit and if by yes.

Women and men(both dong and ding)
summer autumn winter spring
reaped their sowing and went their came
sun moon stars rain

my father moved through dooms of love

my father moved through dooms of love
through sames of am through haves of give,
singing each morning out of each night
my father moved through depths of height

this motionless forgetful where
turned at his glance to shining here;
that if(so timid air is firm)
under his eyes would stir and squirm

newly as from unburied which
floats the first who,his april touch
drove sleeping selves to swarm their fates
woke dreamers to their ghostly roots

and should some why completely weep
my father's fingers brought her sleep:
vainly no smallest voice might cry
for he could feel the mountains grow.

Lifting the valleys of the sea
my father moved through griefs of joy;
praising a forehead called the moon
singing desire into begin

joy was his song and joy so pure
a heart of star by him could steer

and pure so now and now so yes
the wrists of twilight would rejoice

keen as midsummer's keen beyond
conceiving mind of sun will stand,
so strictly(over utmost him
so hugely)stood my father's dream

his flesh was flesh his blood was blood:
no hungry man but wished him food;
no cripple wouldn't creep one mile
uphill to only see him smile.

Scorning the pomp of must and shall
my father moved through dooms of feel;
his anger was as right as rain
his pity was as green as grain

septembering arms of year extend
less humbly wealth to foe and friend
than he to foolish and to wise
offered immeasurable is

proudly and(by octobering flame
beckoned)as earth will downward climb,
so naked for immortal work
his shoulders marched against the dark

his sorrow was as true as bread:
no liar looked him in the head;
if every friend became his foe
he'd laugh and build a world with snow.

My father moved through theys of we,
singing each new leaf out of each tree
(and every child was sure that spring
danced when she heard my father sing)

then let men kill which cannot share,
let blood and flesh be mud and mire,
scheming imagine,passion willed,
freedom a drug that's bought and sold

giving to steal and cruel kind,
a heart to fear,to doubt a mind,

to differ a disease of same,
conform the pinnacle of am

though dull were all we taste as bright,
bitter all utterly things sweet,
maggoty minus and dumb death
all we inherit,all bequeath

and nothing quite so least as truth
—i say though hate were why men breathe—
because my father lived his soul
love is the whole and more than all

Louise Bogan

1897-

Medusa

I had come to the house, in a cave of trees,
Facing a sheer sky.
Everything moved,—a bell hung ready to strike,
Sun and reflection wheeled by.

When the bare eyes were before me
And the hissing hair,
Held up at a window, seen through a door.
The stiff bald eyes, the serpents on the forehead
Formed in the air.

This is a dead scene forever now.
Nothing will ever stir.
The end will never brighten it more than this,
Nor the rain blur.

The water will always fall, and will not fall,
And the tipped bell make no sound.
The grass will always be growing for hay
Deep on the ground.

And I shall stand here like a shadow
Under the great balanced day,
My eyes on the yellow dust that was lifting in the wind,
And does not drift away.

Women

Women have no wilderness in them,
They are provident instead,
Content in the tight hot cell of their hearts
To eat dusty bread.

They do not see cattle cropping red winter grass,
They do not hear
Snow water going down under culverts
Shallow and clear.

They wait, when they should turn to journeys,
They stiffen, when they should bend.
They use against themselves that benevolence
To which no man is friend.

They cannot think of so many crops to a field
Or of clean wood cleft by an ax.
Their love is an eager meaninglessness
Too tense, or too lax.

They hear in every whisper that speaks to them
A shout and a cry.
As like as not, when they take life over their door-sills
They should let it go by.

Decoration

A macaw preens upon a branch outspread
With jewelry of seed. He's deaf and mute.
The sky behind him splits like gorgeous fruit
And claw-like leaves clutch light till it has bled.
The raw diagonal bounty of his wings
Scrapes on the eye color too chafed. He beats
A flattered tail out against gauzy heats;
He has the frustrate look of cheated kings.
And all the simple evening passes by:
A gillyflower spans its little height

And lovers with their mouths press out their grief.
The bird fans wide his striped regality
Prismatic, while against a sky breath-white
A crystal tree lets fall a crystal leaf.

Statue and Birds

Here, in the withered arbor, like the arrested wind,
Straight sides, carven knees,
Stands the statue, with hands flung out in alarm
Or remonstrances.

Over the lintel sway the woven bracts of the vine
In a pattern of angles.
The quill of the fountain falters, woods rake on the sky
Their brusque tangles.

The birds walk by slowly, circling the marble girl,
The golden quails,
The pheasants closed up in their arrowy wings,
Dragging their sharp tails.

The inquietudes of the sap and of the blood are spent.
What is forsaken will rest.
But her heel is lifted,—she would flee,—the whistle of the birds
Fails on her breast.

Simple Autumnal

The measured blood beats out the year's delay.
The tearless eyes and heart forbidden grief,
Watch the burned, restless, but abiding leaf,
The brighter branches arming the bright day.

The cone, the curving fruit should fall away,
The vine-stem crumble, ripe grain know its sheaf.
Bonded to time, fires should have done, be brief,
But, serfs to sleep, they glitter and they stay.

Because not last nor first, grief in its prime
Wakes in the day, and knows of life's intent.
Anguish would break the seal set over time
And bring the baskets where the bough is bent.

Full seasons come, yet filled trees keep the sky,
And never scent the ground where they will lie.

The Dream

O God, in the dream the terrible horse began
To paw at the air, and make for me with his blows.
Fear kept for thirty-five years poured through his mane,
And retribution equally old, or nearly, breathed through his
nose.

Coward complete, I lay and wept on the ground
When some strong creature appeared, and leapt for the rein.
Another woman, as I lay half in a swound
Leapt in the air, and clutched at the leather and chain.

Give him, she said, something of yours as a charm.
Throw him, she said, some poor thing you alone claim.
No, no, I cried, he hates me; he's out for harm,
And whether I yield or not, it is all the same.

But, like a lion in a legend, when I flung the glove
Pulled from my sweating, my cold right hand,
The terrible beast, that no one may understand,
Came to my side, and put down his head in love.

Hart Crane

1899-1932

Repose of Rivers

The willows carried a slow sound,
A sarabande the wind mowed on the mead.
I could never remember
That seething, steady leveling of the marshes
Till age had brought me to the sea.

Flags, weeds. And remembrance of steep alcoves
Where cypresses shared the noon's
Tyranny; they drew me into hades almost.
And mammoth turtles climbing sulphur dreams
Yielded, while sun-silt rippled them
Asunder . . .

How much I would have bartered! the black gorge
And all the singular nestings in the hills
Where beavers learn stitch and tooth.
The pond I entered once and quickly fled—
I remember now its singing willow rim.

And finally, in that memory all things nurse;
After the city that I finally passed
With scalding unguents spread and smoking darts
The monsoon cut across the delta
At gulf gates . . . There, beyond the dykes

I heard wind flaking sapphire, like this summer,
And willows could not hold more steady sound.

Voyages: II

—And yet this great wink of eternity,
Of rimless floods, unfettered leewardings,
Samite sheeted and processioned where
Her undinal vast belly moonward bends,
Laughing the wrapt inflections of our love;

Take this Sea, whose diapason knells
On scrolls of silver snowy sentences,
The sceptered terror of whose sessions rends
As her demeanors motion well or ill,
All but the pieties of lovers' hands.

And onward, as bells off San Salvador
Salute the crocus lusters of the stars,
In these poinsettia meadows of her tides,—
Adagios of islands, O my Prodigal,
Complete the dark confessions her veins spell.

Mark how her turning shoulders wind the hours,
And hasten while her penniless rich palms

Pass superscription of bent foam and wave,—
Hasten, while they are true,—sleep, death, desire,
Close round one instant in one floating flower.

Bind us in time, O seasons clear, and awe.
O minstrel galleons of Carib fire,
Bequeath us to no earthly shore until
Is answered in the vortex of our grave
The seal's wide spindrift gaze toward paradise.

Voyages: VI

Where icy and bright dungeons lift
Of swimmers their lost morning eyes,
And ocean rivers, churning, shift
Green borders under stranger skies,

Steadily as a shell secretes
Its beating leagues of monotone,
Or as many waters trough the sun's
Red kelson past the cape's wet stone;

O rivers mingling toward the sky
And harbor of the phoenix' breast—
My eyes pressed black against the prow,
—Thy derelict and blinded guest

Waiting, afire, what name, unspoke,
I cannot claim: let thy waves rear
More savage than the death of kings,
Some splintered garland for the seer.

Beyond siroccos harvesting
The solstice thunders, crept away,
Like a cliff swinging or a sail
Flung into April's inmost day—

Creation's blithe and petaled word
To the lounged goddess when she rose
Conceding dialogue with eyes
That smile unsearchable repose—

Still fervid covenant, Belle Isle,
—Unfolded floating dais before

Which rainbows twine continual hair—
Belle Isle, white echo of the oar!

The imaged word, it is, that holds
Hushed willows anchored in its glow.
It is the unbetrayable reply
Whose accent no farewell can know.

Praise for an Urn

It was a kind and northern face
That mingled in such exile guise
The everlasting eyes of Pierrot
And, of Gargantua, the laughter.

His thoughts, delivered to me
From the white coverlet and pillow,
I see now, were inheritances—
Delicate riders of the storm.

The slant moon on the slanting hill
Once moved us toward presentiments
Of what the dead keep, living still,
And such assessments of the soul

As, perched in the crematory lobby,
The insistent clock commented on,
Touching as well upon our praise
Of glories proper to the time.

Still, having in mind gold hair,
I cannot see that broken brow
And miss the dry sound of bees
Stretching across a lucid space.

Scatter these well-meant idioms
Into the smoky spring that fills
The suburbs, where they will be lost.
They are no trophies of the sun.

To Brooklyn Bridge

(Proem: From "The Bridge")

How many dawns, chill from his rippling rest
The seagull's wings shall dip and pivot him,
Shedding white rings of tumult, building high
Over the chained bay waters Liberty—

Then, with inviolate curve, forsake our eyes
As apparitional as sails that cross
Some page of figures to be filed away;
—Till elevators drop us from our day . . .

I think of cinemas, panoramic sleights
With multitudes bent toward some flashing scene
Never disclosed, but hastened to again,
Foretold to other eyes on the same screen;

And Thee, across the harbor, silver-paced
As though the sun took step of thee, yet left
Some motion ever unspent in thy stride,—
Implicitly thy freedom staying thee!

Out of some subway scuttle, cell or loft
A bedlamite speeds to thy parapets,
Tilting there momently, shrill shirt ballooning,
A jest falls from the speechless caravan.

Down Wall, from girder into street noon leaks,
A rip-tooth of the sky's acetylene;
All afternoon the cloud-flown derricks turn . . .
Thy cables breathe the North Atlantic still.

And obscure as that heaven of the Jews,
Thy guerdon . . . Accolade thou dost bestow
Of anonymity time cannot raise:
Vibrant reprieve and pardon thou dost show.

O harp and altar, of the fury fused,
(How could mere toil align thy choiring strings!)
Terrific threshold of the prophet's pledge,
Prayer of pariah, and the lover's cry,—

Again the traffic lights that skim thy swift
Unfractioned idiom, immaculate sigh of stars,
Beading thy path—condense eternity:
And we have seen night lifted in thine arms.

Under thy shadow by the piers I waited;
Only in darkness is thy shadow clear.
The City's fiery parcels all undone,
Already snow submerges an iron year . . .

O sleepless as the river under thee,
Vaulting the sea, the prairies' dreaming sod,
Unto us lowliest sometime sweep, descend
And of the curveship lend a myth to God.

Van Winkle

(From "The Bridge")

Macadam, gun-grey as the tunny's belt,
Leaps from Far Rockaway to Golden Gate:
Listen! the miles a hurdy-gurdy grinds—
Down gold arpeggios mile on mile unwinds.

Times earlier, when you hurried off to school
—It is the same hour though a later day—
You walked with Pizarro in a copybook,
And Cortes rode up, reining tautly in—
Firmly as coffee grips the taste,—and away!

There was Priscilla's cheek close in the wind,
And Captain Smith, all beard and certainty,
And Rip Van Winkle, bowing by the way,—
"Is this Sleepy Hollow, friend—?" And he—

And Rip forgot the office hours,
and he forgot the pay;
Van Winkle sweeps a tenement
way down on Avenue A,—

The grind-organ says . . . Remember, remember
The cinder pile at the end of the backyard
Where we stoned the family of young
Garter snakes under . . . And the monoplanes
We launched—with paper wings and twisted

Rubber bands. . . . Recall—recall
the rapid tongues
That flittered from under the ash heap day
After day whenever your stick discovered
Some sunning inch of unsuspecting fiber—
It flashed back at your thrust, as clean as fire.

And Rip was slowly made aware
that he, Van Winkle, was not here
nor there. He woke and swore he'd seen Broadway
a Catskill daisy chain in May—

So memory, that strikes a rhyme out of a box,
Or splits a random smell of flowers through glass—
Is it the whip stripped from the lilac tree
One day in spring my father took to me,
Or is it the Sabbatical, unconscious smile
My mother almost brought me once from church
And once only, as I recall—?

It flickered through the snow screen, blindly
It forsook her at the doorway; it was gone
Before I had left the window. It
Did not return with the kiss in the hall.

Macadam, gun-grey as the tunny's belt,
Leaps from Far Rockaway to Golden Gate . . .
Keep hold of that nickel for car-change, Rip,—
Have you got your *"Times"*—?
And hurry along, Van Winkle—it's getting late!

The River

(From "The Bridge")

Stick your patent name on a signboard
brother—all over—going west—young man
Tintex—Japalac—Certain-teed Overalls ads
and lands sakes! under the new playbill ripped
in the guaranteed corner—see Bert Williams what?
Minstrels when you steal a chicken just
save me the wing for if it isn't
Erie it ain't for miles around a
Mazda—and the telegraphic night coming on Thomas

a Ediford—and whistling down the tracks
a headlight rushing with the sound—can you
imagine—while an EXPRESS makes time like
SCIENCE—COMMERCE and the HOLYGHOST
RADIO ROARS IN EVERY HOME WE HAVE THE NORTHPOLE
WALLSTREET AND VIRGINBIRTH WITHOUT STONES OR
WIRES OR EVEN RUNning brooks connecting ears
and no more sermons windows flashing roar
Breathtaking—as you like it . . . eh?

So the 20th Century—so
whizzed the Limited—roared by and left
three men, still hungry on the tracks, ploddingly
watching the tail lights wizen and converge, slipping gimleted and neatly out of sight.

The last bear, shot drinking in the Dakotas,
Loped under wires that span the mountain stream.
Keen instruments, strung to a vast precision
Bind town to town and dream to ticking dream.
But some men take their liquor slow—and count
—Though they'll confess no rosary nor clue—
The river's minute by the far brook's year.
Under a world of whistles, wires and steam
Caboose-like they go ruminating through
Ohio, Indiana—blind baggage—
To Cheyenne tagging . . . Maybe Kalamazoo.

Time's renderings, time's blendings they construe
As final reckonings of fire and snow;
Strange bird-wit, like the elemental gist
Of unwalled winds they offer, singing low
My Old Kentucky Home and *Casey Jones,*
Some Sunny Day. I heard a road-gang chanting so.
And afterwards, who had a colt's eyes—one said,
"Jesus! O I remember watermelon days!" And sped
High in a cloud of merriment, recalled
"—And when my Aunt Sally Simpson smiled," he drawled—
"It was almost Louisiana, long ago."

"There's no place like Booneville though, Buddy,"
One said, excising a last burr from his vest,
"—For early trouting." Then peering in the can,
"—But I kept on the tracks." Possessed, resigned,
He trod the fire down pensively and grinned,
Spreading dry shingles of a beard. . . .

Behind

My father's cannery works I used to see
Rail-squatters ranged in nomad raillery,
The ancient men—wifeless or runaway
Hobo-trekkers that forever search
An empire wilderness of freight and rails.
Each seemed a child, like me, on a loose perch,
Holding to childhood like some termless play.
John, Jake, or Charley, hopping the slow freight
—Memphis to Tallahassee—riding the rods,
Blind fists of nothing, humpty-dumpty clods.

Yet they touch something like a key perhaps.
From pole to pole across the hills, the states
—They know a body under the wide rain;
Youngsters with eyes like fjords, old reprobates
With racetrack jargon,—dotting immensity
They lurk across her, knowing her yonder breast
Snow-silvered, sumac-stained or smoky blue—
Is past the valley-sleepers, south or west.
—As I have trod the rumorous midnights, too,

And past the circuit of the lamp's thin flame
(O Nights that brought me to her body bare!)
Have dreamed beyond the print that bound her name.
Trains sounding the long blizzards out—I heard
Wail into distances I knew were hers.
Papooses crying on the wind's long mane
Screamed redskin dynasties that fled the brain,
—Dead echoes! But I knew her body there,
Time like a serpent down her shoulder, dark,
And space, an eaglet's wing, laid on her hair.

Under the Ozarks, domed by Iron Mountain,
The old gods of the rain lie wrapped in pools
Where eyeless fish curvet a sunken fountain
And re-descend with corn from querulous crows.
Such pilferings make up their timeless eatage,
Propitiate them for their timber torn
By iron, iron—always the iron dealt cleavage!
They doze now, below axe and powder horn.

And Pullman breakfasters glide glistening steel
From tunnel into field—iron strides the dew—

Straddles the hill, a dance of wheel on wheel.
You have a half-hour's wait at Siskiyou,
Or stay the night and take the next train through.
Southward, near Cairo passing, you can see
The Ohio merging,—borne down Tennessee;
And if it's summer and the sun's in dusk
Maybe the breeze will lift the River's musk
—As though the waters breathed that you might know
Memphis Johnny, Steamboat Bill, Missouri Joe.
Oh, lean from the window, if the train slows down,
As though you touched hands with some ancient clown,
—A little while gaze absently below
And hum *Deep River* with them while they go.

Yes, turn again and sniff once more—look see,
O Sheriff, Brakeman and Authority—
Hitch up your pants and crunch another quid,
For you, too, feed the River timelessly.
And few evade full measure of their fate;
Always they smile out eerily what they seem.
I could believe he joked at heaven's gate—
Dan Midland—jolted from the cold brake-beam.

Down, down—born pioneers in time's despite,
Grimed tributaries to an ancient flow—
They win no frontier by their wayward plight,
But drift in stillness, as from Jordan's brow.

You will not hear it as the sea; even stone
Is not more hushed by gravity . . . But slow,
As loth to take more tribute—sliding prone
Like one whose eyes were buried long ago

The River, spreading, flows—and spends your dream.
What are you, lost within this tideless spell?
You are your father's father, and the stream—
A liquid theme that floating niggers swell.

Damp tonnage and alluvial march of days—
Nights turbid, vascular with silted shale
And roots surrendered down of moraine clays:
The Mississippi drinks the farthest dale.

O quarrying passion, undertowed sunlight!
The basalt surface drags a jungle grace

Ochreous and lynx-barred in lengthening might;
Patience! and you shall reach the biding place!

Over DeSoto's bones the freighted floors
Throb past the City storied of three thrones.
Down two more turns the Mississippi pours
(Anon tall ironsides up from salt lagoons)

And flows within itself, heaps itself free.
All fades but one thin skyline 'round . . . Ahead
No embrace opens but the stinging sea;
The River lifts itself from its long bed,

Poised wholly on its dream, a mustard glow
Tortured with history, its one will—flow!
—The Passion spreads in wide tongues, choked and slow,
Meeting the Gulf, hosannas silently below.

The Dance

(From "The Bridge")

The swift red flesh, a winter king—
Who squired the glacier woman down the sky?
She ran the neighing canyons all the spring;
She spouted arms; she rose with maize—to die.

And in the autumn drouth, whose burnished hands
With mineral wariness found out the stone
Where prayers, forgotten, streamed the mesa sands?
He holds the twilight's dim, perpetual throne.

Mythical brows we saw retiring—loth,
Disturbed and destined, into denser green.
Greeting they sped us, on the arrow's oath:
Now lie incorrigibly what years between . . .

There was a bed of leaves, and broken play;
There was a veil upon you, Pocahontas, bride—
O Princess whose brown lap was virgin May;
And bridal flanks and eyes hid tawny pride.

I left the village for dogwood. By the canoe
Tugging below the mill-race, I could see

Your hair's keen crescent running, and the blue
First moth of evening take wing stealthily.

What laughing chains the water wove and threw!
I learned to catch the trout's moon whisper; I
Drifted how many hours I never knew,
But, watching, saw that fleet young crescent die,—

And one star, swinging, take its place, alone,
Cupped in the larches of the mountain pass—
Until, immortally, it bled into the dawn.
I left my sleek boat nibbling margin grass . . .

I took the portage climb, then chose
A further valley-shed; I could not stop.
Feet nozzled watery webs of upper flows;
One white veil gusted from the very top.

O Appalachian Spring! I gained the ledge;
Steep, inaccessible smile that eastward bends
And northward reaches in that violet wedge
Of Adirondacks!—wisped of azure wands,

Over how many bluffs, tarns, streams I sped!
—And knew myself within some boding shade.
Grey tepees tufting the blue knolls ahead,
Smoke swirling through the yellow chestnut glade . . .

A distant cloud, a thunder-bud—it grew,
That blanket of the skies: the padded foot
Within,—I hear it; 'til its rhythm drew,
—Siphoned the black pool from the heart's hot root!

A cyclone threshes in the turbine crest,
Swooping in eagle feathers down your back;
Know, Maquokeeta, greeting; know death's best;
—Fall, Sachem, strictly as the tamarack!

A birch kneels. All her whistling fingers fly.
The oak grove circles in a crash of leaves;
The long moan of a dance is in the sky.
Dance, Maquokeeta: Pocahontas grieves . . .

And every tendon scurries toward the twangs
Of lightning deltaed down your saber hair.

Now snaps the flint in every tooth; red fangs
And splay tongues thinly busy the blue air . . .

Dance, Maquokeeta! snake that lives before,
That casts his pelt, and lives beyond! Sprout, horn!
Spark, tooth! Medicine-man, relent, restore—
Lie to us—dance us back the tribal morn!

Spears and assemblies: black drums thrusting on—
O yelling battlements,—I, too, was liege
To rainbows currying each pulsant bone:
Surpassed the circumstance, danced out the siege!

And buzzard-circleted, screamed from the stake;
I could not pick the arrows from my side.
Wrapped in that fire, I saw more escorts wake—
Flickering, sprint up the hill, groins like a tide.

I heard the hush of lava wrestling your arms,
And stag teeth foam about the raven throat;
Flame cataracts of heaven in seething swarms
Fed down your anklets to the sunset's moat.

Oh, like the lizard in the furious noon,
That drops his legs and colors in the sun,
—And laughs, pure serpent, Time itself, and moon
Of his own fate, I saw thy change begun!

And saw thee dive to kiss that destiny
Like one white meteor, sacrosanct and blent
At last with all that's consummate and free
There, where the first and last gods keep thy tent

Thewed of the levin, thunder-shod and lean,
Lo, through what infinite seasons dost thou gaze—
Across what bivouacs of thine angered slain,
And see'st thy bride immortal in the maize!

Totem and fire-gall, slumbering pyramid—
Though other calendars now stack the sky,
Thy freedom is her largesse, Prince, and hid
On paths thou knewest best to claim her by.

High unto Labrador the sun strikes free
Her speechless dream of snow, and stirred again,
She is the torrent and the singing tree;
And she is virgin to the last of men . . .

West, west and south! winds over Cumberland
And winds across the llano grass resume
Her hair's warm sibilance. Her breasts are fanned—
O stream by slope and vineyard—into bloom!

And when the caribou slant down for salt
Do arrows thirst and leap? Do antlers shine
Alert, star-triggered in the listening vault
Of dusk?—And are her perfect brows to thine?

We danced, O Brave, we danced beyond their farms,
In cobalt desert closures made our vows . . .
Now is the strong prayer folded in thine arms,
The serpent with the eagle in the boughs.

From "Cape Hatteras"

(From "The Bridge")

The nasal whine of power whips a new universe . . .
Where spouting pillars spoor the evening sky,
Under the looming stacks of the gigantic power house
Stars prick the eyes with sharp ammoniac proverbs,
New verities, new inklings in the velvet hummed
Of dynamos where hearing's leash is strummed . . .
Power's script,—wound, bobbin-bound, refined—
Is stropped to the slap of belts on booming spools, spurred
Into the bulging bouillon, harnessed jelly of the stars.
Towards what? The forked crash of split thunder parts
Our hearing momentwise; but fast in whirling armatures,
As bright as frogs' eyes, giggling in the girth
Of steely gizzards—axle-bound, confined
In coiled precision, bunched in mutual glee
The bearings glint,—O murmurless and shined
In oilrinsed circles of blind ecstasy!

Stars scribble on our eyes the frosty sagas,
The gleaming cantos of unvanquished space . . .
O sinewy silver biplane, nudging the wind's withers!
There, from Kill Devils Hill at Kitty Hawk

Two brothers in their twinship left the dune;
Warping the gale, the Wright windwrestlers veered
Capeward, then blading the wind's flank, banked and spun
What ciphers risen from prophetic script,
What marathons new-set between the stars!
The soul, by naphtha fledged into new reaches
Already knows the closer clasp of Mars,—
New latitudes, unknotting, soon give place
To what fierce schedules, rife of doom apace!

Behold the dragon's covey—amphibian, ubiquitous
To hedge the seaboard, wrap the headland, ride
The blue's unfeathered districts unto ether . . .
While Iliads glimmer through eyes raised in pride
Hell's belt springs wider—into heaven's plumed side.
O bright circumferences, heights employed to fly
War's fiery kennel masked in downy offings,—
This tournament of space, the threshed and chiseled height,
Is baited by marauding circles, bludgeon flail
Of rancorous grenades whose screaming petals carve us
The wounds we wrap with theorems sharp as hail!

Wheeled swiftly, wings emerge from larval-silver hangars.
Taut motors surge, space-gnawing, into flight;
Through sparkling visibility, outspread, unsleeping
Wings clip the last peripheries of light . . .
Tellurian wind-sleuths on dawn patrol,
Each plane a hurtling javelin of winged ordnance,
Bristle the heights above a screeching gale to hover;
Surely no eye that Sunward Escadrille can cover!
There, meaningful, fledged as the Pleiades
With razor sheen they zoom each rapid helix!
Up-chartered choristers of their own speeding
They, cavalcade on escapade, shear Cumulus—
Lay siege and hurdle Cirrus down the skies!
While Cetus-like, O thou Dirigible, enormous Lounger
Of pendulous auroral beaches,—satellited wide
By convoy planes, moonferrets that rejoin thee
On fleeing balconies as thou dost glide,
—Hast splintered space!

The Tunnel

(From "The Bridge")

To find the Western path
Right thro' the Gates of Wrath,
—Blake

Performances, assortments, résumés—
Up Times Square to Columbus Circle lights
Channel the congresses, nightly sessions,
Refractions of the thousand theatres, faces—
Mysterious kitchens. . . . You shall search them all.
Some day by heart you'll learn each famous sight
And watch the curtain lift in hell's despite;
You'll find the garden in the third act dead,
Finger your knees—and wish yourself in bed
With tabloid crime-sheets perched in easy sight.

Then let you reach your hat
and go.
As usual, let you—also
walking down—exclaim
to twelve upward leaving
a subscription praise
for what time slays.

Or can't you quite make up your mind to ride;
A walk is better underneath the L for a brisk
Ten blocks or so before? But you find yourself
Preparing penguin flexions of the arms—
As usual you will meet the scuttle yawn:
The subway yawns the quickest promise home.

Be minimum then, to swim the hiving swarms
Out of the Square, the Circle burning bright—
Avoid the glass doors gyring at your right,
Where boxed alone a second, eyes take fright
—Quite unprepared rush naked back to light:
And down beside the turnstile press the coin
Into the slot. The gongs already rattle.

And so
of cities you bespeak
subways, rivered under streets

and rivers. . . . In the car
the overtone of motion
underground, the monotone
of motion is the sound
of other faces, also underground—

"*Let's* have a pencil Jimmy—living now
at Floral Park
Flatbush—on the fourth of July—
like a pigeon's muddy dream—potatoes
to dig in the field—travlin the town—too—
night after night—the Culver line—the
girls all shaping up—it used to be—"

Our tongues recant like beaten weather vanes.
This answer lives like verdigris, like hair
Beyond extinction, surcease of the bone;
And repetition freezes—"What
what do you want? getting weak on the links?
fandaddle daddy don't ask for change—IS THIS
FOURTEENTH? it's half-past six she said—if
you don't like my gate why did you
swing on it, why *didja*
swing on it
anyhow—"

And somehow anyhow swing- -

The phonographs of hades in the brain
Are tunnels that re-wind themselves, and love
A burnt match skating in a urinal—
Somewhere above Fourteenth TAKE THE EXPRESS
To brush some new presentiment of pain—

"But I want service in this office SERVICE
I said—after
the show she cried a little afterwards but—"

Whose head is swinging from the swollen strap?
Whose body smokes along the bitten rails,
Bursts from a smoldering bundle far behind
In back forks of the chasms of the brain,—
Puffs from a riven stump far out behind
In interborough fissures of the mind . . . ?

And why do I often meet your visage here,
Your eyes like agate lanterns—on and on
Below the toothpaste and the dandruff ads?
—And did their riding eyes right through your side,
And did their eyes like unwashed platters ride?
And Death, aloft—gigantically down
Probing through you toward me, O Evermore!
And when they dragged your retching flesh,
Your trembling hands that night through Baltimore—
That last night on the ballot rounds, did you,
Shaking—did you deny the ticket, Poe?

For Gravesend Manor change at Chambers Street.
The platform hurries along to a dead stop.

The intent escalator lifts a serenade
Stilly
Of shoes, umbrellas, each eye attending its shoe, then
Bolting outright somewhere above where streets
Burst suddenly in rain. . . . The gongs recur:
Elbows and levers, guard and hissing door.
Thunder is galvothermic here below. . . . The car
Wheels off. The train rounds, bending to a scream,
Taking the final level for the dive
Under the river—
And somewhat emptier than before,
Demented, for a hitching second, humps; then
Lets go. . . . Towards corners of the floor
Newspapers wing, revolve and wing.
Blank windows gargle signals through the roar.

And does the Daemon take you home, also,
Wop washerwoman, with the bandaged hair?
After the corridors are swept, the cuspidors—
The gaunt sky-barracks cleanly now, and bare,
O Genoese, do you bring mother eyes and hands
Back home to children and to golden hair?

Daemon, demurring and eventful yawn!
Whose hideous laughter is the bellows mirth
—Or the muffled slaughter of a day in birth—
O cruelly to inoculate the brinking dawn
With antennae toward worlds that spark and sink;—
To spoon us out more liquid than the dim
Locution of the eldest star, and pack

The conscience naveled in the plunging wind,
Umbilical to call—and straightway die!

O caught like pennies beneath soot and steam,
Kiss of our agony thou gatherest;
Condensed, thou takest all—shrill ganglia
Impassioned with some song we fail to keep.
And yet, like Lazarus, to feel the slope,
The sod and billow breaking,—lifting ground,
—A sound of waters bending astride the sky
Unceasing with some word that will not die . . . !

A tugboat, wheezing wreaths of steam,
Lunged past, with one galvanic blare stove up the River.
I counted the echoes assembling, one after one,
Searching, thumbing the midnight on the piers.
Lights, coasting left the oily tympanum of waters;
The blackness somewhere gouged glass on a sky.
And this thy harbor, O my City, I have driven under,
Tossed from the coil of ticking towers. . . . Tomorrow,
And to be. . . . Here by the River that is East—
Here at the waters' edge the hands drop memory;
Shadowless in that abyss they unaccounting lie.
How far away the star has pooled the sea—
Or shall the hands be drawn away, to die?

Kiss of our agony Thou gatherest,
O Hand of Fire
gatherest—

Royal Palm

Green rustlings, more-than-regal charities
Drift coolly from that tower of whispered light.
Amid the noontide's blazed asperities
I watched the sun's most gracious anchorite

Climb up as by communings, year on year
Uneaten of the earth or aught earth holds,
And the gray trunk, that's elephantine, rear
Its frondings sighing in aetherial folds.

Forever fruitless, and beyond that yield
Of sweat the jungle presses with hot love
And tendril till our deathward breath is sealed—
It grazes the horizons, launched above

Mortality—ascending emerald-bright,
A fountain at salute, a crown in view—
Unshackled, casual of its azured height,
As though it soared suchwise through heaven too.

The Air Plant

(Grand Cayman, W. I.)

This tuft that thrives on saline nothingness,
Inverted octopus with heavenward arms
Thrust parching from a palm-bole hard by the cove—
A bird almost—of almost bird alarms,

Is pulmonary to the wind that jars
Its tentacles, horrific in their lurch.
The lizard's throat, held bloated for a fly,
Balloons but warily from this throbbing perch.

The needles and hacksaws of cactus bleed
A milk of earth when stricken off the stalk;
But this—defenseless, thornless, sheds no blood,
Scarce shadow even—but the air's thin talk.

Angelic Dynamo! Ventriloquist of the Blue!
While beachward creeps the shark-swept Spanish Main.
By what conjunctions do the winds appoint
Its apotheosis, at last—the hurricane!

The Hurricane

Lo, Lord, Thou ridest!
Lord, Lord, Thy swifting heart

Naught stayeth, naught now bideth
But's smithereened apart!

Ay! Scripture flee'th stone!
Milk-bright, Thy chisel wind

Rescindeth flesh from bone
To quivering whittlings thinned—

Swept—whistling straw! Battered,
Lord, e'en boulders now out-leap

Rock sockets, levin-lathered!
Nor, Lord, may worm out-deep

Thy drum's gambade, its plunge abscond!
Lord God, while summits crashing

Whip sea-kelp screaming on blond
Sky-seethe, high heaven dashing—

Thou ridest to the door, Lord!
Thou bidest wall nor floor, Lord!

My Grandmother's Love Letters

There are no stars to-night
But those of memory.
Yet how much room for memory there is
In the loose girdle of soft rain.

There is even room enough
For the letters of my mother's mother,
Elizabeth,
That have been pressed so long
Into a corner of the roof
That they are brown and soft,
And liable to melt as snow.

Over the greatness of such space
Steps must be gentle.
It is all hung by an invisible white hair.
It trembles as birch limbs webbing the air.

And I ask myself:

"Are your fingers long enough to play
Old keys that are but echoes:
Is the silence strong enough
To carry back the music to its source
And back to you again
As though to her?"

Yet I would lead my grandmother by the hand
Through much of what she would not understand;
And so I stumble. And the rain continues on the roof
With such a sound of gently pitying laughter.

The Broken Tower

The bell-rope that gathers God at dawn
Dispatches me as though I dropped down the knell
Of a spent day—to wander the cathedral lawn
From pit to crucifix, feet chill on steps from hell.

Have you not heard, have you not seen that corps
Of shadows in the tower, whose shoulders sway
Antiphonal carillons launched before
The stars are caught and hived in the sun's ray?

The bells, I say, the bells break down their tower;
And swing I know not where. Their tongues engrave
Membrane through marrow, my long-scattered score
Of broken intervals. . . . And I, their sexton slave!

Oval encyclicals in canyons heaping
The impasse high with choir. Banked voices slain!
Pagodas, campaniles with reveilles outleaping—
O terraced echoes prostrate on the plain! . . .

And so it was I entered the broken world
To trace the visionary company of love, its voice
An instant in the wind (I know not whither hurled)
But not for long to hold each desperate choice.

My word I poured. But was it cognate, scored
Of that tribunal monarch of the air
Whose thigh embronzes earth, strikes crystal Word
In wounds pledged once to hope—cleft to despair?

The steep encroachments of my blood left me
No answer (could blood hold such a lofty tower
As flings the question true?)—or is it she
Whose sweet mortality stirs latent power?—

And through whose pulse I hear, counting the strokes
My veins recall and add, revived and sure

The angelus of wars my chest evokes:
What I hold healed, original now, and pure . . .

And builds, within, a tower that is not stone
(Not stone can jacket heaven)—but slip
Of pebbles—visible wings of silence sown
In azure circles, widening as they dip

The matrix of the heart, lift down the eye
That shrines the quiet lake and swells a tower . . .
The commodious, tall decorum of that sky
Unseals her earth, and lifts love in its shower.

Allen Tate

1899-

Ode to the Confederate Dead

Row after row with strict impunity
The headstones yield their names to the element,
The wind whirrs without recollection;
In the riven troughs the splayed leaves
Pile up, of nature the casual sacrament
To the seasonal eternity of death,
Then driven by the fierce scrutiny
Of heaven to their business in the vast breath,
They sough the rumor of mortality.

Autumn is desolation in the plot
Of a thousand acres, where these memories grow
From the inexhaustible bodies that are not
Dead, but feed the grass row after rich row:
Remember now the autumns that have gone—
Ambitious November with the humors of the year,
With a particular zeal for every slab,
Staining the uncomfortable angels that rot
On the slabs, a wing chipped here, an arm there:

The brute curiosity of an angel's stare
Turns you like them to stone,
Transforms the heaving air,
Till plunged to a heavier world below
You shift your sea-space blindly,
Heaving, turning like the blind crab.

Dazed by the wind, only the wind
The leaves flying, plunge

You know who have waited by the wall
The twilit certainty of an animal;
Those midnight restitutions of the blood
You know—the immitigable pines, the smoky frieze
Of the sky, the sudden call; you know the rage—
The cold pool left by the mounting flood—
The rage of Zeno and Parmenides.
You who have waited for the angry resolution
Of those desires that should be yours tomorrow,
You know the unimportant shrift of death
And praise the vision
And praise the arrogant circumstance
Of those who fall
Rank upon rank, hurried beyond decision—
Here by the sagging gate, stopped by the wall.

Seeing, seeing only the leaves
Flying, plunge and expire

Turn your eyes to the immoderate past
Turn to the inscrutable infantry rising
Demons out of the earth—they will not last.
Stonewall, Stonewall—and the sunken fields of hemp,
Shiloh, Antietam, Malvern Hill, Bull Run.
Lost in that orient of the thick and fast
You will curse the setting sun.

Cursing only the leaves crying
Like an old man in a storm

You hear the shout—the crazy hemlocks point
With troubled fingers to the silence which
Smothers you, a mummy, in time. The hound bitch
Toothless and dying, in a musty cellar
Hears the wind only.

Now that the salt of their blood
Stiffens the saltier oblivion of the sea,
Seals the malignant purity of the flood,
What shall we, who count our days and bow
Our heads with a commemorial woe,
In the ribboned coats of grim felicity,
What shall we say of the bones, unclean—
Their verdurous anonymity will grow—
The ragged arms, the ragged heads and eyes
Lost in these acres of the insane green?
The gray lean spiders come; they come and go;
In a tangle of willows without light
The singular screech-owl's bright
Invisible lyric seeds the mind
With the furious murmur of their chivalry.

We shall say only, the leaves
Flying, plunge and expire

We shall say only, the leaves whispering
In the improbable mist of nightfall
That flies on multiple wing:
Night is the beginning and the end,
And in between the ends of distraction
Waits mute speculation, the patient curse
That stones the eyes, or like the jaguar leaps
For his own image in a jungle pool, his victim.

What shall we say who have knowledge
Carried to the heart? Shall we take the act
To the grave? Shall we, more hopeful, set up the grave
In the house? The ravenous grave?

Leave now
The turnstile and the old stone wall:
The gentle serpent, green in the mulberry bush,
Riots with his tongue through the hush—
Sentinel of the grave who counts us all!

Mr. Pope

When Alexander Pope strolled in the city
Strict was the glint of pearl and gold sedans.
Ladies leaned out, more out of fear than pity;
For Pope's tight back was rather a goat's than man's.

One often thinks the urn should have more bones
Than skeletons provide for speedy dust;
The urn gets hollow, cobwebs brittle as stones
Weave to the funeral shell a frivolous rust.

And he who dribbled couplets like the snake
Coiled to a lithe precision in the sun,
Is missing. The jar is empty; you may break
It only to find that Mr. Pope is gone.

What requisitions of a verity
Prompted the wit and rage between his teeth
One cannot say: around a crooked tree
A moral climbs whose name should be a wreath.

Death of Little Boys

When little boys grow patient at last, weary,
Surrender their eyes immeasurably to the night,
The event will rage terrific as the sea;
Their bodies fill a crumbling room with light.

Then you will touch at the bedside, torn in two,
Gold curls now deftly intricate with gray
As the windowpane extends a fear to you
From one peeled aster drenched with the wind all day.

And over his chest the covers, in an ultimate dream,
Will mount to the teeth, ascend the eyes, press back
The locks—while round his sturdy belly gleam
The suspended breaths, white spars above the wreck:

Till all the guests, come in to look, turn down
Their palms; and delirium assails the cliff
Of Norway where you ponder, and your little town
Reels like a sailor drunk in his rotten skiff. . . .

The bleak sunshine shrieks its chipped music then
Out to the milkweed amid the fields of wheat.
There is a calm for you where men and women
Unroll the chill precision of moving feet.

Mother and Son

Now all day long the man who is not dead
Hastens the dark with inattentive eyes,
The lady of the white hand, of the erect head
Stares at the cover, leans for the son's replies
At last to her importunate womanhood—
That hand of death laid on the living bed;
Such is the fierce compositor of blood.

She waits; he lies upon the bed of sin
Where greed, avarice, anger writhed and slept
Till to their silence they were gathered in;
There, fallen with time, his tall and wicked kin
Once fired the passions that were never kept
In the permanent heart, and there his mother lay
To bear him on the impenetrable day.

Because of this she cannot will her hand
Up to the bed nor break the manacle
Her exile sets upon her harsh command
That he should say the time is beautiful,
Transfigured with her own devouring light:
The sick man craves the impalpable night.

Loosed betwixt eye and lid, the swimming beams
Of memory, that school of cuttlefish
Rise to the air, plunge to the cold streams,
Rising and plunging the half-forgotten wish
To tear his heart out in some slow disgrace
And freeze the hue of terror to her face.

Hate, misery and fear beat off his heart
To the dry fury of the woman's mind;
The son prone in his autumn, moves apart
A seed blown upon a returning wind:
O child, be vigilant till towards the South
On the flowered wall all the sweet afternoon
That reach of sun, swift as the cottonmouth
Strikes at the black crucifix on her breast
Where the cold dusk comes suddenly to rest—
Mortality will speak the victor soon!

The dreary flies lazy and casual
Stick to the ceiling, buzz along the wall—
O heart, the spider shuffles from the mold
Weaving between the pinks and grapes his pall.
The bright wallpaper imperishably old
Uncurls and flutters; it will never fall.

The Mediterranean

Quem das finem, rex magne, dolorum?

Where we went in the boat was a long bay
A sling-shot wide, walled in by towering stone—
Peaked margin of antiquity's delay,
And we went there out of time's monotone:

Where we went in the black hull no light moved
But a gull white-winged along the feckless wave;
The breeze unseen but fierce as a body loved,
That boat drove onward like a willing slave.

Where we went in the small ship the seaweed
Parted and gave to us the murmuring shore
And we made feast and in our secret need
Devoured the very plates Aeneas bore:

Where derelict you see through the low twilight
The green coast that you thunder-tossed would win,
Drop sail, and hastening to drink all night
Eat dish and bowl—to take that sweet land in!

Where we feasted and caroused on the sandless
Pebbles, affecting our day of piracy,
What prophecy of eaten plates could landless
Wanderers fulfill by the ancient sea?

We for that time might taste the famous age
Eternal here yet hidden from our eyes
When lust of power undid its stuffless rage;
They, in a wineskin, bore earth's paradise.

—Let us lie down once more by the breathing side
Of ocean, where our live forefathers sleep
As if the Known Sea still were a month wide—
Atlantis howls but is no longer steep!

What country shall we conquer, what fair land
Unman our conquest and locate our blood?
We've cracked the hemispheres with careless hand!
Now, from the Gates of Hercules we flood

Westward, westward till the barbarous brine
Whelms us to the tired land where tasseling corn,
Fat beans, grapes sweeter than muscadine
Rot on the vine: in that land were we born.

Léonie Adams

1899-

April Mortality

Rebellion shook an ancient dust,
And bones bleached dry of rottenness
Said: Heart, be bitter still, nor trust
The earth, the sky, in their bright dress.

Heart, heart, dost thou not break to know
This anguish thou wilt bear alone?
We sang of it an age ago,
And traced it dimly upon stone.

With all the drifting race of men
Thou also art begot to mourn
That she is crucified again,
The lonely Beauty yet unborn.

And if thou dreamest to have won
Some touch of her in permanence,
'Tis the old cheating of the sun,
The intricate lovely play of sense.

Be bitter still, remember how
Four petals, when a little breath
Of wind made stir the pear-tree bough,
Blew delicately down to death.

Thought's End

I watched the hills drink the last color of light,
All shapes grow bright and wane on the pale air.
Till down the traitorous east there came the night,
And swept the circle of my seeing bare.
Its intimate beauty like a wanton's veil
Tore from the void as from an empty face.
I felt at being's rim all being fail,
And my one body pitted against space.

O heart more frightened than a wild bird's wings,
Beating at green, now is no fiery mark
Left on the quiet nothingness of things.
Be self no more against the flooding dark:
There thousandwise sown in that cloudy blot
Stars that are worlds look out and see you not.

Death and the Lady

Their bargain told again

Death to the Lady said
While she to dancing-measures still
Would move, while beauties on her lay,
Simply as dews the buds do fill,
Death said: "Stay!
Tell me, Lady,
If in your breast the lively breath
May flicker for a little space,
What ransom will you give to death,
Lady?" he said.
"O not one joy, O not one grace,
And what is your will to my will?
I can outwit parched fancies still."
To Death said the Lady.

Death to that Lady said,
When blood went numb and wearily,
"In innocency dear breath you drew,
And marrow and bloom you rendered me,"
She said: "True."

"How now, Lady?"
"My heart sucked up its sweet at will,
Whose scent when substance' sweet is past,
Is lovely still, is lovely still,
Death," she said.
"For bones' reprieve the dreams go last:
Soon, soon your flowery show did part,
But preciously I cull the heart,"
Death said to the Lady.

Death to that Lady said:
"Is then not all our bargain done?
Or why do you beckon me so fast
To chaffer for a skeleton
Flesh must cast,
Ghostly Lady?"
"For, Death, that I would have you drain
From my dead heart the blood that stands
So chilly in the withered vein.
And, Death," she said,
"Give my due bones into your hands."
"Beauties I claim at morning-prime,
But the lack-luster in good time,"
Death said to the Lady.

Twilit Revelation

This hour was set the time for heaven's descent
Come drooping toward us on the heavy air,
The sky, that's heaven's seat above us bent,
Blue faint as violet-ash, you near me there
In nether space so drenched in goblin blue,
I could touch Hesperus as soon as you.

Now I perceive you lapt in singling light,
Washed by that blue which sucks whole planets in,
And hung like those top jewels of the night,
A mournful gold too high for love to win.
And you, poor brief, poor melting star, you seem
Half sunk, and half to brighten in that stream.

And these rich-bodied hours of our delight
Show like a moth-wing's substance when the fall

Of confine-loosing, blue unending night
Extracts the spirit of this temporal.
So space can pierce the crevice wide between
Fast hearts, skies deep-descended intervene.

Ghostly Tree

O beech, unbind your yellow leaf, for deep
The honeyed time lies sleeping, and lead shade
Seals up the eyelids of its golden sleep.
Long are your flutes, chimes, little bells at rest,
And here is only the cold scream of the fox,
Only the hunter following on the hound,
And your quaint-plumagèd,
The bird that your green happy boughs lapped round,
Bends south its soft bright breast.

Before the winter and the terror break,
Scatter the leaf that broadened with the rose,
Not for a tempest, but a sigh to take.
Four nights to exorcise the thing that stood,
Bound by these frail which dangle at your branch,
They ran a frosty dagger to its heart,
And it, wan substance,
No more remembered it might cry, or start,
Or stain a point with blood.

The Horn

In coming to the feast I found
A venerable silver-throated horn,
Which were I brave enough to sound,
Then all as from that moment born
Would breathe the honey of this clime,
And three times merry in their time,
Would praise the virtue of that horn.

The mist is risen like thin breath,
The young leaves of the ground smell chill,
So faintly are they strewn on death,
The road I came down a west hill.
But none can name as I can name

A little golden-bright thing flame,
Since bones have caught their marrow chill.

And in a thicket passed me by,
In the black brush a running hare,
Having a specter in his eye,
That sped in darkness to the snare;
And who but I can know in pride,
The heart set beating in the side
Has but the wisdom of a hare?

The River in the Meadows

Crystal parting the meads,
A boat drifted up it like a swan,
Tranquil, lovely, its bright front to the waters,
A slow swan is gone.

Full waters, O flowing silver,
Pure, level with the clover,
It will stain drowning a star,
With the moon it will brim over.

Running through lands dewy and shorn,
Cattle stoop at its brink,
And every fawny-colored throat
Will sway its bells and drink.

I saw a boat sailing the river
With a tranced gait; it seemed
Loosed by a spell from its moorings,
Or a thing the helmsman dreamed.

They said it would carry no traveler,
But the vessel would go down,
If a heart were heavy-winged,
Or the bosom it dwelt in, stone.

Country Summer

Now the rich cherry whose sleek wood
And top with silver petals traced,
Like a strict box its gems encased,
Has spilt from out that cunning lid,

All in an innocent green round,
Those melting rubies which it hid;
With moss ripe-strawberry-encrusted,
So birds get half, and minds lapse merry
To taste that deep-red lark's-bite berry,
And blackcap-bloom is yellow-dusted.

The wren that thieved it in the eaves
A trailer of the rose could catch
To her poor droopy sloven thatch,
And side by side with the wren's brood,—
O lovely time of beggars' luck—
Opens the quaint and hairy bud.
And full and golden is the yield
Of cows that never have to house,
But all night nibble under boughs,
Or cool their sides in the moist field.

Into the rooms flow meadow airs,
The warm farm-baking smell blows round;
Inside and out and sky and ground
Are much the same; the wishing star,
Hesperus, kind and early-born,
Is risen only finger-far.
All stars stand close in summer air,
And tremble, and look mild as amber;
When wicks are lighted in the chamber
You might say stars were settling there.

Now straightening from the flowery hay,
Down the still light the mowers look;
Or turn, because their dreaming shook,
And they waked half to other days,
When left alone in yellow-stubble,
The rusty-coated mare would graze.
Yet thick the lazy dreams are born;
Another thought can come to mind,
But like the shivering of the wind,
Morning and evening in the corn.

The Mount

"No, I have tempered haste,"
The joyous traveler said,
"The steed has passed me now
Whose hurrying hooves I fled.
My specter rides thereon,
I learned what mount he has,
Upon what summers fed;
And wept to know again,
Beneath the saddle swung,
Treasure for whose great theft
This breast was wrung.
His bridle bells sang out,
I could not tell their chime,
So brilliantly he rings,
But called his name as Time.
His bin was morning light,
Those straws which gild his bed
Are of the fallen West.
Although green lands consume
Beneath their burning tread,
In everlasting bright
His hooves have rest."

This Measure

This measure was a measure to my mind,
Still musical through the unlikely hush.
The cold goes wide as doors, and in will come
These notes of May set ringing through the brush,
Where every voice by natural law is dumb.

How many seasons I have watched the boughs,
That first are happy-tongued and happy-leaved,
Then bleed, as though an autumn were the last,
While that great life was with them undeceived,
Which all a wintering world seals home more fast.

Now visibly indeed I am assailed,
Yet I seem come clap on my very thing;

And now I learn I only asked as much:
It was in blooming weeks I lacked a spring
Rooted and blowing beyond sense or touch.

Bell Tower

I have seen, O desolate one, the voice has its tower,
The voice also, builded at secret cost,
Its temple of precious tissue; not silent then,
Forever. Casting silence in your hour.

There marble boys are leant from the light throat,
Thick locks that hang with dew, and eyes dew-lashed,
Dazzled with morning,—angels of the wind,
With ear a-point for the enchanted note.

And these at length shall tip the hanging bell,
And first the sound must gather in deep bronze,
Till, rarer than ice, purer than a bubble of gold,
It fill the sky to beat on an airy shell.

Kingdom of Heaven

Bleak the February light
On the dark threshold spread,
The frost stood thick against the lock,
The clock for the great cold stopped dead,
When old wits idle with their luck
Lay singing in the bed,
That heard, while white frost span by night,
A pigeon happy with its bread.

And sang: I wakened to a sound
Which the streams make at thaw,
And pity on the shape I found
Inside a looking-glass with light.
For looking on my heart I saw,
A time before the break of day,
And looking won to second-sight,
And cast my character away.

The fields lie bound beneath the sky,
The hedge-top and the furrow freeze,

And still old plow-wheels sigh,
As sweet as bones which stretch from sleep,
And sooner than their sound is by,
Will come a noise of yellow bees
When the hay is nodding deep,
And some wise throat that laughs for ease.

Till there was a soft voice which spoke:
Hush, for every sound you tell
Is out of an old horn I blew.
I have come down to see who woke
On earth's cold brink when night was through.
No wilder chance befell,
Than the starry breath I drew.
I am Gabriel.

Sundown

This is the time lean woods shall spend
A steeped-up twilight, and the pale evening drink,
And the perilous roe, the leaper to the west brink,
Trembling and bright, to the caverned cloud descend.

Now shall you see pent oak gone gusty and frantic,
Stooped with dry weeping, ruinously unloosing
The sparse disheveled leaf, or reared and tossing
A dreary scarecrow bough in funeral antic.

Then, tatter you and rend,
Oak heart, to your profession mourning, not obscure
The outcome, not crepuscular, on the deep floor,
Sable and gold match lusters and contend.

And rags of shrouding will not muffle the slain.
This is the immortal extinction, the priceless wound
Not to be staunched; the live gold leaks beyond,
And matter's sanctified, dipped in a gold stain.

Night-Piece

The moon above the milky field
Gleaning moves her one slant light,
The wind weeps from the cloud:
Then, weeping wind, unshroud

Pale Cassiopeia, blow
The true-swung pole-lamp bright.
To this room a midnight's come
Which speaks but with the beating clock,
While on glistening paws the mouse
Creeps night-master of the house.
Rust shall eat away the lock,
The door sag from the garner hoard,
And the sleeper lie unsphered.
Time's wheel frets on his finger still,
He bends no more his weight with time's
He wept as long as wind,
And sleeps with an indifferent will.
Not airs, not climes unclose, behind
The lashes' scarcely faltering jet,
Which star he sees since Hesper set.

Lullaby

Hush, lullay,
Your treasures all
        Encrust with rust.
Your trinket pleasures
        Fall
To dust.
Beneath the sapphire arch
Upon the grassy floor
Is nothing more
        To hold,
And play is over old.
Your eyes
        In sleepy fever gleam,
Your lids droop
        To their dream.
You wander late alone,
The flesh frets on the bone,
Your love fails
        In your breast.
Here is the pillow.
        Rest.

Richard Eberhart

1904-

The Horse Chestnut Tree

Boys in sporadic but tenacious droves
Come with sticks, as certainly as Autumn,
To assault the great horse chestnut tree.

There is a law governs their lawlessness.
Desire is in them for a shining amulet
And the best are those that are highest up.

They will not pick them easily from the ground.
With shrill arms they fling to the higher branches,
To hurry the work of nature for their pleasure.

I have seen them trooping down the street
Their pockets stuffed with chestnuts shucked, unshucked.
It is only evening keeps them from their wish.

Sometimes I run out in a kind of rage
To chase the boys away: I catch an arm,
Maybe, and laugh to think of being the lawgiver.

I was once such a young sprout myself
And fingered in my pocket the prize and trophy.
But still I moralize upon the day

And see that we, outlaws on God's property,
Fling out imagination beyond the skies,
Wishing a tangible good from the unknown.

And likewise death will drive us from the scene
With the great flowering world unbroken yet,
Which we held in idea, a little handful.

If I Could Only Live at the Pitch That Is Near Madness

If I could only live at the pitch that is near madness
When everything is as it was in my childhood
Violent, vivid, and of infinite possibility:
That the sun and the moon broke over my head.

Then I cast time out of the trees and fields,
Then I stood immaculate in the Ego;
Then I eyed the world with all delight,
Reality was the perfection of my sight.

And time has big handles on the hands,
Fields and trees a way of being themselves.
I saw battalions of the race of mankind
Standing stolid, demanding a moral answer.

I gave the moral answer and I died
And into a realm of complexity came
Where nothing is possible but necessity
And the truth wailing there like a red babe.

Dam Neck, Virginia

Anti-aircraft seen from a certain distance
On a steely blue night say a mile away
Flowers on the air absolutely dream-like,
The vision has no relation to the reality.

The floating balls of light are tossed easily
And float out into space without a care,
They the sailors of the gentlest parabolas
In a companionship and with a kind of stare.

They are a controlled kind of falling stars,
But not falling, rising and floating and going out,
Teaming together in efflorescent spectacle
Seemingly better than nature's: man is on the lookout.

The men are firing tracers, practising at night.
Each specialist himself precision's instrument,

These expert prestidigitators press the luminence
In knowledge of and ignorance of their doing.

They do not know the dream-like vision ascending
In me, one mile away: they had not thought of that.
Huddled in darkness behind their bright projectors
They are the scientists of the skill to kill.

As this sight and show is gentle and false,
The truth of guns is fierce that aims at death.
Of war in the animal sinews let us speak not,
But of the beautiful disrelation of the spiritual.

The Attic

(From "Burr Oaks")

The attic and the cedar closet—nostalgia!
Who has not dreamed evasive dreams
In the strange disorder of the attic trunks and boxes,
Fantastic clothes, broken dolls, grandfather's canes?
And in that world of broken strangeness
Had glimpses of the profound aberration of the world?
And crept in among mother's old rustling dresses
Overpowered by the cedar ether from the cedar trees?
While from the high tight windows, surveying the vast
World of trees, grove, river and pasture
It was a citadel never the world would cure,
Nor all its years of struggle, philosophy, or knowledge
Divest of a delirium of strange charm.
A special place is the attic where one goes
For special purposes, where anarchy reigns,
Oddness is the prince of disinheritance,
Angularity expresses the confusion of the senses,
Time is suicidally overcome and diverted,
Chaos is come without pain of reality.
O who has not loved hours among attic things?
Who has not grieved to return to the world downstairs?

The Groundhog

In June, amid the golden fields,
I saw a groundhog lying dead.
Dead lay he; my senses shook,
And mind outshot our naked frailty.
There lowly in the vigorous summer
His form began its senseless change,
And made my senses waver dim
Seeing nature ferocious in him.
Inspecting close his maggots' might
And seething cauldron of his being,
Half with loathing, half with a strange love,
I poked him with an angry stick.
The fever rose, became a flame
And Vigour circumscribed the skies,
Immense energy in the sun,
And through my frame a sunless trembling.
My stick had done nor good nor harm.
Then stood I silent in the day
Watching the object, as before;
And kept my reverence for knowledge
Trying for control, to be still,
To quell the passion of the blood;
Until I had bent down on my knees
Praying for joy in the sight of decay.
And so I left; and I returned
In Autumn strict of eye, to see
The sap gone out of the groundhog,
But the bony sodden hulk remained.
But the year had lost its meaning,
And in intellectual chains
I lost both love and loathing,
Mured up in the wall of wisdom.
Another summer took the fields again
Massive and burning, full of life,
But when I chanced upon the spot
There was only a little hair left,
And bones bleaching in the sunlight
Beautiful as architecture;
I watched them like a geometer,
And cut a walking stick from a birch.
It has been three years, now.

There is no sign of the groundhog.
I stood there in the whirling summer,
My hand capped a withered heart,
And thought of China and of Greece,
Of Alexander in his tent;
Of Montaigne in his tower,
Of Saint Theresa in her wild lament.

Seals, Terns, Time

The seals at play off Western Isle
In the loose flowing of the summer tide
And burden of our strange estate—

Resting on the oar and lolling on the sea,
I saw their curious images,
Hypnotic, sympathetic eyes

As the deep elapses of the soul.
O ancient blood, O blurred kind forms
That rise and peer from elemental water:

I loll upon the oar, I think upon the day,
Drawn by strong, by the animal soft bonds
Back to a dim pre-history;

While off the point of Jagged Light
In hundreds, gracefully, the fork-tailed terns
Draw swift esprits across the sky.

Their aspirations dip in mine,
The quick order of their changing spirit,
More freedom than the eye can see.

Resting lightly on the oarlocks,
Pondering, and balanced on the sea,
A gauze and spindrift of the world,

I am in compulsion hid and thwarted,
Pulled back in the mammal water,
Enticed to the release of the sky.

Theodore Roethke

1908-

My Papa's Waltz

The whiskey on your breath
Could make a small boy dizzy;
But I hung on like death:
Such waltzing was not easy.

We romped until the pans
Slid from the kitchen shelf;
My mother's countenance
Could not unfrown itself.

The hand that held my wrist
Was battered on one knuckle;
At every step you missed
My right ear scraped a buckle.

You beat time on my head
With a palm caked hard by dirt,
Then waltzed me off to bed
Still clinging to your shirt.

Elegy for Jane

(My student, thrown by a horse)

I remember the neckcurls, limp and damp as tendrils,
And her quick look, a sidelong pickerel smile;
And how, once startled into talk, the light syllables leaped for
  her,
And she balanced in the delight of her thought,
A wren, happy, tail into the wind,
Her song trembling the twigs and small branches.
The shade sang with her;

The leaves, their whispers turned to kissing;
And the mould sang in the bleached valleys under the rose.

Oh, when she was sad, she cast herself down into such a pure
depth,
Even a father could not find her:
Scraping her cheek against straw;
Stirring the clearest water.

My sparrow, you are not here,
Waiting like a fern, making a spiney shadow.
The sides of wet stones cannot console me,
Nor the moss, wound with the last light.

If only I could nudge you from this sleep,
My maimed darling, my skittery pigeon.
Over this damp grave I speak the words of my love:
I, with no rights in this matter,
Neither father nor lover.

The Shape of the Fire

1

What's this? A dish for fat lips.
Who says? A nameless stranger.
Is he a bird or a tree? Not everyone can tell.

Water recedes to the crying of spiders.
An old scow bumps over black rocks.
A cracked pod calls.

Mother me out of here. What more will the bones allow?
Will the sea give the wind suck? A toad folds into a stone.
These flowers are all fangs. Comfort me, fury.
Wake me, witch, we'll do the dance of rotten sticks.

Shale loosens. Marl reaches into the field. Small birds pass over
water.
Spirit, come near. This is only the edge of whiteness.
I can't laugh at a procession of dogs.

In the hour of ripeness, the tree is barren.
The she-bear mopes under the hill.
Mother, mother, stir from your cave of sorrow.

A low mouth laps water. Weeds, weeds, how I love you.
The arbor is cooler. Farewell, farewell, fond worm.
The warm comes without sound.

II

Where's the eye?
The eye's in the sty.
The ear's not here
Beneath the hair.
When I took off my clothes
To find a nose,
There was only one shoe
For the waltz of To,
The pinch of Where.

Time for the flat-headed man. I recognize that listener,
Him with the platitudes and rubber doughnuts,
Melting at the knees, a varicose horror.
Hello, hello. My nerves knew you, dear boy.
Have you come to unhinge my shadow?
Last night I slept in the pits of a tongue.
The silver fish ran in and out of my special bindings;
I grew tired of the ritual of names and the assistant keeper of the molluscs:
Up over a viaduct I came, to the snakes and sticks of another winter,
A two-legged dog hunting a new horizon of howls.
The wind sharpened itself on a rock:
A voice sang:

Pleasure on ground
Has no sound,
Easily maddens
The uneasy man.

Who, careless, slips
In coiling ooze
Is trapped to the lips,
Leaves more than shoes;

Must pull off clothes
To jerk like a frog
On belly and nose
From the sucking bog.

My meat eats me. Who waits at the gate?
Mother of quartz, your words writhe into my ear.
Renew the light, lewd whisper.

III

The wasp waits.
The edge cannot eat the center.
The grape glistens.
The path tells little to the serpent.
An eye comes out of the wave.
The journey from flesh is longest.
A rose sways least.
The redeemer comes a dark way.

IV

Morning-fair, follow me further back
Into that minnowy world of weeds and ditches,
When the herons floated high over the white houses,
And the little crabs slipped into silvery craters.
When the sun for me glinted the sides of a sand grain.
And my intent stretched over the buds at their first trembling.

That air and shine: and the flicker's loud summer call:
The bearded boards in the stream and the all of apples;
The glad hen on the hill; and the trellis humming.
Death was not. I lived in a simple drowse:
Hands and hair moved through a dream of wakening blossoms.
Rain sweetened the cave and dove still called;
The flowers leaned on themselves, the flowers in hollows;
And love, love sang toward.

V

To have the whole air!
The light, the full sun
Coming down on the flowerheads,
The tendrils turning slowly,
A slow snail-lifting, liquescent;
To be by the rose
Rising slowly out of its bed,
Still as a child in its first loneliness;
To see cyclamen veins become clearer in early sunlight,
And mist lifting out of the brown cattails;
To stare into the after-light, the glitter left on the lake's surface.

When the sun has fallen behind a wooded island;
To follow the drops sliding from a lifted oar,
Held up, while the rower breathes, and the small boat drifts
  quietly shoreward;
To know that light falls and fills, often without our knowing,
As an opaque vase fills to the brim from a quick pouring,
Fills and trembles at the edge yet does not flow over,
Still holding and feeding the stem of the contained flower.

Frau Bauman, Frau Schmidt, and Frau Schwartze

Gone the three ancient ladies
Who creaked on the greenhouse ladders,
Reaching up white strings
To wind, to wind
The sweet-pea tendrils, the smilax,
Nasturtiums, the climbing
Roses, to straighten
Carnations, red
Chrysanthemums; the stiff
Stems, jointed like corn,
They tied and tucked,—
These nurses of nobody else.
Quicker than birds, they dipped
Up and sifted the dirt;
They sprinkled and shook;
They stood astride pipes,
Their skirts billowing out wide into tents,
Their hands twinkling with wet;
Like witches they flew along rows
Keeping creation at ease;
With a tendril for needle
They sewed up the air with a stem;
They teased out the seed that the cold kept asleep,—
All the coils, loops, and whorls.
They trellised the sun; they plotted for more than themselves.

I remember how they picked me up, a spindly kid,
Pinching and poking my thin ribs
Till I lay in their laps, laughing,
Weak as a whiffet;
Now, when I'm alone and cold in my bed,
They still hover over me,

Those ancient leathery crones,
With their bandannas stiffened with sweat,
And their thorn-bitten wrists,
And their snuff-laden breath blowing lightly over me in my
first sleep.

Elizabeth Bishop

1911-

The Fish

I caught a tremendous fish
and held him beside the boat
half out of water, with my hook
fast in a corner of his mouth.
He didn't fight.
He hadn't fought at all.
He hung a grunting weight,
battered and venerable
and homely. Here and there
his brown skin hung in strips
like ancient wall-paper,
and its pattern of darker brown
was like wall-paper:
shapes like full-blown roses
stained and lost through age.
He was speckled with barnacles,
fine rosettes of lime,
and infested
with tiny white sea-lice,
and underneath two or three
rags of green weed hung down.
While his gills were breathing in
the terrible oxygen
—the frightening gills
fresh and crisp with blood,
that can cut so badly—

I thought of the coarse white flesh
packed in like feathers,
the big bones and the little bones,
the dramatic reds and blacks
of his shiny entrails,
and the pink swim-bladder
like a big peony.
I looked into his eyes
which were far larger than mine
but shallower, and yellowed,
the irises backed and packed
with tarnished tinfoil
seen through the lenses
of old scratched isinglass.
They shifted a little, but not
to return my stare.
—It was more like the tipping
of an object toward the light.
I admired his sullen face,
the mechanism of his jaw,
and then I saw
that from his lower lip
—if you could call it a lip—
grim, wet, and weapon-like,
hung five old pieces of fish-line,
or four and a wire leader
with the swivel still attached,
with all their five big hooks
grown firmly in his mouth.
A green line, frayed at the end
where he broke it, two heavier lines,
and a fine black thread
still crimped from the strain and snap
when it broke and he got away.
Like medals with their ribbons
frayed and wavering,
a five-haired beard of wisdom
trailing from his aching jaw.
I stared and stared
and victory filled up
the little rented boat,
from the pool of bilge
where oil had spread a rainbow
around the rusted engine
to the bailer rusted orange,

the sun-cracked thwarts,
the oarlocks on their strings,
the gunnels—until everything
was rainbow, rainbow, rainbow!
And I let the fish go.

The Imaginary Iceberg

We'd rather have the iceberg than the ship,
Although it meant the end of travel.
Although it stood stock still like cloudy rock
And all the sea were moving marble.
We'd rather have the iceberg than the ship;
We'd rather own this breathing plain of snow
Though the ship's sails were laid upon the sea
As the snow lies undissolved upon the water.
O solemn, floating field,
Are you aware an iceberg takes repose
With you, and when it wakes may pasture on your snows?

This is a scene a sailor'd give his eyes for.
The ship's ignored. The iceberg rises
And sinks again; its glassy pinnacles
Correct elliptics in the sky.
This is a scene where he who treads the boards
Is artlessly rhetorical. The curtain
Is light enough to rise on finest ropes
That airy twists of snow provide.
The wits of these white peaks
Spar with the sun. Its weight the iceberg dares
Upon a shifting stage and stands and stares.

This iceberg cuts its facets from within.
Like jewelry from a grave
It saves itself perpetually and adorns
Only itself, perhaps the snows
Which so surprise us lying on the sea.
Goodbye, we say, goodbye, the ship steers off
Where waves give in to one another's waves
And clouds run in a warmer sky.
Icebergs behoove the soul
(Both being self-made from elements least visible)
To see them so: fleshed, fair, erected indivisible.

The Man-Moth [1]

Here, above,
cracks in the buildings are filled with battered moonlight.
The whole shadow of Man is only as big as his hat.
It lies at his feet like a circle for a doll to stand on,
and he makes an inverted pin, the point magnetized to the
moon.
He does not see the moon; he observes only her vast properties,
feeling the queer light on his hands, neither warm nor cold,
of a temperature impossible to record in thermometers.

But when the Man-Moth
pays his rare, although occasional, visits to the surface,
the moon looks rather different to him. He emerges
from an opening under the edge of one of the sidewalks
and nervously begins to scale the faces of buildings.
He thinks the moon is a small hole at the top of the sky,
proving the sky quite useless for protection.
He trembles, but must investigate as high as he can climb.

Up the façades,
his shadow dragging like a photographer's cloth behind him,
he climbs fearfully, thinking that this time he will manage
to push his small head through that round clean opening
and be forced through, as from a tube, in black scrolls on the
light.
(Man, standing below him, has no such illusions.)
But what the Man-Moth fears most he must do, although
he fails, of course, and falls back scared but unhurt.

Then he returns
to the pale subways of cement he calls his home. He flits,
he flutters, and cannot get aboard the silent trains
fast enough to suit him. The doors close swiftly.
The Man-Moth always seats himself facing the wrong way
and the train starts at once at its full, terrible speed,
without a shift in gears or a gradation of any sort.
He cannot tell the rate at which he travels backwards.

Each night he must
be carried through artificial tunnels and dream recurrent
dreams.

[1] Newspaper misprint for "mammoth."

Just as the ties recur beneath his train, these underlie
his rushing brain. He does not dare look out the window,
for the third rail, the unbroken draught of poison,
runs there beside him. He regards it as disease
he has inherited susceptibility to. He has to keep
his hands in pockets, as others must wear mufflers.

If you catch him,
hold up a flashlight to his eye. It's all dark pupil,
an entire night itself, whose haired horizon tightens
as he stares back, and closes up the eye. Then from the lids
one tear, his only possession, like the bee's sting, slips.
Slyly he palms it, and if you're not paying attention
he'll swallow it. However, if you watch, he'll hand it over,
cool as from underground springs and pure enough to drink.

Little Exercise

Think of the storm roaming the sky uneasily
like a dog looking for a place to sleep in,
listen to it growling.

Think how they must look now, the mangrove keys
lying out there unresponsive to the lightning
in dark, coarse-fibred families,

where occasionally a heron may undo his head,
shake up his feathers, make an uncertain comment
when the surrounding water shines.

Think of the boulevard and the little palm trees
all stuck in rows, suddenly revealed
as fistfuls of limp fish-skeletons.

It is raining there. The boulevard
and its broken sidewalks with weeds in every crack,
are relieved to be wet, the sea to be freshened.

Now the storm goes away again in a series
of small, badly lit battle-scenes,
each in "Another part of the field."

Think of someone sleeping in the bottom of a row-boat
tied to a mangrove root or the pile of a bridge;
think of him as uninjured, barely disturbed.

Seascape

This celestial seascape, with white herons got up as angels,
flying as high as they want and as far as they want side-wise
in tiers and tiers of immaculate reflections;
the whole region, from the highest heron
down to the weightless mangrove island
with bright green leaves edged neatly with bird-droppings
like illumination in silver,
and down to the suggestively Gothic arches of the mangrove
    roots
and the beautiful pea-green back-pasture
where occasionally a fish jumps, like a wild-flower
in an ornamental spray of spray;
this cartoon by Raphael for a tapestry for a Pope:
it does look like heaven.
But a skeletal lighthouse standing there
in black and white clerical dress,
who "lives on his nerves," thinks he knows better.
He thinks that Hell rages below his iron feet,
that that is why the shallow water is so warm,
and he knows that heaven is not like this.
Heaven is not like flying or swimming,
but has something to do with blackness and a strong glare
and when it gets dark he will remember something
strongly worded to say on the subject.

The Prodigal

The brown enormous odor he lived by
was too close, with its breathing and thick hair,
for him to judge. The floor was rotten; the sty
was plastered halfway up with glass-smooth dung.
Light-lashed, self-righteous, above moving snouts,
the pigs' eyes followed him, a cheerful stare—
even to the sow that always ate her young—
till, sickening, he leaned to scratch her head.
But sometimes mornings after drinking bouts
(he hid the pints behind a two-by-four),
the sunrise glazed the barnyard mud with red;
the burning puddles seemed to reassure.

And then he thought he almost might endure
his exile yet another year or more.

But evenings the first star came to warn.
The farmer whom he worked for came at dark
to shut the cows and horses in the barn
beneath their overhanging clouds of hay,
with pitchforks, faint forked lightnings, catching light,
safe and companionable as in the Ark.
The pigs stuck out their little feet and snored.
The lantern—like the sun, going away—
laid on the mud a pacing aureole.
Carrying a bucket along a slimy board,
he felt the bats' uncertain staggering flight,
his shuddering insights, beyond his control,
touching him. But it took him a long time
finally to make his mind up to go home.

Delmore Schwartz

1913-

For Rhoda

Calmly we walk through this April's day,
Metropolitan poetry here and there,
In the park sit pauper and *rentier,*
The screaming children, the motor car
Fugitive about us, running away,
Between the worker and the millionaire.
Number provides all distances,
It is Nineteen Thirty-Seven now,
Many great dears are taken away,
What will become of you and me
(This is the school in which we learn . . .)
Besides the photo and the memory?
(. . . that time is the fire in which we burn.)

(This is the school in which we learn . . .)
What is the self amid this blaze?
What am I now that I was then
Which I shall suffer and act again,
The theodicy I wrote in my high school days
Restored all life from infancy,
The children shouting are bright as they run
(This is the school in which they learn . . .)
Ravished entirely in their passing play!
(. . . that time is the fire in which they burn.)

Avid its rush, that reeling blaze!
Where is my father and Eleanor?
Not where are they now, dead seven years,
But what they were then?
                                        No more? No more?
From Nineteen-Fourteen to the present day,
Bert Spira and Rhoda consume, consume
Not where they are now (where are they now?)
But what they were then, both beautiful;
Each minute bursts in the burning room,
The great globe reels in the solar fire,
Spinning the trivial and unique away.
(How all things flash! How all things flare!)
What am I now that I was then?
May memory restore again and again
The smallest color of the smallest day:
Time is the school in which we learn,
Time is the fire in which we burn.

Tired and Unhappy, You Think of Houses

Tired and unhappy, you think of houses
Soft-carpeted and warm in the December evening,
While snow's white pieces fall past the window,
And the orange firelight leaps.
                                        A young girl sings
That song of Gluck where Orpheus pleads with Death;
Her elders watch, nodding their happiness
To see time fresh again in her self-conscious eyes:
The servants bring the coffee, the children retire,
Elder and younger yawn and go to bed,
The coals fade and glow, rose and ashen,

It is time to shake yourself! and break this
Banal dream, and turn your head
Where the underground is charged, where the weight
Of the lean buildings is seen,
Where close in the subway rush, anonymous
In the audience, well-dressed or mean,
So many surround you, ringing your fate,
Caught in an anger exact as a machine!

For the One Who Would Take Man's Life in His Hands

Tiger Christ unsheathed his sword,
Threw it down, became a lamb.
Swift spat upon the species, but
Took two women to his heart.
Samson who was strong as death
Paid his strength to kiss a slut.
Othello that stiff warrior
Was broken by a woman's heart.
Troy burned for a sea-tax, also for
Possession of a charming whore.
What do all examples show?
What must the finished murderer know?

You cannot sit on bayonets,
Nor can you eat among the dead.
When all are killed, you are alone,
A vacuum comes where hate has fed.
Murder's fruit is silent stone,
The gun increases poverty.
With what do these examples shine?
The soldier turned to girls and wine.
Love is the tact of every good,
The only warmth, the only peace.

"What have I said?" asked Socrates,
"Affirmed extremes, cried yes and no,
Taken all parts, denied myself,
Praised the caress, extolled the blow,
Soldier and lover quite deranged
Until their motions are exchanged.

—What do all examples show?
What can any actor know?
The contradiction in every act,
The infinite task of the human heart."

In the Naked Bed, in Plato's Cave

In the naked bed, in Plato's cave,
Reflected headlights slowly slid the wall,
Carpenters hammered under the shaded window,
Wind troubled the window curtains all night long,
A fleet of trucks strained uphill, grinding,
Their freights covered, as usual.
The ceiling lightened again, the slanting diagram
Slid slowly forth.
Hearing the milkman's chop,
His striving up the stair, the bottle's chink,
I rose from bed, lit a cigarette,
And walked to the window. The stony street
Displayed the stillness in which buildings stand,
The street-lamp's vigil and the horse's patience.
The winter sky's pure capital
Turned me back to bed with exhausted eyes.

Strangeness grew in the motionless air. The loose
Film grayed. Shaking wagons, hooves' waterfalls,
Sounded far off, increasing, louder and nearer.
A car coughed, starting. Morning, softly
Melting the air, lifted the half-covered chair
From underseas, kindled the looking-glass,
Distinguished the dresser and the white wall.
The bird called tentatively, whistled, called,
Bubbled and whistled, so! Perplexed, still wet
With sleep, affectionate, hungry and cold. So, so,
O son of man, the ignorant night, the travail
Of early morning, the mystery of beginning
Again and again,
While Time is unforgiven.

Let Us Consider Where the Great Men Are

(From "Shenandoah")

Let us consider where the great men are
Who will obsess the child when he can read:
Joyce teaches in Trieste in a Berlitz school,
Learns to pronounce the puns in *Finnegan's Wake*—
Eliot works in a bank, and there he learns
The profit and the loss,
                    the death of cities—
Pound howls at him, finds what expatriates
Can find,
          culture in chaos all through time,
Like a Picasso show.
                    Rilke endures
Of silence and of solitude the unheard music
In empty castles which great knights have left
(Like Beethoven, hewing in memory
The ineffable forests of the last quartets)—
Trotzky in exile, too, in London walks
With Lenin, hears him speak exile's half-truth:
"Look: that's *their* Westminster there," as if
The father's features were the son's whole soul—
Yeats too, like Rilke, on old lords' estates,
Seeks for the permanent amid the loss,
Daily and desperate, of love, of friends,
Of every thought with which his age began—
Kafka in Prague works in an office, learns
How bureaucratic Life,
                    how far off God,
A white-collar class theology—
Perse is in Asia as a diplomat,
Finding the violent energy with which
Civilization creates itself and moves—
Yet with these images he cannot see
The moral apathy after the Munich Pact,
The unnatural silence on the Maginot Line,
Yet he cannot foresee the Fall of France—
Mann too, in Davos-Platz, finds in the sick
The triumph of the artist and the intellect—
All over Europe these exiles find in art
What exile is: art becomes exile too,
A secret and a code studied in secret,

Declaring the agony of modern life:
This child will learn of life from these great men,
He will participate in their solitude,
And maybe in the end, on such a night
As this, return to the starting-point, his name,
Showing himself as such, among his friends.

The Ballet of the Fifth Year

Where the sea gulls sleep or indeed where they fly
Is a place of different traffic. Although I
Consider the fishing bay (where I see them dip and curve
And purely glide) a place that weakens the nerve
Of will, and closes my eyes, as they should not be
(They should burn like the street-light all night quietly,
So that whatever is present will be known to me),
Nevertheless the gulls and the imagination
Of where they sleep, which comes to creation
In strict shape and color, from their dallying
Their wings slowly, and suddenly rallying
Over, up, down the arabesque of descent,
Is an old act enacted, my fabulous intent
When I skated, afraid of policemen, five years old,
In the winter sunset, sorrowful and cold,
Hardly attained to thought, but old enough to know
Such grace, so self-contained, was the best escape to know.

Muriel Rukeyser

1913-

Effort at Speech Between Two People

Speak to me.   Take my hand.   What are you now?
I will tell you all.   I will conceal nothing.
When I was three, a little child read a story about a rabbit
who died, in the story, and I crawled under a chair:

a pink rabbit: it was my birthday, and a candle
burnt a sore spot on my finger, and I was told to be happy.

Oh, grow to know me.   I am not happy.   I will be open:
Now I am thinking of white sails against a sky like music,
like glad horns blowing, and birds tilting, and an arm about
me.
There was one I loved, who wanted to live, sailing.

Speak to me.   Take my hand.   What are you now?
When I was nine, I was fruitily sentimental,
fluid: and my widowed aunt played Chopin,
and I bent my head on the painted woodwork, and wept.
I want now to be close to you.   I would
link the minutes of my days close, somehow, to your days.

I am not happy.   I will be open.
I have liked lamps in evening corners, and quiet poems.
There has been fear in my life.   Sometimes I speculate
On what a tragedy his life was, really.

Take my hand.   Fist my mind in your hand.   What are
you now?
When I was fourteen, I had dreams of suicide,
and I stood at a steep window, at sunset, hoping toward death:
if the light had not melted clouds and plains to beauty,
if light had not transformed that day, I would have leapt.
I am unhappy.   I am lonely.   Speak to me.

I will be open.   I think he never loved me:
he loved the bright beaches, the little lips of foam
that ride small waves, he loved the veer of gulls:
he said with a gay mouth: I love you.   Grow to know me.

What are you now?   If we could touch one another,
if these our separate entities could come to grips,
clenched like a Chinese puzzle . . . yesterday
I stood in a crowded street that was live with people,
and no one spoke a word, and the morning shone.
Everyone silent, moving. . . . Take my hand.   Speak to me.

Boy with His Hair Cut Short

Sunday shuts down on this twentieth-century evening.
The L passes. Twilight and bulb define
the brown room, the overstuffed plum sofa,
the boy, and the girl's thin hands above his head.
A neighbor radio sings stocks, news, serenade.

He sits at the table, head down, the young clear neck exposed,
watching the drugstore sign from the tail of his eye;
tattoo, neon, until the eye blears, while his
solicitous tall sister, simple in blue, bending
behind him, cuts his hair with her cheap shears.

The arrow's electric red always reaches its mark,
successful neon! He coughs, impressed by that precision.
His child's forehead, forever protected by his cap,
is bleached against the lamplight as he turns head
and steadies to let the snippets drop.

Erasing the failure of weeks with level fingers,
she sleeks the fine hair, combing: "You'll look fine tomorrow!
You'll surely find something, they can't keep turning you down;
the finest gentleman's not so trim as you!" Smiling, he raises
the adolescent forehead wrinkling ironic now.

He sees his decent suit laid out, new-pressed,
his carfare on the shelf. He lets his head fall, meeting
her earnest hopeless look, seeing the sharp blades splitting,
the darkened room, the impersonal sign, her motion,
the blue vein, bright on her temple, pitifully beating.

Ajanta

(The title refers to the caves of that name in India, on whose walls appear the great frescoes, with their religious analogy between space and the space of the body, and their acceptance of reality which may be filled with creation.)

Came in my full youth to the midnight cave
nerves ringing; and this thing I did alone.
Wanting my fulness and not a field of war,
for the world considered annihilation, a star

called Wormwood rose and flickered, shattering
bent light over the dead boiling up in the ground,
the biting yellow of their corrupted lives
streaming to war, denying all our words.
Nothing was left among the tainted weather
but world-walking and the shadowless Ajanta.
Hallucination and the metal laugh
in clouds, and the mountain-spectre riding storm.
Nothing was certain but a moment of peace,
a hollow behind the unbreakable waterfall.
All the way to the cave, the teeming forms of death,
and death, the price of the body, cheap as air.
I blessed my heart on the expiation journey
for it had never been unable to suffer:
when I met the man whose face looked like the future,
when I met the whore with the dying red hair,
the child myself who is my murderer.
So came I between heaven and my grave
past the serene smile of the *voyeur,* to
this cave where the myth enters the heart again.

II. THE CAVE

Space to the mind, the painted cave of dream.
This is not a womb, nothing but good emerges:
this is a stage, neither unreal nor real
where the walls are the world, the rocks and palaces
stand on a borderland of blossoming ground.
If you stretch your hand, you touch the slope of the world
reaching in interlaced gods, animals, and men.
There is no background. The figures hold their peace
in a web of movement. There is no frustration,
every gesture is taken, everything yields connections.
The heavy sensual shoulders, the thighs, the blood-born flesh
and earth turning into color, rocks into their crystals,
water to sound, fire to form; life flickers
uncounted into the supple arms of love.
The space of these walls is the body's living space;
tear open your ribs and breathe the color of time
where nothing leads away, the world comes forward
in flaming sequences. Pillars and prisms. Riders
and horses and the figures of consciousness,
red cow grows long, goes running through the world.
Flung into movement in carnal purity,
these bodies are sealed—warm lip and crystal hand
in a jungle of light. Color-sheeted, seductive

foreboding eyelid lowered on the long eye,
fluid and vulnerable. The spaces of the body
are suddenly limitless, and riding flesh
shapes constellations over the golden breast,
confusion of scents and illuminated touch—
monster touch, the throat printed with brightness,
wide outlined gesture where the bodies ride.
Bells, and the spirit flashing. The religious bells,
bronze under the sunlight like beasts ringing,
bronze in the closed air, the memory of walls,
great sensual shoulders in the web of time.

III. LES TENDRESSES BESTIALES

A procession of caresses alters the ancient sky
until new constellations are the body shining:
There's the Hand to steer by, there the horizon Breast,
and the Great Stars kindling the fluid hill.
All the rooms open into magical boxes,
nothing is tilted, everything flickers
sexual and exquisite.
The panther with its throat along my arm
turns black and flows away.
Deep in all streets passes a faceless whore
and the checkered men are whispering one word.
The face I know becomes the night-black rose.
The sharp face is now an electric fan
and says one word to me.
The dice and the alcohol and the destruction
have drunk themselves and cast.
Broken bottle of loss, and the glass
turned bloody into the face.
Now the scene comes forward, very clear.
Dream-singing, airborne, surrenders the recalled,
the gesture arrives riding over the breast,
singing, singing, tender atrocity,
the silver derelict wearing fur and claws.
Oh love, I stood under the apple branch,
I saw the whipped bay and the small dark islands,
and night sailing the river and the foghorn's word.
My life said to you: I want to love you well.
The wheel goes back and I shall live again,
but the wave turns, my birth arrives and spills
over my breast the world bearing my grave,
and your eyes open in earth. You touched my life.
My life reaches the skin, moves under your smile,

and your shoulders and your throat and your face and your
thighs
flash.
I am haunted by interrupted acts,
introspective as a leper, enchanted
by a repulsive clew,
a gross and fugitive movement of the limbs.
Is this the love that shook the lights to flame?
Sheeted avenues thrash in the wind,
torn streets, the savage parks.
I am plunged deep. Must find the midnight cave.

IV. BLACK BLOOD

A habit leading to murder, smoky laughter
hated at first, but necessary later.
Alteration of motives. To stamp in terror
around the deserted harbor, down the hill
until the woman laced into a harp
screams and screams and the great clock strikes,
swinging its giant figures past the face.
The Floating Man rides on the ragged sunset
asking and asking. Do not say, Which loved?
Which was beloved? Only, Who most enjoyed?
Armored ghost of rage, screaming and powerless.
Only find me and touch my blood again.
Find me. A girl runs down the street
singing Take me, yelling Take me Take
Hang me from the clapper of a bell
and you as hangman ring it sweet tonight,
for nothing clean in me is more than cloud
unless you call it.—As I ran I heard
a black voice beating among all that blood:
"Try to live as if there were a God."

V. THE BROKEN WORLD

Came to Ajanta cave, the painted space of the breast,
the real world where everything is complete,
there are no shadows, the forms of incompleteness.
The great cloak blows in the light, rider and horse arrive,
the shoulders turn and every gift is made.
No shadows fall. There is no source of distortion.
In our world, a tree casts the shadow of a woman,
a man the shadow of a phallus, a hand raised
the shadow of the whip.
Here everything is itself,

here all may stand on summer earth.
Brightness has overtaken every light,
and every myth netted itself in flesh.
New origins, and peace given entire
and the spirit alive.
In the shadowless cave
the naked arm is raised.
Animals arrive,
interlaced, and gods
interlaced, and men
flame-woven.
I stand and am complete.
Crawls from the door,
black at my two feet
the shadow of the world.
World, not yet one,
enters the heart again.
The naked world, and the old noise of tears,
the fear, the expiation and the love,
a world of the shadowed and alone.
The journey, and the struggles of the moon.

Karl Shapiro

1913-

The Leg

Among the iodoform, in twilight-sleep,
What have I lost? he first inquires,
Peers in the middle distance where a pain,
Ghost of a nurse, hazily moves, and day,
Her blinding presence pressing in his eyes
And now his ears. They are handling him
With rubber hands. He wants to get up.

One day beside some flowers near his nose
He will be thinking, *When will I look at it?*

And pain, still in the middle distance, will reply
At what? and he will know it's gone,
O where! and begin to tremble and cry.
He will begin to cry as a child cries
Whose puppy is mangled under a screaming wheel.

Later, as if deliberately, his fingers
Begin to explore the stump. He learns a shape
That is comfortable and tucked in like a sock.
This has a sense of humor, this can despise
The finest surgical limb, the dignity of limping,
The nonsense of wheel-chairs. Now he smiles to the wall:
The amputation becomes an acquisition.

For the leg is wondering where he is (all is not lost)
And surely he has a duty to the leg;
He is its injury, the leg is his orphan,
He must cultivate the mind of the leg,
Pray for the part that is missing, pray for peace
In the image of man, pray, pray for its safety,
And after a little it will die quietly.

The body, what is it, Father, but a sign
To love the force that grows us, to give back
What in Thy palm is senselessness and mud?
Knead, knead the substance of our understanding
Which must be beautiful in flesh to walk,
That if Thou take me angrily in hand
And hurl me to the shark, I shall not die!

The Dome of Sunday

With focus sharp as Flemish-painted face
In film of varnish brightly fixed
And through a polished hand-lens deeply seen,
Sunday at noon through hyaline thin air
Sees down the street,
And in the camera of my eye depicts
Row-houses and row-lives:
Glass after glass, door after door the same,
Face after face the same, the same,
The brutal visibility the same;

As if one life emerging from one house
Would pause, a single image caught between
Two facing mirrors where vision multiplies
Beyond perspective,
A silent clatter in the high-speed eye
Spinning out photo-circulars of sight.

I see slip to the curb the long machines
Out of whose warm and windowed rooms pirouette
Shellacked with silk and light
The hard legs of our women.
Our women are one woman, dressed in black.
The carmine printed mouth
And cheeks as soft as muslin-glass belong
Outright to one dark dressy man
Merely a swagger at her curvy side.

This is their visit to themselves:
All day from porch to porch they weave
A nonsense pattern through the even glare,
Stealing in surfaces
Cold vulgar glances at themselves.

And high up in the heated room all day
I wait behind the plate glass pane for one,
Hot as a voyeur for a glimpse of one,
The vision to blot out this woman's sheen;
All day my sight records expensively
Row-houses and row-lives.

But nothing happens; no diagonal
With melting shadow falls across the curb:
Neither the blinded negress lurching through fatigue
Nor exiles bleeding from their pores,
Nor that bright bomb slipped lightly from its rack
To splinter every silvered glass and crystal prism,
Witch-bowl and perfume bottle
And billion candle-power dressing-bulb,
No direct hit to smash the shatter-proof
And lodge at last the quivering needle
Clean in the eye of one who stands transfixed
In fascination of her brightness.

October 1

That season when the leaf deserts the bole
And half-dead see-saws through the October air
Falling face-downward on the walks to print
The decalcomania of its little soul—
Hardly has the milkman's sleepy horse
On wooden shoes echoed across the blocks,
When with its back jaws open like a dredge
The van comes lumbering up the curb to someone's door and
knocks.

And four black genii muscular and shy
Holding their shy caps enter the first room
Where someone hurriedly surrenders up
The thickset chair, the mirror half awry,
Then to their burdens stoop without a sound.
One with his bare hands rends apart the bed,
One stuffs the china-barrel with stale print,
To bear the sofa toward the door with dark funereal tread.

The corner lamp, the safety eye of night,
Enveloped in the sun blinks and goes blind
And soon the early risers pick their way
Through kitchenware and pillows bolt upright.
The bureau on the sidewalk with bare back
And wrinkling veneer is most disgraced,
The sketch of Paris suffers in the wind,
Only the bike, its nose against the wall, does not show haste.

Two hours—the movers mop their neck and look
Filing through dust and echoes back and forth.
The halls are hollow and all the floors are cleared
Bare to the last board, to the most secret nook;
But on the street a small chaos survives
That slowly now the leviathan ingests,
And schoolboys and stenographers stare at
The truck, the house, the husband in his hat who stands and
rests.

He turns with miserable expectant face
And for the last time enters. On the wall
A picture-stain spreads from the nail-hole down.
Each object live and dead has left its trace.

He leaves his key; but as he quickly goes
This question comes behind: Did someone die?
Is someone rich or poor, better or worse?
What shall uproot a house and bring this care into his eye?

Poet

Il arrive que l'esprit demande la poesie

Left leg flung out, head cocked to the right,
Tweed coat or army uniform, with book,
Beautiful eyes, who is this walking down?
Who, glancing at the pane of glass looks sharp
And thinks it is not he—as when a poet
Comes swiftly on some half-forgotten poem
And loosely holds the page, steady of mind,
Thinking it is not his?

And when will *you* exist?—Oh, it is I,
Incredibly skinny, stooped, and neat as pie,
Ignorant as dirt, erotic as an ape,
Dreamy as puberty—with dirty hair!
Into the room like kangaroo he bounds,
Ears flopping like the most expensive hound's;
His chin receives all questions as he bows
Mouthing a green bon-bon.

Has no more memory than rubber. Stands
Waist-deep in heavy mud of thought and broods
At his own wetness. When he would get out,
To his surprise he lifts in air a phrase
As whole and clean and silvery as a fish.
Which jumps and dangles on his damned hooked grin,
But like a name-card on a man's lapel
Calls him a conscious fool.

And childlike he remembers all his life
And cannily constructs it, fact by fact,
As boys paste postage stamps in careful books,
Denoting pence and legends and profiles,
Nothing more valuable.—And like a thief,
His eyes glassed over and concealed with guilt,
Fondles his secrets like a case of tools,
And waits in empty doors.

By men despised for knowing what he is,
And by himself. But he exists for women.
As dolls to girls, as perfect wives to men,
So he to women. And to himself a thing,
All ages, epicene, without a trade.
To girls and wives always alive and fated;
To men and scholars always dead like Greek
        And always mistranslated.

Towards exile and towards shame he lures himself,
Tongue winding on his arm, and thinks like Eve
By biting apple will become most wise.
Sentio ergo sum: he feels his way
And words themselves stand up for him like Braille
And punch and perforate his parchment ear.
All language falls like Chinese on his soul,
        Image of song unsounded.

This is the coward's coward that in his dreams
Sees shapes of pain grow tall. Awake at night
He peers at sounds and stumbles at a breeze.
And none holds life less dear. For as a youth
Who by some accident observes his love
Naked and in some natural ugly act,
He turns with loathing and with flaming hands,
        Seared and betrayed by sight.

He is the business man, on beauty trades,
Dealer in arts and thoughts who, like the Jew,
Shall rise from slums and hated dialects
A tower of bitterness. Shall be always strange,
Hunted and then sought after. Shall be sat
Like an ambassador from another race
At tables rich with music. He shall eat flowers,
Chew honey and spit out gall. They shall all smile
        And love and pity him.

His death shall be by drowning. In that hour
When the last bubble of pure heaven's air
Hovers within his throat, safe on his bed,
A small eternal figurehead in terror,
He shall cry out and clutch his days of straw
Before the blackest wave. Lastly, his tomb
Shall list and founder in the troughs of grass.
        And none shall speak his name.

Buick

As a sloop with a sweep of immaculate wing on her delicate spine
And a keel as steel as a root that holds in the sea as she leans,
Leaning and laughing, my warm-hearted beauty, you ride, you ride,
You tack on the curves with parabola speed and a kiss of good-bye,
Like a thoroughbred sloop, my new high-spirited spirit, my kiss.

As my foot suggests that you leap in the air with your hips of a girl,
My finger that praises your wheel and announces your voices of song,
Flouncing your skirts, you blueness of joy, you flirt of politeness,
You leap, you intelligence, essence of wheelness with silvery nose,
And your platinum clocks of excitement stir like the hairs of a fern.

But how alien you are from the booming belts of your birth and the smoke
Where you turned on the stinging lathes of Detroit and Lansing at night
And shrieked at the torch in your secret parts and the amorous tests,
But now with your eyes that enter the future of roads you forget;
You are all instinct with your phosphorous glow and your streaking hair.

And now when we stop it is not as the bird from the shell that I leave
Or the leathery pilot who steps from his bird with a sneer of delight,
And not as the ignorant beast do you squat and watch me depart,
But with exquisite breathing you smile, with satisfaction of love,
And I touch you again as you tick in the silence and settle in sleep.

Necropolis

Even in death they prosper; even in the death
Where lust lies senseless and pride fallow
The mouldering owners of rents and labor
Prosper and improve the high hill.

For theirs is the stone whose name is deepest cut,
Theirs the facsimile temple, theirs
The iron acanthus and the hackneyed Latin,
The boxwood rows and all the birds.

And even in death the poor are thickly herded
In intimate congestion under streets and alleys.
Look at the standard sculpture, the cheap
Synonymous slabs, the machined crosses.

Yes, even in death the cities are unplanned.
The heirs govern from the old centers;
They will not remove. And the ludicrous angels,
Remains of the poor, will never fly
But only multiply in the green grass.

The Progress of Faust

He was born in Deutschland, as you would suspect,
And graduated in magic from Cracow
In Fifteen Five. His portraits show a brow
Heightened by science. The eye is indirect,
As of bent light upon a crooked soul,
And that he bargained with the Prince of Shame
For pleasures intellectually foul
Is known by every court that lists his name.

His frequent disappearances are put down
To visits in the regions of the damned
And to the periodic deaths he shammed,
But, unregenerate and in Doctor's gown,
He would turn up to lecture at the fair
And do a minor miracle for a fee.
Many a life he whispered up the stair
To teach the black art of anatomy.

He was as deaf to angels as an oak
When, in the fall of Fifteen Ninety-four,
He went to London and crashed through the floor
In mock damnation of the playgoing folk.
Weekending with the scientific crowd,
He met Sir Francis Bacon and helped draft
"Colours of Good and Evil" and read aloud
An obscene sermon at which no one laughed.

He toured the Continent for a hundred years
And subsidized among the peasantry
The puppet play, his tragic history;
With a white glove he boxed the devil's ears
And with a black his own. Tired of this,
He published penny poems about his sins,
In which he placed the heavy emphasis
On the white glove which, for a penny, wins.

Some time before the hemorrhage of the Kings
Of France, he turned respectable and taught;
Quite suddenly everything that he had thought
Seemed to grow scholars' beards and angels' wings.
It was the Overthrow. On Reason's throne
He sat with the fair Phrygian on his knees
And called all universities his own,
As plausible a figure as you please.

Then back to Germany as the sages' sage
To preach comparative science to the young
Who came from every land in a great throng
And knew they heard the master of the age.
When for a secret formula he paid
The devil another fragment of his soul,
The scholars wept, and several even prayed
That Satan would restore him to them whole.

Backwardly tolerant, Faustus was expelled
From the Third Reich in Nineteen Thirty-nine.
His exit caused the breaching of the Rhine,
Except for which the frontier might have held.
Five years unknown to enemy and friend
He hid, appearing on the sixth to pose
In an American desert at war's end
Where, at his back, a dome of atoms rose.

From "Adam and Eve"

THE SICKNESS OF ADAM

In the beginning, at every step, he turned
As if by instinct to the East to praise
The nature of things. Now every path was learned
He lost the lifted, almost flower-like gaze

Of a temple dancer. He began to walk
Slowly, like one accustomed to be alone.
He found himself lost in the field of talk;
Thinking became a garden of its own.

In it were new things: words he had never said,
Beasts he had never seen and knew were not
In the true garden, terrors, and tears shed
Under a tree by him, for some new thought.

And the first anger. Once he flung a staff
At softly coupling sheep and struck the ram.
It broke away. And God heard Adam laugh
And for his laughter made the creature lame.

And wanderlust. He stood upon the Wall
To search the unfinished countries lying wide
And waste, where not a living thing could crawl,
And yet he would descend, as if to hide.

His thought drew down the guardian at the gate,
To whom man said, "What danger am I in?"
And the angel, hurt in spirit, seemed to hate
The wingless thing that worried after sin,

For it said nothing but marvelously unfurled
Its wings and arched them shimmering overhead,
Which must have been the signal from the world
That the first season of our life was dead.

Adam fell down with labor in his bones,
And God approached him in the cool of day
And said, "This sickness in your skeleton
Is longing. I will remove it from your clay."

He said also, "I made you strike the sheep."
It began to rain and God sat down beside
The sinking man. When he was fast asleep
He wet his right hand deep in Adam's side

And drew the graceful rib out of his breast.
Far off, the latent streams began to flow
And birds flew out of Paradise to nest
On earth. Sadly the angel watched them go.

THE RECOGNITION OF EVE

Whatever it was she had so fiercely fought
Had fled back to the sky, but still she lay
With arms outspread, awaiting its assault,
Staring up through the branches of the tree,
The fig tree. Then she drew a shuddering breath
And turned her head instinctively his way.
She had fought birth as dying men fight death.

Her sigh awakened him. He turned and saw
A body swollen, as though formed of fruits,
White as the flesh of fishes, soft and raw.
He hoped she was another of the brutes
So he crawled over and looked into her eyes,
The human wells that pool all absolutes.
It was like looking into double skies.

And when she spoke the first word (it was *thou*)
He was terror-stricken, but she raised her hand
And touched his wound where it was fading now,
For he must feel the place to understand.
Then he recalled the longing that had torn
His side, and while he watched it whitely mend,
He felt it stab him suddenly like a thorn.

He thought the woman had hurt him. Was it she
Or the same sickness seeking to return;
Or was there any difference, the pain set free
And she who seized him now as hard as iron?
Her fingers bit his body. She looked old
And involuted, like the newly born.
He let her hurt him till she loosed her hold.

Then she forgot him and she wearily stood
And went in search of water through the grove.

Adam could see her wandering through the wood,
Studying her footsteps as her body wove
In light and out of light. She found a pool
And there he followed shyly to observe.
She was already turning beautiful.

Randall Jarrell

1914-

Burning the Letters

(The wife of a pilot killed in the Pacific is speaking several years after his death. She was once a Christian, a Protestant.)

Here in my head, the home that is left for you,
You have not changed; the flames rise from the sea
And the sea changes: the carrier, torn in two,
Sinks to its planes—the corpses of the carrier
Are strewn like ashes on the star-reflecting sea;
Are gathered, sewn with weights, are sunk.
The gatherers disperse.
Here to my hands
From the sea's dark, incalculable calm,
The unchanging circle of the universe,
The letters float: the set yellowing face
Looks home to me, a child's at last,
From the cut-out paper; and the licked
Lips part in their last questioning smile.
The poor labored answers, still unanswering;
The faded questions—questioning so much,
I thought then—questioning so little;
Grew younger, younger, as my eyes grew old,
As that dreamed-out and wept-for wife,
Your last unchanging country, changed
Out of your own rejecting life—a part
Of accusation and of loss, a child's eternally—
Into my troubled separate being.

A child has her own faith, a child's.
In its savage figures—worn down, now, to death—
Men's one life issues, neither out of earth
Nor from the sea, the last dissolving sea,
But out of death: by man came death
And his Life wells from death, the death of Man.
The hunting flesh, the broken blood
Glimmer within the tombs of earth, the food
Of the lives that burrow under the hunting wings
Of the light, of the darkness: dancing, dancing,
The flames grasp flesh with their last searching grace—
Grasp as the lives have grasped: the hunted
Pull down the hunter for his unused life
Parted into the blood, the dark, veined bread
Later than all law. The child shudders, aging:
The peering savior, stooping to her clutch,
His talons cramped with his own bartered flesh,
Pales, flickers, and flares out. In the darkness—darker
With the haunting after-images of light—
The dying God, the eaten Life
Are the nightmare I awaken from to night.

(The flames dance over life. The mourning slaves
In their dark secrecy, come burying
The slave bound in another's flesh, the slave
Freed once, forever, by another's flesh:
The Light flames, flushing the passive face
With its eternal life.)
                                        The lives are fed
Into the darkness of their victory;
The ships sink, forgotten; and the sea
Blazes to darkness: the unsearchable
Death of the lives lies dark upon the life
That, bought by death, the loved and tortured lives,
Stares westward, passive, to the blackening sea.
In the tables of the dead, in the unopened almanac,
The head, charred, featureless—the unknown mean—
Is thrust from the waters like a flame, is torn
From its last being with the bestial cry
Of its pure agony. O death of all my life,
Because of you, because of you, I have not died,
By your death I have lived.
                                        The sea is empty.
As I am empty, stirring the charred and answered
Questions about your home, your wife, your cat

That stayed at home with me—that died at home
Gray with the years that gleam above you there
In the great green grave where you are young
And unaccepting still. Bound in your death,
I choose between myself and you, between your life
And my own life: it is finished.

Here in my head
There is room for your black body in its shroud,
The dog-tags welded to your breastbone, and the flame
That winds above your death and my own life
And the world of my life. The letters and the face
That stir still, sometimes, with your fiery breath—
Take them, O grave! Great grave of all my years,
The unliving universe in which all life is lost,
Make yours the memory of that accepting
And accepted life whose fragments I cast here.

Hope

The spirit killeth, but the
letter giveth life.

The week is dealt out like a hand
That children pick up card by card.
One keeps getting the same hand.
One keeps getting the same card.

But twice a day—except on Saturday—
But every day—except on Sunday—
The wheel stops, there is a catch in Time:
With a hiss of soles, a rattle of tin,
My own gray Daemon pauses on the stair,
My own bald Fortune lifts me by the hair.

Woe's me! Woe's me! In Folly's mailbox
Still laughs the postcard, Hope:
Your uncle in Australia
Has died and you are Pope.
For many a soul has entertained
A Mailman unawares—
And as you cry, "Impossible,"
A step is on the stairs.

One keeps getting the same dream
Delayed, marked Postage Due,
The bill that one has paid
Delayed, marked Payment Due,

Twice a day, in a rotting mailbox,
The white grubs are new:
And Faith once more is mine
Faithfully, but Charity
Writes hopefully about a new
Asylum—but Hope is as good as new.

Woe's me! Woe's me! In Folly's mailbox
Still laughs the postcard, Hope:
Your uncle in Australia
Has died and you are Pope.
For many a soul has entertained
A Mailman unawares—
And as you cry, "Impossible,"
A step is on the stairs.

The Refugees

In the shabby train no seat is vacant.
The child in the ripped mask
Sits undisturbed in the waste
Of the smashed compartment. But how shall I escape?
These had lives like mine. What was it they possessed
That they were willing to trade for this?

There is blood, dried now, along the mask
Of the child who yesterday possessed
A country welcomer than this.
Did he? All night into the waste
The train moves silently, the vacant
Breath rises, vanishes—Escape, escape!

One pays, for this freedom, all that one possessed;
Here all the purses are vacant.
Sleep; and the emptying hearts escape
Even their own wish—turn back to this
Nothing that hides, with its calm cancelling mask,
The days and the faces: the world they waste.

What else are the lives but a journey to the vacant
Satisfaction of death? And the mask
They wear tonight through their waste
Is death's rehearsal. *For I too shall escape,*
We read in the faces; and what is there we possessed
That we were unwilling to trade for this?

90 North

At home, in my flannel gown, like a bear to its floe,
I clambered to bed; up the globe's impossible sides
I sailed all night—till at last, with my black beard,
My furs and my dogs, I stood at the northern pole.

There in the childish night my companions lay frozen,
The stiff furs knocked at my starveling throat,
And I gave my great sigh—the flakes came huddling;
Were they really my end? In the darkness I turned to my rest.

Here, the flag snaps in the glare and silence
Of the unbroken ice. And I stand here,
The dogs bark, my beard is black, and I stare
At the North Pole. And now what? Why, go back.

Turn as I please, my step is to the south.
The world—my world—spins on this final point
Of cold and wretchedness: all lines, all winds
End in this whirlpool I at last discover.

And it is meaningless. In the child's bed
After the night's voyage, in that warm world
Where people work and suffer till the death
That crowns the pain—in that Cloud-Cuckoo-Land

I reached my North and it had meaning.
Here at the actual pole of my existence,
Where all that I have done is meaningless,
Where I live or die by accident alone—

Where, living or dying, I am still alone;
Here where North, the night, the berg of death
Crowd to me out of the ignorant darkness,
I see at last that all the knowledge

I wrung from the darkness—that the darkness flung me—
Is worthless as ignorance: nothing comes from nothing,
The darkness from the darkness. Pain comes from the darkness
And we call it wisdom. It is pain.

Pilots, Man Your Planes

(A Jill is a Japanese torpedo-plane.)

Dawn; and the jew's-harp's sawing seesaw song
Plucks at the starlight where the planes are folded
At the lee of their blank, wind-whipped, hunting road—
A road in air, the road to nowhere
Turreted and bucketed with guns, long undermined
With the thousand necessary deaths that breathe
Like fire beside a thousand men, who sleep
Hunched in the punk of Death: slow, dreaming sparks
That burrow through the block-long, light-split gloom
Of their great hangar underground and oversea
Into the great tanks, dark forever; past the steam
Of turbines, laundries—under rockets,
Bakeries, war-heads, the steel watch-like fish,
To the hull's last plates and atmosphere:
The sea sways with the dazed, blind, groping sway
Of the raw soul drugged with sleep, the chancy life
Troubling with dreams its wars, its owned earned sea
That stretches year on year, death after death,
And hemisphere on blind black hemisphere
Into the stubborn corners of its earth.

Here in the poor, bleak, guessing haze of dawn
The giant's jew's-harp screeches its two notes
Over and over, over and over, from the roar
Of the fighters waved into the blazing clouds
The lookout lifts his scrubbed tetanic stare
Into the East of light, the empty day.
But on the tubes the raiders oscillate
A mile in every nine or thirteen seconds
To the target's first premonitory bursts;
To the boy with a ball of coffee in his stomach,
Snapping the great light buckles on his groin,
Shifting his raft's hot-water-bottle weight

As he breasts the currents of the bellowing deck
And, locked at last into the bubble, Hope,
Is borne along the foaming windy road
To the air where he alone is still
Above the world's cold, absent, searching roll.

The carrier meshed in its white whirling wake,
The gray ship sparkling from the blue-black sea,
The little carrier—erupts in flak,
One hammering, hysterical, tremendous fire.
Flickering through flashes, the stained rolling clouds,
The air jarred like water tilted in a bowl,
The red wriggling tracers—colonies
Whose instant life annexes the whole sky—
Hunt out the one end they have being for,
Are metamorphosed into one pure smear
Of flame, and die
In the maniacal convulsive spin
Of the raider with a wing snapped off, the plane
Trailing its flaming kite's-tail to the wave.
A miss's near, near bloom, a hill of foam,
Is bulged skyward, crashes back; crest after crest
Patterns the ships' cat's-cradle wakes, the racing
Swells that hiss outward from a plane's quenched flame:
There is traced in the thousand meetings of the grave
Of matter and of matter, man and man,
The print of the running feet upon the waves . . .
The Jill threads her long, blind, unbearable
Way into fire (the waves lick past her, her whole sky
Is tracer and the dirt of flak, the fire
Flung from the muzzles riddling sea and sky),
Comes on, comes on, comes on; and the fighter flames to her
Through his own flak, the hammering guns
Stitch one long line along his wing, his gear
Falls, his dive staggers as his tracer strikes,
And he breaks off and somersaults into the sea.
Under the canopy's dark strangling green,
The darkening canopy, he struggles free
To float into the choking white, to breathe—
His huge leg floating and immovable,
His goggles blackened with his own bright blood—
On the yellow raft, to see his carrier
Still firing, but itself a fire, its planes
Flung up like matches from the stern's white burst.
Now rockets arch above the deck's great blaze,

Shells break from it, trail after trail; its steel
Melts in steam into the sea, its tanks explode
In one last overwhelming sound; and silently
The ship, a flame, sinks home into the sea.
The pilot holds his striped head patiently
Up out of the dancing smother of the sea
And weeps with hatred, longing, agony—
The sea rises and settles; and the ship is gone.

The planes fly off looking for a carrier,
Destroyers curve in their long hunting arcs
Through the dead of the carrier: the dazed, vomiting,
Oil-blackened and fire-blistered, saved or dying men
Cling with cramped shaking fingers to the lines
Lowered from their old life: the pilot,
Drugged in a blanket, straining up to gulp
From the mug that scrapes like chalk against his mouth,
Knows, knows at last; he yawns the chattering yawn
Of effort and anguish, of hurt hating helplessness—
Yawns sobbingly, his head falls back, he sleeps.

John Malcolm Brinnin

1916-

At the Airport

Here, at the airport, waiting,
Watching the schedule by
The opulent calm of a match,
I think: the cold, unpeopled stars
This hutch of night that wears
A floodlight for an eye,
Have turned against my hope.

When silence broadens: swinging,
Whipped by the wind, the little
Zeppelins report a change;
And from the glassy tower goes
Immediately its subtle news:
Over the moonlike lakes
Whose wings? Whose ancient name?

On margins of the field, cattle
Make their slow and noiseless rounds,
Imprinting daisies or
A singular cleft hoof in mud;
Degenerate, soft-eyed, they plod
Without expectancy;
Sometimes, even, they sleep.

A signal's up! The humming
Imminence of wings
Berates the thoughtful ear;
I underline my schedule with
A fingernail; across the path
Of light, and lazily,
The great eyes land with pride.

All those I've loved in any
History have come;
Their presence, like a wreath
Of pain, sits coldly on my skull;
Puzzled, resigned to good or ill,
Yet fearing recognition,
I watch them evilly.

Do I dare to greet them, calling
"This is the place, this is
The one who telegraphed?"
Emerging single file, they seem
Like statues scissored from a dream,
Except that in their eyes
The past has turned to stone.

I turn into the City;
Let them wonder who it was
That brought them here, who called
Across the distances as if
Their presence meant his very life;

The City is more kind
With stranger citizens.

Now when I hear my pillow
Hum with those approaching wings,
I remember how they came
Out of the heavenly dark that night;
Only a ghost would choose to wait,
Among the quiet cattle,
Their coming down again.

Nuns at Eve

On St. Martin's evening green
Imaginary diamond, between
The vestry buttress and the convent wall,
Solemn as sea-birds in a sanctuary,
Under the statue of the Virgin they play baseball.
They are all named Mary,
Sister Mary, Mary Anthony, or Mary Rose,
And when the softball flies
In the shadow of the cross
The little chaplet of the Virgin's hands
Contains their soft excitements like a house.

A flying habit traces
The unprecedented rounding of the bases
By Sister Mary Agatha, who thanks God
For the easy triple and turns her eyes toward home;
As *Mary, Mother, Help Me* echoes in her head,
Mild cries from the proud team
Encourage her, and the obliging sun,
Dazzling the pitcher's box
With a last celestial light upon
The gold-spiked halo of the Virgin in her niche,
Leads Sister Mary John to a wild pitch.

Prayer wins the game.
As Sister Mary Agatha comes sailing home
Through infield dusk, like birds fan-wise
In the vague cloisters of slow-rising mist,
Winners and losers gather in to praise
The fleetness of a bride of Christ.
Flushed and humble, Agatha collects the bats

And balls, while at her belt
Catcher's and pitcher's mitts
—Brute fingers, toes and gross lopsided heads—
Fumble the ropes of her long swinging beads.

Views of the Favorite Colleges

Approaching by the gate, (Class of '79,
All dead) the unimpressed new scholars find
Halls of archaic brick and, if it is April,
Three dazzling magnolias behind bars, like lions.

Unsettling winds among the pillars of wisdom
Assure them of harmonious extremes,
However academic. The bells, in key,
Covered with singing birds, ring on the hour.

Towering, but without aspiration, the campanile
Is known to sway an inch in a high wind;
But that, like the statue's changeable complexion,
Is natural. To find the unnatural,

Gradually absorb the industry
Of ten o'clock: the embryo pig slit through
With the proper instruments by embryos;
And Sophocles cut, for speed, with a blue pencil.

Prehensile sophomores in the tree of learning
Stare at the exiled blossoming trees, vaguely puzzled;
The lecturer, especially if bearded,
Enhances those druidical undertones.

What is the terminus of books? sing the birds.
Tell us about Sophocles! cry the trees.
And a crazy child on roller-skates skates through
The campus like a one-man thunderstorm.

Robert Lowell

1917-

The Holy Innocents

Listen, the hay-bells tinkle as the cart
Wavers on rubber tires along the tar
And cindered ice below the burlap mill
And ale-wife run. The oxen drool and start
In wonder at the fenders of a car
And blunder hugely up St. Peter's hill.
These are the undefiled by woman—their
Sorrow is not the sorrow of this world:
King Herod shrieking vengeance at the curled
Up knees of Jesus choking in the air,

A king of speechless clods and infants. Still
The world out-Herods Herod; and the year,
The nineteen-hundred forty-fifth of grace,
Lumbers with losses up the clinkered hill
Of our purgation; and the oxen near
The worn foundations of their resting place,
The holy manger where their bed is corn
And holly torn for Christmas. If they die,
As Jesus, in the harness, who will mourn?
Lamb of the shepherds, Child, how still you lie.

Colloquy in Black Rock

Here the jack-hammer jabs into the ocean;
My heart, you race and stagger and demand
More blood-gangs for your nigger-brass percussions,
Till I, the stunned machine of your devotion,
Clanging upon this cymbal of a hand,
Am rattled screw and footloose. All discussions

End in the mud-flat detritus of death.
My heart, beat faster, faster. In Black Mud
Hungarian workmen give their blood
For the martyre Stephen, who was stoned to death.

Black Mud, a name to conjure with: O mud
For watermelons gutted to the crust,
Mud for the mole-tide harbor, mud for mouse,
Mud for the armored Diesel fishing tubs that thud
A year and a day to wind and tide; the dust
Is on this skipping heart that shakes my house,

House of our Savior who was hanged till death.
My heart, beat faster, faster. In Black Mud
Stephen the martyre was broken down to blood:
Our ransom is the rubble of his death.

Christ walks on the black water. In Black Mud
Darts the kingfisher. On Corpus Christi, heart,
Over the drum-beat of St. Stephen's choir
I hear him, *Stupor Mundi,* and the mud
Flies from his hunching wings and beak—my heart,
The blue kingfisher dives on you in fire.

As a Plane Tree by the Water

Darkness has called to darkness, and disgrace
Elbows about our windows in this planned
Babel of Boston where our money talks
And multiplies the darkness of a land
Of preparation where the Virgin walks
And roses spiral her enamelled face
Or fall to splinters on unwatered streets.
Our Lady of Babylon, go by, go by,
I was once the apple of your eye;
Flies, flies are on the plane tree, on the streets.

The flies, the flies, the flies of Babylon
Buzz in my ear-drums while the devil's long
Dirge of the people detonates the hour
For floating cities where his golden tongue
Enchants the masons of the Babel Tower
To raise tomorrow's city to the sun
That never sets upon these hell-fire streets

Of Boston, where the sunlight is a sword
Striking at the withholder of the Lord:
Flies, flies are on the plane tree, on the streets.

Flies strike the miraculous waters of the iced
Atlantic and the eyes of Bernadette
Who saw Our Lady standing in the cave
At Massabielle, saw her so squarely that
Her vision put out reason's eyes. The grave
Is open-mouthed and swallowed up in Christ.
O walls of Jericho! And all the streets
To our Atlantic wall are singing: "Sing,
Sing for the resurrection of the King."
Flies, flies are on the plane tree, on the streets.

The Death of the Sheriff

"forsitan et Priami fuerint quae fata, requiras?"

Noli Me Tangere

We park and stare. A full sky of the stars
Wheels from the pumpkin setting of the moon
And sparks the windows of the yellow farm
Where the red-flannelled madmen look through bars
At windmills thrashing snowflakes by an arm
Of that Atlantic. Soon
The undertaker who collects antiques
Will let his motor idle at the door
And set his pine-box on the parlor floor.
Our homicidal sheriff howled for weeks;
We kiss. The State had reasons: on the whole,
It acted out of kindness when it locked
Its servant in this place and had him watched
Until an ordered darkness left his soul
A *tabula rasa;* when the Angel knocked
The sheriff laid his notched
Revolver on the table for the guest.
Night draws us closer in its bearskin wrap
And our loved sightless smother feels the tap
Of the blind stars descending to the west
To lay the Devil in the pit our hands
Are draining like a windmill. Who'll atone
For the unsearchable quicksilver heart
Where spiders stare their eyes out at their own

Spitting and knotted likeness? We must start:
Our aunt, his mother, stands
Singing *O Rock of Ages,* as the light
Wanderers show a man with a white cane
Who comes to take the coffin in his wain,
The thirsty Dipper on the arc of night.

Where the Rainbow Ends

I saw the sky descending, black and white,
Not blue, on Boston where the winters wore
The skulls to jack-o'-lanterns on the slates,
And Hunger's skin-and-bone retrievers tore
The chickadee and shrike. The thorn tree waits
Its victim and tonight
The worms will eat the deadwood to the foot
Of Ararat: the scythers, Time and Death,
Helmed locusts, move upon the tree of breath;
The wild ingrafted olive and the root

Are withered, and a winter drifts to where
The Pepperpot, ironic rainbow, spans
Charles River and its scales of scorched-earth miles
I saw my city in the Scales, the pans
Of judgment rising and descending. Piles
Of dead leaves char the air—
And I am a red arrow on this graph
Of Revelations. Every dove is sold.
The Chapel's sharp-shinned eagle shifts its hold
On serpent-Time, the rainbow's epitaph.

In Boston serpents whistle at the cold.
The victim climbs the altar steps and sings:
"Hosannah to the lion, lamb, and beast
Who fans the furnace-face of IS with wings:
I breathe the ether of my marriage feast."
At the high altar, gold
And a fair cloth. I kneel and the wings beat
My cheek. What can the dove of Jesus give
You now but wisdom, exile? Stand and live,
The dove has brought an olive branch to eat.

Children of Light

Our fathers wrung their bread from stocks and stones
And fenced their gardens with the Redman's bones;
Embarking from the Nether Land of Holland,
Pilgrims unhouseled by Geneva's night,
They planted here the Serpent's seeds of light;
And here the pivoting searchlights probe to shock
The riotous glass houses built on rock,
And candles gutter by an empty altar,
And light is where the landless blood of Cain
Is burning, burning the unburied grain.

Mr. Edwards and the Spider

I saw the spiders marching through the air,
Swimming from tree to tree that mildewed day
In latter August when the hay
Came creaking to the barn. But where
The wind is westerly,
Where gnarled November makes the spiders fly
Into the apparitions of the sky,
They purpose nothing but their ease and die
Urgently beating east to sunrise and the sea;

What are we in the hands of the great God?
It was in vain you set up thorn and briar
In battle array against the fire
And treason crackling in your blood;
For the wild thorns grow tame
And will do nothing to oppose the flame;
Your lacerations tell the losing game
You play against a sickness past your cure.
How will the hands be strong? How will the heart endure?

A very little thing, a little worm,
Or hourglass-blazoned spider, it is said,
Can kill a tiger. Will the dead
Hold up his mirror and affirm
To the four winds the smell

And flash of his authority? It's well
If God who holds you to the pit of hell,
Much as one holds a spider, will destroy,
Baffle and dissipate your soul. As a small boy

On Windsor Marsh, I saw the spider die
When thrown into the bowels of fierce fire:
There's no long struggle, no desire
To get up on its feet and fly—
It stretches out its feet
And dies. This is the sinner's last retreat;
Yes, and no strength exerted on the heat
Then sinews the abolished will, when sick
And full of burning, it will whistle on a brick.

But who can plumb the sinking of that soul?
Josiah Hawley, picture yourself cast
Into a brick-kiln where the blast
Fans your quick vitals to a coal—
If measured by a glass
How long would it seem burning! Let there pass
A minute, ten, ten trillion; but the blaze
Is infinite, eternal: this is death,
To die and know it. This is the Black Widow, death.

The Quaker Graveyard in Nantucket

(For Warren Winslow, dead at sea)

Let man have dominion over the fishes of the sea and the fowls of the air and the beasts and the whole earth, and every creeping creature that moveth upon the earth.

I

A brackish reach of shoal off Madaket,—
The sea was still breaking violently and night
Had steamed into our North Atlantic Fleet,
When the drowned sailor clutched the drag-net. Light
Flashed from his matted head and marble feet,
He grappled at the net
With the coiled, hurdling muscles of his thighs:
The corpse was bloodless, a botch of reds and whites,
Its open, staring eyes

Were lustreless dead-lights
Or cabin-windows on a stranded hulk
Heavy with sand. We weigh the body, close
Its eyes and heave it seaward whence it came,
Where the heel-headed dogfish barks its nose
On Ahab's void and forehead; and the name
Is blocked in yellow chalk.
Sailors, who pitch this portent at the sea
Where dreadnaughts shall confess
Its hell-bent deity,
When you are powerless
To sand-bag this Atlantic bulwark, faced
By the earth-shaker, green, unwearied, chaste
In his steel scales: ask for no Orphean lute
To pluck life back. The guns of the steeled fleet
Recoil and then repeat
The hoarse salute.

II

Whenever winds are moving and their breath
Heaves at the roped-in bulwarks of this pier,
The terns and sea-gulls tremble at your death
In these home waters. Sailor, can you hear
The Pequod's sea wings, beating landward, fall
Headlong and break on our Atlantic wall
Off 'Sconset, where the yawing S-boats splash
The bellbuoy, with ballooning spinnakers,
As the entangled, screeching mainsheet clears
The blocks: off Madaket, where lubbers lash
The heavy surf and throw their long lead squids
For blue-fish? Sea-gulls blink their heavy lids
Seaward. The winds' wings beat upon the stones,
Cousin, and scream for you and the claws rush
At the sea's throat and wring it in the slush
Of this old Quaker graveyard where the bones
Cry out in the long night for the hurt beast
Bobbing by Ahab's whaleboats in the East.

III

All you recovered from Poseidon died
With you, my cousin, and the harrowed brine
Is fruitless on the blue beard of the god,
Stretching beyond us to the castles in Spain,
Nantucket's westward haven. To Cape Cod
Guns, cradled on the tide,

Blast the eelgrass about a waterclock
Of bilge and backwash, roil the salt and sand
Lashing earth's scaffold, rock
Our warships in the hand
Of the great God, where time's contrition blues
Whatever it was these Quaker sailors lost
In the mad scramble of their lives. They died
When time was open-eyed,
Wooden and childish; only bones abide
There, in the nowhere, where their boats were tossed
Sky-high, where mariners had fabled news
Of Is, the swashing castle. What it cost
Them is their secret. In the monster's slick
I see the Quakers drown and hear their cry:
"If God himself had not been on our side,
If God himself had not been on our side,
When the Atlantic rose against us, why,
Then it had swallowed us up quick."

IV

This is the end of the whaleroad and the whale
Who spewed Nantucket bones on the thrashed swell
And stirred the troubled waters to whirlpools
To send the Pequod packing off to hell:
This is the end of them, three-quarters fools,
Snatching at straws to sail
Seaward and seaward on the turntail whale,
Spouting out blood and water as it rolls,
Sick as a dog to these Atlantic shoals:
Clamavimus, O depths. Let the sea-gulls wail

For water, for the deep where the high tide
Mutters to its hurt self, mutters and ebbs.
Waves wallow in their wash, go out and out,
Leave only the death-rattle of the crabs,
The beach increasing, its enormous snout
Sucking the ocean's side.
This is the end of running on the waves;
We are poured out like water. Who will dance
The mast-lashed master of Leviathans
Up from this field of Quakers in their unstoned graves?

V

When the whale's viscera go and the roll
Of its corruption overruns this world

Beyond tree-swept Nantucket and Wood's Hole
And Martha's Vineyard, Sailor, will your sword
Whistle and fall and sink into the fat?
In the great ash-pit of Jehoshaphat
The bones cry for the blood of the white whale,
The fat flukes arch and whack about its ears,
The death-lance churns into the sanctuary, tears
The gun-blue swingle, heaving like a flail,
And hacks the coiling life out: it works and drags
And rips the sperm-whale's midriff into rags,
Gobbets of blubber spill to wind and weather,
Sailor, and gulls go round the stoven timbers
Where the morning stars sing out together
And thunder shakes the white surf and dismembers
The red flag hammered in the mast-head. Hide
Our steel, Jonas Messias, in Thy side.

VI

Our Lady of Walsingham

There once the penitents took off their shoes
And then walked barefoot the remaining mile;
And the small trees, a stream and hedgerows file
Slowly along the munching English lane,
Like cows to the old shrine, until you lose
Track of your dragging pain.
The stream flows down under the druid tree,
Shiloah's whirlpools gurgle and make glad
The castle of God. Sailor, you were glad
And whistled Sion by that stream. But see:
Our Lady, too small for her canopy,
Sits near the altar. There's no comeliness
At all or charm in that expressionless
Face with its heavy eyelids. As before,
This face, for centuries a memory,
Non est species, neque decor,
Expressionless, expresses God: it goes
Past castled Sion. She knows what God knows,
Not Calvary's Cross nor crib at Bethlehem
Now, and the world shall come to Walsingham.

VII

The empty winds are creaking and the oak
Splatters and splatters on the cenotaph,

The boughs are trembling and a gaff
Bobs on the untimely stroke
Of the greased wash exploding on a shoal-bell
In the old mouth of the Atlantic. It's well;
Atlantic, you are fouled with the blue sailors,
Sea-monsters, upward angel, downward fish:
Unmarried and corroding, spare of flesh,
Mart once of supercilious, wing'd clippers;
Atlantic, where your bell-trap guts its spoil
You could cut the brackish winds with a knife
Here in Nantucket, and cast up the time
When the Lord God formed man from the sea's slime
And breathed into his face the breath of life,
And blue-lung'd combers lumbered to the kill.
The Lord survives the rainbow of his will.

Richard Wilbur

1921-

Potato

An underground grower, blind and a common brown;
Got a misshapen look, it's nudged where it could;
Simple as soil yet crowded as earth with all.

Cut open raw, it looses a cool clean stench,
Mineral acid seeping from pores of prest meal;
It is like breaching a strangely refreshing tomb:

Therein the taste of first stones, the hands of dead slaves,
Waters men drank in the earliest frightful woods,
Flint chips, and peat, and the cinders of buried camps.

Scrubbed under faucet water the planet skin
Polishes yellow, but tears to the plain insides;
Parching, the white's blue-hearted like hungry hands.

All of the cold dark kitchens, and war-frozen gray
Evening at window; I remember so many
Peeling potatoes quietly into chipt pails.

"It was potatoes saved us, they kept us alive."
Then they had something to say akin to praise
For the mean earth-apples, too common to cherish or steal.

Times being hard, the Sikh and the Senegalese,
Hobo and Okie, the body of Jesus the Jew,
Vestigial virtues, are eaten; we shall survive.

What has not lost its savor shall hold us up,
And we are praising what saves us, what fills the need.
(Soon there'll be packets again, with Algerian fruits.)

Oh, it will not bear polish, the ancient potato,
Needn't be nourished by Caesars, will blow anywhere,
Hidden by nature, counted-on, stubborn and blind.

You may have noticed the bush that it pushes to air,
Comical-delicate, sometimes with second-rate flowers
Awkward and milky and beautiful only to hunger.

Bell Speech

The selfsame toothless voice for death or bridal:
It has been long since men would give the time
To tell each someone's-change with a special chime,
And a toll for every year the dead walked through.
And mostly now, above this urgent idle
Town, the bells mark time, as they can do.

This bavardage of early and of late
Is what is wanted, and yet the bells beseech
By some excess that's in their stricken speech
Less meanly to be heard. Were this not so,
Why should Great Paul shake every window plate
To warn me that my pocket watch is slow?

Whether or not attended, bells will chant
With a clear dumb sound, and wide of any word
Expound our hours, clear as the waves are heard

Crashing at Mount Desert, from far at sea,
And dumbly joining, as the night's descent
Makes deltas into dark of every tree.

Great Paul, great pail of sound, still dip and draw
Dark speech from the deep and quiet steeple well,
Bring dark for doctrine, do but dim and quell
All voice in yours, while earth will give you breath.
Still gather to a language without flaw
Our loves, and all the hours of our death.

Juggler

A ball will bounce, but less and less. It's not
A light-hearted thing, resents its own resilience.
Falling is what it loves, and the earth falls
So in our hearts from brilliance,
Settles and is forgot.
It takes a sky-blue juggler with five red balls

To shake our gravity up. Whee, in the air
The balls roll round, wheel on his wheeling hands,
Learning the ways of lightness, alter to spheres
Grazing his finger ends,
Cling to their courses there,
Swinging a small heaven about his ears.

But a heaven is easier made of nothing at all
Than the earth regained, and still and sole within
The spin of worlds, with a gesture sure and noble
He reels that heaven in,
Landing it ball by ball,
And trades it all for a broom, a plate, a table.

Oh, on his toe the table is turning, the broom's
Balancing up on his nose, and the plate whirls
On the tip of the broom! Damn, what a show, we cry:
The boys stamp, and the girls
Shriek, and the drum booms
And all comes down, and he bows and says good-bye.

If the juggler is tired now, if the broom stands
In the dust again, if the table starts to drop

Through the daily dark again, and though the plate
Lies flat on the table top,
For him we batter our hands
Who has won for once over the world's weight.

Tywater

Death of Sir Nihil, book the *nth,*
Upon the charred and clotted sward,
Lacking the lily of our Lord,
Alases of the hyacinth.

Could flicker from behind his ear
A whistling silver throwing knife
And with a holler punch the life
Out of a swallow in the air.

Behind the lariat's butterfly
Shuttled his white and gritted grin,
And cuts of sky would roll within
The noose-hole, when he spun it high.

The violent, neat and practiced skill
Was all he loved and all he learned;
When he was hit, his body turned
To clumsy dirt before it fell.

And what to say of him, God knows.
Such violence. And such repose.

In the Elegy Season

Haze, char, and the weather of All Souls':
A giant absence mopes upon the trees:
Leaves cast in casual potpourris
Whisper their scents from pits and cellar-holes.

Or brewed in gulleys, steeped in wells, they spend
In chilly steam their last aromas, yield
From shallow hells a revenance of field
And orchard air. And now the envious mind

Which could not hold the summer in my head
While bounded by that blazing circumstance
Parades these barrens in a golden trance,
Remembering the wealthy season dead,

And by an autumn inspiration makes
A summer all its own. Green boughs arise
Through all the boundless backward of the eyes,
And the soul bathes in warm conceptual lakes.

Less proud than this, my body leans an ear
Past cold and colder weather after wings'
Soft commotion, the sudden race of springs,
The goddess' tread heard on the dayward stair,

Longs for the brush of the freighted air, for smells
Of grass and cordial lilac, for the sight
Of green leaves building into the light
And azure water hoisting out of wells.

Still, Citizen Sparrow

Still, citizen sparrow, this vulture which you call
Unnatural, let him but lumber again to air
Over the rotten office, let him bear
The carrion ballast up, and at the tall

Tip of the sky lie cruising. Then you'll see
That no more beautiful bird is in heaven's height,
No wider more placid wings, no watchfuller flight;
He shoulders nature there, the frightfully free,

The naked-headed one. Pardon him, you
Who dart in the orchard aisles, for it is he
Devours death, mocks mutability,
Has heart to make an end, keeps nature new.

Thinking of Noah, childheart, try to forget
How for so many bedlam hours his saw
Soured the song of birds with its wheezy gnaw,
And the slam of his hammer all the day beset

The people's ears. Forget that he could bear
To see the towns like coral under the keel,

And the fields so dismal deep. Try rather to feel
How high and weary it was, on the waters where

He rocked his only world, and everyone's.
Forgive the hero, you who would have died
Gladly with all you knew; he rode that tide
To Ararat; all men are Noah's sons.

After the Last Bulletins

After the last bulletins the windows darken
And the whole city founders easily and deep,
Sliding on all its pillows
To the thronged Atlantis of personal sleep,

And the wind rises. The wind rises and bowls
The day's litter of news in the alleys. Trash
Tears itself on the railings,
Soars and falls with a soft crash,

Tumbles and soars again. In empty lots
Our journals spiral in a fierce noyade
Of all we thought to think,
Or caught in corners cramp and wad

And twist our words. And some from gutters flail
Their tatters at the tired patrolman's feet
Like all that fisted snow
That cried beside his long retreat

Damn you! damn you! to the emperor's horses' heels.
Oh none too soon through the air white and dry
Will the clear announcer's voice
Beat like a dove, and you and I

From the heart's anarch and responsible town
Rise by the subway-mouth to life again,
Bearing the morning papers,
And cross the park where saintlike men,

White and absorbed, with stick and bag remove
The litter of the night, and footsteps rouse
With confident morning sound
The songbirds in the public boughs.

A Black November Turkey

Nine white chickens come
With haunchy walk and heads
Jabbing among the chips, the chaff, the stones
And the cornhusk-shreds,

And bit by bit infringe
A pond of dusty light,
Spectral in shadow until they bobbingly one
By one ignite.

Neither pale nor bright,
The turkey-cock parades
Through radiant squalors, darkly auspicious as
The ace of spades,

Himself his own cortège
And puffed with the pomp of death,
Rehearsing over and over with strangled râle
His latest breath.

The vast black body floats
Above the crossing knees
As a cloud over thrashed branches, a calm ship
Over choppy seas,

Shuddering its fan and feathers
In fine soft clashes
With the cold sound that the wind makes, fondling
Paper-ashes.

The pale-blue bony head
Set on its shepherd's-crook
Like a saint's death-mask, turns a vague, superb
And timeless look

Upon these clocking hens
And the cocks that one by one,
Dawn after mortal dawn, with vulgar joy
Acclaim the sun.

Howard Moss

1922-

The Lie

Some bloodied sea-bird's hovering decay
Assails us where we lie, and lie
To make that symbol go away,
To mock the true north of the eye.
But lie to me, lie next to me;
The world is an infirmity.

Too much of sun's been said, too much
Of sea, and of the lover's touch,
Whole volumes that old men debauch.
But we, at the sea's edge curled,
Hurl back their bloody world.
Lie to me, lie next to me,

For there is nothing here to see
But the mirror of ourselves, the day,
Clear with the odors of the sea.
Lie to me. And lie to me.

A Lesson from Van Gogh

Speechless tree and animal and bird
Vein dreams with meaning, often blurred.
If we could but connect the beast and word!

"The end of life," life callously repeats,
"Is love and its renewal," yet it cheats
Us all in graveyards of eternal streets.

Unharmed by guilt or will, day after day,
The silly fish, performing in the bay,
The simple serpent, lion, pig, and jay,

Are not more separate in each other's sight
Than we who speak—our speech engraves the night
With all the hieroglyphics of delight

That daylight cannot translate. "Take my ear,"
One painter said, who painted out his fear.
Madness has a poetry that comes too near

Truth for comfort: though the mind goes numb,
Thinking of that severance, the deaf and dumb
Communicate by signs, and everyone

Can follow the plain meaning: "Talk to me,"
Van Gogh was saying, "I am not a tree,
A fish, a serpent, lion, pig, or jay."

Venice

Its wingéd lion stands up straight to hide
The source of pain: the reign of the unnatural.
One cannot tell how really false the real is.
One cannot tell how real the really false is.
Seen in one light, we apprehend the Beautiful:
The thinnest minarets of lattice lacework
Tangibly recovered from the hardest natural
Elements command our endless homage:
One doorway makes our human lives seem trivial.
In yet another light, a scabrous limb of Venus,
Dangling in rank water, rots to golden bone—
The swank and stink of the imagination
Beautifully gone bad. Its waterways re-weave
The only city that has seen itself
Reflected in the mirror of its very eye,
Made-up, each century, in vain for views
No one can now remember. How the painters lie,
Taken altogether, in their fabrication!
Even the Adriatic, static in its green,
Evokes no known sea. From the campanile,
One sees, face down, a short, ceramic fish
Glittering its red-tiled scales below.
Exquisite emphases and subtle losses
Make up its tide. For power, four bronze horses,
Brought from Byzantium, outpace the sun.

Dwindling to our shadows in outside salons
Where orchestras of afternoon rehearse our evening,
We sound the very history of fear we felt
Through all the shorter histories of fear we feel.
Is it true, we think, our sorry otherness
Is to fall in love with beasts whose beauty ruins us?
Those beasts are everywhere, though Venice says
Lions to be golden must be painted gold.

James Merrill

1926-

Transfigured Bird

I

That day the eggshell of appearance split
And weak of its own translucence lay in the dew.
A child fond of natural things discovered it.

Though it was broken it was very blue,
Pearly within, and lit by sun enough
For it to glow, though broken clean in two.

He ran home with it wrapped in a handkerchief
To where he kept his findings. Here, in a nest,
Robins' eggs hollowed with a pin and a puff;

Moths spread like ferns, then ferns and flowers pressed
Like moths on cotton; a bullfrog, once green;
Minerals, and a few smutched feathers—lest

The world be part forgotten if part unseen.
No longer glowing, but blue as the sky that day,
The shell went on the top shelf. What had been

Inside was nimble and hungry and far away,
And had left behind only this envelope
For a child to find and fancy it was gay.

II

As one who watches two days in some hope
A fertile yolk, until there throbs at last
The point of blood beneath his microscope,

Then rises rinsed with the thought of what has passed,
I watched the big yolk of remembrance swallowed
By the throbbing legend there, that broke its fast,

Grew into shape, now to be hatched and hallowed,
Whether a bugling bird or cockatrice;
And when the wild wings rose, on foot I followed.

And much was legend long days after this.
I mean that much was read and read aright.
Where the bird went gold plumes fell, which were his.

III

Philippa raised her elbows to the light
As though to lean there watching the red deer
Leap through it, blond as her hair unpinned at night

When by her bed she took a comb to her hair
And gave it lessons in simplicity
Till each long strand was docile and severe;

Then turned as if to smile, smiled then at me,
And in the sudden dark stretched with no fear,
For whom the night was a warm nubility.

Reynard, Cock Robin, Bruin and Chanticleer,
Dreaming she ruled these clever animals
She had laughed aloud in her sleep when they came near.

And had herself shown other valuables:
Fabergé's royal Easter eggs she kept
To look at in her moods. The enameled shells

Sprang wide at her touch, and out each marvel stepped:
In one, some great-grandchildren's miniatures
That a Russian prince smiled at before he slept;

Then from a gold yolk with sharp ruby spurs
A little rooster flaps gold wings and crows
—Inside of it a thumbnail engine whirs;

"And this I think has a fox, but one never knows."
Nor did she know, nor would I tell her ever
How close she was to the flood of time that flows,

Or rather flies, a yellow bird, forever
Beyond, stops only if we stop, to trill
In the thicket yonder, loudest to a lover.

Close in the thicket under her windowsill
The bird of prophecy no song decoys
Sang, while she dreamed and I was somewhat still;

Sang, while the darkness would not mute its noise,
First of its past, the teeming yolk; sang then
Of fables, findings, shelves of fabulous toys,

Its various images in the minds of men;
Of love. At which she woke. The bird in me
Sang on, a panic in my blood, a pain.

Strange how that music made a woman's beauty,
Most notable for being frail, of such
A power one could have wept for frailty;

Her hair too much like sun, her love too much
Like ignorance, perhaps. I must begin
To tell her of this music in my touch:

Of God who like a little boy with a pin
Shall prick a hole in either end of the sky
And blow it clean away, the thing within,

Away, before it waste, or hatching fly
Out of his reach in noisy solitude,
Or kill him with the oracle in its eye;

Blow all away, the yolk with its X of blood,
The shelves of jewels away, this drowsing girl
At whose hand, away, the shapely animals fed;

Till the egg is void of all but pearl-on-pearl
Reflections and their gay meanderings;
Shall, tiring, burst the shell, let the fragments whirl.

IV

That day the year, eager to hatch new springs,
Nested in russet feathers by the bare lake.
That day a child who was fond of natural things

Went where light dangled like a bait to take
And found a blue egg which had airily dropped,
A freak of season, down to the hooked brake,

Lifted it out, as children will, but stopped:
He had thought to blow it clean, but there had broken
From the cold shell his chilly fingers cupped

The claw of the dead bird, clutching air, a token
Of how there should be nothing cleanly for years to come,
Nor godly, nor reasons found, nor prayers spoken.

And though it was still early morning he went home
And slept and would not till nearly dusk be woken.

Hotel de l'Univers et Portugal

The strange bed, whose recurrent dream we are,
Basin, and shutters guarding with their latch
The hour of arrivals, the reputed untouched Square.
Bleakly with ever fewer belongings we watch
And have never, it each time seems, so coldly before

Steeped the infant membrane of our clinging
In a strange city's clear grave acids;
Or thought how like a pledge the iron key-ring
Slid overboard, one weighty calm at Rhodes,
Down to the vats of its eventual rusting.

And letters moulting out of memory, lost
Seasons of the breast of a snowbird . . .
One morning on the pillow shall at last
Lie strands of age, and many a crease converge
Where the ambitious dreaming head has tossed

The world away and turned, and taken dwelling
Within the pillow's dense white dark, has heard

The lover's speech from cool walls peeling
To the white bed, whose dream they were.
Bare room, forever feeling and annulling,

Bare room, bleak problem set for space,
Fold us ever and over in less identity
Than six walls hold, the oval mirror face
Showing us vacantly how to become only
Bare room, mere air, no hour and no place,

Lodging of chance, and bleak as all beginning.
We had begun perhaps to lack a starlit Square.
But now our very poverties are dissolving,
Are swallowed up, strong powders to ensure
Sleep, by a strange bed in the dark of dreaming.

MODERN BRITISH POETRY

Thomas Hardy

1840-1928

In Time of "The Breaking of Nations"

Only a man harrowing clods
  In a slow silent walk,
With an old horse that stumbles and nods
  Half asleep as they stalk.

Only thin smoke without flame
  From the heaps of couch grass:
Yet this will go onward the same
  Though Dynasties pass.

Yonder a maid and her wight
  Come whispering by;
War's annals will fade into night
  Ere their story die.

The Darkling Thrush

I leaned upon a coppice gate
  When Frost was specter-gray,
And Winter's dregs made desolate
  The weakening eye of day.
The tangled bine-stems scored the sky
  Like strings from broken lyres,
And all mankind that haunted nigh
  Had sought their household fires.

The land's sharp features seemed to be
  The Century's corpse outleant;
His crypt the cloudy canopy,
  The wind his death-lament.
The ancient pulse of germ and birth
  Was shrunken hard and dry,
And every spirit upon earth
  Seemed fervorless as I.

At once a voice burst forth among
  The bleak twigs overhead
In a full-hearted evensong
  Of joy illimited;
An aged thrush, frail, gaunt and small,
  In blast-beruffled plume,
Had chosen thus to fling his soul
  Upon the growing gloom.

So little cause for carolings
  Of such ecstatic sound
Was written on terrestrial things
  Afar or nigh around,
That I could think there trembled through
  His happy good-night air
Some blessed hope, whereof he knew
  And I was unaware.

The Man He Killed

"Had he and I but met
  By some old ancient inn,
We should have sat us down to wet
  Right many a nipperkin!

"But ranged as infantry,
  And staring face to face,
I shot at him as he at me,
  And killed him in his place.

"I shot him dead because—
  Because he was my foe,
Just so: my foe of course he was;
  That's clear enough; although

"He thought he'd 'list, perhaps,
  Off-hand-like—just as I—
Was out of work—had sold his traps—
  No other reason why.

"Yes; quaint and curious war is!
  You shoot a fellow down
You'd treat, if met where any bar is,
  Or help to half-a-crown."

In the Servants' Quarters

"Man, you too, aren't you, one of these rough followers of the
criminal?
All hanging hereabout to gather how he's going to bear
Examination in the hall." She flung disdainful glances on
The shabby figure standing at the fire with others there,
Who warmed them by its flare.

"No, indeed, my skipping maiden: I know nothing of the trial
here,
Or criminal, if so he be.—I chanced to come this way,
And the fire shone out into the dawn, and morning airs are
cold now;
I, too, was drawn in part by charms I see before me play,
That I see not every day."

"Ha, ha!" then laughed the constables who also stood to warm
themselves,
The while another maiden scrutinized his features hard,
As the blaze threw into contrast every knot and line that
wrinkled them,
Exclaiming, "Why, last night when he was brought in by the
guard,
You were with him in the yard!"

"Nay, nay, you teasing wench, I say! You know you speak
mistakenly.
Cannot a tired pedestrian who has legged it long and far
Here on his way from northern parts, engrossed in humble
marketings,
Come in and rest awhile, although judicial doings are
Afoot by morning star?"

"O come, come!" laughed the constables. "Why, man, you
speak the dialect
He uses in his answers; you can hear him up the stairs.
So own it. We sha'n't hurt ye. There, he's speaking now! His
syllables
Are those you sound yourself when you are talking unawares,
As this pretty girl declares."

"And you shudder when his chain clinks!" she rejoined. "O yes,
I noticed it.

And you winced, too, when those cuffs they gave him echoed to
us here.
They'll soon be coming down, and you may then have to defend yourself
Unless you hold your tongue, or go away and keep you clear
When he's led to judgment near!"

"No! I'll be damned in hell if I know anything about the man!
No single thing about him more than everybody knows!
Must not I even warm my hands but I am charged with
blasphemies?" . . .
—His face convulses as the morning cock that moment crows,
And he droops, and turns, and goes.

Weathers

This is the weather the cuckoo likes,
And so do I;
When showers betumble the chestnut spikes,
And nestlings fly;
And the little brown nightingale bills his best,
And they sit outside the "Traveler's Rest,"
And maids come forth sprig-muslin drest,
And citizens dream of the South and West,
And so do I.

This is the weather the shepherd shuns,
And so do I;
When beeches drip in browns and duns,
And thresh, and ply;
And hill-hid tides throb, throe on throe,
And meadow rivulets overflow,
And drops on gate-bars hang in a row,
And rooks in families homeward go,
And so do I.

"Ah, Are You Digging on My Grave?"

"Ah, are you digging on my grave
My beloved one?—planting rue?"
—"No: yesterday he went to wed
One of the brightest wealth has bred,
'It cannot hurt her now,' he said,
'That I should not be true.' "

"Then who is digging on my grave?
  My nearest, dearest kin?"
—"Ah, no: they sit and think, 'What use!
What good will planting flowers produce?
No tendance of her mound can loose
  Her spirit from Death's gin.' "

"But someone digs upon my grave?
  My enemy?—prodding sly?"
—"Nay: when she heard you had passed the Gate
That shuts on all flesh soon or late,
She thought you no more worth her hate,
  And cares not where you lie."

"Then, who is digging on my grave?
  Say—since I have not guessed!"
—"O it is I, my mistress dear,
Your little dog, who still lives near,
And much I hope my movements here
  Have not disturbed your rest?"

"Ah, yes! *You* dig upon my grave. . . .
  Why flashed it not on me
That one true heart was left behind!
What feeling do we ever find
To equal among human kind
  A dog's fidelity!"

"Mistress, I dug upon your grave
  To bury a bone, in case
I should be hungry near this spot
When passing on my daily trot.
I am sorry, but I quite forgot
  It was your resting-place."

Five "Satires of Circumstance"

IN CHURCH

"And now to God the Father," he ends,
And his voice thrills up to the topmost tiles:
Each listener chokes as he bows and bends,
And emotion pervades the crowded aisles.
Then the preacher glides to the vestry-door,
And shuts it, and thinks he is seen no more.

The door swings softly ajar meanwhile,
And a pupil of his in the Bible class,
Who adores him as one without gloss or guile,
Sees her idol stand with a satisfied smile
And reënact at the vestry-glass
Each pulpit gesture in deft dumb-show
That had moved the congregation so.

BY HER AUNT'S GRAVE

"Sixpence a week," says the girl to her lover,
"Aunt used to bring me, for she could confide
In me alone, she vowed. It was to cover
The cost of her headstone when she died.
And that was a year ago last June;
I've not yet fixed it. But I must soon."

"And where is the money now, my dear?"
"O, snug in my purse. . . . Aunt was *so* slow
In saving it—eighty weeks, or near." . . .
"Let's spend it," he hints. "For she won't know.
There's a dance tonight at the *Load of Hay.*"
She passively nods. And they go that way.

AT THE ALTAR-RAIL

"My bride is not coming, alas!" says the groom,
And the telegram shakes in his hand. "I own
It was hurried! We met at a dancing-room
When I went to the Cattle-Show alone,
And then, next night, where the Fountain leaps,
And the Street of the Quarter-Circle sweeps.

"Aye, she won me to ask her to be my wife—
'Twas foolish perhaps!—to forsake the ways
Of the flaring town for a farmer's life.
She agreed. And we fixed it. Now she says:
'It's sweet of you, dear, to prepare me a nest,
But a swift, short, gay life suits me best.
What I really am you have never gleaned;
I had eaten the apple ere you were weaned.' "

IN THE RESTAURANT

"But hear. If you stay, and the child be born,
It will pass as your husband's with the rest,
While, if we fly, the teeth of scorn
Will be gleaming at us from east to west;

And the child will come as a life despised.
I feel an elopement is ill-advised!"

"O you realize not what it is, my dear,
To a woman! Daily and hourly alarms
Lest the truth should out. How can I stay here
And nightly take him into my arms!
Come to the child no name or fame,
Let us go, and face it, and bear the shame."

AT THE DRAPER'S

"I stood at the back of the shop, my dear,
  But you did not perceive me.
Well, when they deliver what you were shown
  I shall know nothing of it, believe me!"

And he coughed and coughed as she paled and said,
  "O, I didn't see you come in there—
Why couldn't you speak?"—"Well, I didn't. I left
  That you should not notice I'd been there.

"You were viewing some lovely things. *'Soon required*
  For a widow, of latest fashion';
And I knew 'twould upset you to meet the man
  Who had to be cold and ashen

"And screwed in a box before they could dress you
  'In the last new note in mourning,'
As they defined it. So, not to distress you,
  I left you to your adorning."

The Dark-Eyed Gentleman

I pitched my day's leazings [1] in Crimmercrock Lane,
To tie up my garter and jog on again,
When a dear dark-eyed gentleman passed there and said,
In a way that made all o' me color rose-red,
    "What do I see—
    O pretty knee!"
And he came and he tied up my garter for me.

'Twixt sunset and moonrise it was, I can mind:
Ah, 'tis easy to lose what we nevermore find!—

[1] Leazings: bundles of gleaned corn.

Of the dear stranger's home, of his name, I knew nought,
But I soon knew his nature and all that it brought.
Then bitterly
Sobbed I that he
Should ever have tied up my garter for me!

Yet now I've beside me a fine lissom lad,
And my slip's nigh forgot, and my days are not sad;
My own dearest joy is he, comrade, and friend,
He it is who safe-guards me, on him I depend;
No sorrow brings he,
And thankful I be
That his daddy once tied up my garter for me!

The Subalterns

"Poor wanderer," said the leaden sky,
"I fain would lighten thee,
But there be laws in force on high
Which say it must not be."

"I would not freeze thee, shorn one," cried
The North, "knew I but how
To warm my breath, to slack my stride;
But I am ruled as thou."

"Tomorrow I attack thee, wight,"
Said Sickness. "Yet I swear
I bear thy little ark no spite,
But am bid enter there."

"Come hither, Son," I heard Death say;
"I did not will a grave
Should end thy pilgrimage today,
But I, too, am a slave!"

We smiled upon each other then,
And life to me wore less
Of that fell guise it wore ere when
They owned their passiveness.

The Oxen

Christmas Eve, and twelve of the clock,
  "Now they are all on their knees,"
An elder said as we sat in a flock
  By the embers in hearthside ease.

We pictured the meek mild creatures where
  They dwelt in their strawy pen,
Nor did it occur to one of us there
  To doubt they were kneeling then.

So fair a fancy few would weave
  In these years! Yet, I feel,
If someone said on Christmas Eve,
  "Come; see the oxen kneel

"In the lonely barton [1] by yonder coomb [2]
  Our childhood used to know,"
I should go with him in the gloom,
  Hoping it might be so.

The Tree and the Lady

  I have done all I could
For that lady I knew! Through the heats I have shaded her,
Drawn to her songsters when summer has jaded her,
  Home from the heath or the wood.

  At the mirth-time of May,
When my shadow first lured her, I'd donned my new bravery
Of greenth: 'twas my all. Now I shiver in slavery,
  Icicles grieving me gray.

  Plumed to every twig's end
I could tempt her chair under me. Much did I treasure her
During those days she had nothing to pleasure her;
  Mutely she used me as friend.

[1] Barton: farmyard.
[2] Coomb: valley, hollow.

I'm a skeleton now,
And she's gone, craving warmth. The rime sticks like skin to
me;
Through me Arcturus peers; Nor'lights shoot into me;
Gone is she, scorning my bough!

Snow in the Suburbs

Every branch big with it,
Bent every twig with it;
Every fork like a white web-foot;
Every street and pavement mute:
Some flakes have lost their way, and grope back upward, when
Meeting those meandering down they turn and descend again.
The palings are glued together like a wall,
And there is no waft of wind with the fleecy fall.

A sparrow enters the tree
Whereon immediately
A snow-lump thrice his own slight size
Descends on him and showers his head and eyes.
And overturns him,
And near inurns him,
And lights on a nether twig, when its brush
Starts off a volley of other lodging lumps with a rush.

The steps are a blanched slope,
Up which, with feeble hope,
A black cat comes, wide-eyed and thin;
And we take him in.

The Convergence of the Twain

(Lines on the loss of the "Titanic")

I

In a solitude of the sea
Deep from human vanity,
And the Pride of Life that planned her, stilly couches she.

II

Steel chambers, late the pyres
Of her salamandrine fires,
Cold currents thrid, and turn to rhythmic tidal lyres.

III

Over the mirrors meant
To glass the opulent
The sea-worm crawls—grotesque, slimed, dumb, indifferent.

IV

Jewels in joy designed
To ravish the sensuous mind
Lie lightless, all their sparkles bleared and black and blind.

V

Dim moon-eyed fishes near
Gaze at the gilded gear
And query: "What does this vaingloriousness down here?"

VI

Well: while was fashioning
This creature of cleaving wing,
The Immanent Will that stirs and urges everything

VII

Prepared a sinister mate
For her—so gaily great
A Shape of Ice, for the time far and dissociate.

VIII

And as the smart ship grew
In stature, grace, and hue,
In shadowy silent distance grew the Iceberg too.

IX

Alien they seemed to be;
No mortal eye could see
The intimate welding of their later history,

X

Or sign that they were bent
By paths coincident
On being anon twin halves of one august event,

XI

Till the Spinner of the Years
Said "Now!" And each one hears,
And consummation comes, and jars two hemispheres.

Rome

(At the Pyramid of Cestius near the Graves of Shelley and Keats)

Who, then was Cestius
And what is he to me?—
Amid thick thoughts and memories multitudinous
One thought alone brings he.

I can recall no word
Of anything he did;
For me he is a man who died and was interred
To leave a pyramid

Whose purpose was exprest
Not with its first design,
Nor till, far down in Time, beside it found their rest
Two countrymen of mine.

Cestius in life, maybe,
Slew, breathed out threatening;
I know not. This I know: in death all silently
He does a finer thing,

In beckoning pilgrim feet
With marble finger high
To where, by shadowy wall and history-haunted street,
Those matchless singers lie. . . .

—Say, then, he lived and died
That stones which bear his name
Should mark, through Time, where two immortal Shades abide;
It is an ample fame.

Before Waterloo

(From "The Dynasts")

Chorus of the Years

The eyelids of eve fall together at last,
And the forms so foreign to field and tree
Lie down as though native, and slumber fast!

Chorus of the Pities

Sore are the thrills of misgiving we see
In the artless champaign at this harlequinade,
Distracting a vigil where calm should be!

The green seems opprest, and the plain afraid
Of a Something to come, whereof these are the proofs,—
Neither earthquake, nor storm, nor eclipse's shade!

Chorus of the Years

Yes, the coneys are scared by the thud of hoofs,
And their white scuts flash at their vanishing heels,
And swallows abandon the hamlet-roofs.

The mole's tunnelled chambers are crushed by wheels,
The lark's eggs scattered, their owners fled;
And the hedgehog's household the sapper unseals.

The snail draws in at the terrible tread,
But in vain; he is crushed by the fellow-rim;
The worm asks what can be overhead,

And wriggles deep from a scene so grim,
And guesses him safe; for he does not know
What a foul red flood will be soaking him!

Beaten about by the heel and toe
Are butterflies, sick of the day's long rheum,
To die of a worse than the weather-foe.

Trodden and bruised to a miry tomb
Are ears that have greened but will never be gold,
And flowers in the bud that will never bloom.

Chorus of the Pities

So the season's intent, ere its fruit unfold,
Is frustrate, and mangled, and made succumb,
Like a youth of promise struck stark and cold! . . .

And what of these who tonight have come?

Chorus of the Years

The young sleep sound; but the weather awakes
In the veterans, pains from the past that numb;

Old stabs of Ind, old Peninsular aches,
Old Friedland chills, haunt their moist mud bed,
Cramps from Austerlitz; till their slumber breaks.

Chorus of Sinister Spirits

And each soul sighs as he shifts his head
On the loam his to lease with the other dead
From to-morrow's mist-fall till Time be sped!

Waiting Both

A star looks down at me,
And says: "Here I and you
Stand, each in our degree:
What do you mean to do–
Mean to do?"

I say: "For all I know,
Wait, and let Time go by,
Till my change come."–"Just so,"
The star says: "So mean I–
So mean I."

Afterwards

When the Present has latched its postern behind my tremulous stay,
And the May month flaps its glad green leaves like wings,
Delicate-filmed as new-spun silk, will the neighbors say,
"He was a man who used to notice such things"?

If it be in the dusk when, like an eyelid's soundless blink,
The dewfall-hawk comes crossing the shades to alight
Upon the wind-warped upland thorn, a gazer may think,
"To him this must have been a familiar sight."

If I pass during some nocturnal blackness, mothy and warm,
When the hedgehog travels furtively over the lawn,
One may say, "He strove that such innocent creatures should come to no harm,
But he could do little for them; and now he is gone."

If, when hearing that I have been stilled at last, they stand at
the door,
Watching the full-starred heavens that winter sees,
Will this thought rise on those who will meet my face no more,
"He was one who had an eye for such mysteries"?

And will any say when my bell of quittance is heard in the
gloom,
And a crossing breeze cuts a pause in its outrollings,
Till they rise again, as they were a new bell's boom,
"He hears it not now, but used to notice such things"?

Gerard Manley Hopkins

1844-1889

Pied Beauty

Glory be to God for dappled things—
For skies of couple-color as a brinded cow;
For rose-moles all in stipple upon trout that swim;
Fresh-firecoal chestnut-falls; finches' wings;
Landscapes plotted and pieced—fold, fallow, and plow;
And all trades, their gear and tackle and trim.
All things counter, original, spare, strange;
Whatever is fickle, freckled (who knows how?)
With swift, slow; sweet, sour; adazzle, dim;
He fathers-forth whose beauty is past change:
Praise Him.

Thou Art Indeed Just, Lord

Thou art indeed just, Lord, if I contend
With thee; but, sir, so what I plead is just.
Why do sinners' ways prosper? and why must
Disappointment all I endeavour end?
Wert thou my enemy, O thou my friend,
How wouldst thou worse, I wonder, than thou dost
Defeat, thwart me? Oh, the sots and thralls of lust
Do in spare hours more thrive than I that spend,
Sir, life upon thy cause. See, banks and brakes
Now, leavèd how thick! lacèd they are again
With fretty chervil, look, and fresh wind shakes
Them; birds build—but not I build; no, but strain,
Time's eunuch, and not breed one work that wakes.
Mine, O thou lord of life, send my roots rain.

The Habit of Perfection

Elected Silence, sing to me
And beat upon my whorlèd ear,
Pipe me to pastures still, and be
The music that I care to hear.

Shape nothing, lips; be lovely-dumb;
It is the shut, the curfew sent
From there where all surrenders come
Which only makes you eloquent.

Be shellèd, eyes, with double dark
And find the uncreated light:
This ruck and reel which you remark
Coils, keeps, and teases simple sight.

Palate, the hutch of tasty lust,
Desire not to be rinsed with wine:
The can must be so sweet, the crust
So fresh that come in fasts divine!

Nostrils, your careless breath that spend
Upon the stir and keep of pride,
What relish shall the censers send
Along the sanctuary side!

O feel-of-primrose hands, O feet
That want the yield of plushy sward,
But you shall walk the golden street
And you unhouse and house the Lord.

And, Poverty, be thou the bride
And now the marriage feast begun,
And lily-colored clothes provide
Your spouse, not labored-at nor spun.

The Leaden Echo

How to keep—is there any, any, is there none such, nowhere known, some bow or brooch or braid or brace, lace, latch or catch or key to keep
Back beauty, keep it, beauty, beauty, beauty, . . . from vanishing away?
Oh, is there no frowning of these wrinkles, ranked wrinkles deep,
Down? no waving-off of these most mournful messengers, still messengers, sad and stealing messengers of gray?
No, there's none, there's none—oh, no, there's none!
Nor can you long be, what you now are, called fair—
Do what you may do, do what you may,
And wisdom is early to despair:
Be beginning; since, no, nothing can be done
To keep at bay
Age and age's evils—hoar hair,
Ruck and wrinkle, drooping, dying, death's worst, winding sheets, tombs and worms, and tumbling to decay;
So be beginning, be beginning to despair.
Oh, there's none—no, no, no, there's none:
Be beginning to despair, to despair,
Despair, despair, despair, despair.

The Golden Echo

Spare!
There is one, yes, I have one (Hush there!);
Only not within seeing of the sun,
Not within the singeing of the strong sun,
Tall sun's tingeing, or treacherous the tainting of the earth's air,

Somewhere elsewhere there is ah, well, where! one,
One. Yes, I can tell such a key, I do know such a place,
Where whatever's prized and passed of us, everything that's fresh and fast-flying of us, seems to us sweet of us and swiftly away with, done away with, undone,
Undone, done with, soon done with, and yet dearly and dangerously sweet
Of us, the wimpled-water-dimpled, not-by-morning-matchèd face,
The flower of beauty, fleece of beauty, too too apt to, ah! to fleet,
Never fleets more, fastened with the tenderest truth
To its own best being and its loveliness of youth: it is an everlastingness of, O it is an all youth!
Come then, your ways and airs and looks, locks, maiden gear, gallantry and gayety and grace,
Winning ways, airs innocent, maiden manners, sweet looks, loose locks, long locks, lovelocks, gaygear, going gallant, girlgrace—
Resign them, sign them, seal them, send them, motion them with breath,
And with sighs soaring, soaring sighs deliver
Them; beauty-in-the-ghost, deliver it, early now, long before death
Give beauty back, beauty, beauty, beauty, back to God, beauty's self and beauty's giver.
See; not a hair is, not an eyelash, not the least lash lost; every hair
Is, hair of the head, numbered.
Nay, what we had lighthanded left in surely the mere mold
Will have waked and have waxed and have walked with the wind whatwhile we slept,
This side, that side hurling a heavyheaded hundredfold
Whatwhile we, while we slumbered.
O then, weary then why should we tread? O why are we so haggard at the heart, so care-coiled, care-killed, so fagged, so fashed, so cogged, so cumbered,
When the thing we freely forfeit is kept with fonder a care,
Fonder a care kept than we could have kept it, kept
Far with fonder a care (and we, we should have lost it) finer, fonder
A care kept.—Where kept? Do but tell us where kept, where.—
Yonder.—What high as that! We follow, now we follow.—Yonder, yes, yonder, yonder,
Yonder.

God's Grandeur

The world is charged with the grandeur of God.
  It will flame out, like shining from shook foil;
  It gathers to a greatness, like the ooze of oil
Crushed. Why do men then now not reck his rod?
Generations have trod, have trod, have trod;
  And all is seared with trade; bleared, smeared with toil;
  And wears man's smudge and shares man's smell: the soil
Is bare now, nor can foot feel, being shod.

And for all this, nature is never spent;
  There lives the dearest freshness deep down things;
And though the last lights off the black West went
  Oh, morning, at the brown brink eastward, springs—
Because the Holy Ghost over the bent
  World broods with warm breast and with ah! bright wings.

The Starlight Night

Look at the stars! look, look up at the skies!
  O look at all the fire-folk sitting in the air!
  The bright boroughs, the circle-citadels there!
Down in dim woods the diamond delves! the elves'-eyes!
The gray lawns cold where gold, where quickgold lies!
  Wind-beat whitebeam! airy abeles set on a flare!
  Flake-doves sent floating forth at a farmyard scare!
Ah, well! it is all a purchase, all is a prize.

Buy then! bid then!—What?—Prayer, patience, alms, vows.
Look, look: a May-mess, like on orchard boughs!
  Look! March-bloom, like on mealed-with-yellow sallows!
These are indeed the barn; withindoors house
The shocks. This piece-bright paling shuts the spouse
  Christ home, Christ and his mother and all his hallows.

Spring

Nothing is so beautiful as spring—
  When weeds, in wheels, shoot long and lovely and lush;
  Thrush's eggs look like low heavens, and thrush
Through the echoing timber does so rinse and wring

The ear, it strikes like lightning to hear him sing;
  The glassy peartree leaves and blooms, they brush
  The descending blue; that blue is all in a rush
With richness; the racing lambs too have fair their fling.

What is all this juice and all this joy?
  A strain of the earth's sweet being in the beginning
In Eden garden.—Have, get, before it cloy,
  Before it cloud, Christ, lord, and sour with sinning,
Innocent mind and Mayday in girl and boy,
  Most, O maid's child, thy choice and worthy the winning.

Hurrahing in Harvest

Summer ends now; now, barbarous in beauty, the stooks arise
  Around; up above, what wind-walks! what lovely behavior
  Of silk-sack clouds! has wilder, willful-wavier
Meal-drift molded ever and melted across skies?

I walk, I lift up, I lift up heart, eyes,
  Down all that glory in the heavens to glean our Saviour;
  And, eyes, heart, what looks, what lips yet gave you a
Rapturous love's greeting of realer, of rounder replies?

And the azurous hung hills are his world-wielding shoulder
  Majestic—as a stallion stalwart, very-violet-sweet!—
These things, these things were here and but the beholder
  Wanting; which two when they once meet,
The heart rears wings bold and bolder
  And hurls for him, O half hurls earth for him off under his
    feet.

The Caged Skylark

As a dare-gale skylark scanted in a dull cage
  Man's mounting spirit in his bone-house, mean house,
    dwells—
  That bird beyond the remembering his free fells;
This in drudgery, day-laboring-out life's age.

Though aloft on turf or perch or poor low stage,
  Both sing sometimes the sweetest, sweetest spells,
  Yet both droop deadly sometimes in their cells
Or wring their barriers in bursts of fear or rage.

Not that the sweet-fowl, song-fowl, needs no rest—
Why, hear him, hear him babble and drop down to his nest,
  But his own nest, wild nest, no prison.

Man's spirit will be flesh-bound when found at best,
But uncumbered: meadow-down is not distressed
  For a rainbow footing it nor he for his bones risen.

Moonrise

I awoke in the Midsummer not to call night, in the white and the walk of the morning:
The moon, dwindled and thinned to the fringe of a finger-nail held to the candle,
Or paring of paradisaïcal fruit, lovely in waning but lusterless,
Stepped from the stool, drew back from the barrow, of dark Maenefa the mountain;
A cusp still clasped him, a fluke yet fanged him, entangled him, not quit utterly.
This was the prized, the desirable sight, unsought, presented so easily,
Parted me leaf and leaf, divided me, eyelid and eyelid of slumber.

Felix Randal

Felix Randal the farrier, O he is dead then? my duty all ended,
Who have watched his mold of man, big-boned and hardy-handsome
Pining, pining, till time when reason rambled in it and some
Fatal four disorders, fleshed there, all contended?

Sickness broke him. Impatient he cursed at first, but mended
Being anointed and all; though a heavenlier heart began some
Months earlier, since I had our sweet reprieve and ransom
Tendered to him. Ah, well, God rest him all road ever he offended!

This seeing the sick endears them to us, us too it endears.
My tongue had taught thee comfort, touch had quenched thy tears,
Thy tears that touched my heart, child, Felix, poor Felix Randal;

How far from then forethought of, all thy more boisterous
years,
When thou at the random grim forge, powerful amidst peers,
Didst fettle for the great gray drayhorse his bright and battering sandal!

To His Watch

(unfinished)

Mortal my mate, bearing my rock-a-heart
Warm beat with cold beat company, shall I
Earlier or you fail at our force, and lie
The ruins of, rifled, once a world of art?
The telling time our task is; time's some part,
Not all, but we were framed to fail and die—
One spell and well that one. There, ah, thereby
Is comfort's carol of all or woe's worst smart.

Field-flown the departed day no morning brings
Saying "This was yours" with her, but new one, worse,
And then that last and shortest . . .

The Cuckoo

Repeat that, repeat,
Cuckoo, bird, and open ear wells, heart-springs, delightfully sweet,
With a ballad, with a ballad, a rebound
Off trundled timber and scoops of the hillside ground, hollow hollow hollow ground:
The whole landscape flushes on a sudden at a sound.

The Windhover

To Christ Our Lord

I caught this morning morning's minion, king-
dom of daylight's dauphin, dapple-dawn-drawn Falcon, in his riding
Of the rolling level underneath him steady air, and striding
High there, how he rung upon the rein of a wimpling wing

In his ecstasy! then off, off forth on swing,
  As a skate's heel sweeps smooth on a bow-bend: the hurl
    and gliding
  Rebuffed the big wind. My heart in hiding
Stirred for a bird,—the achieve of, the mastery of the thing!

Brute beauty and valor and act, oh, air, pride, plume, here
  Buckle! AND the fire that breaks from thee then, a billion
Times told lovelier, more dangerous, O my chevalier!

  No wonder of it: sheer plod makes plough down sillion
Shine, and blue-bleak embers, ah my dear,
  Fall, gall themselves, and gash gold-vermilion.

Inversnaid

This darksome burn, horseback brown,
His rollrock highroad roaring down,
In coop and in comb the fleece of his foam
Flutes and low to the lake falls home.

A windpuff-bonnet of fawn-froth
Turns and twindles over the broth
Of a pool so pitchblack, fell-frowning,
It rounds and rounds Despair to drowning.

Degged with dew, dappled with dew
Are the groins of the braes that the brook treads through,
Wiry heathpacks, flitches of fern,
And the beadbonny ash that sits over the burn.

What would the world be, once bereft
Of wet and of wildness? Let them be left,
O let them be left, wildness and wet;
Long live the weeds and the wilderness yet.

Heaven-Haven

A Nun Takes the Veil

I have desired to go
  Where springs not fail,
To fields where flies no sharp and sided hail,
  And a few lilies blow.

And I have asked to be
Where no storms come,
Where the green swell is in the havens dumb
And out of the swing of the sea.

What I Do Is Me

As kingfishers catch fire, dragonflies draw flame;
As tumbled over rim in roundy wells
Stones ring; like each tucked string tells, each hung bell's
Bow swung finds tongue to fling out broad its name;
Each mortal thing does one thing and the same:
Deals out that being indoors each one dwells;
Selves—goes itself; *myself* it speaks and spells,
Crying *What I do is me: for that I came.*

I say more: the just man justices;
Keeps grace: that keeps all his goings graces;
Acts in God's eye what in God's eye he is—
Christ—for Christ plays in ten thousand places,
Lovely in limbs, and lovely in eyes not his
To the Father through the features of men's faces.

No Worst, There Is None

No worst, there is none. Pitched past pitch of grief,
More pangs will, schooled at forepangs, wilder wring.
Comforter, where, where is your comforting?
Mary, mother of us, where is your relief?
My cries heave, herds-long; huddle in a main, a chief
Woe, world-sorrow; on an age-old anvil wince and sing-
Then lull, then leave off. Fury had shrieked "No ling-
ering! Let me be fell: force I must be brief."

O the mind, mind has mountains; cliffs of fall
Frightful, sheer, no-man-fathomed. Hold them cheap
May who ne'er hung there. Nor does long our small
Durance deal with that steep or deep. Here! creep,
Wretch, under a comfort serves in a whirlwind: all
Life death does end and each day dies with sleep.

My Own Heart

My own heart let me more have pity on; let
Me live to my sad self hereafter kind,
Charitable; not live this tormented mind
With this tormented mind tormenting yet.
I cast for comfort I can no more get
By groping round my comfortless, than blind
Eyes in their dark can day or thirst can find
Thirst's all-in-all in all a world of wet.

Soul, self; come, poor Jackself, I do advise
You, jaded, let be; call off thoughts awhile
Elsewhere; leave comfort root-room; let joy size
At God knows when to God knows what; whose smile
's not wrung, see you; unforeseen times rather—as skies
Betweenpie mountains—lights a lovely mile.

Spring and Fall: To a Young Child

Márgarét, are you gríeving
Over Goldengrove unleaving?
Leáves, líke the things of man, you
With your fresh thoughts care for, can you?
Ah! ás the heart grows older
It will come to such sights colder
By and by, nor spare a sigh
Though worlds of wanwood leafmeal lie;
And yet you wíll weep and know why.
Now no matter, child, the name:
Sórrow's spríngs áre the same.
Nor mouth had, no nor mind, expressed
What heart heard of, ghost guessed:
It ís the blight man was born for,
It is Margaret you mourn for.

That Nature Is a Heraclitean Fire and of the Comfort of the Resurrection

Cloud-puffball, torn tufts, tossed pillows flaunt forth, then chevy on an air-
built thoroughfare: heaven-roysterers, in gay-gangs they throng; they glitter in marches.
Down roughcast, down dazzling whitewash, wherever an elm arches,
Shivelights and shadowtackle in long lashes lace, lance, and pair.
Delightfully the bright wind boisterous ropes, wrestles, beats earth bare
Of yestertempest's creases; in pool and rut peel parches
Squandering ooze to squeezed dough, crust, dust; stanches, starches
Squadroned masks and manmarks treadmire toil there
Footfretted in it. Million-fuelèd, nature's bonfire burns on.
But quench her bonniest, dearest to her, her clearest-selvèd spark
Man, how fast his firedint, his mark on mind, is gone!
Both are in an unfathomable, all is in an enormous dark
Drowned. O pity and indignation! Manshape, that shone
Sheer off, disseveral, a star, death blots black out; nor mark
Is any of him at all so stark
But vastness blurs and time beats level. Enough! the Resurrection,
A heart's-clarion! Away grief's gasping, joyless days, dejection.
Across my foundering deck shone
A beacon, an eternal beam. Flesh fade, and mortal trash
Fall to the residuary worm; world's wildfire, leave but ash:
In a flash, at a trumpet crash,
I am all at once what Christ is, since he was what I am, and
This Jack, joke, poor potsherd, patch, matchwood, immortal diamond,
Is immortal diamond.

Robert Bridges

1844-1930

A Passer-By

Whither, O splendid ship, thy white sails crowding,
Leaning across the bosom of the urgent West,
That fearest nor sea rising nor sky clouding,
Whither away, fair rover, and what thy quest?
Ah! soon, when Winter has all our vales opprest,
When skies are cold and misty, and hail is hurling,
Wilt thou glide on the blue Pacific, or rest
In a summer haven asleep, thy white sails furling.

I there before thee, in the country that well thou knowest,
Already arrived am inhaling the odorous air:
I watch thee enter unerringly where thou goest,
And anchor queen of the strange shipping there,
Thy sails for awnings spread, thy masts bare;
Nor is aught from the foaming reef to the snow-capp'd, grandest
Peak, that is over the feathery palms, more fair
Than thou, so upright, so stately, and still thou standest.

And yet, O splendid ship, unhail'd and nameless,
I know not if, aiming a fancy, I rightly divine
That thou hast a purpose joyful, a courage blameless,
Thy port assured in a happier land than mine.
But for all I have given thee, beauty enough is thine,
As thou, aslant with trim tackle and shrouding,
From the proud nostril curve of a prow's line
In the offing scatterest foam, thy white sails crowding.

Awake, My Heart, To Be Loved

Awake, my heart, to be loved, awake, awake!
The darkness silvers away, the morn doth break,
It leaps in the sky: unrisen lusters slake
The o'ertaken moon. Awake, O heart, awake!

She too that loveth awaketh and hopes for thee;
Her eyes already have sped the shades that flee,
Already they watch the path thy feet shall take:
Awake, O heart, to be loved, awake, awake!

And if thou tarry from her,—if this could be,—
She cometh herself, O heart, to be loved, to thee;
For thee would unashamèd herself forsake:
Awake to be loved, my heart, awake, awake!

Awake! the land is scattered with light, and see,
Uncanopied sleep is flying from field and tree:
And blossoming boughs of April in laughter shake;
Awake, O heart, to be loved, awake, awake!

Lo all things wake and tarry and look for thee:
She looketh and saith, "O sun, now bring him to me.
Come more adored, O adored, for his coming's sake,
And awake, my heart, to be loved: awake, awake!"

O Weary Pilgrims

(From "The Growth of Love")

O weary pilgrims, chanting of your woe,
That turn your eyes to all the peaks that shine,
Hailing in each the citadel divine
The which ye thought to have entered long ago;
Until at length your feeble steps and slow
Falter upon the threshold of the shrine,
And your hearts overburdened doubt in fine
Whether it be Jerusalem or no:
Disheartened pilgrims, I am one of you;
For, having worshiped many a barren face,

I scarce now greet the goal I journeyed to:
I stand a pagan in the holy place;
Beneath the lamp of truth I am found untrue,
And question with the God that I embrace.

Thou Didst Delight My Eyes

Thou didst delight my eyes:
Yet who am I? nor first
Nor last nor best, that durst
Once dream of thee for prize;
Nor this the only time
Thou shalt set love to rhyme.

Thou didst delight my ear:
Ah! little praise; thy voice
Makes other hearts rejoice,
Makes all ears glad that hear;
And short my joy: but yet,
O song, do not forget.

For what wert thou to me?
How shall I say? The moon,
That poured her midnight noon
Upon his wrecking sea;—
A sail, that for a day
Has cheered the castaway.

Winter Nightfall

The day begins to droop,—
  Its course is done:
But nothing tells the place
  Of the setting sun.

The hazy darkness deepens,
  And up the lane
You may hear, but cannot see,
  The homing wain.

An engine pants and hums
  In the farm hard by:

Its lowering smoke is lost
  In the lowering sky.

The soaking branches drip,
  And all night through
The dropping will not cease
  In the avenue.

A tall man there in the house
  Must keep his chair:
He knows he will never again
  Breathe the spring air:

His heart is worn with work;
  He is giddy and sick
If he rise to go as far
  As the nearest rick:

He thinks of his morn of life,
  His hale, strong years;
And braves as he may the night
  Of darkness and tears.

London Snow

When men were all asleep the snow came flying,
In large white flakes falling on the city brown,
Stealthily and perpetually settling and loosely lying,
  Hushing the latest traffic of the drowsy town;
Deadening, muffling, stifling its murmurs failing;
Lazily and incessantly floating down and down;
  Silently sifting and veiling road, roof and railing;
Hiding difference, making unevenness even,
Into angles and crevices softly drifting and sailing.
  All night it fell, and when full inches seven
It lay in the depth of its uncompacted lightness,
The clouds blew off from a high and frosty heaven;
  And all woke earlier for the unaccustomed brightness
Of the winter dawning, the strange unheavenly glare:
The eye marveled—marveled at the dazzling whiteness;
  The ear hearkened to the stillness of the solemn air;
No sound of wheel rumbling nor of foot falling,
And the busy morning cries came thin and spare.
  Then boys I heard, as they went to school, calling;

They gathered up the crystal manna to freeze
Their tongues with tasting, their hands with snow-balling;
  Or rioted in a drift, plunging up to the knees;
Or peering up from under the white-mossed wonder,
"O look at the trees!" they cried. "O look at the trees!"
  With lessened load, a few carts creak and blunder,
Following along the white deserted way,
A country company long dispersed asunder:
  When now already the sun, in pale display
Standing by Paul's high dome, spread forth below
His sparkling beams, and awoke the stir of the day.
  For now doors open, and war is waged with the snow;
And trains of somber men, past tale of number,
Tread long brown paths, as toward their toil they go:
  But even for them awhile no cares encumber
Their minds diverted; the daily word is unspoken,
The daily thoughts of labor and sorrow slumber
At the sight of the beauty that greets them, for the charm they
    have broken.

Nightingales

Beautiful must be the mountains whence ye come,
And bright in the fruitful valleys the streams wherefrom
      Ye learn your song:
Where are those starry woods? O might I wander there,
  Among the flowers, which in that heavenly air
      Bloom the year long!

Nay, barren are those mountains and spent the streams:
Our song is the voice of desire, that haunts our dreams,
      A throe of the heart,
Whose pining visions dim, forbidden hopes profound,
  No dying cadence nor long sigh can sound,
      For all our art.

Alone, aloud in the raptured ear of men
We pour our dark nocturnal secret; and then,
      As night is withdrawn
From these sweet-springing meads and bursting boughs of May,
  Dream, while the innumerable choir of day
      Welcome the dawn.

I Have Loved Flowers

I have loved flowers that fade,
Within whose magic tents
Rich hues have marriage made
With sweet unmemoried scents:
A honeymoon delight,—
A joy of love at sight,
That ages in an hour:—
My song be like a flower!

I have loved airs that die
Before their charm is writ
Along a liquid sky
Trembling to welcome it.
Notes that with pulse of fire
Proclaim the spirit's desire,
Then die, and are nowhere:—
My song be like an air!

Die, song, die like a breath,
And wither as a bloom:
Fear not a flowery death,
Dread not an airy tomb!
Fly with delight, fly hence!
'Twas thine love's tender sense
To feast; now on thy bier
Beauty shall shed a tear.

Nimium Fortunatus

I have lain in the sun,
I have toil'd as I might,
I have thought as I would,
And now it is night.

My bed full of sleep,
My heart of content
For friends that I met
The way that I went.

I welcome fatigue
While frenzy and care

Like thin summer clouds
Go melting in air.

To dream as I may
And awake when I will
With the song of the birds
And the sun on the hill.

Or death—were it death—
To what should I wake
Who loved in my home
All life for its sake?

What good have I wrought?
I laugh to have learned
That joy cannot come
Unless it be earned;

For a happier lot
Than God giveth me
It never hath been
Nor ever shall be.

Francis Thompson

1859-1907

Daisy

Where the thistle lifts a purple crown
  Six foot out of the turf,
And the harebell shakes on the windy hill—
  O breath of the distant surf!—

The hills look over on the South,
  And southward dreams the sea;
And with the sea-breeze hand in hand
  Came innocence and she.

Where 'mid the gorse the raspberry
  Red for the gatherer springs;
Two children did we stray and talk
  Wise, idle, childish things.

She listened with big-lipped surprise,
  Breast-deep 'mid flower and spine:
Her skin was like a grape whose veins
  Run snow instead of wine.

She knew not those sweet words she spake,
  Nor knew her own sweet way;
But there's never a bird, so sweet a song
  Thronged in whose throat all day.

Oh, there were flowers in Storrington
  On the turf and on the spray;
But the sweetest flower on Sussex hills
  Was the Daisy-flower that day!

Her beauty smoothed earth's furrowed face.
  She gave me tokens three:—
A look, a word of her winsome mouth,
  And a wild raspberry.

A berry red, a guileless look,
  A still word,—strings of sand!
And yet they made my wild, wild heart
  Fly down to her little hand.

For standing artless as the air
  And candid as the skies,
She took the berries with her hand
  And the love with her sweet eyes.

The fairest things have fleetest end,
  Their scent survives their close:
But the rose's scent is bitterness
  To him that loved the rose.

She looked a little wistfully,
  Then went her sunshine way:—
The sea's eye had a mist on it,
  And the leaves fell from the day.

She went her unremembering way,
  She went and left in me
The pang of all the partings gone,
  And partings yet to be.

She left me marveling why my soul
  Was sad that she was glad;
At all the sadness in the sweet,
  The sweetness in the sad.

Still, still I seemed to see her, still
  Look up with soft replies,
And take the berries with her hand,
  And the love with her lovely eyes.

Nothing begins, and nothing ends,
  That is not paid with moan,
For we are born in other's pain,
  And perish in our own.

To a Snowflake

What heart could have thought you?—
Past our devisal
(O filigree petal!)
Fashioned so purely,
Fragilely, surely,
From what Paradisal
Imagineless metal,
Too costly for cost?
Who hammered you, wrought you,
From argentine vapor?—

"God was my shaper.
Passing surmisal,
He hammered, He wrought me,
From curled silver vapor,
To lust of his mind:—
Thou couldst not have thought me!
So purely, so palely,
Tinily, surely,
Mightily, frailly,

Insculped and embossed,
With His hammer of wind,
And His graver of frost."

An Arab Love-Song

The hunchèd camels of the night [1]
Trouble the bright
And silver waters of the moon.
The Maiden of the Morn will soon
Through Heaven stray and sing,
Star gathering.
Now while the dark about our loves is strewn,
Light of my dark, blood of my heart, O come!
And night will catch her breath up, and be dumb.

Leave thy father, leave thy mother
And thy brother;
Leave the black tents of thy tribe apart!
Am I not thy father and thy brother,
And thy mother?
And thou—what needest with thy tribe's black tents
Who hast the red pavilion of my heart?

All's Vast

O nothing, in this corporal earth of man,
  That to the imminent heaven of his high soul
Responds with color and with shadow, can
  Lack correlated greatness. If the scroll
Where thoughts lie fast in spell of hieroglyph
  Be mighty through its mighty inhabitants;
If God be in His Name; grave potence if
  The sounds unbind of hieratic chants;
All's vast that vastness means. Nay, I affirm
  Nature is whole in her least things exprest,
Nor know we with what scope God builds the worm.
  Our towns are copied fragments from our breast;
    And all man's Babylons strive but to impart
    The grandeurs of his Babylonian heart.

[1] Cloud-shapes observed by travelers in the East.

Epilogue

(From "A Judgment in Heaven")

Heaven, which man's generations draws,
Nor deviates into replicas,
Must of as deep diversity
In judgment as creation be.
There is no expeditious road
To pack and label men for God,
And save them by the barrel-load.
Some may perchance, with strange surprise,
Have blundered into Paradise.
In vasty dusk of life abroad,
They fondly thought to err from God,
Nor knew the circle that they trod;
And, wandering all the night about,
Found them at morn where they set out.
Death dawned; Heaven lay in prospect wide:—
Lo! they were standing by His side!

The Sun

(From "Ode to the Setting Sun")

Who lit the furnace of the mammoth's heart?
  Who shagged him like Pilatus' ribbèd flanks?
        Who raised the columned ranks
Of that old pre-diluvian forestry,
Which like a continent torn oppressed the sea,
  When the ancient heavens did in rains depart,
      While the high-dancèd whirls
Of the tossed scud made hiss thy drenchèd curls?
      Thou rear'dst the enormous brood;
    Who hast with life imbued
  The lion maned in tawny majesty,
    The tiger velvet-barred,
    The stealthy-stepping pard,
  And the lithe panther's flexous symmetry?

How came the entombèd tree a light-bearer,
      Though sunk in lightless lair?
      Friend of the forgers of earth,

Mate of the earthquake and thunders volcanic,
Clasped in the arms of the forces Titanic
Which rock like a cradle the girth
Of the ether-hung world;
Swart son of the swarthy mine,
When flame on the breath of his nostrils feeds
How is his countenance half-divine,
Like thee in thy sanguine weeds?
Thou gavest him his light,
Though sepultured in night
Beneath the dead bones of a perished world;
Over his prostrate form
Though cold, and heat, and storm,
The mountainous wrack of a creation hurled.

Who made the splendid rose
Saturate with purple glows;
Cupped to the marge with beauty; a perfume-press
Whence the wind vintages
Gushes of warmèd fragrance richer far
Than all the flavorous ooze of Cyprus' vats?
Lo, in yon gale which waves her green cymar,
With dusky cheeks burnt red
She sways her heavy head,
Drunk with the must of her own odorousness;
While in a moted trouble the vexed gnats
Maze, and vibrate, and tease the noontide hush.
Who girt dissolvèd lightnings in the grape?
Summered the opal with an Irised flush?
Is it not thou that dost the tulip drape,
And huest the daffodilly,
Yet who hast snowed the lily,
And her frail sister, whom the waters name,
Dost vestal-vesture 'mid the blaze of June,
Cold as the new-sprung girlhood of the moon
Ere Autumn's kiss sultry her cheek with flame?
Thou sway'st thy sceptered beam
O'er all delight and dream,
Beauty is beautiful but in thy glance:
And like a jocund maid
In garland-flowers arrayed,
Before thy ark Earth keeps her sacred dance.

A Fallen Yew

It seemed corrival of the world's great prime,
Made to un-edge the scythe of Time,
And last with stateliest rhyme.

No tender Dryad ever did indue
That rigid chiton of rough yew,
To fret her white flesh through:

But some god like to those grim Asgard lords,
Who walk the fables of the hordes
From Scandinavian fjords,

Upheaved its stubborn girth, and raised unriven,
Against the whirl-blast and the levin,
Defiant arms to Heaven.

When doom puffed out the stars, we might have said,
It would decline its heavy head,
And see the world to bed.

For this firm yew did from the vassal leas,
And rain and air, its tributaries,
Its revenues increase,

And levy impost on the golden sun,
Take the blind years as they might run,
And no fate seek or shun.

But now our yew is strook, is fallen—yea,
Hacked like dull wood of every day
To this and that, men say.

Never!—To Hades' shadowy shipyards gone,
Dim barge of Dis, down Acheron
It drops, or Lethe wan.

Stirred by its fall—poor destined bark of Dis!—
Along my soul a bruit there is
Of echoing images,

Reverberations of mortality:
Spelt backward from its death, to me
Its life reads saddenedly.

Its breast was hollowed as the tooth of eld;
  And boys, there creeping unbeheld,
    A laughing moment dwelled.

Yet they, within its very heart so crept,
  Reached not the heart that courage kept
    With winds and years beswept.

And in its boughs did close and kindly nest
  The birds, as they within its breast,
    By all its leaves caressed.

But bird nor child might touch by any art
  Each other's or the tree's hid heart,
    A whole God's breadth apart;

The breadth of God, the breadth of death and life!
  Even so, even so, in undreamed strife
    With pulseless Law, the wife,—

The sweetest wife on sweetest marriage-day,—
  Their souls at grapple in mid-way,
    Sweet to her sweet may say:

"I take you to my inmost heart, my true!"
  Ah, fool! but there is one heart you
    Shall never take him to!

The hold that falls not when the town is got,
  The heart's heart, whose immurèd plot
    Hath keys yourself keep not!

Its ports you cannot burst—you are withstood—
  For him that to your listening blood
    Sends precepts as he would.

Its gates are deaf to Love, high summoner;
  Yea, love's great warrant runs not there:
    You are your prisoner.

Yourself are with yourself the sole consortress
  In that unleaguerable fortress;
    It knows you not for portress.

Its keys are at the cincture hung of God;
  Its gates are trepidant to His nod;
    By Him its floors are trod.

And if His feet shall rock those floors in wrath,
Or blest aspersion sleek His path,
Is only choice it hath.

Yea, in that ultimate heart's occult abode
To lie as in an oubliette of God,
Or in a bower untrod,

Built by a secret Lover for His Spouse;—
Sole choice is this your life allows,
Sad tree, whose perishing boughs
So few birds house!

The Hound of Heaven

I fled Him, down the nights and down the days;
I fled Him, down the arches of the years;
I fled Him, down the labyrinthine ways
Of my own mind; and in the mist of tears
I hid from Him, and under running laughter.
Up vistaed hopes I sped;
And shot, precipitatèd,
Adown Titanic glooms of chasmèd fears,
From those strong Feet that followed, followed after.
But with unhurrying chase,
And unperturbèd pace,
Deliberate speed, majestic instancy,
They beat—and a Voice beat
More instant than the Feet—
"All things betray thee, who betrayest Me."

I pleaded, outlaw-wise,
By many a hearted casement, curtained red,
Trellised with intertwining charities
(For, though I knew His love Who followèd,
Yet was I sore adread
Lest, having Him, I must have naught beside);
But, if one little casement parted wide,
The gust of His approach would clash it to:
Fear wist not to evade, as Love wist to pursue.
Across the margent of the world I fled,
And troubled the gold gateways of the stars,
Smiting for shelter on their clangèd bars;
Fretted to dulcet jars

And silvern chatter the pale ports o' the moon.
I said to Dawn: Be sudden—to Eve: Be soon;
With thy young skiey blossoms heap me over
From this tremendous Lover—
Float thy vague veil about me, lest He see!
I tempted all His servitors, but to find
My own betrayal in their constancy,
In faith to Him their fickleness to me,
Their traitorous trueness, and their loyal deceit.
To all swift things for swiftness did I sue;
Clung to the whistling mane of every wind.
But whether they swept, smoothly fleet,
The long savannahs of the blue;
Or whether, Thunder-driven,
They clanged his chariot 'thwart a heaven,
Plashy with flying lightnings round the spurn o' their feet:—
Fear wist not to evade as Love wist to pursue.
Still with unhurrying chase,
And unperturbèd pace,
Deliberate speed, majestic instancy,
Came on the following Feet,
And a Voice above their beat—
"Naught shelters thee, who wilt not shelter Me."

I sought no more that after which I strayed
In face of man or maid;
But still within the little children's eyes
Seems something, something that replies,
They at least are for me, surely for me!
I turned me to them very wistfully;
But just as their young eyes grew sudden fair
With dawning answers there,
Their angel plucked them from me by the hair.
"Come then, ye other children, Nature's—share
With me" (said I) "your delicate fellowship;
Let me greet you lip to lip,
Let me twine with you caresses,
Wantoning
With our Lady-Mother's vagrant tresses.
Banqueting
With her in her wind-walled palace,
Underneath her azured daïs,
Quaffing, as your taintless way is,
From a chalice
Lucent-weeping out of the dayspring."

So it was done:
I in their delicate fellowship was one—
Drew the bolt of Nature's secrecies.
I knew all the swift importings
On the willful face of skies;
I knew how the clouds arise
Spumèd of the wild sea-snortings;
All that's born or dies
Rose and drooped with; made them shapers
Of mine own moods, or wailful or divine;
With them joyed and was bereaven.
I was heavy with the even,
When she lit her glimmering tapers
Round the day's dead sanctities.
I laughed in the morning's eyes.
I triumphed and I saddened with all weather,
Heaven and I wept together,
And its sweet tears were salt with mortal mine;
Against the red throb of its sunset-heart
I laid my own to beat,
And share commingling heat;
But not by that, by that, was eased my human smart.
In vain my tears were wet on Heaven's gray cheek.
For ah! we know not what each other says,
These things and I; in sound *I* speak—
Their sound is but their stir, they speak by silences.
Nature, poor stepdame, cannot slake my drouth;
Let her, if she would owe me,
Drop yon blue bosom-veil of sky, and show me
The breasts o' her tenderness:
Never did any milk of hers once bless
My thirsting mouth.
Nigh and nigh draws the chase,
With unperturbèd pace,
Deliberate speed, majestic instancy;
And past those noisèd Feet
A Voice comes yet more fleet—
"Lo! naught contents thee, who content'st not Me."

Naked I wait Thy love's uplifted stroke!
My harness piece by piece Thou hast hewn from me,
And smitten me to my knee;
I am defenseless utterly.
I slept, methinks, and woke,
And, slowly gazing, find me stripped in sleep.

In the rash lustihead of my young powers,
  I shook the pillaring hours
And pulled my life upon me; grimed with smears,
I stand amid the dust o' the mounded years—
My mangled youth lies dead beneath the heap.
My days have crackled and gone up in smoke,
Have puffed and burst as sun-starts on a stream.
  Yea, faileth now even dream
The dreamer, and the lute the lutanist;
Even the linked fantasies, in whose blossomy twist
I swung the earth a trinket at my wrist,
Are yielding; cords of all too weak account
For earth with heavy griefs so overplused.
  Ah! is Thy love indeed
A weed, albeit an amaranthine weed,
Suffering no flowers except its own to mount?
  Ah! must—
  Designer infinite!—
Ah! must Thou char the wood ere Thou canst limn with it?
My freshness spent its wavering shower i' the dust;
And now my heart is as a broken fount,
Wherein tear-drippings stagnate, spilt down ever
  From the dank thoughts that shiver
Upon the sighful branches of my mind.
  Such is; what is to be?
The pulp so bitter, how shall taste the rind?
I dimly guess what Time in mists confounds;
Yet ever and anon a trumpet sounds
From the hid battlements of Eternity;
Those shaken mists a space unsettle, then
Round the half-glimpsèd turrets slowly wash again.
  But not ere him who summoneth
  I first have seen, enwound
With glooming robes purpureal, cypress-crowned;
His name I know, and what his trumpet saith.
Whether man's heart or life it be which yields
  Thee harvest, must Thy harvest-fields
  Be dunged with rotten death?

   Now of that long pursuit
   Comes on at hand the bruit;
  That Voice is round me like a bursting sea:
   "And is thy earth so marred,
   Shattered in shard on shard?
  Lo, all things fly thee, for thou fliest Me!

Strange, piteous, futile thing!
Wherefore should any set thee love apart?
Seeing none but I makes much of naught" (He said),
"And human love needs human meriting:
How hast thou merited—
Of all man's clotted clay the dingiest clot?
Alack, thou knowest not
How little worthy of any love thou art!
Whom wilt thou find to love ignoble thee
Save Me, save only Me?
All which I took from thee I did but take,
Not for thy harms,
But just that thou might'st seek it in My arms.
All which thy child's mistake
Fancies as lost, I have stored for thee at home:
Rise, clasp My hand, and come!"

Halts by me that footfall:
Is my gloom, after all,
Shade of His hand, outstretched caressingly?
"Ah, fondest, blindest, weakest,
I am He Whom thou seekest!
Thou dravest love from thee, who dravest Me."

From "Grace of the Way"

Now of that vision I, bereaven,
This knowledge keep, that may not dim:
Short arm needs man to reach to Heaven,
So ready is Heaven to stoop to him.

"In No Strange Land"

O world invisible, we view thee,
O world intangible, we touch thee,
O world unknowable, we know thee,
Inapprehensible, we clutch thee!

Does the fish soar to find the ocean,
The eagle plunge to find the air—
That we ask of the stars in motion
If they have rumor of thee there?

Not where the wheeling systems darken,
And our benumbed conceiving soars!—
The drift of pinions, would we hearken,
Beats at our own clay-shuttered doors.

The angels keep their ancient places;
Turn but a stone, and start a wing!
'Tis ye, 'tis your estrangèd faces,
That miss the many-splendored thing.

But, when so sad thou canst not sadder,
Cry;—and upon thy so sore loss
Shall shine the traffic of Jacob's ladder
Pitched betwixt Heaven and Charing Cross.

Yea, in the night, my Soul, my daughter,
Cry,—clinging Heaven by the hems;
And lo, Christ walking on the water
Not of Gennesareth, but Thames!

A. E. Housman

1859-1936

Reveillé

Wake: the silver dusk returning
  Up the beach of darkness brims,
And the ship of sunrise burning
  Strands upon the eastern rims.

Wake: the vaulted shadow shatters,
  Trampled to the floor it spanned,
And the tent of night in tatters
  Straws the sky-pavilioned land.

Up, lad, up, 'tis late for lying:
  Hear the drums of morning play;

Hark, the empty highways crying
  "Who'll beyond the hills away?"

Towns and countries woo together,
  Forelands beacon, belfries call;
Never lad that trod on leather
  Lived to feast his heart with all.

Up, lad: thews that lie and cumber
  Sunlit pallets never thrive;
Morns abed and daylight slumber
  Were not meant for man alive.

Clay lies still, but blood's a rover;
  Breath's a ware that will not keep.
Up, lad: when the journey's over
  There'll be time enough to sleep.

With Rue My Heart Is Laden

With rue my heart is laden
  For golden friends I had,
For many a rose-lipt maiden
  And many a lightfoot lad.

By brooks too broad for leaping
  The lightfoot boys are laid;
The rose-lipt girls are sleeping
  In fields where roses fade.

Into My Heart

Into my heart an air that kills
  From yon far country blows:
What are those blue remembered hills,
  What spires, what farms are those?

That is the land of lost content,
  I see it shining plain:
The happy highways where I went
  And cannot come again.

When I Was One-and-Twenty

When I was one-and-twenty
I heard a wise man say,
"Give crowns and pounds and guineas
But not your heart away;
Give pearls away and rubies
But keep your fancy free."
But I was one-and-twenty,
No use to talk to me.

When I was one-and-twenty
I heard him say again,
"The heart out of the bosom
Was never given in vain;
'Tis paid with sighs a-plenty
And sold for endless rue."
And I am two-and-twenty,
And oh, 'tis true, 'tis true.

To an Athlete Dying Young

The time you won your town the race
We chaired you through the market-place;
Man and boy stood cheering by,
And home we brought you shoulder-high.

Today, the road all runners come,
Shoulder-high we bring you home,
And set you at your threshold down,
Townsman of a stiller town.

Smart lad, to slip betimes away
From fields where glory does not stay,
And early though the laurel grows
It withers quicker than the rose.

Eyes the shady night has shut
Cannot see the record cut,
And silence sounds no worse than cheers
After earth has stopped the ears:

Now you will not swell the rout
Of lads that wore their honors out,
Runners whom renown outran
And the name died before the man.

So set, before its echoes fade,
The fleet foot on the sill of shade,
And hold to the low lintel up
The still-defended challenge-cup.

And round that early-laureled head
Will flock to gaze the strengthless dead,
And find unwithered on its curls
The garland briefer than a girl's.

Loveliest of Trees

Loveliest of trees, the cherry now
Is hung with bloom along the bough,
And stands about the woodland ride
Wearing white for Eastertide.

Now, of my threescore years and ten,
Twenty will not come again,
And take from seventy springs a score,
It only leaves me fifty more.

And since to look at things in bloom
Fifty springs are little room,
About the woodlands I will go
To see the cherry hung with snow.

Is My Team Ploughing

"Is my team ploughing,
  That I was used to drive
And hear the harness jingle
  When I was man alive?"

Aye, the horses trample,
  The harness jingles now;
No change though you lie under
  The land you used to plough.

"Is football playing
  Along the river shore,
With lads to chase the leather,
  Now I stand up no more?"

Aye, the ball is flying,
  The lads play heart and soul;
The goal stands up, the keeper
  Stands up to keep the goal.

"Is my girl happy,
  That I thought hard to leave,
And has she tired of weeping
  As she lies down at eve?"

Aye, she lies down lightly,
  She lies not down to weep:
Your girl is well contented.
  Be still, my lad, and sleep.

"Is my friend hearty,
  Now I am thin and pine;
And has he found to sleep in
  A better bed than mine?"

Aye, lad, I lie easy,
  I lie as lads would choose;
I cheer a dead man's sweetheart.
  Never ask me whose.

On Wenlock Edge

On Wenlock Edge the wood's in trouble;
His forest fleece the Wrekin heaves;
The gale, it plies the saplings double,
And thick on Severn snow the leaves.

'Twould blow like this through hold and hangar
When Uricon the city stood:
'Tis the old wind in the old anger,
But then it threshed another wood.

Then, 'twas before my time, the Roman
At yonder heaving hill would stare:

The blood that warms an English yeoman,
The thoughts that hurt him, they were there.

There, like the wind through woods in riot,
Through him the gale of life blew high;
The tree of man was never quiet:
Then 'twas the Roman, now 'tis I.

The gale, it plies the saplings double,
It blows so hard, 'twill soon be gone:
Today the Roman and his trouble
Are ashes under Uricon.

Along the Field As We Came By

Along the field as we came by
A year ago, my love and I,
The aspen over stile and stone
Was talking to itself alone.
"Oh, who are these that kiss and pass?
A country lover and his lass;
Two lovers looking to be wed;
And time shall put them both to bed,
But she shall lie with earth above,
And he beside another love."

And sure enough beneath the tree
There walks another love with me,
And overhead the aspen heaves
Its rainy-sounding silver leaves;
And I spell nothing in their stir,
But now perhaps they speak to her,
And plain for her to understand
They talk about a time at hand
When I shall sleep with clover clad,
And she beside another lad.

Bredon Hill

In summertime on Bredon
  The bells they sound so clear;
Round both the shires they ring them
  In steeples far and near,
  A happy noise to hear.

Here of a Sunday morning
  My love and I would lie,
And see the colored counties,
  And hear the larks so high
  About us in the sky.

The bells would ring to call her
  In valleys miles away:
"Come all to church, good people;
  Good people, come and pray."
  But here my love would stay.

And I would turn and answer
  Among the springing thyme,
"Oh, peal upon our wedding,
  And we will hear the chime,
  And come to church in time."

But when the snows at Christmas
  On Bredon top were strown,
My love rose up so early
  And stole out unbeknown
  And went to church alone.

They tolled the one bell only,
  Groom there was none to see,
The mourners followed after,
  And so to church went she,
  And would not wait for me.

The bells they sound on Bredon,
  And still the steeples hum.
"Come all to church, good people,—"
  Oh, noisy bells, be dumb;
  I hear you. I will come.

The Chestnut Casts His Flambeaux

The chestnut casts his flambeaux, and the flowers
  Stream from the hawthorn on the wind away,
The doors clap to, the pane is blind with showers.
  Pass me the can, lad; there's an end of May.

There's one spoilt spring to scant our mortal lot,
  One season ruined of our little store.

May will be fine next year as like as not:
  Oh, aye, but then we shall be twenty-four.

We for a certainty are not the first
  Have sat in taverns while the tempest hurled
Their hopeful plans to emptiness, and cursed
  Whatever brute and blackguard made the world.

It is in truth iniquity on high
  To cheat our sentenced souls of aught they crave,
And mar the merriment as you and I
  Fare on our long fool's errand to the grave.

Iniquity it is; but pass the can.
  My lad, no pair of kings our mothers bore;
Our only portion is the estate of man:
  We want the moon, but we shall get no more.

If here today the cloud of thunder lours
  Tomorrow it will hie on far behests;
The flesh will grieve on other bones than ours
  Soon, and the soul will mourn in other breasts.

The troubles of our proud and angry dust
  Are from eternity, and shall not fail.
Bear them we can, and if we can we must.
  Shoulder the sky, my lad, and drink your ale.

The Carpenter's Son

Here the hangman stops his cart:
Now the best of friends must part
Fare you well, for ill fare I:
Live, lads, and I will die.

"Oh, at home had I but stayed
'Prenticed to my father's trade,
Had I stuck to plane and adze,
I had not been lost, my lads.

"Then I might have built perhaps
Gallows-trees for other chaps,
Never dangled on my own,
Had I but left ill alone.

"Now, you see, they hang me high,
And the people passing by
Stop to shake their fists and curse;
So 'tis come from ill to worse.

"Here hang I, and right and left
Two poor fellows hang for theft:
All the same's the luck we prove,
Though the midmost hangs for love.

"Comrades all, that stand and gaze,
Walk henceforth in other ways;
See my neck and save your own:
Comrades all, leave ill alone.

"Make some day a decent end,
Shrewder fellows than your friend.
Fare you well, for ill fare I:
Live, lads, and I will die."

Be Still, My Soul, Be Still

Be still, my soul, be still; the arms you bear are brittle,
  Earth and high heaven are fixt of old and founded strong.
Think rather,—call to thought, if now you grieve a little,
  The days when we had rest, O soul, for they were long.

Men loved unkindness then, but lightless in the quarry
  I slept and saw not; tears fell down, I did not mourn;
Sweat ran and blood sprang out and I was never sorry:
  Then it was well with me, in days ere I was born.

Now, and I muse for why and never find the reason,
  I pace the earth, and drink the air, and feel the sun.
Be still, be still, my soul; it is but for a season:
  Let us endure an hour and see injustice done.

Ay, look: high heaven and earth ail from the prime foundation;
  All thoughts to rive the heart are here, and all are vain:
Horror and scorn and hate and fear and indignation—
  Oh, why did I awake? When shall I sleep again?

I Hoed and Trenched and Weeded

I hoed and trenched and weeded,
  And took the flowers to fair:
I brought them home unheeded;
  The hue was not the wear.

So up and down I sow them
  For lads like me to find,
When I shall lie below them,
  A dead man out of mind.

Some seeds the birds devour,
  And some the season mars,
But here and there will flower
  The solitary stars,

And fields will yearly bear them
  As light-leaved spring comes on,
And luckless lads will wear them
  When I am dead and gone.

The Laws of God, the Laws of Man

The laws of God, the laws of man,
He may keep that will and can;
Not I: let God and man decree
Laws for themselves and not for me;
And if my ways are not as theirs
Let them mind their own affairs.
Their deed I judge and much condemn,
Yet when did I make laws for them?
Please yourselves, say I, and they
Need only look the other way.
But no, they will not; they must still
Wrest their neighbour to their will,
And make me dance as they desire
With jail and gallows and hell-fire.
And how am I to face the odds
Of man's bedevilment and God's?
I, a stranger and afraid
In a world I never made.

They will be master, right or wrong;
Though both are foolish, both are strong
And since, my soul, we cannot fly
To Saturn nor to Mercury,
Keep we must, if keep we can,
These foreign laws of God and man.

Farewell

"Farewell to barn and stack and tree,
  Farewell to Severn shore.
Terence, look your last at me,
  For I come home no more.

"The sun burns on the half-mown hill,
  By now the blood is dried;
And Maurice among the hay lies still
  And my knife is in his side.

"My mother thinks us long away;
  'Tis time the field were mown.
She had two sons at rising day,
  To-night she'll be alone.

"And here's a bloody hand to shake,
  And oh, man, here's good-bye;
We'll sweat no more on scythe and rake,
  My bloody hands and I.

"I wish you strength to bring you pride,
  And love to keep you clean,
And I wish you luck, come Lammastide,
  At racing on the green.

"Long for me the rick will wait,
  And long will wait the fold,
And long will stand the empty plate,
  And dinner will be cold."

Epilogue

"Terence, this is stupid stuff;
You eat your victuals fast enough;
There can't be much amiss, 'tis clear,
To see the rate you drink your beer.
But oh, good Lord, the verse you make,
It gives a chap the belly-ache.
The cow, the old cow, she is dead;
It sleeps well, the hornèd head:
We poor lads, 'tis our turn now
To hear such tunes as killed the cow.
Pretty friendship 'tis to rhyme
Your friends to death before their time
Moping melancholy mad:
Come, pipe a tune to dance to, lad."

Why, if 'tis dancing you would be,
There's brisker pipes than poetry.
Say, for what were hop-yards meant,
Or why was Burton built on Trent?
Oh, many a peer of England brews
Livelier liquor than the Muse,
And malt does more than Milton can
To justify God's ways to man.
Ale, man, ale's the stuff to drink
For fellows whom it hurts to think:
Look into the pewter pot
To see the world as the world's not.
And faith, 'tis pleasant till 'tis past:
The mischief is that 'twill not last.
Oh, I have been to Ludlow fair
And left my necktie God knows where,
And carried half way home, or near,
Pints and quarts of Ludlow beer:
Then the world seemed none so bad,
And I myself a sterling lad;
And down in lovely muck I've lain,
Happy till I woke again.
Then I saw the morning sky:
Heigho, the tale was all a lie;
The world, it was the old world yet,
I was I, my things were wet,

And nothing now remained to do
But begin the game anew.

Therefore, since the world has still
Much good, but much less good than ill,
And while the sun and moon endure
Luck's a chance, but trouble's sure,
I'd face it as a wise man would,
And train for ill and not for good.
'Tis true, the stuff I bring for sale
Is not so brisk a brew as ale:
Out of a stem that scored the hand
I wrung it in a weary land.
But take it: if the smack is sour,
The better for the embittered hour;
It should do good to heart and head
When your soul is in my soul's stead;
And I will friend you, if I may,
In the dark and cloudy day.

There was a king reigned in the East:
There, when kings will sit to feast,
They get their fill before they think
With poisoned meat and poisoned drink.
He gathered all that springs to birth
From the many-venomed earth;
First a little, thence to more,
He sampled all her killing store;
And easy, smiling, seasoned sound,
Sate the king when healths went round.
They put arsenic in his meat
And stared aghast to watch him eat;
They poured strychnine in his cup
And shook to see him drink it up:
They shook, they stared as white's their shirt:
Them it was their poison hurt.
—I tell the tale that I heard told.
Mithridates, he died old.

Eight O'clock

He stood, and heard the steeple
  Sprinkle the quarters on the morning town.
One, two, three, four, to market-place and people
  It tossed them down.

Strapped, noosed, nighing his hour,
  He stood and counted them and cursed his luck;
And then the clock collected in the tower
  Its strength, and struck.

Epitaph on an Army of Mercenaries

These, in the day when heaven was falling,
  The hour when earth's foundations fled,
Followed their mercenary calling
  And took their wages and are dead.

Their shoulders held the sky suspended;
  They stood, and earth's foundations stay;
What God abandoned, these defended,
  And saved the sum of things for pay.

Easter Hymn

If in that Syrian garden, ages slain,
You sleep, and know not you are dead in vain,
Nor even in dreams behold how dark and bright
Ascends in smoke and fire by day and night
The hate you died to quench and could but fan,
Sleep well and see no morning, son of man.

But if, the grave rent and the stone rolled by,
At the right hand of majesty on high
You sit, and sitting so remember yet
Your tears, your agony and bloody sweat,
Your cross and passion and the life you gave,
Bow hither out of heaven and see and save.

William Butler Yeats

1865-1939

The Lake Isle of Innisfree

I will arise and go now, and go to Innisfree,
And a small cabin build there, of clay and wattles made;
Nine bean rows will I have there, a hive for the honey bee,
And live alone in the bee-loud glade.

And I shall have some peace there, for peace comes dropping slow,
Dropping from the veils of the morning to where the cricket sings;
There midnight's all a glimmer, and noon a purple glow,
And evening full of the linnet's wings.

I will arise and go now, for always night and day
I hear lake water lapping with low sounds by the shore;
While I stand on the roadway, or on the pavements gray,
I hear it in the deep heart's core.

The Song of Wandering Aengus

I went out to the hazel wood,
Because a fire was in my head,
And cut and peeled a hazel wand,
And hooked a berry to a thread,
And when white moths were on the wing,
And moth-like stars were flickering out,
I dropped the berry in a stream
And caught a little silver trout.

When I had laid it on the floor
I went to blow the fire a-flame,

But something rustled on the floor,
And someone called me by my name:
It had become a glimmering girl
With apple blossoms in her hair
Who called me by my name and ran
And faded through the brightening air.

Though I am old with wandering
Through hollow lands and hilly lands,
I will find out where she has gone,
And kiss her lips and take her hands;
And walk among long dappled grass,
And pluck, till time and times are done,
The silver apples of the moon,
The golden apples of the sun.

When You Are Old

When you are old and gray and full of sleep,
And nodding by the fire, take down this book,
And slowly read, and dream of the soft look
Your eyes had once, and of their shadows deep;

How many loved your moments of glad grace,
And loved your beauty with love false or true;
But one man loved the pilgrim soul in you,
And loved the sorrows of your changing face.

And bending down beside the glowing bars
Murmur, a little sadly, how love fled
And paced upon the mountains overhead
And hid his face amid a crowd of stars.

The Cap and Bells

A Queen was beloved by a jester,
  And once when the owls grew still
He made his soul go upward
  And stand on her window sill.

In a long and straight blue garment,
  It talked before morn was white,

And it had grown wise by thinking
  Of a footfall hushed and light.

But the young queen would not listen;
  She rose in her pale nightgown,
She drew in the brightening casement
  And pushed the brass bolt down.

He bade his heart go to her,
  When the bats cried out no more,
In a red and quivering garment
  It sang to her through the door.

The tongue of it sweet with dreaming
  Of a flutter of flower-like hair,
But she took up her fan from the table
  And waved it off on the air.

"I've cap and bells," he pondered,
  "I will send them to her and die."
And as soon as the morn had whitened
  He left them where she went by.

She laid them upon her bosom,
  Under a cloud of her hair,
And her red lips sang them a love song.
  The stars grew out of the air.

She opened her door and her window,
  And the heart and the soul came through,
To her right hand came the red one,
  To her left hand came the blue.

They set up a noise like crickets,
  A chattering wise and sweet,
And her hair was a folded flower,
  And the quiet of love her feet.

An Old Song Resung [1]

Down by the salley gardens my love and I did meet;
She passed the salley gardens with little snow-white feet.
She bid me take love easy, as the leaves grow on the tree;
But I, being young and foolish, with her would not agree.

[1] "This," Yeats wrote in a footnote in one of the early editions, "is an extension of three lines sung to me by an old woman of Ballisodare."

In a field by the river my love and I did stand,
And on my leaning shoulder she laid her snow-white hand.
She bid me take life easy, as the grass grows on the weirs;
But I was young and foolish, and now am full of tears.

The Rose of the World

Who dreamed that beauty passes like a dream?
For these red lips, with all their mournful pride,
Mournful that no new wonder may betide,
Troy passed away in one high funeral gleam,
And Usna's children died.

We and the laboring world are passing by:
Amid men's souls, that waver and give place,
Like the pale waters in their wintry race,
Under the passing stars, frame of the sky,
Lives on this lonely face.

Bow down, archangels, in your dim abode:
Before you were, or any hearts to beat,
Weary and kind, one lingered by His seat;
He made the world to be a grassy road
Before her wandering feet.

The Sorrow of Love

The quarrel of the sparrows in the eaves,
The full round moon and the star-laden sky,
And the loud song of the ever-singing leaves,
Has hid away earth's old and weary cry.

And then you came with those red mournful lips,
And with you came the whole of the world's tears,
And all the trouble of her laboring ships,
And all the trouble of her myriad years.

And now the sparrows warring in the eaves,
The curd-pale moon, the white stars in the sky,
And the loud chaunting of the unquiet leaves,
Are shaken with earth's old and weary cry.

The Wild Swans at Coole

The trees are in their autumn beauty,
The woodland paths are dry,
Under the October twilight the water
Mirrors a still sky;
Upon the brimming water among the stones
Are nine and fifty swans.

The nineteenth Autumn has come upon me
Since I first made my count;
I saw, before I had well finished,
All suddenly mount
And scatter, wheeling, in great broken rings
Upon their clamorous wings.

I have looked upon those brilliant creatures,
And now my heart is sore.
All's changed since I, hearing at twilight,
The first time on this shore,
The bell-beat of their wings above my head,
Trod with a lighter tread.

Unwearied still, lover by lover,
They paddle in the cold,
Companionable streams or climb the air;
Their hearts have not grown old;
Passion or conquest, wander where they will,
Attend upon them still.

But now they drift on the still water
Mysterious, beautiful;
Among what rushes will they build,
By what lake's edge or pool
Delight men's eyes, when I awake some day
To find they have flown away?

Leda and the Swan

A sudden blow: the great wings beating still
Above the staggering girl, her thighs caressed
By the dark webs, her nape caught in his bill,
He holds her helpless breast upon his breast.

How can those terrified vague fingers push
The feathered glory from her loosening thighs?
And how can body, laid in that white rush,
But feel the strange heart beating where it lies?

A shudder in the loins engenders there
The broken wall, the burning roof and tower
And Agamemnon dead.
Being so caught up,
So mastered by the brute blood of the air,
Did she put on his knowledge with his power
Before the indifferent beak could let her drop?

Sailing to Byzantium

I

That is no country for old men. The young
In one another's arms, birds in the trees,
—Those dying generations—at their song,
The salmon-falls, the mackerel-crowded seas,
Fish, flesh, or fowl, commend all summer long
Whatever is begotten, born, and dies.
Caught in that sensual music all neglect
Monuments of unaging intellect.

II

An aged man is but a paltry thing,
A tattered coat upon a stick, unless
Soul clap its hands and sing, and louder sing
For every tatter in its mortal dress,
Nor is there singing school but studying
Monuments of its own magnificence;
And therefore I have sailed the seas and come
To the holy city of Byzantium.

III

O sages standing in God's holy fire
As in the gold mosaic of a wall,
Come from the holy fire, perne in a gyre,
And be the singing-masters of my soul.
Consume my heart away; sick with desire
And fastened to a dying animal

It knows not what it is; and gather me
Into the artifice of eternity.

IV

Once out of nature I shall never take
My bodily form from any natural thing,
But such a form as Grecian goldsmiths make
Of hammered gold and gold enameling
To keep a drowsy Emperor awake;
Or set upon a golden bough to sing
To lords and ladies of Byzantium
Of what is past, or passing, or to come.

Among School Children

I

I walk through the long schoolroom questioning;
A kind old nun in a white hood replies;
The children learn to cipher and to sing,
To study reading-books and history,
To cut and sew, be neat in everything
In the best modern way—the children's eyes
In momentary wonder stare upon
A sixty-year-old smiling public man.

II

I dream of a Ledaean body, bent
Above a sinking fire, a tale that she
Told of a harsh reproof, or trivial event
That changed some childish day to tragedy—
Told, and it seemed that our two natures blent
Into a sphere from youthful sympathy,
Or else, to alter Plato's parable,
Into the yolk and white of the one shell.

III

And thinking of that fit of grief or rage
I look upon one child or t'other there
And wonder if she stood so at that age—
For even daughters of the swan can share
Something of every paddler's heritage—
And had that color upon cheek or hair,

And thereupon my heart is driven wild:
She stands before me as a living child.

IV

Her present image floats into the mind—
Did Quattrocento finger fashion it
Hollow of cheek as though it drank the wind
And took a mess of shadows for its meat?
And I though never of Ledaean kind
Had pretty plumage once—enough of that,
Better to smile on all that smile, and show
There is a comfortable kind of old scarecrow.

V

What youthful mother, a shape upon her lap
Honey of generation had betrayed,
And that must sleep, shriek, struggle to escape
As recollection or the drug decide,
Would think her son, did she but see that shape
With sixty or more winters on its head,
A compensation for the pang of his birth,
Or the uncertainty of his setting forth?

VI

Plato thought nature but a spume that plays
Upon a ghostly paradigm of things;
Solider Aristotle played the taws
Upon the bottom of a king of kings;
World-famous golden-thighed Pythagoras
Fingered upon a fiddle-stick or strings
What a star sang and careless Muses heard:
Old clothes upon old sticks to scare a bird.

VII

Both nuns and mothers worship images,
But those the candles light are not as those
That animate a mother's reveries,
But keep a marble or a bronze repose.
And yet they too break hearts—O Presences
That passion, piety or affection knows,
And that all heavenly glory symbolize—
O self-born mockers of man's enterprise;

VIII

Labor is blossoming or dancing where
The body is not bruised to pleasure soul,
Nor beauty born out of its own despair,
Nor blear-eyed wisdom out of midnight oil.
O chestnut tree, great rooted blossomer,
Are you the leaf, the blossom or the bole?
O body swayed to music, O brightening glance,
How can we know the dancer from the dance?

The Leaders of the Crowd

They must to keep their certainty accuse
All that are different of a base intent;
Pull down established honor; hawk for news
Whatever their loose phantasy invent
And murmur it with bated breath, as though
The abounding gutter had been Helicon
Or calumny a song. How can they know
Truth flourishes where the student's lamp has shone,
And there alone, that have no solitude?
So the crowd come they care not what may come.
They have loud music, hope every day renewed
And heartier loves; that lamp is from the tomb.

An Irish Airman Foresees His Death

I know that I shall meet my fate
Somewhere among the clouds above;
Those that I fight I do not hate,
Those that I guard I do not love;
My country is Kiltartan Cross,
My countrymen Kiltartan's poor,
No likely end could bring them loss
Or leave them happier than before.
Nor law, nor duty bade me fight,
Nor public men, nor cheering crowds,
A lonely impulse of delight
Drove to this tumult in the clouds;
I balanced all, brought all to mind,
The years to come seemed waste of breath,
A waste of breath the years behind
In balance with this life, this death.

To a Friend Whose Work Has Come to Nothing

Now all the truth is out,
Be secret and take defeat
From any brazen throat,
For how can you compete,
Being honor bred, with one
Who, were it proved he lies,
Were neither shamed in his own
Nor in his neighbors' eyes?
Bred to a harder thing
Than Triumph, turn away
And like a laughing string
Whereon mad fingers play
Amid a place of stone,
Be secret and exult,
Because of all things known
That is most difficult.

Song from "The Only Jealousy of Emer"

A woman's beauty is like a white
Frail bird, like a white sea-bird alone
At daybreak after stormy night
Between two furrows upon the ploughed land:
A sudden storm and it was thrown
Between dark furrows upon the ploughed land.
How many centuries spent
The sedentary soul
In toils of measurement
Beyond eagle or mole,
Beyond hearing or seeing,
Or Archimedes' guess,
To raise into being
That loveliness?

A strange unserviceable thing,
A fragile, exquisite, pale shell,
That the vast troubled waters bring
To the loud sands before day has broken.
The storm arose and suddenly fell
Amid the dark before day had broken.

What death? what discipline?
What bonds no man could unbind,
Being imagined within
The labyrinth of the mind,
What pursuing or fleeing,
What wounds, what bloody press
Dragged into being
This loveliness?

In Memory of Eva Gore-Booth and Con Markiewicz

The light of evening, Lissadell,
Great windows open to the south,
Two girls in silk kimonos, both
Beautiful, one a gazelle.
But a raving autumn shears
Blossom from the summer's wreath;
The older is condemned to death,
Pardoned, drags out lonely years
Conspiring among the ignorant.
I know not what the younger dreams—
Some vague Utopia—and she seems,
When withered old and skeleton-gaunt,
An image of such politics.
Many a time I think to seek
One or the other out and speak
Of that old Georgian mansion, mix
Pictures of the mind, recall
That table and the talk of youth,
Two girls in silk kimonos, both
Beautiful, one a gazelle.
Dear shadows, now you know it all,
All the folly of a fight
With a common wrong or right.
The innocent and the beautiful
Have no enemy but time;
Arise and bid me strike a match
And strike another till time catch;
Should the conflagration climb,
Run till all the sages know.
We the great gazebo built,
They convicted us of guilt;
Bid me strike a match and blow.

A Prayer for My Daughter

Once more the storm is howling, and half hid
Under this cradle-hood and coverlid
My child sleeps on. There is no obstacle
But Gregory's wood and one bare hill
Whereby the haystack- and roof-levelling wind,
Bred on the Atlantic, can be stayed;
And for an hour I have walked and prayed
Because of the great gloom that is in my mind.

I have walked and prayed for this young child an hour
And heard the sea-wind scream upon the tower,
And under the arches of the bridge, and scream
In the elms above the flooded stream;
Imagining in excited reverie
That the future years had come,
Dancing to a frenzied drum,
Out of the murderous innocence of the sea.

May she be granted beauty and yet not
Beauty to make a stranger's eye distraught,
Or hers before a looking-glass, for such,
Being made beautiful overmuch,
Consider beauty a sufficient end,
Lose natural kindness and maybe
The heart-revealing intimacy
That chooses right, and never find a friend.

Helen being chosen found life flat and dull
And later had much trouble from a fool,
While that great Queen, that rose out of the spray,
Being fatherless could have her way
Yet chose a bandy-leggèd smith for man.
It's certain that fine women eat
A crazy salad with their meat
Whereby the Horn of Plenty is undone.

In courtesy I'd have her chiefly learned;
Hearts are not had as a gift but hearts are earned
By those that are not entirely beautiful;
Yet many, that have played the fool
For beauty's very self, has charm made wise,
And many a poor man that has roved,

Loved and thought himself beloved,
From a glad kindness cannot take his eyes.

May she become a flourishing hidden tree
That all her thoughts may like the linnet be,
And have no business but dispensing round
Their magnanimities of sound,
Nor but in merriment begin a chase,
Nor but in merriment a quarrel.
O may she live like some green laurel
Rooted in one dear perpetual place.

My mind, because the minds that I have loved,
The sort of beauty that I have approved,
Prosper but little, has dried up of late,
Yet knows that to be choked with hate
May well be of all evil chances chief.
If there's no hatred in a mind
Assault and battery of the wind
Can never tear the linnet from the leaf.

An intellectual hatred is the worst,
So let her think opinions are accursed.
Have I not seen the loveliest woman born
Out of the mouth of Plenty's horn,
Because of her opinionated mind
Barter that horn and every good
By quiet natures understood
For an old bellows full of angry wind?

Considering that, all hatred driven hence,
The soul recovers radical innocence
And learns at last that it is self-delighting,
Self-appeasing, self-affrighting,
And that its own sweet will is Heaven's will;
She can, though every face should scowl
And every windy quarter howl
Or every bellows burst, be happy still.

And may her bridegroom bring her to a house
Where all's accustomed, ceremonious;
For arrogance and hatred are the wares
Peddled in the thoroughfares.

How but in custom and in ceremony
Are innocence and beauty born?
Ceremony's a name for the rich horn,
And custom for the spreading laurel tree.

Crazy Jane on God

That lover of a night
Came when he would,
Went in the dawning light
Whether I would or no;
Men come, men go;
All things remain in God.

Banners choke the sky:
Men-at-arms tread;
Armoured horses neigh
Where the great battle was
In the narrow pass:
All things remain in God.

Before their eyes a house
That from childhood stood
Uninhabited, ruinous,
Suddenly lit up
From door to top:
All things remain in God.

I had wild Jack for a lover;
Though like a road
That men pass over
My body makes no moan
But sings on:
All things remain in God.

John Kinsella's Lament for Mrs. Mary Moore

A bloody and a sudden end,
Gunshot or a noose,
For death who takes what man would keep,
Leaves what man would lose.
He might have had my sister,
My cousins by the score,

But nothing satisfied the fool
But my dear Mary Moore;
None other knows what pleasures man
At table or in bed.
What shall I do for pretty girls
Now my old bawd is dead?

Though stiff to strike a bargain,
Like an old Jew man,
Her bargain struck we laughed and talked
And emptied many a can;
And O! but she had stories,
Though not for the priest's ear,
To keep the soul of man alive,
Banish age and care,
And being old she put a skin
On everything she said.
What shall I do for pretty girls
Now my old bawd is dead?

The priests have got a book that says
But for Adam's sin
Eden's Garden would be there
And I there within.
No expectation fails there,
No pleasing habit ends,
No man grows old, no girl grows cold,
But friends walk by friends.
Who quarrels over halfpennies
That plucks the trees for bread?
What shall I do for pretty girls
Now my old bawd is dead?

Easter, 1916

I have met them at close of day
Coming with vivid faces
From counter or desk among grey
Eighteenth-century houses.
I have passed with a nod of the head
Or polite meaningless words,
Or have lingered awhile and said
Polite meaningless words,
And thought before I had done

Of a mocking tale or a gibe
To please a companion
Around the fire at the club,
Being certain that they and I
But lived where motley is worn:
All changed, changed utterly:
A terrible beauty is born.

That woman's days were spent
In ignorant good-will,
Her nights in argument
Until her voice grew shrill.
What voice more sweet than hers
When, young and beautiful,
She rode to harriers?
This man had kept a school
And rode our wingèd horse;
This other his helper and friend
Was coming into his force;
He might have won fame in the end,
So sensitive his nature seemed,
So daring and sweet his thought.
This other man I had dreamed
A drunken, vainglorious lout.
He had done most bitter wrong
To some who are near my heart,
Yet I number him in the song;
He, too, has resigned his part
In the casual comedy;
He, too, has been changed in his turn,
Transformed utterly:
A terrible beauty is born.

Hearts with one purpose alone
Through summer and winter seem
Enchanted to a stone
To trouble the living stream.
The horse that comes from the road,
The rider, the birds that range
From cloud to tumbling cloud,
Minute by minute they change;
A shadow of cloud on the stream
Changes minute by minute;
A horse-hoof slides on the brim,
And a horse plashes within it;

The long-legged moor-hens dive,
And hens to moor-cocks call;
Minute by minute they live:
The stone's in the midst of all.

Too long a sacrifice
Can make a stone of the heart.
O when may it suffice?
That is Heaven's part, our part
To murmur name upon name,
As a mother names her child
When sleep at last has come
On limbs that had run wild.
What is it but nightfall?
No, no, not night but death;
Was it needless death after all?
For England may keep faith
For all that is done and said.
We know their dream; enough
To know they dreamed and are dead;
And what if excess of love
Bewildered them till they died?
I write it out in a verse—
MacDonagh and MacBride
And Connolly and Pearse
Now and in time to be,
Wherever green is worn,
Are changed, changed utterly:
A terrible beauty is born.

Byzantium

The unpurged images of day recede;
The Emperor's drunken soldiery are abed;
Night resonance recedes, night-walkers' song
After great cathedral gong;
A starlit or a moonlit dome disdains
All that man is,
All mere complexities,
The fury and the mire of human veins.

Before me floats an image, man or shade,
Shade more than man, more image than a shade;
For Hades' bobbin bound in mummy-cloth

May unwind the winding path;
A mouth that has no moisture and no breath
Breathless mouths may summon;
I hail the superhuman;
I call it death-in-life and life-in-death.

Miracle, bird or golden handiwork,
More miracle than bird or handiwork,
Planted on the star-lit golden bough,
Can like the cocks of Hades crow,
Or, by the moon embittered, scorn aloud
In glory of changeless metal
Common bird or petal
And all complexities of mire or blood.

At midnight on the Emperor's pavement flit
Flames that no faggot feeds, nor steel has lit,
Nor storm disturbs, flames begotten of flame,
Where blood-begotten spirits come
And all complexities of fury leave,
Dying into a dance,
An agony of trance,
An agony of flame that cannot singe a sleeve.

Astraddle on the dolphin's mire and blood,
Spirit after spirit! The smithies break the flood,
The golden smithies of the Emperor!
Marbles of the dancing floor
Break bitter furies of complexity,
Those images that yet
Fresh images beget,
That dolphin-torn, that gong-tormented sea.

Nineteen Hundred and Nineteen

I

Many ingenious lovely things are gone
That seemed sheer miracle to the multitude,
Protected from the circle of the moon
That pitches common things about. There stood
Amid the ornamental bronze and stone
An ancient image made of olive wood—
And gone are Phidias' famous ivories
And all the golden grasshoppers and bees.

We too had many toys when young;
A law indifferent to blame or praise,
To bribe or threat; habits that made old wrong
Melt down, as it were wax in the sun's rays;
Public opinion ripening for so long
We thought it would outlive all future days.
O what fine thought we had because we thought
That the worst rogues and rascals had died out.

All teeth were drawn, all ancient tricks unlearned,
And a great army but a showy thing;
What matter that no cannon had been turned
Into a ploughshare? Parliament and king
Thought that unless a little powder burned
The trumpeters might burst with trumpeting
And yet it lack all glory; and perchance
The guardsmen's drowsy chargers would not prance.

Now days are dragon-ridden, the nightmare
Rides upon sleep: a drunken soldiery
Can leave the mother, murdered at her door,
To crawl in her own blood, and go scot-free;
The night can sweat with terror as before
We pieced our thoughts into philosophy,
And planned to bring the world under a rule,
Who are but weasels fighting in a hole.

He who can read the signs nor sink unmanned
Into the half-deceit of some intoxicant
From shallow wits; who knows no work can stand,
Whether health, wealth or peace of mind were spent
On master-work of intellect or hand,
No honour leave its mighty monument,
Has but one comfort left: all triumph would
But break upon his ghostly solitude.

But is there any comfort to be found?
Man is in love and loves what vanishes,
What more is there to say? That country round
None dared admit, if such a thought were his,
Incendiary or bigot could be found
To burn that stump on the Acropolis,
Or break in bits the famous ivories
Or traffic in the grasshoppers or bees.

II

When Loie Fuller's Chinese dancers enwound
A shining web, a floating ribbon of cloth,
It seemed that a dragon of air
Had fallen among dancers, had whirled them round
Or hurried them off on its own furious path;
So the Platonic Year
Whirls out new right and wrong,
Whirls in the old instead;
All men are dancers and their tread
Goes to the barbarous clangour of a gong.

III

Some moralist or mythological poet
Compares the solitary soul to a swan;
I am satisfied with that,
Satisfied if a troubled mirror show it,
Before that brief gleam of its life be gone,
An image of its state;
The wings half spread for flight,
The breast thrust out in pride
Whether to play, or to ride
Those winds that clamour of approaching night.

A man in his own secret meditation
Is lost amid the labyrinth that he has made
In art or politics;
Some Platonist affirms that in the station
Where we should cast off body and trade
The ancient habit sticks,
And that if our works could
But vanish with our breath
That were a lucky death,
For triumph can but mar our solitude.

The swan has leaped into the desolate heaven:
That image can bring wildness, bring a rage
To end all things, to end
What my laborious life imagined, even
The half-imagined, the half-written page;
O but we dreamed to mend
What ever mischief seemed
To afflict mankind, but now

That winds of winter blow
Learn that we were crack-pated when we dreamed.

IV

We, who seven years ago
Talked of honour and of truth,
Shriek with pleasure if we show
The weasel's twist, the weasel's tooth.

V

Come let us mock at the great
That had such burdens on the mind
And toiled so hard and late
To leave some monument behind,
Nor thought of the levelling wind.

Come let us mock at the wise;
With all those calendars whereon
They fixed old aching eyes,
They never saw how seasons run,
And now but gape at the sun.

Come let us mock at the good
That fancied goodness might be gay,
And sick of solitude
Might proclaim a holiday:
Wind shrieked—and where are they?

Mock mockers after that
That would not lift a hand maybe
To help good, wise or great
To bar that foul storm out, for we
Traffic in mockery.

VI

Violence upon the roads: violence of horses;
Some few have handsome riders, are garlanded
On delicate sensitive ear or tossing mane,
But wearied running round and round in their courses
All break and vanish, and evil gathers head:
Herodias' daughters have returned again,
A sudden blast of dusty wind and after
Thunder of feet, tumult of images,
Their purpose in the labyrinth of the wind;

And should some crazy hand dare touch a daughter
All turn with amorous cries, or angry cries,
According to the wind, for all are blind.
But now wind drops, dust settles; thereupon
There lurches past, his great eyes without thought
Under the shadow of stupid straw-pale locks,
That insolent fiend Robert Artisson —
To whom the love-lorn Lady Kyteler brought
Bronzed peacock feathers, red combs of her cocks.

The Second Coming

Turning and turning in the widening gyre
The falcon cannot hear the falconer;
Things fall apart; the centre cannot hold;
Mere anarchy is loosed upon the world,
The blood-dimmed tide is loosed, and everywhere
The ceremony of innocence is drowned;
The best lack all conviction, while the worst
Are full of passionate intensity.

Surely some revelation is at hand;
Surely the Second Coming is at hand.
The Second Coming! Hardly are those words out
When a vast image out of *Spiritus Mundi*
Troubles my sight: somewhere in sands of the desert
A shape with lion body and the head of a man,
A gaze blank and pitiless as the sun,
Is moving its slow thighs, while all about it
Reel shadows of the indignant desert birds.
The darkness drops again; but now I know
That twenty centuries of stony sleep
Were vexed to nightmare by a rocking cradle,
And what rough beast, its hour come round at last,
Slouches towards Bethlehem to be born?

Charlotte Mew

1869-1928

In the Fields

Lord, when I look at lovely things which pass,
Under old trees the shadow of young leaves
Dancing to please the wind along the grass,
Or the gold stillness of the August sun on the August sheaves;
Can I believe there is a heavenlier world than this?
And if there is
Will the strange heart of any everlasting thing
Bring me these dreams that take my breath away?
They come at evening with the home-flying rooks and the scent of hay,
Over the fields. They come in Spring.

Sea Love

Tide be runnin' the great world over:
'Twas only last June month I mind that we
Was thinkin' the toss and the call in the breast of the lover
So everlastin' as the sea.

Here's the same little fishes that sputter and swim,
Wi' the moon's old glim on the gray, wet sand;
An' him no more to me nor me to him
Than the wind goin' over my hand.

I Have Been Through the Gates

His heart, to me, was a place of palaces and pinnacles and shining towers;
I saw it then as we see things in dreams,—I do not remember how long I slept;

I remember the trees, and the high, white walls, and how the
sun was always on the towers;
The walls are standing today, and the gates: I have been
through the gates, I have groped, I have crept
Back, back. There is dust in the streets, and blood; they are
empty; darkness is over them;
His heart is a place with the lights gone out, forsaken by great
winds and the heavenly rain, unclean and unswept,
Like the heart of the holy city, old, blind, beautiful Jerusalem,
Over which Christ wept.

To a Child in Death

You would have scoffed if we had told you yesterday
Love made us feel—or so it was with me—like some great bird
Trying to hold and shelter you in its strong wing;—
A gay little shadowy smile would have tossed us back such a
solemn word,
And it was not for that you were listening
When so quietly you slipped away
With half the music of the world unheard.
What shall we do with this strange Summer, meant for you,—
Dear, if we see the Winter through
What shall be done with Spring—?
This, this is the victory of the grave; here is death's sting.
That it is not strong enough, our strongest wing.

But what of His who like a Father pitieth—?
His Son was also, once, a little thing,
The wistfulest child that ever drew breath,
Chased by a sword from Bethlehem and in the busy house at
Nazareth
Playing with little rows of nails, watching the carpenter's
hammer swing,
Long years before His hands and feet were tied
And by a hammer and the three great nails He died,
Of youth, of Spring,
Of sorrow, of loneliness, of victory the king,
Under the shadow of that wing.

The Farmer's Bride

Three Summers since I chose a maid,
Too young maybe—but more's to do
At harvest-time than bide and woo.
  When us was wed she turned afraid
Of love and me and all things human;
Like the shut of a winter's day.
Her smile went out, and 'twasn't a woman—
  More like a little frightened fay.
    One night, in the Fall, she runned away.

"Out 'mong the sheep, her be," they said,
'Should properly have been abed;
But sure enough she wasn't there
Lying awake with her wide brown stare.
So over seven-acre field and up-along across the down
We chased her, flying like a hare
Before our lanterns. To Church-Town
  All in a shiver and a scare
We caught her, fetched her home at last
  And turned the key upon her, fast.

She does the work about the house
As well as most, but like a mouse:
  Happy enough to chat and play
  With birds and rabbits and such as they,
  So long as men-folk keep away.
"Not near, not near!" her eyes beseech
When one of us comes within reach.
  The women say that beasts in stall
  Look round like children at her call.
  I've hardly heard her speak at all.

Shy as a leveret, swift as he,
Straight and slight as a young larch tree,
Sweet as the first wild violets, she
To her wild self. But what to me?

The short days shorten and the oaks are brown,
  The blue smoke rises to the low gray sky,
One leaf in the still air falls slowly down,
  A magpie's spotted feathers lie

On the black earth spread white with rime,
The berries redden up to Christmas-time.
What's Christmas-time without there be
Some other in the house than we!

She sleeps up in the attic there
Alone, poor maid. 'Tis but a stair
Betwixt us. Oh! my God! the down,
The soft young down of her, the brown,
The brown of her—her eyes, her hair, her hair . . .

Beside the Bed

Someone has shut the shining eyes, straightened and folded
The wandering hands quietly covering the unquiet breast:
So, smoothed and silenced you lie, like a child, not again to be questioned or scolded:
But, for you, not one of us believes that this is rest.

Not so to close the windows down can cloud and deaden
The blue beyond: or to screen the wavering flame subdue its breath:
Why, if I lay my cheek to your cheek, your gray lips, like dawn, would quiver and redden,
Breaking into the old, odd smile at this fraud of death.

Because all night you have not turned to us or spoken
It is time for you to wake; your dreams were never very deep:
I, for one, have seen the thin bright, twisted threads of them dimmed suddenly and broken.
This is only a most piteous pretense of sleep!

From "Madeleine in Church"

How old was Mary out of whom you cast
So many devils? Was she young or perhaps for years
She had sat staring, with dry eyes, at this and that man going past
Till suddenly she saw You on the steps of Simon's house
And stood and looked at You through tears.
I think she must have known by those

The thing, for what it was that had come to her.
For some of us there is a passion, I suppose,
So far from earthly cares and earthly fears
That in its stillness you can hardly stir
Or in its nearness lift your hand,
So great that you have simply got to stand
Looking at it through tears, through tears.
Then straight from these there broke the kiss.
I think You must have known by this
The thing, for what it was that had come to You:
She did not love You like the rest,
It was in her own way, but at the worst, the best,
She gave you something altogether new.
And through it all, from her, no word,
She scarcely saw You, scarcely heard:
Surely You knew when she so touched You with her hair,
Or by the wet cheek lying there,
And while her perfume clung to You from head to feet all through the day
That You can change the things for which we care,
But even You, unless You kill us, not the way.

This then was peace for her, but passion too.
I wonder was it like a kiss that once I knew,
The only one that I would care to take
Into the grave with me, to which if there were afterwards, to wake
Almost as happy as the carven dead
In some dim chancel lying head to head
We slept with it, but face to face, the whole night through—
One breath, one throbbing quietness, as if the thing behind our lips was endless life,
Lost, as I woke, to hear in the strange earthly dawn, his "Are you there?"
And lie still, listening to the wind outside, among the firs.

So Mary chose the dream of Him for what was left to her of night and day.
It is the only truth: it is the dream in us that neither life nor death nor any other thing can take away:
But if she had not touched Him in the doorway of the dream could she have cared so much?
She was a sinner, we are what we are: the spirit afterwards, but first, the touch.

And He has never shared with me my haunted house beneath the trees
Of Eden and Calvary, with its ghosts that have not any eyes for tears,
And the happier guests, who would not see, or if they did, remember these,
Though they lived here a thousand years.
Outside, too gravely looking at me, He seems to stand,
And looking at Him if my forgotten spirit came
Unwillingly back, what could it claim
Of those calm eyes, that quiet speech,
Breaking like a slow tide upon the beach,
The scarred, not quite human hand?—
Unwillingly back to the burden of old imaginings
When it has learned so long not to think, not to be,
Again, again it would speak as it has spoken to me of things
That I shall not see!

Again

One day, not here, you will find a hand
Stretched out to you as you walk down some heavenly street;
You will see a stranger scarred from head to feet;
But when he speaks to you you will not understand,
Nor yet who wounded him nor why his wounds are sweet.
And saying nothing, letting go his hand,
You will leave him in the heavenly street—
So we shall meet!

Old Shepherd's Prayer

Up to the bed by the window, where I be lyin',
Comes bells and bleats of the flock wi' they two children's clack.
Over, from under the eaves there's the starlings flyin',
And down in yard, fit to burst his chain, yapping out at Sue I do hear young Mac.

Turning around like a falled-over sack
I can see team plowin' in Whithy-bush field and meal carts startin' up road to Church-Town;
Saturday arternoon then men goin' back
And the women from market, trapin' home over the down.

Heavenly Master, I wud like to wake to they same green places
Where I be know'd for breakin' dogs and follerin' sheep.
And if I may not walk in th' old ways and look on th' old faces
I wud sooner sleep.

The Trees Are Down

—and he cried with a loud voice:
Hurt not the earth, neither the sea, nor the trees—
(*Revelation.*)

They are cutting down the great plane-trees at the end of the
gardens.
For days there has been the grate of the saw, the swish of the
branches as they fall,
The crash of trunks, the rustle of trodden leaves,
With the "Whoops" and the "Whoas," the loud common talk,
the loud common laughs of the men, above it all.

I remember one evening of a long past Spring
Turning in at a gate, getting out of a cart, and finding a large
dead rat in the mud of the drive.
I remember thinking: alive or dead, a rat was a god-forsaken
thing,
But at least, in May, that even a rat should be alive.

The week's work here is as good as done. There is just one
bough
On the roped bole, in the fine gray rain,
Green and high
And lonely against the sky.
(Down now!—)
And but for that,
If an old dead rat
Did once, for a moment, unmake the Spring, I might never
have thought of him again.

It is not for a moment the Spring is unmade today;
These were great trees, it was in them from root to stem:
When the men with the "Whoops" and the "Whoas" have
carted the whole of the whispering loveliness away
Half the Spring, for me, will have gone with them.

It is going now, and my heart has been struck with the hearts
of the planes;

Half my life it has beat with these, in the sun, in the rains,
In the March wind, the May breeze,
In the great gales that came over to them across the roofs from
the great seas.
There was only a quiet rain when they were dying;
They must have heard the sparrows flying,
And the small creeping creatures in the earth where they were
lying—
But I, all day, I heard an angel crying:
"Hurt not the trees."

Absence

Sometimes I know the way
You walk, up over the bay;
It is a wind from that far sea
That blows the fragrance of your hair to me.

Or in this garden when the breeze
Touches my trees
To stir their dreaming shadows on the grass
I see you pass.

In sheltered beds, the heart of every rose
Serenely sleeps tonight. As shut as those
Your guarded heart; as safe as they from the beat, beat
Of hooves that tread dropped roses in the street.

Turn never again
On these eyes blind with a wild rain
Your eyes; they were stars to me.
There are things stars may not see.

But call, call, and though Christ stands
Still with scarred hands
Over my mouth, I must answer. So,
I will come—He shall let me go!

Ralph Hodgson

1871-

Eve

Eve, with her basket, was
Deep in the bells and grass,
Wading in bells and grass
Up to her knees.
Picking a dish of sweet
Berries and plums to eat,
Down in the bells and grass
Under the trees.

Mute as a mouse in a
Corner the cobra lay,
Curled round a bough of the
Cinnamon tall. . . .
Now to get even and
Humble proud heaven and
Now was the moment or
Never at all.

"Eva!" Each syllable
Light as a flower fell,
"Eva!" he whispered the
Wondering maid,
Soft as a bubble sung
Out of a linnet's lung,
Soft and most silverly
"Eva!" he said.

Picture that orchard sprite;
Eve, with her body white,
Supple and smooth to her
Slim finger tips;

Wondering, listening,
Listening, wondering,
Eve with a berry
Half-way to her lips.

Oh, had our simple Eve
Seen through the make-believe!
Had she but known the
Pretender he was!
Out of the boughs he came,
Whispering still her name,
Tumbling in twenty rings
Into the grass.

Here was the strangest pair
In the world anywhere,
Eve in the bells and grass
Kneeling, and he
Telling his story low. . . .
Singing birds saw them go
Down the dark path to
The Blasphemous Tree.

Oh, what a clatter when
Titmouse and Jenny Wren
Saw him successful and
Taking his leave!
How the birds rated him,
How they all hated him!
How they all pitied
Poor motherless Eve!

Picture her crying
Outside in the lane,
Eve, with no dish of sweet
Berries and plums to eat,
Haunting the gate of the
Orchard in vain. . . .
Picture the lewd delight
Under the hill tonight—
"Eva!" the toast goes round,
"Eva!" again.

Time, You Old Gypsy Man

Time, you old gypsy man,
  Will you not stay,
Put up your caravan
  Just for one day?

All things I'll give you
Will you be my guest,
Bells for your jennet
Of silver the best,
Goldsmiths shall beat you
A great golden ring,
Peacocks shall bow to you,
Little boys sing,
Oh, and sweet girls will
Festoon you with may.
Time, you old gypsy,
Why hasten away?

Last week in Babylon,
Last night in Rome,
Morning, and in the crush
Under Paul's dome;
Under Paul's dial
You tighten your rein—
Only a moment,
And off once again;
Off to some city
Now blind in the womb,
Off to another
Ere that's in the tomb.

Time, you old gypsy man,
  Will you not stay,
Put up your caravan
  Just for one day?

The Bull

See an old unhappy bull,
Sick in soul and body both,
Slouching in the undergrowth
Of the forest beautiful,
Banished from the herd he led,
Bulls and cows a thousand head.

Cranes and gaudy parrots go
Up and down the burning sky;
Tree-top cats purr drowsily
In the dim-day green below;
And troops of monkeys, nutting some,
All disputing, go and come;
And things abominable sit
Picking offal buck or swine,
On the mess and over it
Burnished flies and beetles shine,
And spiders big as bladders lie
Under hemlocks ten foot high;

And a dotted serpent curled
Round and round and round a tree,
Yellowing its greenery,
Keeps a watch on all the world,
All the world and this old bull
In the forest beautiful.

Bravely by his fall he came:
One he led, a bull of blood
Newly come to lustihood,
Fought and put his prince to shame,
Snuffed and pawed the prostrate head
Tameless even while it bled.

There they left him, every one,
Left him there without a lick,
Left him for the birds to pick,
Left him for the carrion,
Vilely from their bosom cast
Wisdom, worth and love at last.
When the lion left his lair

And roared his beauty through the hills,
And the vultures pecked their quills
And flew into the middle air,
Then this prince no more to reign
Came to life and lived again.
He snuffed the herd in far retreat,
He saw the blood upon the ground,
And snuffed the burning airs around
Still with beevish odors sweet,
While the blood ran down his head
And his mouth ran slaver red.
Pity him, this fallen chief,
All his splendor, all his strength
All his beauty's breadth and length
Dwindled down with shame and grief,
Half the bull he was before,
Bones and leather, nothing more.

See him standing dewlap-deep
In the rushes at the lake,
Surly, stupid, half asleep,
Waiting for his heart to break
And the birds to join the flies
Feasting at his bloodshot eyes,—
Standing with his head hung down
In a stupor, dreaming things:
Green savannas, jungles brown,
Battlefields and bellowings,
Bulls undone and lions dead
And vultures flapping overhead.
Dreaming things: of days he spent
With his mother gaunt and lean
In the valley warm and green,
Full of baby wonderment,
Blinking out of silly eyes
At a hundred mysteries;
Dreaming over once again
How he wandered with a throng
Of bulls and cows a thousand strong,
Wandered on from plain to plain,
Up the hill and down the dale,
Always at his mother's tail;
How he lagged behind the herd,
Lagged and tottered, weak of limb,

And she turned and ran to him
Blaring at the loathly bird
Stationed always in the skies,
Waiting for the flesh that dies.

Dreaming maybe of a day,
When her drained and drying paps
Turned him to the sweets and saps,
Richer fountains by the way,
And she left the bull she bore
And he looked to her no more;
And his little frame grew stout,
And his little legs grew strong,
And the way was not so long;
And his little horns came out,
And he played at butting trees
And bowlder-stones and tortoises,
Joined a game of knobby skulls
With the youngsters of his year,
All the other little bulls,
Learning both to bruise and bear,
Learning how to stand a shock
Like a little bull of rock.

Dreaming of a day less dim,
Dreaming of a time less far,
When the faint but certain star
Of destiny burned clear for him,
And a fierce and wild unrest
Broke the quiet of his breast,
And the gristles of his youth
Hardened in his comely pow,
And he came to fighting growth,
Beat his bull and won his cow,
And flew his tail and trampled off
Past the tallest, vain enough.
And curved about in splendor full
And curved again and snuffed the airs
As who should say, Come out who dares!
And all beheld a bull, a Bull,
And knew that here was surely one
That backed for no bull, fearing none.
And the leader of the herd
Looked and saw, and beat the ground,

And shook the forest with his sound,
Bellowed at the loathly bird
Stationed always in the skies,
Waiting for the flesh that dies.

Dreaming, this old bull forlorn,
Surely dreaming of the hour
When he came to sultan power,
And they owned him master-horn,
Chiefest bull of all among
Bulls and cows a thousand strong,
And in all the trampling herd
Not a bull that barred his way,
Not a cow that said him nay,
Not a bull or cow that erred
In the furnace of his look
Dared a second, worse rebuke;
Not in all the forest wide,
Jungle, thicket, pasture, fen,
Not another dared him then,
Dared him and again defied;
Not a sovereign buck or boar
Came a second time for more.
Not a serpent that survived
Once the terrors of his hoof,
Risked a second time reproof,
Came a second time and lived,
Not a serpent in its skin
Came again for discipline;

Not a leopard bright as flame,
Flashing fingerhooks of steel,
That a wooden tree might feel,
Met his fury once and came
For a second reprimand,
Not a leopard in the land,
Not a lion of them all,
Not a lion of the hills,
Hero of a thousand kills,
Dared a second fight and fall,
Dared that ram terrific twice,
Paid a second time the price. . . .

Pity him, this dupe of dream,
Leader of the herd again

Only in his daft old brain,
Once again the bull supreme
And bull enough to bear the part
Only in his tameless heart.

Pity him that he must wake.
Even now the swarm of flies
Blackening his bloodshot eyes
Bursts and blusters round the lake,
Scattered from the feast half-fed,
By great shadows overhead,
And the dreamer turns away
From his visionary herds
And his splendid yesterday,
Turns to meet the loathly birds
Flocking round him from the skies,
Waiting for the flesh that dies.

The Bells of Heaven

'Twould ring the bells of Heaven
The wildest peal for years,
If Parson lost his senses
And people came to theirs,
And he and they together
Knelt down with angry prayers
For tamed and shabby tigers
And dancing dogs and bears,
And wretched, blind pit ponies,
And little hunted hares.

Stupidity Street

I saw with open eyes
Singing birds sweet
Sold in the shops
For the people to eat,
Sold in the shops of
Stupidity Street.

I saw in a vision
The worm in the wheat,

And in the shops nothing
For people to eat:
Nothing for sale in
Stupidity Street.

The Mystery

He came and took me by the hand
  Up to a red rose tree,
He kept His meaning to Himself
  But gave a rose to me.

I did not pray Him to lay bare
  The mystery to me,
Enough the rose was Heaven to smell,
  And His own face to see.

Walter de la Mare

1873-1956

The Listeners

"Is there anybody there?" said the Traveler,
  Knocking on the moonlit door;
And his horse in the silence champed the grasses
  Of the forest's ferny floor.
And a bird flew up out of the turret,
  Above the Traveler's head:
And he smote upon the door again a second time;
  "Is there anybody there?" he said.
But no one descended to the Traveler;
  No head from the leaf-fringed sill
Leaned over and looked into his gray eyes,
  Where he stood perplexed and still.
But only a host of phantom listeners
  That dwelt in the lone house then

Stood listening in the quiet of the moonlight
  To that voice from the world of men:
Stood thronging the faint moonbeams on the dark stair
  That goes down to the empty hall,
Hearkening in an air stirred and shaken
  By the lonely Traveler's call.
And he felt in his heart their strangeness,
  Their stillness answering his cry,
While his horse moved, cropping the dark turf,
  'Neath the starred and leafy sky;
For he suddenly smote on the door, even
  Louder, and lifted his head:—
"Tell them I came, and no one answered,
  That I kept my word," he said.
Never the least stir made the listeners,
  Though every word he spake
Fell echoing through the shadowiness of the still house
  From the one man left awake:
Aye, they heard his foot upon the stirrup,
  And the sound of iron on stone,
And how the silence surged softly backward,
  When the plunging hoofs were gone.

An Epitaph

Here lies a most beautiful lady,
Light of step and heart was she;
I think she was the most beautiful lady
That ever was in the West Country.

But beauty vanishes; beauty passes;
However rare—rare it be;
And when I crumble, who will remember
This lady of the West Country?

The Sleeper

As Ann came in one summer's day,
  She felt that she must creep,
So silent was the clear cool house,
  It seemed a house of sleep.
And sure, when she pushed open the door,
  Rapt in the stillness there,

Her mother sat with stooping head,
  Asleep upon a chair;
Fast—fast asleep; her two hands laid
  Loose-folded on her knee,
So that her small unconscious face
  Looked half unreal to be:
So calmly lit with sleep's pale light
  Each feature was; so fair
Her forehead—every trouble was
  Smooth'd out beneath her hair.
But though her mind in dream now moved,
  Still seemed her gaze to rest
From out beneath her fast-sealed lids,
  Above her moving breast,
On Ann, as quite, quite still she stood;
  Yet slumber lay so deep
Even her hands upon her lap
  Seemed saturate with sleep.
And as Ann peeped, a cloudlike dread
  Stole over her, and then,
On stealthy, mouselike feet she trod,
  And tiptoed out again.

The Old Men

Old and alone sit we,
Caged, riddle-rid men,
Lost to earth's "Listen!" and "See!"
Thought's "Wherefore?" and "When?"
Only far memories stray
Of a past once lovely, but now
Wasted and faded away,
Like green leaves from the bough.
Vast broods the silence of night;
And the ruinous moon
Lifts on our faces her light,
Whence all dreaming is gone.
We speak not; trembles each head;
In their sockets our eyes are still;
Desire as cold as the dead,
Without wonder or will.
And one, with a lanthorn, draws near,
At clash with the moon in our eyes:

"Where art thou?" he asks: "I am here!"
One by one we arise.
And none lifts a hand to withhold
A friend from the touch of that foe:
Heart cries unto heart, "Thou art old!"
Yet reluctant we go.

At the Keyhole

"Grill me some bones," said the Cobbler,
"Some bones, my pretty Sue;
I'm tired of my lonesome with heels and soles,
Springsides and uppers too;
A mouse in the wainscot is nibbling;
A wind in the keyhole drones;
And a sheet webbed over my candle, Susie,
Grill me some bones!"

"Grill me some bones," said the Cobbler,
"I sat at my tic-tac-to;
And a footstep came to my door and stopped,
And a hand groped to and fro;
And I peered up over my boot and last;
And my feet went cold as stones:—
I saw an eye at the keyhole, Susie!—
Grill me some bones!"

Sam

When Sam goes back in memory,
It is to where the sea
Breaks on the shingle, emerald-green,
In white foam, endlessly;
He says—with small brown eye on mine—
"I used to keep awake,
And lean from my window in the moon,
Watching those billows break.
And half a million tiny hands,
And eyes, like sparks of frost,
Would dance and come tumbling into the moon,
On every breaker tossed.
And all across from star to star,
I've seen the watery sea,

With not a single ship in sight,
  Just ocean there, and me;
And heard my father snore. And once,
  As sure as I'm alive,
Out of those wallowing, moon-flecked waves
  I saw a mermaid dive;
Head and shoulders above the wave,
  Plain as I now see you,
Combing her hair, now back, now front,
  Her two eyes peeping through;
Calling me, 'Sam!'—quietlike—'Sam!' . . .
  But me . . . I never went,
Making believe I kind of thought
  'Twas someone else she meant . . .
Wonderful lovely there she sat,
  Singing the night away,
All in the solitudinous sea
  Of that there lonely bay.
P'raps," and he'd smooth his hairless mouth,
  "P'raps, if 'twere now, my son,
P'raps, if I heard a voice say, 'Sam!'
  Morning would find me gone."

All but Blind

All but blind
  In his chambered hole
Gropes for worms
  The four-clawed Mole.

All but blind
  In the evening sky,
The hooded Bat
  Twirls softly by.

All but blind
  In the burning day
The Barn-Owl blunders
  On her way.

And blind as are
  These three to me,
So, blind to Someone
  I must be.

Summer Evening

The sandy cat by the Farmer's chair
Mews at his knee for dainty fare;
Old Rover in his moss-greened house
Mumbles a bone, and barks at a mouse.
In the dewy fields the cattle lie
Chewing the cud 'neath a fading sky.
Dobbin at manger pulls his hay:
Gone is another summer's day.

There Blooms No Bud in May

There blooms no bud in May
Can for its white compare
With snow at break of day,
On fields forlorn and bare.

For shadow it hath rose,
Azure, and amethyst;
And every air that blows
Dies out in beauteous mist.

It hangs the frozen bough
With flowers on which the night
Wheeling her darkness through
Scatters a starry light.

Fearful of its pale glare
In flocks the starlings rise;
Slide through the frosty air,
And perch with plaintive cries.

Only the inky rook,
Hunched cold in ruffled wings,
Its snowy nest forsook,
Caws of unnumbered Springs.

The Ghost

"Who knocks?" "I, who was beautiful,
Beyond all dreams to restore,
I, from the roots of the dark thorn am hither,
And knock on the door."

"Who speaks?" "I—once was my speech
Sweet as the bird's on the air,
When echo lurks by the waters to heed;
'Tis I speak thee fair."

"Dark is the hour!" "Aye, and cold."
"Lone is my house." "Ah, but mine?"
"Sight, touch, lips, eyes yearned in vain."
"Long dead these to thine. . . ."

Silence. Still faint on the porch
Brake the flames of the stars.
In gloom groped a hope-wearied hand
Over keys, bolts, and bars.

A face peered. All the grey night
In chaos of vacancy shone;
Nought but vast sorrow was there—
The sweet cheat gone.

Silver

Slowly, silently, now the moon
Walks the night in her silver shoon;
This way, and that, she peers, and sees
Silver fruit upon silver trees;
One by one the casements catch
Her beams beneath the silvery thatch;
Couched in his kennel, like a log,
With paws of silver sleeps the dog;
From their shadowy cote the white breasts peep
Of doves in a silver-feathered sleep;
A harvest mouse goes scampering by,
With silver claws and a silver eye;
And moveless fish in the water gleam,
By silver reeds in a silver stream.

Nod

Softly along the road of evening,
  In a twilight dim with rose,
Wrinkled with age, and drenched with dew
  Old Nod, the shepherd, goes.

His drowsy flock streams on before him,
  Their fleeces charged with gold,
To where the sun's last beam leans low
  On Nod the shepherd's fold.

The hedge is quick and green with briar,
  From their sand the conies creep;
And all the birds that fly in heaven
  Flock singing home to sleep.

His lambs outnumber a noon's roses,
  Yet, when night's shadows fall,
His blind old sheep-dog, Slumber-soon,
  Misses not one of all.

His are the quiet steeps of dreamland,
  The waters of no-more-pain;
His ram's bell rings 'neath an arch of stars,
  "Rest, rest, and rest again."

Peace

Night arches England, and the winds are still;
Jasmine and honeysuckle steep the air;
Softly the stars that are all Europe's fill
Her heaven-wide dark with radiancy fair;
That shadowed moon now waxing in the west,
Stirs not a rumor in her tranquil seas;
Mysterious sleep has lulled her heart to rest,
Deep even as theirs beneath her churchyard trees.

Secure, serene; dumb now the nighthawk's threat;
The gun's low thunder drumming o'er the tide;
The anguish pulsing in her stricken side . . .

All is at peace. Ah, never, heart, forget
For this her youngest, best, and bravest died,
These bright dews once were mixed with blood and sweat.

All That's Past

Very old are the woods;
  And the buds that break
Out of the brier's boughs,
  When March winds wake,
So old with their beauty are—
  Oh, no man knows
Through what wild centuries
  Roves back the rose.

Very old are the brooks;
  And the rills that rise
Where snow sleeps cold beneath
  The azure skies
Sing such a history
  Of come and gone,
Their every drop is as wise
  As Solomon.

Very old are we men;
  Our dreams are tales
Told in dim Eden
  By Eve's nightingales;
We wake and whisper awhile,
  But, the day gone by,
Silence and sleep like fields
  Of amaranth lie.

Edward Thomas

1878-1917

The New House

Now first, as I shut the door,
  I was alone
In the new house; and the wind
  Began to moan.

Old at once was the house,
  And I was old;
My ears were teased with the dread
  Of what was foretold,

Nights of storm, days of mist, without end;
  Sad days when the sun
Shone in vain; old griefs and griefs
  Not yet begun.

All was foretold me; naught
  Could I foresee;
But I learned how the wind would sound
  After these things should be.

Tall Nettles

Tall nettles cover up, as they have done
These many springs, the rusty harrow, the plow
Long worn out, and the roller made of stone:
Only the elm butt tops the nettles now.

This corner of the farmyard I like most:
As well as any bloom upon a flower
I like the dust on the nettles, never lost
Except to prove the sweetness of a shower.

If I Should Ever by Chance

If I should ever by chance grow rich
I'll buy Codham, Cockridden, and Childerditch,
Roses, Pyrgo, and Lapwater,
And let them all to my elder daughter.
The rent I shall ask of her will be only
Each year's first violets, white and lonely,
The first primroses and orchises—
She must find them before I do, that is.
But if she finds a blossom on furze
Without rent they shall all for ever be hers,
Codham, Cockridden, and Childerditch,
Roses, Pyrgo, and Lapwater,—
I shall give them all to my elder daughter.

Cock-Crow

Out of the wood of thoughts that grows by night
To be cut down by the sharp ax of light,—
Out of the night, two cocks together crow,
Cleaving the darkness with a silver blow:

And bright before my eyes twin trumpeters stand,
Heralds of splendor, one at either hand,
Each facing each as in a coat of arms:—
The milkers lace their boots up at the farms.

The Penny Whistle

The new moon hangs like an ivory bugle
  In the naked frosty blue;
And the ghylls of the forest, already blackened
  By Winter, are blackened anew.

The brooks that cut up and increase the forest,
  As if they had never known
The sun, are roaring with black hollow voices
  Betwixt rage and a moan.

But still the caravan-hut by the hollies
  Like a kingfisher gleams between;

Round the mossed old hearths of the charcoal-burners,
First primroses ask to be seen.

The charcoal-burners are black, but their linen
Blows white on the line;
And white the letter the girl is reading
Under that crescent fine:

And her brother who hides apart in a thicket,
Slowly and surely playing
On a whistle an olden nursery melody,
Says far more than I am saying.

Digging

Today I think
Only with scents,—scents dead leaves yield,
And bracken and wild carrot's seed,
And the square mustard field;

Odors that rise
When the spade wounds the root of a tree,
Rose, currant, raspberry, or goutweed,
Rhubarb or celery;

The smoke's smell, too,
Flowing from where a bonfire burns
The dead, the waste, the dangerous,
And all to sweetness turns.

It is enough
To smell, to crumble the dark earth,
While the robin sings over again
Sad songs of Autumn mirth.

Thaw

Over the land freckled with snow half-thawed
The speculating rooks at their nests cawed,
And saw from elm-tops, delicate as flower of grass,
What we below could not see, Winter pass.

Gallows

There was a weasel lived in the sun
With all his family,
Till a keeper shot him with his gun
And hung him up on a tree,
Where he swings in the wind and the rain,
In the sun and in the snow,
Without pleasure, without pain
On the dead oak tree bough.

There was a crow who was no sleeper,
But a thief and a murderer
Till a very late hour; and this keeper
Made him one of the things that were,
To hang and flap in the rain and wind,
In the sun and in the snow.
There are no more sins to be sinned
On the dead oak tree bough.

There was a magpie, too,
Had a long tongue and a long tail;
He could both talk and do—
But what did that avail?
He, too, flaps in the wind and rain
Alongside weasel and crow.
Without pleasure, without pain,
On the dead oak tree bough.

And many other beasts
And birds, skin, bone and feather,
Have been taken from their feasts
And hung up there together,
To swing and have endless leisure
In the sun and in the snow,
Without pain, without pleasure,
On the dead oak tree bough.

Fifty Faggots

There they stand, on their ends, the fifty faggots
That once were underwood of hazel and ash
In Jenny Pink's copse. Now, by the hedge
Close packed they make a thicket fancy alone
Can creep through with the mouse and wren. Next Spring
A blackbird or a robin will nest there,
Accustomed to them, thinking they will remain
Whatever is forever to a bird:
This Spring it is too late; the swift has come.
'Twas a hot day for carrying them up:
Better they will never warm me, though they must
Light several Winters' fires. Before they are done
The war will have ended, many other things
Have ended, maybe, that I can no more
Foresee or more control than robin and wren.

Out in the Dark

Out in the dark over the snow
The fallow fawns invisible go
With the fallow doe;
And the winds blow
Fast as the stars are slow.

Stealthily the dark haunts round
And, when a lamp goes, without sound
At a swifter bound
Than the swiftest hound,
Arrives, and all else is drowned;

And I and star and wind and deer,
Are in the dark together,—near,
Yet far,—and fear
Drums on my ear
In that sage company drear.

How weak and little is the light,
All the universe of sight,
Love and delight,
Before the might,
If you love it not, of night.

Haymaking

After night's thunder far away had rolled,
The fiery day had a sweet kernel of cold,
And in the perfect blue the clouds uncurled,
Like the first gods before they made the world
And misery, swimming the stormless sea
In beauty and in divine gayety.
The smooth white empty road was lightly strewn
With leaves—the holly's Autumn falls in June—
And fir cones standing stiff up in the heat.
The mill-foot water tumbled white and lit
With tossing crystals, happier than any crowd
Of children pouring out of school aloud.
And in the little thickets where a sleeper
For ever might lie lost, the nettle-creeper
And garden warbler sang unceasingly;
While over them shrill shrieked in his fierce glee
The swift with wings and tail as sharp and narrow
As if the bow had flown off with the arrow.
Only the scent of woodbine and hay new-mown
Traveled the road. In the field sloping down,
Park-like to where its willows showed the brook,
Haymakers rested. The tosser lay forsook
Out in the sun; and the long wagon stood
Without its team, it seemed it never would
Move from the shadow of that single yew.
The team, as still, until their task was due,
Beside the laborers enjoyed the shade
That three squat oaks mid-field together made
Upon a circle of grass and weed uncut,
And on the hollow, once a chalk-pit, but
Now brimmed with nut and elder-flower so clean.
The men leaned on their rakes, about to begin,
But still. And all were silent. All was old,
This morning time, with a great age untold,
Older than Clare and Cobbett, Morland and Crome,
Than, at the field's far edge, the farmer's home,
A white house crouched at the foot of a great tree.
Under the heavens that know not what years be
The men, the beasts, the trees, the implements
Uttered even what they will in times far hence—
All of us gone out of the reach of change—
Immortal in a picture of an old grange.

Liberty

The last light has gone out of the world, except
This moonlight lying on the grass like frost
Beyond the brink of the tall elm's shadow.
It is as if everything else had slept
Many an age, unforgotten and lost
The men that were, the things done, long ago.
All I have thought; and, but the moon and I
Live yet and here stand idle over a grave
Where all is buried. Both have liberty
To dream what we could do if we were free
To do something we had desired long,
The moon and I. There's none less free than who
Does nothing and has nothing else to do,
Being free only for what is not to his mind,
And nothing is to his mind. If every hour
Like this one passing that I have spent among
The wiser others when I have forgot
To wonder whether I was free or not,
Were piled before me, and not lost behind,
And I could take and carry them away
I should be rich; or if I had the power
To wipe out every one and not again
Regret, I should be rich to be so poor.
And yet I still am half in love with pain,
With what is imperfect, with both tears and mirth,
With things that have an end, with life and earth,
And this moon that leaves me dark within the door.

John Masefield

1878-

A Consecration

Not of the princes and prelates with periwigged charioteers
Riding triumphantly laureled to lap the fat of the years,—
Rather the scorned—the rejected—the men hemmed in with the
 spears;

The men of the tattered battalion which fights till it dies,
Dazed with the dust of the battle, the din and the cries.
The men with the broken heads and the blood running into
 their eyes.

Not the be-medaled Commander, beloved of the throne,
Riding cock-horse to parade when the bugles are blown,
But the lads who carried the koppie and cannot be known.

Not the ruler for me, but the ranker, the tramp of the road,
The slave with the sack on his shoulders pricked on with the
 goad,
The man with too weighty a burden, too weary a load.

The sailor, the stoker of steamers, the man with the clout,
The chantyman bent at the halliards putting a tune to the
 shout,
The drowsy man at the wheel and the tired look-out.

Others may sing of the wine and the wealth and the mirth,
The portly presence of potentates goodly in girth;—
Mine be the dirt and the dross, the dust and scum of the earth!

Theirs be the music, the color, the glory, the gold;
Mine be a handful of ashes, a mouthful of mold.
Of the maimed, of the halt and the blind in the rain and the
 cold—
Of these shall my songs be fashioned, my tales be told.

Sea-Fever

I must down to the seas again, to the lonely sea and the sky,
And all I ask is a tall ship and a star to steer her by,
And the wheel's kick and the wind's song and the white sail's
shaking,
And a gray mist on the sea's face and a gray dawn breaking.

I must down to the seas again, for the call of the running tide
Is a wild call and a clear call that may not be denied;
And all I ask is a windy day with the white clouds flying,
And the flung spray and the blown spume, and the sea-gulls
crying.

I must down to the seas again to the vagrant gypsy life.
To the gull's way and the whale's way where the wind's like a
whetted knife;
And all I ask is a merry yarn from a laughing fellow-rover,
And quiet sleep and a sweet dream when the long trick's over.

A Wanderer's Song

A wind's in the heart of me, a fire's in my heels,
I am tired of brick and stone and rumbling wagon-wheels;
I hunger for the sea's edge, the limits of the land,
Where the wild old Atlantic is shouting on the sand.

Oh I'll be going, leaving the noises of the street,
To where a lifting foresail-foot is yanking at the sheet;
To a windy, tossing anchorage where yawls and ketches ride,
Oh I'll be going, going, until I meet the tide.

And first I'll hear the sea-wind, the mewing of the gulls,
The clucking, sucking of the sea about the rusty hulls,
The songs at the capstan in the hooker warping out,
And then the heart of me'll know I'm there or thereabout.

Oh I am sick of brick and stone, the heart of me is sick,
For windy green, unquiet sea, the realm of Moby Dick;
And I'll be going, going, from the roaring of the wheels,
For a wind's in the heart of me, a fire's in my heels.

The West Wind

It's a warm wind, the west wind, full of birds' cries;
I never hear the west wind but tears are in my eyes.
For it comes from the west lands, the old brown hills,
And April's in the west wind, and daffodils.

It's a fine land, the west land, for hearts as tired as mine,
Apple orchards blossom there, and the air's like wine.
There is cool green grass there, where men may lie at rest,
And the thrushes are in song there, fluting from the nest.

"Will ye not come home, brother? ye have been long away,
It's April, and blossom time, and white is the may;
And bright is the sun, brother, and warm is the rain,—
Will ye not come home, brother, home to us again?

"The young corn is green, brother, where the rabbits run,
It's blue sky, and white clouds, and warm rain and sun.
It's song to a man's soul, brother, fire to a man's brain,
To hear the wild bees and see the merry spring again.

"Larks are singing in the west, brother, above the green wheat,
So will ye not come home, brother, and rest your tired feet?
I've a balm for bruised hearts, brother, sleep for aching eyes,"
Says the warm wind, the west wind, full of birds' cries.

It's the white road westwards is the road I must tread
To the green grass, the cool grass, and rest for heart and head,
To the violets and the warm hearts and the thrushes' song,
In the fine land, the west land, the land where I belong.

Rounding the Horn

(From "Dauber")

Then came the cry of "Call all hands on deck!"
The Dauber knew its meaning; it was come:
Cape Horn, that tramples beauty into wreck,
And crumples steel and smites the strong man dumb.
Down clattered flying kites and staysails; some
Sang out in quick, high calls: the fair-leads skirled,
And from the south-west came the end of the world . . .

"Lay out!" the Bosun yelled. The Dauber laid
Out on the yard, gripping the yard, and feeling
Sick at the mighty space of air displayed
Below his feet, where mewing birds were wheeling.
A giddy fear was on him; he was reeling.
He bit his lip half through, clutching the jack.
A cold sweat glued the shirt upon his back.

The yard was shaking, for a brace was loose.
He felt that he would fall; he clutched, he bent,
Clammy with natural terror to the shoes
While idiotic promptings came and went.
Snow fluttered on a wind-flaw and was spent;
He saw the water darken. Someone yelled,
"Frap it; don't stay to furl! Hold on!" He held.

Darkness came down—half darkness—in a whirl;
The sky went out, the waters disappeared.
He felt a shocking pressure of blowing hurl
The ship upon her side. The darkness speared
At her with wind; she staggered, she careered;
Then down she lay. The Dauber felt her go,
He saw her yard tilt downwards. Then the snow

Whirled all about—dense, multitudinous, cold—
Mixed with the wind's one devilish thrust and shriek,
Which whiffled out men's tears, defeated, took hold,
Flattening the flying drift against the cheek.
The yards buckled and bent, man could not speak.
The ship lay on her broadside; the wind's sound
Had devilish malice at having got her downed.

How long the gale had blown he could not tell,
Only the world had changed, his life had died.
A moment now was everlasting hell.
Nature an onslaught from the weather side,
A withering rush of death, a frost that cried,
Shrieked, till he withered at the heart; a hail
Plastered his oilskins with an icy mail. . . .

"Up!" yelled the Bosun; "up and clear the wreck!"
The Dauber followed where he led; below
He caught one giddy glimpsing of the deck

Filled with white water, as though heaped with snow.
He saw the streamers of the rigging blow
Straight out like pennons from the splintered mast,
Then, all sense dimmed, all was an icy blast.

Roaring from nether hell and filled with ice,
Roaring and crashing on the jerking stage,
An utter bridle given to utter vice,
Limitless power mad with endless rage
Withering the soul; a minute seemed an age.
He clutched and hacked at ropes, at rags of sail,
Thinking that comfort was a fairy tale,

Told long ago—long, long ago—long since
Heard of in other lives—imagined, dreamed—
There where the basest beggar was a prince.
To him in torment where the tempest screamed,
Comfort and warmth and ease no longer seemed
Things that a man could know; soul, body, brain,
Knew nothing but the wind, the cold, the pain.

Cargoes

Quinquireme of Nineveh from distant Ophir
Rowing home to haven in sunny Palestine,
With a cargo of ivory,
And apes and peacocks,
Sandalwood, cedarwood, and sweet white wine.

Stately Spanish galleon coming from the Isthmus,
Dipping through the Tropics by the palm-green shores,
With a cargo of diamonds,
Emeralds, amethysts,
Topazes, and cinnamon, and gold moidores.

Dirty British coaster with a salt-caked smoke-stack
Butting through the Channel in the mad March days,
With a cargo of Tyne coal,
Road-rail, pig-lead,
Firewood, iron-ware, and cheap tin trays.

On Growing Old

Be with me, Beauty, for the fire is dying;
My dog and I are old, too old for roving.
Man, whose young passion sets the spindrift flying,
Is soon too lame to march, too cold for loving.
I take the book and gather to the fire,
Turning old yellow leaves; minute by minute
The clock ticks to my heart. A withered wire,
Moves a thin ghost of music in the spinet.
I cannot sail your seas, I cannot wander
Your cornland, nor your hill-land, nor your valleys
Ever again, nor share the battle yonder
Where the young knight the broken squadron rallies.
Only stay quiet while my mind remembers
The beauty of fire from the beauty of embers.

Beauty, have pity! for the strong have power,
The rich their wealth, the beautiful their grace,
Summer of man its sunlight and its flower,
Spring-time of man all April in a face.
Only, as in the jostling in the Strand,
Where the mob thrusts or loiters or is loud,
The beggar with the saucer in his hand
Asks only a penny from the passing crowd,
So, from this glittering world with all its fashion,
Its fire, and play of men, its stir, its march,
Let me have wisdom, Beauty, wisdom and passion,
Bread to the soul, rain when the summers parch.
Give me but these, and though the darkness close
Even the night will blossom as the rose.

The Choice

The Kings go by with jeweled crowns;
Their horses gleam, their banners shake, their spears are many.
The sack of many-peopled towns
Is all their dream:
The way they take
Leaves but a ruin in the brake,
And, in the furrow that the plowmen make,
A stampless penny; a tale, a dream.

The Merchants reckon up their gold,
Their letters come, their ships arrive, their freights are glories;
The profits of their treasures sold
They tell and sum;
Their foremen drive
Their servants, starved to half-alive,
Whose labors do but make the earth a hive
Of stinking stories; a tale, a dream.

The Priests are singing in their stalls,
Their singing lifts, their incense burns, their praying clamors;
Yet God is as the sparrow falls,
The ivy drifts;
The votive urns
Are all left void when Fortune turns,
The god is but a marble for the kerns
To break with hammers; a tale, a dream.

O Beauty, let me know again
The green earth cold, the April rain, the quiet waters figuring sky,
The one star risen.
So shall I pass into the feast
Not touched by King, Merchant, or Priest;
Know the red spirit of the beast,
Be the green grain;
Escape from prison.

The Passing Strange

Out of the earth to rest or range
Perpetual in perpetual change,
The unknown passing through the strange.

Water and saltness held together
To tread the dust and stand the weather,
And plow the field and stretch the tether,

To pass the wine-cup and be witty,
Water the sands and build the city,
Slaughter like devils and have pity,

Be red with rage and pale with lust,
Make beauty come, make peace, make trust,
Water and saltness mixed with dust;

Drive over earth, swim under sea,
Fly in the eagle's secrecy,
Guess where the hidden comets be;

Know all the deathy seeds that still
Queen Helen's beauty, Caesar's will,
And slay them even as they kill;

Fashion an altar for a rood,
Defile a continent with blood,
And watch a brother starve for food:

Love like a madman, shaking, blind,
Till self is burnt into a kind
Possession of another mind;

Brood upon beauty, till the grace
Of beauty with the holy face
Brings peace into the bitter place;

Prove in the lifeless granites, scan
The stars for hope, for guide, for plan;
Live as a woman or a man;

Fasten to lover or to friend,
Until the heart break at the end
The break of death that cannot mend:

Then to lie useless, helpless, still,
Down in the earth, in dark, to fill
The roots of grass or daffodil.

Down in the earth, in dark, alone,
A mockery of the ghost in bone,
The strangeness, passing the unknown.

Time will go by, that outlasts clocks,
Dawn in the thorps will rouse the cocks,
Sunset be glory on the rocks:

But it, the thing, will never heed
Even the rootling from the seed
Thrusting to suck it for its need.

Since moons decay and suns decline,
How else should end this life of mine?
Water and saltness are not wine.

But in the darkest hour of night,
When even the foxes peer for sight,
The byre-cock crows; he feels the light.

So, in this water mixed with dust,
The byre-cock spirit crows from trust
That death will change because it must.

For all things change: the darkness changes,
The wandering spirits change their ranges,
The corn is gathered to the granges.

The corn is sown again, it grows;
The stars burn out, the darkness goes;
The rhythms change, they do not close.

They change, and we, who pass like foam,
Like dust blown through the streets of Rome,
Change ever, too; we have no home,

Only a beauty, only a power,
Sad in the fruit, bright in the flower,
Endlessly erring for its hour,

But gathering as we stray, a sense
Of Life, so lovely and intense,
It lingers when we wander hence,

That those who follow feel behind
Their backs, when all before is blind,
Our joy, a rampart to the mind.

James Stephens

1882-1950

The Shell

And then I pressed the shell
Close to my ear
And listened well,
And straightway like a bell
Came low and clear
The slow, sad murmur of the distant seas,
Whipped by an icy breeze
Upon a shore
Wind-swept and desolate.
It was a sunless strand that never bore
The footprint of a man,
Nor felt the weight
Since time began
Of any human quality or stir
Save what the dreary winds and waves incur.
And in the hush of waters was the sound
Of pebbles rolling round,
For ever rolling with a hollow sound.
And bubbling sea-weeds as the waters go
Swish to and fro
Their long, cold tentacles of slimy gray.
There was no day,
Nor ever came a night
Setting the stars alight
To wonder at the moon:
Was twilight only and the frightened croon,
Smitten to whimpers, of the dreary wind
And waves that journeyed blind—
And then I loosed my ear . . . O, it was sweet
To hear a cart go jolting down the street.

What Thomas an Buile Said in a Pub

I saw God. Do you doubt it?
  Do you dare to doubt it?
I saw the Almighty Man. His hand
Was resting on a mountain, and
He looked upon the World and all about it:
I saw Him plainer than you see me now,
  You mustn't doubt it.

He was not satisfied;
  His look was all dissatisfied.
His beard swung on a wind far out of sight
Behind the world's curve, and there was light
Most fearful from His forehead, and He sighed,
"That star went always wrong, and from the start
  I was dissatisfied."

He lifted up His hand—
  I say He heaved a dreadful hand
Over the spinning Earth. Then I said, "Stay,
You must not strike it, God; I'm in the way;
And I will never move from where I stand."
He said, "Dear child, I feared that you were dead,"
  And stayed His hand.

To the Four Courts, Please

The driver rubbed at his nettly chin
With a huge, loose forefinger, crooked and black,
And his wobbly, violent lips sucked in,
And puffed out again and hung down slack:
One fang shone through his lop-sided smile,
In his little pouched eye flickered years of guile.

And the horse, poor beast, it was ribbed and forked,
And its ears hung down, and its eyes were old,
And its knees were knuckly, and as we talked
It swung the stiff neck that could scarcely hold
Its big, skinny head up—then I stepped in,
And the driver climbed to his seat with a grin.

God help the horse and the driver too,
And the people and beasts who have never a friend,
For the driver easily might have been you,
And the horse be me by a different end.
And nobody knows how their days will cease,
And the poor, when they're old, have little of peace.

Hate

My enemy came nigh,
And I
Stared fiercely in his face.
My lips went writhing back in a grimace,
And stern I watched him with a narrow eye.
Then, as I turned away, my enemy,
That bitter heart and savage, said to me:
"Some day, when this is past,
When all the arrows that we have are cast,
We may ask one another why we hate,
And fail to find a story to relate.
It may seem to us then a mystery
That we could hate each other."
Thus said he,
And did not turn away,
Waiting to hear what I might have to say.
But I fled quickly, fearing if I stayed
I might have kissed him as I would a maid.

Odell

My mind is sad and weary thinking how
The griffins of the Gael went over the sea
From noble Eiré, and are fighting now
In France and Flanders and in Germany.

If they, 'mid whom I sported without dread,
Were home I would not mind what foe might do,
Or fear tax-man Odell would seize my bed
To pay the hearth-rate that is overdue.

I pray to Him who, in the haughty hour
Of Babel, threw confusion on each tongue,
That I may see our princes back in power,
And see Odell, the tax-collector, hung.

Righteous Anger

(After O'Bruaidar)

The lanky hank of a she in the inn over there
Nearly killed me for asking the loan of a glass of beer:
May the devil grip the whey-faced slut by the hair,
And beat bad manners out of her skin for a year.

That parboiled imp, with the hardest jaw you will see
On virtue's path, and a voice that would rasp the dead,
Came roaring and raging the minute she looked at me,
And threw me out of the house on the back of my head!

If I asked her master he'd give me a cask a day;
But she with the beer at hand, not a gill would arrange!
May she marry a ghost and bear him a kitten and may
The High King of Glory permit her to get the mange.

Blue Blood

(After O'Bruaidar)

We thought at first, this man is a king for sure,
Or the branch of a mighty and ancient and famous lineage—
That silly, sulky, illiterate, black-avised boor
Who was hatched by foreign vulgarity under a hedge.

The good men of Clare were drinking his health in a flood,
And gazing with me in awe of the princely lad,
And asking each other from what bluest blueness of blood
His daddy was squeezed, and the pa of the da of his dad?

We waited there, gaping and wondering, anxiously,
Until he'd stop eating and let the glad tidings out,
And the slack-jawed booby proved to the hilt that he
Was lout, son of lout, by old lout, and was da to a lout!

In Waste Places

As a naked man I go
Through the desert, sore afraid;
Holding high my head, although
I'm as frightened as a maid.

The lion crouches there! I saw
In barren rocks his amber eye!
He parts the cactus with his paw!
He stares at me as I go by!

He would pad upon my trace
If he thought I was afraid!
If he knew my hardy face
Veils the terrors of a maid.

He rises in the night-time, and
He stretches forth! He snuffs the air!
He roars! He leaps along the sand!
He creeps! He watches everywhere!

His burning eyes, his eyes of bale
Through the darkness I can see!
He lashes fiercely with his tail!
He makes again to spring at me!

I am the lion, and his lair!
I am the fear that frightens me!
I am the desert of despair!
And the night of agony!

Night or day, whate'er befall,
I must walk that desert land,
Until I dare my fear and call
The lion out to lick my hand.

The Crest Jewel

I

The leaf will wrinkle to decay
And crumble into dust away!

The rose, the lily, grow to eld,
And are, and are no more, beheld!

Nothing will stay! For, as the eye
Rests upon an object nigh,

It is not there to look upon!
It is mysteriously gone!

And, in its place, another thing
Apes its shape and fashioning!

II

All that the sun will breathe today
The moon will lip and wear away

Tonight. And all will re-begin
Tomorrow as the dawn comes in.

Is no beginning, middle-trend
Or argument to that or end.

No cause and no effect, and no
Reason why it should be so.

Or why it might be otherwise
To other minds or other eyes.

III

The soul can dream itself to be
Adrift upon an endless sea

Of day and night. The soul can seem
To be all things that it can dream!

Yet needs but look within to find
That which is steady in the wind,

That which the fire does not appal,
Which good and ill mourn not at all

Which does not seek, or lack, or try.
And was not born, and cannot die!

IV

It has been writ in wisdom old—
This is the last word to be told:

—There is no dissolution! No
Creation! There are none in woe!

There is no teacher, teaching, taught!
Are none who long for, lack for aught!

Are none who pine for freedom! None
Are liberated under sun!

—And this is absolutely true
In Him who dreams in me and you.

D. H. Lawrence

1885-1930

A Youth Mowing

There are four men mowing down by the Isar;
I can hear the swish of the scythe-strokes, four
Sharp breaths taken; yea, and I
Am sorry for what's in store.

The first man out of the four that's mowing
Is mine, I claim him once and for all;
Though it's sorry I am, on his young feet, knowing
None of the trouble he's led to stall.

As he sees me bringing the dinner, he lifts
His head as proud as a deer that looks
Shoulder-deep out of the corn; and wipes
His scythe-blade bright, unhooks

The scythe-stone and over the stubble to me.
Lad, thou hast gotten a child in me,
Laddie, a man thou'lt ha'e to be,
Yea, though I'm sorry for thee.

Lightning

I felt the lurch and halt of her heart
  Next my breast, where my own heart was beating;
And I laughed to feel it plunge and bound,
And strange in my blood-swept ears was the sound
  Of the words I kept repeating,
Repeating with tightened arms, and the hot blood's blind-fold
    art.

Her breath flew warm against my neck,
  Warm as a flame in the close night air;
And the sense of her clinging flesh was sweet
Where her arms and my neck's blood-surge could meet.
  Holding her thus, did I care
That the black night hid her from me, blotted out every speck?

I leaned me forward to find her lips,
  And claim her utterly in a kiss,
When the lightning flew across her face,
And I saw her for the flaring space
  Of a second, afraid of the clips
Of my arms, inert with dread, wilted in fear of my kiss.

A moment, like a wavering spark,
  Her face lay there before my breast,
Pale love lost in a snow of fear,
And guarded by a glittering tear,
  And lips apart with dumb cries;
A moment, and she was taken again in the merciful dark.

I heard the thunder, and felt the rain,
  And my arms fell loose, and I was dumb.

Almost I hated her, she was so good,
Hated myself, and the place, and my blood,
  Which burned with rage, as I bade her come
Home, away home, ere the lightning floated forth again.

Cherry Robbers

Under the long dark boughs, like jewels red
  In the hair of an Eastern girl
Hang strings of crimson cherries, as if had bled
  Blood-drops beneath each curl.

Under the glistening cherries, with folded wings
  Three dead birds lie:
Pale-breasted throstles and a blackbird, robberlings
  Stained with red dye.

Against the haystack a girl stands laughing at me,
  Cherries hung round her ears.
Offers me her scarlet fruit: I will see
  If she has any tears.

A Winter's Tale

Yesterday the fields were only gray with scattered snow,
And now the longest grass-leaves hardly emerge;
Yet her deep footsteps mark the snow, and go
On toward the pines at the hill's white verge.

I cannot see her, since the mist's pale scarf
Obscures the dark wood and the dull orange sky;
But she's waiting, I know, impatient and cold, half
Sobs struggling into her frosty sigh.

Why does she come so promptly, when she must know
She's only the nearer to the inevitable farewell?
The hill is steep, on the snow my steps are slow—
Why does she come, when she knows what I have to tell?

Love on the Farm

What large, dark hands are those at the window
Grasping in the golden light
Which weaves its way through the evening wind
  At my heart's delight?

Ah, only the leaves! But in the west
I see a redness suddenly come
Into the evening's anxious breast—
  'Tis the wound of love goes home!

The woodbine creeps abroad
Calling low to her lover:
  The sun-lit flirt who all the day
  Has poised above her lips in play
  And stolen kisses, shallow and gay
  Of pollen, now has gone away—
    She woos the moth with her sweet, low word;
And when above her his moth-wings hover
Then her bright breast she will uncover
And yield her honey-drop to her lover.

Into the yellow, evening glow
Saunters a man from the farm below;
Leans, and looks in at the low-built shed
Where the swallow has hung her marriage bed.
  The bird lies warm against the wall.
  She glances quick her startled eyes
  Towards him, then she turns away
  Her small head, making warm display
  Of red upon the throat. Her terrors sway
  Her out of the nest's warm, busy ball,
  Whose plaintive cry is heard as she flies
  In one blue stoop from out the sties
  Into the twilight's empty hall.

Oh, water-hen, beside the rushes,
Hide your quaintly scarlet blushes,
Still your quick tail, lie still as dead,
Till the distance folds over his ominous tread!

The rabbit presses back her ears,
Turns back her liquid, anguished eyes

And crouches low; then with wild spring
Spurts from the terror of his oncoming;
To be choked back, the wire ring
Her frantic effort throttling:
  Piteous brown ball of quivering fears!
Ah, soon in his large, hard hands she dies,
And swings all loose from the swing of his walk!
Yet calm and kindly are his eyes
And ready to open in brown surprise
Should I not answer to his talk
Or should he my tears surmise.

I hear his hand on the latch, and rise from my chair
Watching the door open; he flashes bare
His strong teeth in a smile, and flashes his eyes
In a smile like triumph upon me; then careless-wise
He flings the rabbit soft on the table board
And comes toward me: he! the uplifted sword
Of his hand against my bosom! and oh, the broad
Blade of his glance that asks me to applaud
His coming! With his hand he turns my face to him
And caresses me with his fingers that still smell grim
Of rabbit's fur! God, I am caught in a snare!
I know not what fine wire is round my throat;
I only know I let him finger there
My pulse of life, and let him nose like a stoat
Who sniffs with joy before he drinks the blood.

And down his mouth comes to my mouth! and down
His bright dark eyes come over me, like a hood
Upon my mind! his lips meet mine, and a flood
Of sweet fire sweeps across me, so I drown
Against him, die, and find death good.

Piano

Softly, in the dusk, a woman is singing to me;
Taking me back down the vista of years, till I see
A child sitting under the piano, in the boom of the tingling
    strings
And pressing the small, poised feet of a mother who smiles as
    she sings.

In spite of myself, the insidious mastery of song
Betrays me back, till the heart of me weeps to belong

To the old Sunday evenings at home, with winter outside
And hymns in the cozy parlor, the tinkling piano our guide.

So now it is vain for the singer to burst into clamor
With the great black piano appassionato. The glamour
Of childish days is upon me, my manhood is cast
Down in the flood of remembrance, I weep like a child for the
past.

Hymn to Priapus

My love lies underground
With her face upturned to mine,
And her mouth unclosed in a last long kiss
That ended her life and mine.

I danced at the Christmas party
Under the mistletoe
Along with a ripe, slack country lass
Jostling to and fro.

The big, soft country lass,
Like a loose sheaf of wheat
Slipped through my arms on the threshing floor
At my feet.

The warm, soft country lass,
Sweet as an armful of wheat
At threshing-time broken, was broken
For me, and ah, it was sweet!

Now I am going home
Fulfilled and alone,
I see the great Orion standing
Looking down.

He's the star of my first beloved
Love-making.
The witness of all that bitter-sweet
Heart-aching.

Now he sees this as well,
This last commission.
Nor do I get any look
Of admonition.

He can add the reckoning up
I suppose, between now and then,
Having walked himself in the thorny, difficult
Ways of men.

He has done as I have done
No doubt:
Remembered and forgotten
Turn and about.

My love lies underground
With her face upturned to mine,
And her mouth unclosed in the last long kiss
That ended her life and mine.

She fares in the stark immortal
Fields of death;
I in these goodly, frozen
Fields beneath.

Something in me remembers
And will not forget.
The stream of my life in the darkness
Deathward set!

And something in me has forgotten,
Has ceased to care.
Desire comes up, and contentment
Is debonair.

I, who am worn and careful,
How much do I care?
How is it I grin then, and chuckle
Over despair?

Grief, grief, I suppose and sufficient
Grief makes us free
To be faithless and faithful together
As we have to be.

Wedding Morn

The morning breaks like a pomegranate
In a shining crack of red;
Ah, when tomorrow the dawn comes late
Whitening across the bed
It will find me at the marriage gate
And waiting while light is shed
On him who is sleeping satiate
With a sunk, unconscious head.

And when the dawn comes creeping in,
Cautiously I shall raise
Myself to watch the daylight win
On my first of days,
As it shows him sleeping a sleep he got
With me, as under my gaze
He grows distinct, and I see his hot
Face freed of the wavering blaze.

Then I shall know which image of God
My man is made toward;
And I shall see my sleeping rod
Or my life's reward;
And I shall count the stamp and worth
Of the man I've accepted as mine,
Shall see an image of heaven or of earth
On his minted metal shine.

Oh, and I long to see him sleep
In my power utterly;
So I shall know what I have to keep. . . .
I long to see
My love, that spinning coin, laid still
And plain at the side of me
For me to reckon—for surely he will
Be wealth of life to me.

And then he will be mine, he will lie
Revealed to me;
Patent and open beneath my eye
He will sleep of me;

He will lie negligent, resign
  His truth to me, and I
Shall watch the dawn light up for me
  This fate of mine.

And as I watch the wan light shine
  On his sleep that is filled of me,
On his brow where the curved wisps clot and twine
  Carelessly,
On his lips where the light breaths come and go
  Unconsciously,
On his limbs in sleep at last laid low
  Helplessly,
I shall weep, oh, I shall weep, I know
  For joy or for misery.

Kisses in the Train

I saw the midlands
  Revolve through her hair;
The fields of autumn
  Stretching bare,
And sheep on the pasture
  Tossed back in a scare.

And still as ever
  The world went round,
My mouth on her pulsing
  Neck was found,
And my breast to her beating
  Breast was bound.

But my heart at the center
  Of all, in a swound
Was still as a pivot,
  As all the ground
On its prowling orbit
  Shifted round.

And still in my nostrils
  The scent of her flesh,
And still my wet mouth
  Sought her afresh;

And still one pulse
  Through the world did thresh.

And the world all whirling
  Around in joy
Like the dance of a dervish
  Did destroy
My sense—and my reason
  Spun like a toy.

But firm at the center
  My heart was found;
Her own to my perfect
  Heart-beat bound,
Like a magnet's keeper
  Closing the round.

Spring Morning

Ah, through the open door
Is there an almond tree
Aflame with blossom!
    —Let us fight no more.

Among the pink and blue
Of the sky and the almond flowers
A sparrow flutters.
    —We have come through.

It is really spring!—See,
When he thinks himself alone
How he bullies the flowers.
    —You and me

How happy we'll be!—See him,
He clouts the tufts of flowers
In his impudence.
    —But, did you dream

It would be so bitter? Never mind
It is finished, the spring is here.
And we're going to be summer-happy
    And summer-kind.

We have died, we have slain and been slain
We are not our old selves any more.
I feel new and eager
To start again.

It is gorgeous to live and forget.
And to feel quite new.
See the bird in the flowers?—he's making
A rare to-do!

He thinks the whole blue sky
Is much less than the bit of blue egg
He's got in his nest—we'll be happy
You and I, I and you.

With nothing to fight any more—
In each other, at least.
See, how gorgeous the world is
Outside the door!

Trees in the Garden

Ah in the thunder air
how still the trees are!

And the lime-tree, lovely and tall, every leaf silent
hardly looses even a last breath of perfume.

And the ghostly, creamy colored little tree of leaves
white, ivory white among the rambling greens,
how evanescent, variegated elder, she hesitates on the green grass
as if, in another moment, she would disappear
with all her grace of foam!

And the larch that is only a column, it goes up too tall to see:
and the balsam-pines that are blue with the gray-blue blueness of things from the sea,
and the young copper beech, its leaves red-rosy at the ends
how still they are together, they stand so still
in the thunder air, all strangers to one another
as the green grass glows upwards, strangers in the garden.

Morning Work

A gang of labourers on the piled wet timber
That shines blood-red beside the railway siding
Seem to be making out of the blue of the morning
Something faery and fine, the shuttles sliding,
The red-gold spools of their hands and faces shuttling
Hither and thither across the morn's crystalline frame
Of blue: trolls at the cave of ringing cerulean mining,
And laughing with work, living their work like a game.

Snake

A snake came to my water-trough
On a hot, hot day, and I in pyjamas for the heat,
To drink there.

In the deep, strange-scented shade of the great dark carob-tree
I came down the steps with my pitcher
And must wait, must stand and wait, for there he was at the trough before me.

He reached down from a fissure in the earth-wall in the gloom
And trailed his yellow-brown slackness soft-bellied down, over the edge of the stone trough
And rested his throat upon the stone bottom,
And where the water had dripped from the tap, in a small clearness,
He sipped with his straight mouth,
Softly drank through his straight gums, into his slack long body,
Silently.

Someone was before me at my water-trough,
And I, like a second comer, waiting.

He lifted his head from his drinking, as cattle do,
And looked at me vaguely, as drinking cattle do,
And flickered his two-forked tongue from his lips, and mused a moment,
And stooped and drank a little more,

Being earth-brown, earth-golden from the burning bowels of
the earth
On the day of Sicilian July, with Etna smoking.

The voice of my education said to me
He must be killed,
For in Sicily the black, black snakes are innocent, the gold are
venomous.

And voices in me said, If you were a man
You would take a stick and break him now, and finish him off.

But must I confess how I liked him,
How glad I was he had come like a guest in quiet, to drink at
my water-trough
And depart peaceful, pacified, and thankless,
Into the burning bowels of this earth?

Was it cowardice, that I dared not kill him?
Was it perversity, that I longed to talk to him?
Was it humility, to feel so honoured?
I felt so honoured.

And yet those voices:
If you were not afraid, you would kill him!

And truly I was afraid, I was most afraid,
But even so, honoured still more
That he should seek my hospitality
From out the dark door of the secret earth.

He drank enough
And lifted his head, dreamily, as one who has drunken,
And flickered his tongue like a forked night on the air, so
black,
Seeming to lick his lips,
And looked around like a god, unseeing, into the air,
And slowly turned his head,
And slowly, very slowly, as if thrice adream,
Proceeded to draw his slow length curving round
And climb again the broken bank of my wall-face.

And as he put his head into that dreadful hole,
And as he slowly drew up, snake-easing his shoulders, and entered farther,

A sort of horror, a sort of protest against his withdrawing into
that horrid black hole,
Deliberately going into the blackness, and slowly drawing himself after,
Overcame me now his back was turned.

I looked round, I put down my pitcher,
I picked up a clumsy log
And threw it at the water-trough with a clatter.

I think it did not hit him,
But suddenly that part of him that was left behind convulsed
in undignified haste,
Writhed like lightning, and was gone
Into the black hole, the earth-lipped fissure in the wall-front,
At which, in the intense still noon, I stared with fascination.

And immediately I regretted it.
I thought how paltry, how vulgar, what a mean act!
I despised myself and the voices of my accursed human edu-
cation.

And I thought of the albatross,
And I wished he would come back, my snake.

For he seemed to me again like a king,
Like a king in exile, uncrowned in the underworld,
Now due to be crowned again.

And so, I missed my chance with one of the lords
Of life.
And I have something to expiate:
A pettiness.

Ship of Death

I sing of autumn and the falling fruit
and the long journey towards oblivion.

The apples falling like great drops of dew
to bruise themselves an exit from themselves.

Have you built your ship of death, oh, have you?
Build then your ship of death, for you will need it!

Can man his own quietus make
with a bare bodkin?

With daggers, bodkins, bullets, man can make
a bruise or break of exit for his life
but is that a quietus, oh tell me, is it quietus?

Quietus is the goal of the long journey
the longest journey towards oblivion.

Slips out the soul, invisible one, wrapped still
in the white shirt of the mind's experiences
and folded in the dark-red, unseen
mantle of the body's still mortal memories.

Frightened and alone, the soul slips out of the house
or is pushed out
to find himself on the crowded, arid margins of existence.

Oh, it is not so easy, I tell you it is not so easy
to set softly forth on the longest journey, the longest journey.

It is easy to be pushed out of the silvery city of the body
through any breach in the wall,
thrust out onto the grey grey beaches of shadow
the long marginal stretches of existence, crowded with lost souls
that intervene between our tower and the shaking sea of the beyond.

Oh build your ship of death, oh build it in time
and build it lovingly, and put it between the hands of your soul.

Once outside the gate of the walled silvery life of days
once outside, upon the grey marsh beaches, where lost souls moan
in millions, unable to depart
having no boat to launch upon the shaken, soundless
deepest and longest of seas,
once outside the gate
what will you do, if you have no ship of the soul?

Oh pity the dead that are dead, but cannot take
the journey, still they moan and beat
against the silvery adamant walls of this our exclusive existence.

They moan and beat, they gnash, they rage
they fall upon the new outcoming souls with rage
and they send arrows of anger, bullets and bombs of frustration
over the adamant walls of this, our by-no-means impregnable
existence.

Pity, oh pity the poor dead that are only ousted from life
and crowd there on the grey mud beaches of the margins
gaunt and horrible
waiting, waiting till at last the ancient boatman with the
common barge
shall take them abroad, towards the great goal of oblivion.

Pity the poor gaunt dead that cannot die
into the distance with receding oars
but must roam like outcast dogs on the margins of life,
and think of them, and with the soul's deep sigh
waft nearer to them the bark of delivery.

But for myself, but for my soul, dear soul
let me build a little ship with oars and food
and little dishes, and all accoutrements
dainty and ready for the departing soul.

And put it between the hands of the trembling soul.
So that when the hour comes, and the last door closes behind
him
he shall slip down the shores invisible
between the half-visible hordes
to where the furthest and the longest sea
touches the margins of our life's existence
with wincing unwilling waves.

And launching there his little ship,
wrapped in the dark-red mantle of the body's memories
the little, slender soul sits swiftly down, and takes the oars
and draws away, away, away, towards the dark depths
fathomless deep ahead, far, far from the grey shores
that fringe with shadow all this world's existence.

Over the sea, over the farthest sea
on the longest journey
past the jutting rocks of shadow
past the lurking, octopus arms of agonised memory
past the strange whirlpools of remembered greed

through the dead weed of a life-time's falsity,
slow, slow my soul, in his little ship
on the most soundless of all seas
taking the longest journey.

Pulling the long oars of a life-time's courage,
drinking the confident water from the little jug
and eating the brave bread of a wholesome knowledge
row, little soul, row on
on the longest journey, towards the greatest goal

Neither straight nor crooked, neither here nor there
but shadows folded on deeper shadows
and deeper, to a core of sheer oblivion
like the convolutions of shadow-shell
or deeper, like the foldings and involvings of a womb.

Drift on, drift on, my soul, towards the most pure
most dark oblivion.
And at the penultimate porches, the dark-red mantle
of the body's memories slips and is absorbed
into the shell-like, womb-like convoluted shadow.

And round the great final bend of unbroken dark
the skirt of the spirit's experience has melted away
the oars have gone from the boat, and the little dishes
gone, gone, and the boat dissolves like pearl
as the soul at last slips perfect into the goal, the core
of sheer oblivion and of utter peace,
the womb of silence in the living night.

Ah peace, ah lovely peace, most lovely lapsing
of this my soul into the plasm of peace.

Oh lovely last, last lapse of death, into pure oblivion
at the end of the longest journey
peace, complete peace!
But can it be that also it is procreation?

Oh build your ship of death
oh build it!
Oh, nothing matters but the longest journey.

Edith Sitwell

1887-

Interlude

Amid this hot green glowing gloom
A word falls with a raindrop's boom.

Like baskets of ripe fruit in air
The bird-songs seem, suspended where

Those goldfinches—the ripe warm lights
Peck slyly at them—take quick flights.

My feet are feathered like a bird
Among the shadows scarcely heard;

I bring you branches green with dew
And fruits that you may crown anew

Your whirring waspish-gilded hair
Amid this cornucopia—

Until your warm lips bear the stains
And bird-blood leap within your veins.

Aubade

Jane, Jane,
Tall as a crane,
The morning light creaks down again.

Comb your cockscomb-ragged hair;
Jane, Jane, come down the stair.

Each dull blunt wooden stalactite
Of rain creaks, hardened by the light,

Sounding like an overtone
From some lonely world unknown.

But the creaking empty light
Will never harden into sight,

Will never penetrate your brain
With overtones like the blunt rain.

The light would show (if it could harden)
Eternities of kitchen-garden,

Cockscomb flowers that none will pluck,
And wooden flowers that 'gin to cluck.

In the kitchen you must light
Flames as staring, red and white

As carrots or as turnips, shining
Where the cold dawn light lies whining.

Cockscomb hair on the cold wind
Hangs limp, turns the milk's weak mind. . . .

Jane, Jane,
Tall as a crane,
The morning light creaks down again!

Sir Beelzebub

WHEN
Sir
Beelzebub called for his syllabub in the hotel in Hell
Where Proserpine first fell,
Blue as the gendarmerie were the waves of the sea,

(Rocking and shocking the bar-maid.)

Nobody comes to give him his rum but the
Rim of the sky hippopotamus-glum
Enhances the chances to bless with a benison
Alfred Lord Tennyson crossing the bar laid
With cold vegetation from pale deputations

Of temperance workers (all signed In Memoriam)
Hoping with glory to trip up the Laureate's feet,

(Moving in classical meters). . . .

Like Balaclava, the lava came down from the
Roof, and the sea's blue wooden gendarmerie
Took them in charge while Beelzebub roared for his rum.

. . . None of them come!

Solo for Ear-Trumpet

The carriage brushes through the bright
Leaves (violent jets from life to light).
Strong polished speed is plunging, heaves
Between the showers of bright hot leaves.
The window-glasses glaze our faces
And jar them to the very basis,—
But they could never put a polish
Upon my manners, or abolish
My most distinct disinclination
For calling on a rich relation!
In her house,—bulwark built between
The life man lives and visions seen,—
The sunlight hiccups white as chalk,
Grown drunk with emptiness of talk,
And silence hisses like a snake,
Invertebrate and rattling ache. . . .

Till suddenly, Eternity
Drowns all the houses like a sea,
And down the street the Trump of Doom
Blares,—barely shakes this drawing-room
Where raw-edged shadows sting forlorn
As dank dark nettles. Down the horn
Of her ear-trumpet I convey
The news that: "It is Judgment Day!"
"Speaker louder; I don't catch, my dear."
I roared: *"It is the Trump we hear!"*
"The *What?"*—"The T R U M P !" . . .
"I shall complain—
Those boy-scouts practicing again!"

Gardener Janus Catches a Naiad

Baskets of ripe fruit in air
The bird-songs seem suspended where

Between the hairy leaves trills dew
All tasting of fresh green anew.

Ma'am, I've heard your laughter flare
Through your waspish-gilded hair:

Feathered masks,
Pots of peas,—
Janus asks
Nought of these,
Creaking water
Brightly stripèd
Now I've caught her—
Shrieking biped.
Flute sounds jump
And turn together,
Changing clumps
Of glassy feather.
In among the
Pots of peas
Naiad changes—
Quick as these.

Spinning Song

The miller's daughter
Combs her hair,
Like flocks of dove
As soft as vair. . . .

Oh, how those soft flocks flutter down
Over the empty grassy town.

Like a queen in a crown
Of gold light, she
Sits 'neath the shadows'
Flickering tree—

Till the old dame went the way she came,
Playing bobcherry with a candle-flame.

Now Min the cat
With her white velvet gloves
Watches where sat
The mouse with her loves—

(Old and malicious Mrs. Grundy
Whose washing day is from Monday to Monday.)

"Not a crumb," said Min,
"To a mouse I'll be giving.
For a mouse must spin
To earn her living."

So poor Mrs. Mouse and her three cross Aunts
Nibble snow that rustles like gold wheat plants.

And the miller's daughter
Combs her locks,
Like running water
Those dove-soft flocks;

And her mouth is sweet as a honey flower cold
But her heart is heavy as bags of gold.

The shadow-mice said
"We will line with down
From those doves, our bed
And our slippers and gown,

For everything comes to the shadows at last
If the spinning-wheel Time move slow or fast."

Panope

How lovely are the tombs of the dead nymphs
On the heroic shore—the glittering plinths
Of jacynth . . . hyacinthine waves profound
Sigh of the beauty out of sight and sound

And many a golden foot that pressed the sand—
Panope walking like the pomp of waves

With plumaged helmet near the fountain caves
The panoply of suns on distant strand—

Is only now an arena for the worm,
Her golden flesh lies in the dust's frail storm

And beauty water-bright for long is laid
Deep in the empire of eternal shade—

Only the sighing waves know now the plinth
Of those deep tombs that were of hyacinth.

But still the echoes of that helmeted bright hair
Are like the pomp of tropic suns, the blare
That from the inaccessible horizon runs—
The eternal music of heroic suns
When their strong youth comes freshened from deep seas—
And the first music heard among the trees.

Colonel Fantock

Thus spoke the lady underneath the tree:
I was a member of a family
Whose legend was of hunting—(all the rare
And unattainable brightness of the air)—
A race whose fabled skill in falconry
Was used on the small song-birds and a winged
And blinded Destiny. . . . I think that only
Winged ones know the highest eyrie is so lonely.

There in a land austere and elegant
The castle seemed an arabesque in music;
We moved in an hallucination born
Of silence, which like music gave us lotus
To ear, perfuming lips and our long eyelids
As we trailed over the sad summer grass
Or sat beneath a smooth and mournful tree.

And Time passed, suavely, imperceptibly.

But Dagobert and Peregrine and I
Were children then; we walked like shy gazelles
Among the music of thin flower-bells.
And life still held some promise,—never ask

Of what,—but life seemed less a stranger then
Than ever after in this cold existence.
I always was a little outside life,—
And so the things we touch could comfort me,
I loved the shy dreams we could hear and see—
For I was like one dead, like a small ghost,
A little cold air wandering and lost.

All day within the straw-roofed arabesque
Of the towered castle and the sleepy gardens wandered
We; those delicate paladins, the waves
Told us fantastic legends that we pondered.
And the soft leaves were breasted like a dove,
Crooning old mournful tales of untrue love.

When night came sounding like the growth of trees,
My great-grandmother bent to say good night,
And the enchanted moonlight seemed transformed
Into the silvery tinkling of an old
And gentle music-box that played a tune
Of Circean enchantments and far seas.
Her voice was lulling like the splash of these
When she had given me her good night kiss
There, in her lengthened shadow, I saw this
Old military ghost with mayfly whiskers,—
Poor harmless creature, blown by the cold wind,
Boasting of unseen, unreal victories
To a harsh unbelieving world unkind,—
For all the battles that this warrior fought
Were with cold poverty and helpless age—
His spoils were shelters from the winter's rage.
And so forever through his braggart voice,
Through all that martial trumpet's sound, his soul
Wept a little sound, so pitiful,
Knowing that he is outside life for ever
With no one that will warm or comfort him. . . .
He is not even dead, but Death's buffoon
On a bare stage, a shrunken pantaloon.—
His military banner never fell,
Nor his account of victories, the stories
Of old apocryphal misfortunes, glories
Which comforted his heart in later life
When he was the Napoleon of the schoolroom
And all the victories he gained were over
Little boys who would not learn to spell.

All day within the sweet and ancient gardens
He had my childish self for audience—
Whose body flat and strange, whose pale straight hair
Made me appear as though I had been drowned—
(We all have the remote air of a legend)—
And Dagobert my brother whose large strength,
Great body and grave beauty still reflect
The Angevin dead kings from whom we spring;
And sweet as the young tender winds that stir
In thickets where the earliest flower-bells sing
Upon the boughs, was his just character;
And Peregrine the youngest with a naïve
Shy grace like a faun's, whose slant eyes seemed
The warm green light beneath eternal boughs.
His hair was like the fronds of feathers, life
In him was changing ever, springing fresh
As the dark songs of birds . . . the furry warmth
And purring sound of fires was in his voice
Which never failed to warm and comfort me.

And there were haunted summers in Troy Park
When all the stillness budded into leaves;
We listened like Ophelia drowned in blond
And fluid hair, beneath stag-antlered trees;
Then in the ancient park the country-pleasant
Shadows fell as brown as any pheasant,
And Colonel Fantock seemed like one of these.
Sometimes for comfort in the castle kitchen
He drowsed, where with a sweet and velvet lip
The snapdragons within the fire
Of their red summer never tire.
And Colonel Fantock liked our company.
For us he wandered over each old lie,
Changing the flowering hawthorn full of bees
Into the silver helm of Hercules,
For us defended Troy from the top stair
Outside the nursery, when the calm full moon
Was like the sound within the growth of trees.
But then came one cruel day in deepest June
When pink flowers seemed a sweet Mozartian tune,
And Colonel Fantock pondered o'er a book.
A gay voice like a honeysuckle nook,—
So sweet,—said, "It is Colonel Fantock's age
Which makes him babble." . . . Blown by winter's rage
The poor old man then knew his creeping fate,

The darkening shadow that would take his sight
And hearing; and he thought of his saved pence
Which scarce would rent a grave . . . that youthful voice
Was a dark bell which ever clanged "Too late"—
A creeping shadow that would steal from him
Even the little boys who would not spell—
His only prisoners. . . . On that June day
Cold Death had taken his first citadel.

Still Falls the Rain

The Raids, 1940. Night and Dawn

Still falls the Rain—
Dark as the world of man, black as our loss—
Blind as the nineteen hundred and forty nails
Upon the Cross.

Still falls the Rain
With a sound like the pulse of the heart that is changed to the
hammer-beat
In the Potter's Field, and the sound of the impious feet

On the Tomb:
Still falls the Rain
In the Field of Blood where the small hopes breed and the
human brain
Nurtures its greed, that worm with the brow of Cain.

Still falls the Rain
At the feet of the Starved Man hung upon the Cross.
Christ that each day, each night, nails there, have mercy on us—
On Dives and on Lazarus:
Under the rain the sore and the gold are as one.

Still falls the Rain—
Still falls the blood from the Starved Man's wounded Side:
He bears in His Heart all wounds,—those of the light that died,
The last faint spark
In the self-murdered heart, the wounds of the sad uncompre-
hending dark,

The wounds of the baited bear,—
The blind and weeping bear whom the keepers beat
On his helpless flesh . . . the tears of the hunted hare.

Still falls the Rain—
Then—O Ile leape up to my God: who pulles me doune—
See, see where Christ's blood streames in the firmament:
It flows from the Brow we nailed upon the tree
Deep to the dying, to the thirsting heart
That holds the fires of the world,—dark-smirched with pain
As Caesar's laurel crown.

Then sounds the voice of One who like the heart of man
Was once a child who among beasts has lain—
"Still do I love, still shed my innocent light, my Blood, for
thee."

Song

Now that Fate is dead and gone
And that Madness reigns alone,
Still the Furies shake the fires
Of their torches in the street
Of my blood. . . . And still they stand
In the city's street that tires
Of the tread of Man.

Three old rag-pickers are they—
Clothed with grandeur by the light
As a queen, but blind as Doom
Fumbling for the rag of Man
In an empty room.

Now they take the place of Fate
In whom the flames of Madness ran
Since her lidless eyes were cursed
With the world-expunging sight
Of the heart of Man.

How simple was the time of Cain
Before the latter Man-made Rain
Washed away all loss and gain
And the talk of right and wrong—
Murdered now and gone!

And the Ghost of Man is red
From the sweep of the world's blood . . .
In this late equality
Would you know the Ghost of Man
From the Ghost of the Flea?

But still the fires of the great Spring
In the desolate fields proclaim
Eternity . . . those wild fires shout
Of Christ the New Song.

Run those fires from field to field;
I walk alone and ghostily
Burning with Eternity's
Fires, and quench the Furies' song
In flame that never tires.

Dirge for the New Sunrise

(Fifteen minutes past eight o'clock, on the morning of Monday, the 6th of August, 1945.)

Bound to my heart as Ixion to the wheel,
Nailed to my heart as the thief upon the cross,
I hang between our Christ and the gap where the world was lost

And watch the phantom Sun in Famine Street—
The ghost of the heart of Man . . . red Cain,
And the more murderous brain
Of Man, still redder Nero that conceived the death
Of his mother Earth, and tore
Her womb, to know the place where he was conceived.

But no eyes grieved—
For none were left for tears:
They were blinded as the years
Since Christ was born. Mother or Murderer, you have given or taken life—
Now all is one!

There was a morning when the holy Light
Was young. . . . The beautiful First Creature came
To our water-springs, and thought us without blame.

Our hearts seemed safe in our breasts and sang to the Light—
The marrow in the bone
We dreamed was safe . . . the blood in the veins, the sap in the tree
Were springs of Deity.

But I saw the little Ant-men as they ran
Carrying the world's weight of the world's filth
And the filth in the heart of Man—
Compressed till those lusts and greeds had a greater heat than
that of the Sun.

And the ray from the heat came soundless, shook the sky
As if in search for food, and squeezed the stems
Of all that grows on the earth till they were dry.
—And drank the marrow of the bone:
The eyes that saw, the lips that kissed, are gone,
Or black as thunder lie and grin at the murdered Sun.

The living blind and seeing dead together lie
As if in love . . . There was no more hating then—
And no more love: Gone is the heart of Man.

Wilfred Owen

1893-1918

Futility

Move him into the sun—
Gently its touch awoke him once,
At home, whispering of fields unsown.
Always it woke him, even in France.
Until this morning and this snow.
If anything might rouse him now
The kind old sun will know.

Think how it wakes the seeds—
Woke, once, the clay of a cold star.
Are limbs so dear-achieved, are sides
Full-nerved,—still warm,—too hard to stir?
Was it for this the clay grew tall?
—Oh, what made fatuous sunbeams toil
To break earth's sleep at all?

Apologia pro Poemate Meo

I, too, saw God through mud–
The mud that cracked on cheeks when wretches smiled.
War brought more glory to their eyes than blood,
And gave their laughs more glee than shakes a child.

Merry it was to laugh there–
Where death becomes absurd and life absurder.
For power was on us as we slashed bones bare
Not to feel sickness or remorse of murder.

I, too, have dropped off fear–
Behind the barrage, dead as my platoon,
And sailed my spirit surging, light and clear,
Past the entanglement where hopes lay strewn;

And witnessed exultation–
Faces that used to curse me, scowl for scowl,
Shine and lift up with passion of oblation,
Seraphic for an hour, though they were foul.

I have made fellowships–
Untold of happy lovers in old song.
For love is not the binding of fair lips
With the soft silk of eyes that look and long,

By Joy, whose ribbon slips,–
But wound with war's hard wire whose stakes are strong;
Bound with the bandage of the arm that drips;
Knit in the welding of the rifle-thong.

I have perceived much beauty
In the hoarse oaths that kept our courage straight;
Heard music in the silentness of duty;
Found peace where shell-storms spouted reddest spate.

Nevertheless, except you share
With them in hell the sorrowful dark of hell,
Whose world is but the trembling of a flare,
And heaven but as the highway for a shell,

You shall not hear their mirth:
You shall not come to think them
By any jest of mine. These men a
Your tears: You are not worth the

Anthem for Doomed Y

What passing-bells for these who die as cattle?
Only the monstrous anger of the guns.
Only the stuttering rifles' rapid rattle
Can patter out their hasty orisons.
No mockeries for them; no prayers nor bells,
Nor any voice of mourning save the choirs,—
The shrill, demented choirs of wailing shells;
And bugles calling for them from sad shires.

What candles may be held to speed them all?
Not in the hands of boys, but in their eyes
Shall shine the holy glimmers of good-bys.
The pallor of girls' brows shall be their pall;
Their flowers the tenderness of patient minds,
And each slow dusk a drawing-down of blinds.

Dulce et Decorum Est

Bent double, like old beggars under sacks,
Knock-kneed, coughing like hags, we cursed through sludge,
Till on the haunting flares we turned our backs,
And towards our distant rest began to trudge.
Men marched asleep. Many had lost their boots,
But limped on, blood-shod. All went lame, all blind;
Drunk with fatigue; deaf even to the hoots
Of gas-shells dropping softly behind.

Gas! Gas! Quick, boys!—An ecstasy of fumbling,
Fitting the clumsy helmets just in time,
But someone still was yelling out and stumbling
And flound'ring like a man in fire or lime.
Dim through the misty panes and thick green light,
As under a green sea, I saw him drowning.

In all my dreams before my helpless sight
He plunges at me, guttering, choking, drowning.

[illegible] some smothering dreams, you too could pace
[illegible]ehind the wagon that we flung him in,
And watch the white eyes wilting in his face,
His hanging face, like a devil's sick of sin,
If you could hear, at every jolt, the blood
Come gargling from the froth-corrupted lungs
Bitten as the cud
Of vile, incurable sores on innocent tongues,—
My friend, you would not tell with such high zest
To children ardent for some desperate glory,
The old lie: *Dulce et decorum est*
Pro patria mori.

From My Diary, July 1914

Leaves
  Murmuring by myriads in the shimmering trees.
Lives
  Wakening with wonder in the Pyrenees.
Birds
  Cheerily chirping in the early day.
Bards
  Singing of summer scything thro' the hay.
Bees
  Shaking the heavy dews from bloom and frond.
Boys
  Bursting the surface of the ebony pond.
Flashes
  Of swimmers carving thro' the sparkling cold.
Fleshes
  Gleaming with wetness to the morning gold.
A mead
  Bordered about with warbling water brooks.
A maid
  Laughing the love-laugh with me; proud of looks.
The heat
  Throbbing between the upland and the peak.
Her heart
  Quivering with passion to my pressed cheek.
Braiding
  Of floating flames across the mountain brow.
Brooding
  Of stillness; and a sighing of the bough.

Stirs
  Of leaflets in the gloom; soft petal-showers;
Stars
  Expanding with the starr'd nocturnal flowers.

Greater Love

Red lips are not so red
    As the stained stones kissed by the English dead.
Kindness of wooed and wooer
Seems shame to their love pure.
O Love, your eyes lose lure
    When I behold eyes blinded in my stead!

Your slender attitude
    Trembles not exquisite like limbs knife-skewed,
Rolling and rolling there
Where God seems not to care;
Till the fierce love they bear
    Cramps them in death's extreme decrepitude.

Your voice sings not so soft,—
    Though even as wind murmuring through raftered loft,—
Your dear voice is not dear,
Gentle, and evening clear,
As theirs whom none now hear
    Now earth has stopped their piteous mouths that coughed.

Heart, you were never hot,
    Nor large, nor full like hearts made great with shot;
And though your hand be pale,
Paler are all which trail
Your cross through flame and hail:
    Weep, you may weep, for you may touch them not.

Miners

There was a whispering in my hearth,
  A sigh of the coal,
Grown wistful of a former earth
  It might recall.

I listened for a tale of leaves
  And smothered ferns,
Proud forests, and the low sly lives
  Before the fawns.

My fire might show steam-phantoms simmer
  From Time's old caldron,
Before the birds made nests in summer,
  Or men had children.

But the coals were murmuring of their mine.
  And moans down there,
Of boys that slept wry sleep, and men
  Writhing for air.

I saw white bones in the cinder-shard,
  Bones without number.
For many hearts with coal are charred,
  And few remember.

I thought of all that worked dark pits
  Of war, and died
Digging the rock where Death reputes
  Peace lies indeed:

Comforted years will sit soft-chaired,
  In rooms of amber,
The years will stretch their hands, well cheered
  By our life's ember;

The centuries will burn rich loads
  With which we groaned,
Whose warmth shall lull their dreamy lids,
  While songs are crooned;
But they will not dream of us poor lads
  Lost in the ground.

Arms and the Boy

Let the boy try along this bayonet-blade
How cold steel is, and keen with hunger of blood;
Blue with all malice, like a madman's flash;
And thinly drawn with famishing for flesh.

Lend him to stroke these blind, blunt bullet-heads
Which long to nuzzle in the heart of lads,
Or give him cartridges of fine zinc teeth,
Sharp with the sharpness of grief and death.

For his teeth seem for laughing round an apple.
There lurk no claws behind his fingers supple;
And god will grow no talons at his heels,
Nor antlers through the thickness of his curls.

Strange Meeting

It seemed that out of the battle I escaped
Down some profound dull tunnel, long since scooped
Through granites which Titanic wars had groined.
Yet also there encumbered sleepers groaned,
Too fast in thought or death to be bestirred.
Then, as I probed them, one sprang up, and stared
With piteous recognition in fixed eyes,
Lifting distressful hands as if to bless.
And by his smile, I knew that sullen hall;
By his dead smile I knew I stood in Hell.
With a thousand fears that vision's face was grained;
Yet no blood reached there from the upper ground,
And no guns thumped, or down the flues made moan.
"Strange, friend," I said, "here is no cause to mourn."
"None," said the other, "save the undone years,
The hopelessness. Whatever hope is yours,
Was my life also; I went hunting wild
After the wildest beauty in the world,
Which lies not calm in eyes, or braided hair,
But mocks the steady running of the hour,
And if it grieves, grieves richlier than here.
For by my glee might many men have laughed,
And of my weeping something has been left,
Which must die now. I mean the truth untold,
The pity of war, the pity war distilled.
Now men will go content with what we spoiled,
Or, discontent, boil bloody, and be spilled.
They will be swift with swiftness of the tigress,
None will break ranks, though nations trek from progress.
Courage was mine, and I had mystery,
Wisdom was mine, and I had mastery;

To miss the march of this retreating world
Into vain citadels that are not walled.
Then when much blood had clogged their chariot-wheels
I would go up and wash them from sweet wells,
Even with truths that lie too deep for taint.
I would have poured my spirit without stint
But not through wounds; not on the cess of war.
Foreheads of men have bled where no wounds were.
I am the enemy you killed, my friend.
I knew you in this death; for so you frowned
Yesterday through me as you jabbed and killed.
I parried; but my hands were loath and cold.
Let us sleep now. . . ."

Insensibility

Happy are men who yet before they are killed
Can let their veins run cold.
Whom no compassion fleers
Or makes their feet
Sore on the alleys cobbled with their brothers.
The front line withers,
But they are troops who fade, not flowers
For poets' tearful fooling:
Men, gaps for filling:
Losses who might have fought
Longer; but no one bothers.

And some cease feeling
Even themselves or for themselves.
Dullness best solves
The tease and doubt of shelling,
And Chance's strange arithmetic
Comes simpler than the reckoning of their shilling.
They keep no check on armies' decimation.

Happy are these who lose imagination:
They have enough to carry with ammunition.
Their spirit drags no pack,
Their old wounds save with cold can not more ache.
Having seen all things red,
Their eyes are rid
Of the hurt of the colour of blood for ever.
And terror's first constriction over,

Their hearts remain small-drawn.
Their senses in some scorching cautery of battle
Now long since ironed,
Can laugh among the dying, unconcerned.

Happy the soldier home, with not a notion
How somewhere, every dawn, some men attack,
And many sighs are drained.
Happy the lad whose mind was never trained:
His days are worth forgetting more than not.
He sings along the march
Which we march taciturn, because of dusk,
The long, forlorn, relentless trend
From larger day to huger night.

We wise, who with a thought besmirch
Blood over all our soul,
How should we see our task
But through his blunt and lashless eyes?
Alive, he is not vital overmuch;
Dying, not mortal overmuch;
Nor sad, nor proud,
Nor curious at all.
He cannot tell
Old men's placidity from his.

But cursed are dullards whom no cannon stuns,
That they should be as stones;
Wretched are they, and mean
With paucity that never was simplicity.
By choice they make themselves immune
To pity and whatever moans in man
Before the last sea and the hapless stars;
Whatever mourns when many leave these shores;
Whatever shares
The eternal reciprocity of tears.

The Send-Off

Down the close, darkening lanes they sang their way
To the siding-shed,
And lined the train with faces grimly gay.
Their breasts were stuck all white with wreath and spray
As men's are, dead.

Dull porters watched them, and a casual tramp
Stood staring hard,
Sorry to miss them from the upland camp.
Then, unmoved, signals nodded, and a lamp
Winked to the guard.

So secretly, like wrongs hushed-up, they went.
They were not ours:
We never heard to which front these were sent.
Nor there if they yet mock what women meant
Who gave them flowers.

Shall they return to beatings of great bells
In wild trainloads?
A few, a few, too few for drums and yells,
May creep back, silent, to still village wells
Up half-known roads.

The Show

My soul looked down from a vague height with Death,
As unremembering how I rose or why,
And saw a sad land, weak with sweats of dearth,
Gray, cratered like the moon with hollow woe,
And fitted with great pocks and scabs of plagues.

Across its beard, that horror of harsh wire,
There moved thin caterpillars, slowly uncoiled.
It seemed they pushed themselves to be as plugs
Of ditches, where they writhed and shrivelled, killed.

By them had slimy paths been trailed and scraped
Round myriad warts that might be little hills.
From gloom's last dregs these long-strung creatures crept,
And vanished out of dawn down hidden holes.

(And smell came up from those foul openings
As out of mouths, or deep wounds deepening.)

On dithering feet upgathered, more and more,
Brown strings towards strings of gray, with bristling spines,
All migrants from green fields, intent on mire.

Those that were gray, of more abundant spawns,
Ramped on the rest and ate them and were eaten.
I saw their bitten backs curve, loop, and straighten,
I watched those agonies curl, lift, and flatten.

Whereat, in terror what that sight might mean,
I reeled and shivered earthward like a feather.
And Death fell with me, like a deepening moan.
And He, picking a manner of worm, which half had hid
Its bruises in the earth, but crawled no further,
Showed me its feet, the feet of many men,
And the fresh-severed head of it, my head.

Sylvia Townsend Warner

1893-

Nelly Trim

"Like men riding,
The mist from the sea
Drives down the valley
And baffles me."
"Enter, traveler,
Whoever you be."

By lamplight confronted
He staggered and peered;
Like a wet bramble
Was his beard.
"Sit down, stranger,
You look a-feared."

Shudders rent him
To the bone,

The wet ran off him
And speckled the stone.
"Dost bide here alone, maid?"
"Yes, alone."

As he sat down
In the chimney-nook
Over his shoulder
He cast a look,
As if the night
Were pursuing; she took

A handful of brash
To mend the fire,
He eyed her close
As the flame shot higher;
He spoke—and the cattle
Moved in the byre.

"Though you should heap
Your fire with wood,
'Twouldn't warm me
Nor do no good,
Unless you first warm me
As a maiden should."

With looks unwavering,
With breath unstirred,
She took off her clothes
Without a word,
And stood up naked
And white as a curd.

He breathed her to him
With famished sighs,
Against her bosom
He sheltered his eyes,
And warmed his hands
Between her thighs.

Strangely assembled
In the quiet room,
Alone alight
Amidst leagues of gloom,
So brave a bride,
So sad a groom;

And strange love-traffic
Between these two;
Nor mean, nor shamefaced—
As though they'd do
Something more solemn
Than they knew:

As though by this greeting
Which chance had willed
'Twixt him so silent
And her so stilled,
Some pledge or compact
Were fulfilled,

Made for all time
In times unknown,
'Twixt man and woman
Standing alone
In mirk night
By a tall stone.

His wayfaring terrors
All cast aside,
Brave now the bridegroom
Quitted the bride;
As he came, departing—
Undenied.

But once from darkness
Turned back his sight
To where in the doorway
She held a light:
"Good-by to you, maiden."
"Stranger, good night."

Long time has this woman
Been bedded alone.
The house where she slept
Lies stone on stone:
She'd not know her ash-tree,
So warped has it grown.

But yet this story
Is told of her
As a memorial;

And some aver
She'd comfort thus any
Poor traveler.

A wanton, you say—
Yet where's the spouse,
However true
To her marriage-vows,
To whom the lot
Of the earth-born allows

More than this?—
To comfort the care
Of a stranger, bound
She knows not where,
And afraid of the dark,
As his fathers were.

Elizabeth

"Elizabeth the Beloved"—
So much says the stone
That is all with weather defaced,
With moss overgrown.

But if to husband or child,
Brother or sire, most dear
Is past deciphering;
This only is clear:

That once she was beloved,
Was Elizabeth,
And is now beloved no longer,
If it be not of Death.

Triumph of Sensibility

"Tiger, strolling at my side,
Why have you unbound the zone
Of your individual pride?
Why so meek did you come sneaking
After me as I walked alone?

"Since the goat and since the deer
Wait the shattering death you wield
In a constancy of fear,
By your stripes, my strange disciple,
Am I also to be healed?"

"Woman, it was your tender heart
Did my bloody heart compel.
Master-mistress of my art,
Past my wit of wrath your pity,
Ruthless and inexorable.

"I hunt flesh by fallible sense;
You a more exquisite prey pursue
With a finer prescience,
And lap up another's unhappiness:
Woman, let me learn of you."

Song

She has left me, my pretty,
Like a fleeting of apple-blows
She has left her loving husband.
And who she has gone to
The Lord only knows.

She has left me, my pretty,
A needle in a shirt,
Her pink flannelette bedgown,
And a pair of pattens
Caked over with dirt.

I care not for the pattens,
Let 'em lie in the mold;
But the pretty pink bedgown
Will comfort my lumbago
When midnights are cold;

And the shirt I will wear it,
And the needle may bide.
Let it prick, let it rankle,
Let my flesh remember
How she lay against my side!

The Rival

The farmer's wife looked out of the dairy:
She saw her husband in the yard;
She said: "A woman's life is hard,
The chimney smokes, the churn's contrary."
  She said:
"I of all women am the most ill-starred.

"Five sons I've borne and seven daughters,
And the last of them is on my knee.
Finer children you could not see.
Twelve times I've put my neck in the halter:
  You'd think
So much might knit my husband's love to me.

"But no! Though I should serve him double
He keeps another love outdoors,
Who thieves his strength, who drains his stores,
Who haunts his mind with fret and trouble;
  I pray
God's curse may light on such expensive whores.

"I am grown old before my season,
Weather and care have worn me down;
Each year delves deeper in my frown,
I've lost my shape and for good reason:
  But she
Yearly puts on young looks like an Easter gown.

"And year by year she has betrayed him
With blight and mildew, rain and drought,
Smut, scab, and murrain, all the rout;
But he forgets the tricks she's played him
  When first
The fields give a good smell and the leaves put out.

"Aye, come the Spring, and the gulls keening,
Over her strumpet lap he'll ride,
Watching those wasteful fields and wide,
Where the darkened tilth will soon be greening,
  With looks
Fond and severe, as looks the groom on bride."

Robert Graves

1895-

It's a Queer Time

It's hard to know if you're alive or dead
When steel and fire go roaring through your head.
One moment you'll be crouching at your gun
Traversing, mowing heaps down half in fun:
The next, you choke and clutch at your right breast—
No time to think—leave all—and off you go . . .
To Treasure Island where the Spice winds blow,
To lovely groves of mango, quince and lime—
Breathe no good-by, but ho, for the Red West!
 It's a queer time.

You're charging madly at them yelling "Fag!"
When somehow something gives and your feet drag.
You fall and strike your head; yet feel no pain
And find . . . you're digging tunnels through the hay
In the Big Barn, 'cause it's a rainy day.
Oh, springy hay, and lovely beams to climb!
You're back in the old sailor suit again.
 It's a queer time.

Or you'll be dozing safe in your dug-out—
A great roar—the trench shakes and falls about—
You're struggling, gasping, struggling, then . . . *hullo!*
Elsie comes tripping gayly down the trench,
Hanky to nose—that lyddite makes a stench—
Getting her pinafore all over grime.
Funny! because she died ten years ago!
 It's a queer time.

The trouble is, things happen much too quick;
Up jump the Boches, rifles thump and click,

You stagger, and the whole scene fades away:
Even good Christians don't like passing straight
From Tipperary or their Hymn of Hate
To Alleluiah-chanting, and the chime
Of golden harps . . . and . . . I'm not well today . . .
It's a queer time.

The Traveler's Curse After Misdirection

(from the Welsh)

May they wander stage by stage
Of the same vain pilgrimage,
Stumbling on, age after age,
Night and day, mile after mile,
At each and every step, a stile;
At each and every stile, withal,
May they catch their feet and fall;
At each and every fall they take,
May a bone within them break;
And may the bones that break within
Not be, for variation's sake,
Now rib, now thigh, now arm, now shin,
But always, without fail, THE NECK.

Song: One Hard Look

Small gnats that fly
In hot July
And lodge in sleeping ears,
Can rouse therein
A trumpet's din
With Day of Judgment fears.

Small mice at night
Can wake more fright
Than lions at midday.
A straw will crack
The camel's back;
There is no easier way.

One smile relieves
A heart that grieves

Though deadly sad it be,
And one hard look
Can close the book
That lovers love to see.

A Frosty Night

Mother

Alice, dear, what ails you,
  Dazed and white and shaken?
Has the chill night numbed you?
  Is it fright you have taken?

Alice

Mother, I am very well,
  I felt never better,
Mother, do not hold me so,
  Let me write my letter.

Mother

Sweet, my dear, what ails you?

Alice

  No, but I am well;
The night was cold and frosty,
  There's no more to tell.

Mother

Aye, the night was frosty,
  Coldly gaped the moon,
Yet the birds seemed twittering
  Through green boughs of June.

Soft and thick the snow lay,
  Stars danced in the sky.
Not all the lambs of May-day
  Skip so bold and high.

Your feet were dancing, Alice,
  Seemed to dance on air,

You looked a ghost or angel
  In the starlight there.

Your eyes were frosted starlight,
  Your heart fire and snow.
Who was it said, "I love you"?

Alice

Mother, let me go!

In the Wilderness

Christ of His gentleness
Thirsting and hungering,
Walked in the wilderness;
Soft words of grace He spoke
Unto lost desert-folk
That listened wondering.
He heard the bitterns call
From ruined palace-wall,
Answered them brotherly.
He held communion
With the she-pelican
Of lonely piety.
Basilisk, cockatrice,
Flocked to his homilies,
With mail of dread device,
With monstrous barbèd slings,
With eager dragon-eyes;
Great bats on leathern wings
And poor blind broken things,
Foul in their miseries.
And ever with Him went,
Of all His wanderings
Comrade, with ragged coat,
Gaunt ribs—poor innocent—
Bleeding foot, burning throat,
The guileless old scapegoat;
For forty nights and days
Followed in Jesus' ways,
Sure guard behind Him kept,
Tears like a lover wept.

Lost Love

His eyes are quickened so with grief,
He can watch a grass or leaf
Every instant grow; he can
Clearly through a flint wall see,
Or watch the startled spirit flee
From the throat of a dead man:
Across two counties he can hear,
And catch your words before you speak;
The woodlouse or the maggot's weak
Clamor rings in his sad ear;
And noise so slight it would surpass
Credence:—drinking sound of grass,
Worm-talk, clashing jaws of moth
Chumbling tiny holes in cloth:
The groan of ants who undertake
Gigantic loads for honor's sake,
Their sinews creak, their breath comes thin:
Whir of spiders when they spin,
And minute, whispering, mumbling sighs
Of idle grubs and flies.
This man is quickened so with grief,
He wanders god-like or like thief
Inside and out, below, above,
Without relief seeking lost love.

Mid-Winter Waking

Stirring suddenly from long hibernation
I knew myself once more a poet
Guarded by timeless principalities
Against the worm of death, this hillside haunting;
And presently dared open both my eyes.

O gracious, lofty, shone against from under,
Back-of-the-mind-far clouds like towers;
And you, sudden warm airs that blow
Before the expected season of new blossom,
While sheep still gnaw at roots and lambless go—

Be witness that on waking, this mid-winter,
I found her hand in mine laid closely

Who shall watch out the spring with me.
We stared in silence all around us
But found no winter anywhere to see.

The Pier-Glass

Lost manor where I walk continually
A ghost, though yet in woman's flesh and blood,
Up your broad stairs mounting with outspread fingers
And gliding steadfast down your corridors
I come by nightly custom to this room,
And even on sultry afternoons I come
Drawn by a thread of time-sunk memory.

Empty, unless for a huge bed of state
Shrouded with rusty curtains drooped awry
(A puppet theatre where malignant fancy
Peoples the wings with fear). At my right hand
A ravelled bell-pull hangs in readiness
To summon me from attic glooms above
Service of elder ghosts; here, at my left,
A sullen pier-glass, cracked from side to side,
Scorns to present the face (as do new mirrors)
With a lying flush, but shows it melancholy
And pale, as faces grow that look in mirrors.

Is there no life, nothing but the thin shadow
And blank foreboding, never a wainscot rat
Rasping a crust? Or at the window-pane
No fly, no bluebottle, no starveling spider?
The windows frame a prospect of cold skies
Half-merged with sea, as at the first creation—
Abstract, confusing welter. Face about,
Peer in the glass once more, take note
Of self, the grey lips and long hair dishevelled,
Sleep-staring eyes. Ah, mirror, for Christ's love
Give me one token that there still abides
Remote—beyond this island mystery,
So be it only this side Hope, somewhere,
In streams, on sun-warm mountain pasturage—
True life, natural breath; not this phantasma.

Intercession in Late October

How hard the year dies: no frost yet.
On drifts of yellow sand Midas reclines,
Fearless of moaning reed or sullen wave.
Firm and fragrant still the brambleberries.
On ivy-bloom butterflies wag.

Spare him a little longer, Crone,
For his clean hands and love-submissive heart.

Pure Death

We looked, we loved, and therewith instantly
Death became terrible to you and me.
By love we disenthralled our natural terror
Of every comfortable philosopher
Or tall, grey doctor of divinity:
Death stood at last in his true rank and order.

It happened soon, so wild of heart were we,
Exchange of gifts grew to a malady:
Their worth rose always higher on each side
Till there seemed nothing but ungivable pride
That yet remained ungiven, and this degree
Called a conclusion not to be denied.

Then we at last bethought ourselves, made shift
And simultaneously this final gift
Gave: each with shaking hands unlocks
The sinister, long, brass-bound coffin-box,
Unwraps pure death, with such bewilderment
As greeted our love's first accomplishment.

Trudge, Body

Trudge, body, and climb, trudge and climb,
But not to stand again on any peak of time:
Trudge, body.

I'll cool you, body, with a hot sun, that draws the sweat,
I'll warm you, body, with ice-water, that stings the blood,

I'll enrage you, body, with idleness, to do
And having done to sleep the long night through:
Trudge, body.

But in such cooling or warming, doing or sleeping,
No pause for satisfaction: henceforth you make address
Beyond heat to the heat, beyond cold to the cold,
Beyond enraged idleness to enraged idleness.
Here no more crowns of hope, and none of regret:
Before each sun may rise, you salute it for set.
The hills hang above you, they smile or glare,
But shall have dropped behind before you lord it there.

Trudge, body, and climb, trudge and climb,
But not to stand again on any peak of time:
Trudge, body.

The Climate of Thought

The climate of thought has seldom been described.
It is no terror of Caucasian frost,
Nor yet that brooding Hindu heat
For which a loin-rag and a dish of rice
Suffice until the pestilent monsoon.
But, without winter, blood would run too thin;
Or, without summer, fires would burn too long.
In thought the seasons run concurrently.

Thought has a sea to gaze, not voyage on;
And hills, to rough the edge of the bland sky,
Not to be climbed in search of blander prospect;
Few birds, sufficient for such caterpillars
As are not fated to turn butterflies;
Few butterflies, sufficient for the flowers
That are the luxury of a full orchard;
Wind, sometimes, in the evening chimneys; rain
On the early morning roof, on sleepy night;
Snow streaked upon the hilltop, feeding
The fond brook at the valley-head
That greens the valley and that parts the lips;
The sun, simple, like a country neighbour;
The moon, grand, not fanciful with clouds.

Austin Clarke

1896-

Night and Morning

I know the injured pride of sleep,
The strippers at the mocking-post,
The insult in the house of Caesar
And every moment that can hold
In brief the miserable act
Of centuries. Thought can but share
Belief—and the tormented soul,
Changing confession to despair,
Must wear a borrowed robe.

Morning has moved the dreadful candle,
Appointed shadows cross the nave;
Unlocked by the secular hand,
The very elements remain
Appearances upon the altar.
Adoring priest has turned his back
Of gold upon the congregation.
All saints have had their day at last,
But thought still lives in pain.

How many councils and decrees
Have perished in the simple prayer
That gave obedience to the knee;
Trampling of rostrum, feathering
Of pens at cock-rise, sum of reason
To elevate a common soul:
Forgotten as the minds that bled
For us, the miracle that raised
A language from the dead.

O when all Europe was astir
With echo of learned controversy,

The voice of logic led the choir.
Such quality was in all being,
The forks of heaven and this earth
Had met, town-walled, in mortal view
And in the pride that we ignore,
The holy rage of argument,
God was made man once more.

The Straying Student

On a holy day when sails were blowing southward,
A bishop sang the Mass at Inishmore,
Men took one side, their wives were on the other
But I heard the woman coming from the shore:
And wild in despair my parents cried aloud
For they saw the vision draw me to the doorway.

Long had she lived in Rome when Popes were bad,
The wealth of every age she makes her own,
Yet smiled on me in eager admiration,
And for a summer taught me all I know,
Banishing shame with her great laugh that rang
As if a pillar caught it back alone.

I learned the prouder counsel of her throat,
My mind was growing bold as light in Greece:
And when in sleep her stirring limbs were shown,
I blessed the noonday rock that knew no tree:
And for an hour the mountain was her throne,
Although her eyes were bright with mockery.

They say I was sent back from Salamanca
And failed in logic, but I wrote her praise
Nine times upon a college wall in France.
She laid her hand at darkfall on my page
That I might read the heavens in a glance
And I knew every star the Moors have named.

Awake or in my sleep, I have no peace now,
Before the ball is struck, my breath has gone,
And yet I tremble lest she may deceive me
And leave me in this land, where every woman's son
Must carry his own coffin and believe,
In dread, all that the clergy teach the young.

The Jewels

The crumbling centuries are thrust
In hands that are too frail for them
And we, who squabble with our dust,
Have learned in anguish to dissemble;
Yet taken in the darkest need
Of mind, no faith makes me ashamed.
Whether the truth is foul or sweet
The truth is still the same.

If ordinary thought prevail
In all this knocking of the ribs
And the dead heat of mortal haste,
Why should I hesitate at morning
Or wake a memory of myself,
All eyes, terrible as the jewels
And carbons of the consciousness
That waste the night in falsehood?

The sanctuary lamp is lowered
In witness of our ignorance;
Greed of religion makes us old
Before our time. We are undone
Within the winking of an eyelid,
The very heavens are assailed
And there is nothing can be hidden:
Love darts and thunders from the rail.

The misery of common faith
Was ours before the age of reason.
Hurrying years cannot mistake
The smile for the decaying teeth,
The last confusion of our senses.
But O to think, when I was younger
And could not tell the difference,
God lay upon this tongue.

C. Day Lewis

1904-

Nearing Again the Legendary Isle

Nearing again the legendary isle
Where sirens sang and mariners were skinned,
We wonder now what was there to beguile
That such stout fellows left their bones behind.

Those chorus-girls are surely past their prime,
Voices grow shrill and paint is wearing thin,
Lips that sealed up the sense from gnawing time
Now beg the favor with a graveyard grin.

We have no flesh to spare and they can't bite,
Hunger and sweat have stripped us to the bone;
A skeleton crew we toil upon the tide
And mock the theme-song meant to lure us on:

No need to stop the ears, avert the eyes
From purple rhetoric of evening skies.

Do Not Expect Again a Phoenix Hour

Do not expect again a phoenix hour,
The triple-towered sky, and dove complaining,
Sudden the rain of gold and heart's first ease
Tranced under trees by the eldritch light of sundown.

By a blazed trail our joy will be returning:
One burning hour throws light a thousand ways,
And hot blood stays into familiar gestures.
The best years wait, the body's plenitude.

Consider then, my lover, this is the end
Of the lark's ascending, the hawk's unearthly hover:

Spring season is over soon and first heatwave;
Grave-browed with cloud ponders the huge horizon.

Draw up the dew. Swell with pacific violence.
Take shape in silence. Grow as the clouds grew.
Beautiful brood the cornlands, and you are heavy;
Leafy the boughs—they also hide big fruit.

Chiefly to Mind Appears

Chiefly to mind appears
That hour on Silverhowe
When evening's lid hung low
And the sky was about our ears.
Buoyed between fear and love
We watched in eastward form
The armadas of the storm
And sail superbly above;
So near, they'd split and founder
On the least jag of sense,
One false spark fire the immense
Broadside, the confounding thunder.
They pass, give not a salvo,
And in their rainy wash
We hear the horizons crash
With monitors of woe.

Only at highest power
Can love and fear become
Their equilibrium,
And in that eminent hour
A virtue is made plain
Of passionate cleavage
Like the hills' cutting edge
When the sun sets to rain.
This is the single mind,
This is the star-solved equation
Of life with life's negation:
A deathless cell designed
To demonstrate death's act,
Which, the more surely it moves
To earth's influence, but proves
Itself the more intact.

Tempt Me No More

Tempt me no more; for I
Have known the lightning's hour,
The poet's inward pride,
The certainty of power.

Bayonets are closing round.
I shrink; yet I must wring
A living from despair
And out of steel a song.

Though song, though breath be short,
I'll share not the disgrace
Of those that ran away
Or never left the base.

Comrades, my tongue can speak
No comfortable words;
Calls to a forlorn hope
Give work and not rewards.

Oh keep the sickle sharp
And follow still the plow:
Others may reap, though some
See not the winter through.

Father who endest all,
Pity our broken sleep;
For we lie down with tears
And waken but to weep.

And if our blood alone
Will melt this iron earth,
Take it. It is well spent
Easing a savior's birth.

The Conflict

I sang as one
Who on a tilting deck sings
To keep their courage up, though the wave hangs
That shall cut off their sun.

As storm-cocks sing,
Flinging their natural answer in the wind's teeth,
And care not if it is waste of breath
Or birth-carol of spring.

As ocean-flyer clings
To height, to the last drop of spirit driving on
While yet ahead is land to be won
And work for wings.

Singing I was at peace,
Above the clouds, outside the ring:
For sorrow finds a swift release in song
And pride its poise.

Yet living here,
As one between two massing powers I live
Whom neutrality cannot save
Nor occupation cheer.

None such shall be left alive:
The innocent wing is soon shot down,
And private stars fade in the blood-red dawn
Where two worlds strive.

The red advance of life
Contracts pride, calls out the common blood,
Beats song into a single blade,
Makes a depth-charge of grief.

Move then with new desires,
For where we used to build and love
Is no man's land, and only ghosts can live
Between two fires.

When They Have Lost

When they have lost the little that they looked for,
The poor allotment of ease, custom, fame:
When the consuming star their fathers worked for
Has guttered into death, a fatuous flame:
When love's a cripple, faith a bed-time story,
Hope eats her heart out and peace walks on knives,
And suffering men cry an end to this sorry

World of whose children want alone still thrives:
Then shall the mounting stages of oppression
Like mazed and makeshift scaffolding torn down
Reveal his unexampled, best creation–
The shape of man's necessity full-grown.
Built from their bone, I see a power-house stand
To warm men's hearts again and light the land.

Newsreel

Enter the dream-house, brothers and sisters, leaving
Your debts asleep, your history at the door:
This is the home for heroes, and this loving
Darkness a fur you can afford.

Fish in their tank electrically heated
Nose without envy the glass wall: for them
Clerk, spy, nurse, killer, prince, the great and the defeated,
Move in a mute day-dream.

Bathed in this common source, you gape incurious
At what your active hours have willed–
Sleep-walking on that silver wall, the furious
Sick shapes and pregnant fancies of your world.

There is the mayor opening the oyster season:
A society wedding: the autumn hats look swell:
An old crock's race, and a politician
In fishing-waders to prove that all is well.

Oh, look at the warplanes! Screaming hysteric treble
In the long power-dive, like gannets they fall steep.
But what are they to trouble–
These silver shadows to trouble your watery, womb-deep sleep?

See the big guns, rising, groping, erected
To plant death in your world's soft womb.
Fire-bud, smoke-blossom, iron seed projected–
Are these exotics? They will grow nearer home:

Grow nearer home–and out of the dream-house stumbling
One night into a strangling air and the flung
Rags of children and thunder of stone niagaras tumbling,
You'll know you slept too long.

Bombers

Through the vague morning, the heart preoccupied,
A deep in air buried grain of sound
Starts and grows, as yet unwarning—
The tremor of baited deepsea line.

Swells the seed, and now tight sound-buds
Vibrate, upholding their paean flowers
To the sun. There are bees in sky-bells droning,
Flares of crimson at the heart unfold.

Children look up, and the elms spring-garlanded
Tossing their heads and marked for the axe.
Gallant or woebegone, alike unlucky—
Earth shakes beneath us: we imagine loss.

Black as vermin, crawling in echelon
Beneath the cloud-floor, the bombers come:
The heavy angels, carrying harm in
Their wombs that ache to be rid of death.

This is the seed that grows for ruin,
The iron embryo conceived in fear.
Soon or late its need must be answered
In fear delivered and screeching fire.

Choose between your child and this fatal embryo.
Shall your guilt bear arms, and the children you want
Be condemned to die by the powers you paid for
And haunt the houses you never built?

Patrick Kavanagh

1904-

Pegasus

My soul was an old horse
Offered for sale in twenty fairs.
I offered him to the Church—the buyers
Were little men who feared his unusual airs.
One said: "Let him remain unbid
In the wind and rain and hunger
Of sin and we will get him—
With the winkers thrown in—for nothing."

Then the men of State looked at
What I'd brought for sale.
One minister, wondering if
Another horse-body would fit the tail
That he'd kept for sentiment—
The relic of his own soul—
Said, "I will graze him in lieu of his labour."
I lent him for a week or more
And he came back a hurdle of bones,
Starved, overworked, in despair.
I nursed him on the roadside grass
To shape him for another fair.

I lowered my price. I stood him where
The broken-winded, spavined stand
And crooked shopkeepers said that he
Might do for a season on the land—
But not for high-paid work in towns.
He'd do a tinker, possibly.
I begged, "O make some offer now,
A soul is a poor man's tragedy.
He'll draw your dungiest cart," I said,

"Show you short cuts to Mass,
Teach weather lore, at night collect
Bad debts from poor men's grass."
And they would not.

Where the
Tinkers quarrel I went down
With my horse, my soul.
I cried, "Who will bid me half a crown?"
From their rowdy bargaining
Not one turned. "Soul," I prayed,
"I have hawked you through the world
Of Church and State and meanest trade.
But this evening, halter off,
Never again will it go on.
On the south side of ditches
There is grazing of the sun.
No more haggling with the world. . . ."

As I said these words he grew
Wings upon his back. Now I may ride him
Every land my imagination knew.

From "Father Mat"

In a meadow
Beside the chapel three boys were playing football.
At the forge door an old man was leaning
Viewing a hunter-hoe. A man could hear
If he listened to the breeze the fall of wings—
How wistfully the sin-birds come home!

It was Confession Saturday, the first
Saturday in May; the May Devotions
Were spread like leaves to quieten
The excited armies of conscience.
The knife of penance fell so like a blade
Of grass that no one was afraid.

Father Mat came slowly walking, stopping to
Stare through gaps at ancient Ireland sweeping
In again with all its unbaptized beauty:
In calm evening,
The whitethorn blossoms,

The smell from ditches that were not Christian.
The dancer that dances in the hearts of men cried:
Look! I have shown this to you before—
The rags of living surprised
The joy in things you cannot forget.

His heavy hat was square upon his head,
Like a Christian Brother's;
His eyes were an old man's watery eyes,
Out of his flat nose grew spiky hairs.
He was a part of the place,
Natural as a round stone in a grass field;
He could walk through a cattle fair
And the people would only notice his odd spirit there.

His curate passed on a bicycle—
He had the haughty intellectual look
Of the man who never reads in brook or book;
A man designed
To wear a mitre,
To sit on committees—
For will grows strongest in the emptiest mind.

The old priest saw him pass
And, seeing, saw
Himself a mediaeval ghost.
Ahead of him went Power,
One who was not afraid when the sun opened a flower,
Who was never astonished
At a stick carried down a stream
Or at the undying difference in the corner of a field.

From "The Great Hunger"

Health and wealth and love he too dreamed of in May
As he sat on the railway slope and watched the children of the
place
Picking up a primrose here and a daisy there—
They were picking up life's truth singly. But he dreamt of the
Absolute envased bouquet—

All or nothing. And it was nothing. For God is not all
In one place, complete
Till Hope comes in and takes it on his shoulder—

O Christ, that is what you have done for us:
In a crumb of bread the whole mystery is.

He read the symbol too sharply and turned
From the five simple doors of sense
To the door whose combination lock has puzzled
Philosopher and priest and common dunce.

Men build their heavens as they build their circles
Of friends. God is the bits and pieces of Everyday—
A kiss here and a laugh again, and sometimes tears,
A pearl necklace round the neck of poverty.

He sat on the railway slope and watched the evening,
Too beautifully perfect to use,
And his three wishes were three stones too sharp to sit on,
Too hard to carve. Three frozen idols of a speechless muse.

Memory of Brother Michael

It would never be morning, always evening,
Golden sunset, golden age—
When Shakespeare, Marlowe, and Jonson were writing
The future of England page by page
A nettle-wild grave was Ireland's stage.

It would never be spring, always autumn
After a harvest always lost,
When Drake was winning seas for England
We sailed in puddles of the past
Chasing the ghost of Brendan's mast.

The seeds among the dust were less than dust,
Dust we sought, decay,
The young sprout rising smothered in it,
Cursed for being in the way—
And the same is true to-day.

Culture is always something that was,
Something pedants can measure,
Skull of bard, thigh of chief,
Depth of dried-up river.
Shall we be thus for ever?
Shall we be thus for ever?

William Empson

1906-

Homage to the British Museum

There is a Supreme God in the ethnological section;
A hollow toad shape, faced with a blank shield.
He needs his belly to include the Pantheon,
Which is inserted through a hole behind.
At the navel, at the points formally stressed, at the organs of
    sense,
Lice glue themselves, dolls, local deities,
His smooth wood creeps with all the creeds of the world.

Attending there let us absorb the cultures of nations
And dissolve into our judgment all their codes.
Then, being clogged with a natural hesitation
(People are continually asking one the way out),
Let us stand here and admit that we have no road.
Being everything, let us admit that is to be something,
Or give ourselves the benefit of the doubt;
Let us offer our pinch of dust all to this God,
And grant his reign over the entire building.

This Last Pain

This last pain for the damned the Fathers found:
"They knew the bliss with which they were not crowned."
    Such, but on earth, let me foretell,
    Is all, of heaven or of hell.

Man, as the prying housemaid of the soul,
May know her happiness by eye to hole:
    He's safe; the key is lost; he knows
    Door will not open, nor hole close.

"What is conceivable can happen too,"
Said Wittgenstein, who had not dreamt of you;
  But wisely; if we worked it long
  We should forget where it was wrong.

Those thorns are crowns which, woven into knots,
Crackle under and soon boil fool's pots;
  And no man's watching, wise and long,
  Would ever stare them into song.

Thorns burn to a consistent ash, like man;
A splendid cleanser for the frying-pan:
  And those who leap from pan to fire
  Should this brave opposite admire.

All those large dreams by which men long live well
Are magic-lanterned on the smoke of hell;
  This then is real, I have implied,
  A painted, small, transparent slide.

These the inventive can hand-paint at leisure,
Or most emporia would stock or measure;
  And feasting in their dappled shade
  We should forget how they were made.

Feign then what's by a decent tact believed
And act that state is only so conceived,
  And build an edifice of form
  For house where phantoms may keep warm.

Imagine, then, by miracle, with me,
(Ambiguous gifts, as what gods give must be)
  What could not possibly be there,
  And learn a style from a despair.

Missing Dates

Slowly the poison the whole blood stream fills.
It is not the effort nor the failure tires.
The waste remains, the waste remains and kills.

It is not your system or clear sight that mills
Down small to the consequence a life requires;
Slowly the poison the whole blood stream fills.

They bled an old dog dry yet the exchange rills
Of young dog blood gave but a month's desires;
The waste remains, the waste remains and kills.

It is the Chinese tombs and the slag hills
Usurp the soil, and not the soil retires.
Slowly the poison the whole blood stream fills.

Not to have fire is to be a skin that shrills.
The complete fire is death. From partial fires
The waste remains, the waste remains and kills.

It is the poems you have lost, the ills
From missing dates, at which the heart expires.
Slowly the poison the whole blood stream fills.
The waste remains, the waste remains and kills.

To an Old Lady

Ripeness is all; her in her cooling planet
Revere; do not presume to think her wasted.
Project her no projectile, plan nor man it;
Gods cool in turn, by the sun long outlasted.

Our earth alone given no name of god
Gives, too, no hold for such a leap to aid her;
Landing, you break some palace and seem odd;
Bees sting their need, the keeper's queen invader.

No, to your telescope; spy out the land;
Watch while her ritual is still to see,
Still stand her temples emptying in the sand
Whose waves o'erthrew their crumpled tracery;

Still stand uncalled-on her soul's appanage;
Much social detail whose successor fades,
Wit used to run a house and to play Bridge,
And tragic fervour, to dismiss her maids.

Years her precession do not throw from gear.
She reads a compass certain of her pole;
Confident, finds no confines on her sphere,
Whose failing crops are in her sole control.

Stars how much further from me fill my night,
Strange that she too should be inaccessible,
Who shares my sun. He curtains her from sight,
And but in darkness is she visible.

Louis MacNeice

1907-

The British Museum Reading Room

Under the hive-like dome the stooping haunted readers
Go up and down the alleys, tap the cells of knowledge—
    Honey and wax, the accumulation of years—
Some on commission, some for the love of learning,
Some because they have nothing better to do
Or because they hope these walls of books will deaden
    The drumming of the demon in their ears.

Cranks, hacks, poverty-stricken scholars,
In pince-nez, period hats or romantic beards
    And cherishing their hobby or their doom.
Some are too much alive and some are asleep
Hanging like bats in a world of inverted values,
Folded up in themselves in a world which is safe and silent:
    This is the British Museum Reading Room.

Out on the steps in the sun the pigeons are courting,
Puffing their ruffs and sweeping their tails or taking
    A sun-bath at their ease
And under the totem poles—the ancient terror—
Between the enormous fluted Ionic columns
There seeps from heavily jowled or hawk-like foreign faces
    The guttural sorrow of the refugees.

Cradle Song

The clock's untiring fingers wind the wool of darkness
And we all lie alone, having long outgrown our cradles
(Sleep, sleep, Miriam)
And the flames like faded ladies always unheeded simper
And all is troubledness.

Soft the wool, dark the wool
Is gathered slowly, wholly up
Into a ball, all of it.

And yet in the back of the mind, lulled all else,
There is something unsleeping, un-tamperable-with,
Something that whines and scampers
And like the ladies in the grate will not sleep nor forget itself,
Clawing at the wool like a kitten.

The clock's fingers wind, wind the wool of Lethe,
(Sleep, sleep, Miriam)
It glides across the floor drawn by hidden fingers
And the beast droops his head
And the fire droops its flounces
And winks a final ogle out of the fading embers
But no one pays attention;

This is too much, the flames say, insulted,
We who were once the world's beauties and now
No one pays attention
No one remembers us.

Sleep, sleep, Miriam.
And as for this animal of yours
He must be cradled also.
That he may not unravel this handiwork of forgetfulness.
That he may not philander with the flames before they die.

The world like a cradle rises and falls
On a wave of confetti and funerals
And sordor and stinks and stupid faces
And the deity making bored grimaces.

Oh what a muddle he has made of the wool,
(God will tomorrow have his hands full),

You must muzzle your beast, you must fasten him
For the whole of life—the interim.

Through the interim we pass
Everyone under an alias
Till they gather the strands of us together
And wind us up for ever and ever.

Sunday Morning

Down the road someone is practicing scales,
The notes like little fishes vanish with a wink of tails,
Man's heart expands to tinker with his car
For this is Sunday morning, Fate's great bazaar,
Regard these means as ends, concentrate on this Now,
And you may grow to music or drive beyond Hindhead any-
 how,
Take corners on two wheels until you go so fast
That you can clutch a fringe or two of the windy past,
That you can abstract this day and make it to the week of time
A small eternity, a sonnet self-contained in rhyme.

But listen, up the road, something gulps, the church spire
Opens its eight bells out, skulls' mouths which will not tire
To tell how there is no music or movement which secures
Escape from the weekday time. Which deadens and endures.

Morning Sun

Shuttles of trains going north, going south, drawing threads of
 blue
The shining of the lines of trams like swords
Thousands of posters asserting a monopoly of the good, the
 beautiful, the true
Crowds of people all in the vocative, you and you,
The haze of the morning shot with words.

Yellow sun comes white off the wet streets but bright
Chromium yellows in the gay sun's light
Filleted sun streaks the purple mist,
Everything is kissed and reticulated with sun
Scooped-up and cupped in the open fronts of shops
And bouncing on the traffic which never stops.

And the street fountain blown across the square
Rainbow-trellises the air and sunlight blazons
The red butcher's and scrolls of fish on marble slabs
Whistled bars of music crossing silver sprays
And horns of cars, touché, touché, rapiers' retort, a moving cage,
A turning page of shine and sound, the day's maze.

But when the sun goes out, the streets go cold, the hanging meat
And tiers of fish are colorless and merely dead
And the hoots of cars neurotically repeat and the tiptoed feet
Of women hurry and falter whose faces are dead
And I see in the air but not belonging there
The blown gray powder of the fountain gray as the ash
That forming on a cigarette covers the red.

Birmingham

Smoke from the train-gulf hid by hoardings blunders upward, the brakes of cars
Pipe as the policeman pivoting round raises his flat hands, bars
With his figure of a monolith Pharaoh the queue of fidgety machines
(Chromium dogs on the bonnet, faces behind the triplex screens)
Behind him the streets run away between the proud glass of shops
Cubical scent-bottles artificial legs arctic foxes and electric mops
But beyond this center the slumward vista thins like a diagram:
There, unvisited, are Vulcan's forges who doesn't care a tinker's damn.

Splayed outwards through the suburbs houses, houses for rest
Seducingly rigged by the builder, half-timbered houses with lips pressed
So tightly and eyes staring at the traffic through bleary haws
And only a six-inch grip of the racing earth in their concrete claws;
In these houses men as in a dream pursue the Platonic Forms
With wireless and cairn terriers and gadgets approximating to the fickle norms

And endeavor to find God and score one over the neighbor
By climbing tentatively upward on jerry-built beauty and
sweated labor.

The lunch hour: the shops empty, shopgirls' faces relax
Diaphanous as green glass empty as old almanacs
As incoherent with ticketed gewgaws tiered behind their heads
As the Burne-Jones windows in St. Philip's broken by crawling
leads
Insipid color, patches of emotion, Saturday thrills—
(This theater is sprayed with "June")—the gutter take our old
playbills,
Next week-end it is likely in the heart's funfair we shall pull
Strong enough on the handle to get back our money; or at any
rate it is possible.

On shining lines the trams like vast sarcophagi move
Into the sky, plum after sunset, merging to duck's egg, barred
with mauve
Zeppelin clouds, and pentecost-like the cars' headlights bud
Out from sideroads and the traffic signals, crême-de-menthe or
bull's blood,
Tell one to stop, the engine gently breathing, or to go on
To where like black pipes of organs in the frayed and fading
zone
Of the West the factory chimneys on sullen sentry will all night
wait
To call, in the harsh morning, sleep-stupid faces through the
daily gate.

Nuts in May

May come up with bird-din
And May come up with sun-dint,
May come up with water-wheels
And May come up with iris.

In the sun-peppered meadow the shepherds are old,
Their flutes are broken and their tales are told,
And their ears are deaf when the guns unfold
The new philosophy over the wold.

May come up with pollen of death,
May come up with cordite,

May come up with a chinagraph
And May come up with a stopwatch.

In the high court of heaven Their tail-feathers shine
With cowspit and bullspit and spirits of wine,
They know no pity, being divine,
And They give no quarter to thine or mine.

May come up with Very lights,
May come up with duty,
May come up with a bouncing cheque,
An acid-drop and a bandage.

Yes, angels are frigid and shepherds are dumb,
There is no holy water when the enemy come,
The trees are askew and the skies are a-hum
And you have to keep mum and go to it and die for
your life and keep mum.

May come up with fiddle-bows,
May come up with blossom,
May come up the same again,
The same again but different.

Brother Fire

When our brother Fire was having his dog's day
Jumping the London streets with millions of tin cans
Clanking at his tail, we heard some shadow say
"Give the dog a bone"—and so we gave him ours;
Night after night we watched him slaver and crunch away
The beams of human life, the tops of topless towers.

Which gluttony of his for us was Lenten fare
Who mother-naked, suckled with sparks, were chill
Though cotted in a grill of sizzling air
Striped like a convict—black, yellow and red;
Thus were we weaned to knowledge of the Will
That wills the natural world but wills us dead.

O delicate walker, babbler, dialectician Fire,
O enemy and image of ourselves,
Did we not on those mornings after the All Clear,

When you were looting shops in elemental joy
And singing as you swarmed up city block and spire,
Echo your thoughts in ours? "Destroy! Destroy!"

Jehu

Peace on New England, on the shingled white houses, on golden
Rod and the red Turkey carpet spikes of sumach. The little
American flags are flapping in the graveyard. Continuous
Chorus of grasshoppers. Fleece
Of quiet around the mind. Honeysuckle, phlox and smoke-bush,
Hollyhocks and nasturtium and corn on the cob. And the pine wood
Smelling of outmoded peace.

A king sat over the gate looking to the desert. A spiral
Of dust came towards him, a special messenger asking
Anxiously "Is it peace?" The heavy eyebrows lowered,
He answered "What have I
To do with peace?" and the messenger mopped the sweat and obedient
Took his place behind the king who still sat scanning
Miles of desert and sky.

Negative prospect; sand in the lungs; blood in the sand; deceiving
Mirage of what were once ideals or even motives
And in this desert even a ghost can hardly
Live—but in the long run what
Have I to do with life? He got up blandly, harnessed his horses
And furiously drove, his eyeballs burning and the chariot's
Axles burning hot.

Someone sat in a window with a new coiffure, her raddled
Face, a Muse's possibly once but now a harlot's,
Smirked at the charioteer who, looking past her, signalled
To the maids to throw her down
And they threw her down and the wheels went over her ribs and the carcase,
The one-time inspiration of artists, the toast of kings, was abandoned
To the scavenger dogs of the town.

And now the sand blows over Kent and Wales where we may
shortly
Learn the secret of the desert's purge, of the mad driving,
The cautery of the gangrened soul, though we are not certain
Whether we shall stand beside
The charioteer, the surgeon, or shall be one with the pampered
Queen who tittered in the face of death, unable to imagine
The meaning of the flood-tide.

W. H. Auden

1907-

Who's Who

A shilling life will give you all the facts:
How Father beat him, how he ran away,
What were the struggles of his youth, what acts
Made him the greatest figure of his day:
Of how he fought, fished, hunted, worked all night;
Though giddy, climbed new mountains; named a sea:
Some of the last researchers even write
Love made him weep his pints like you and me.

With all his honors on, he sighed for one
Who, say astonished critics, lived at home;
Did little jobs about the house with skill
And nothing else; could whistle; would sit still
Or potter round the garden; answered some
Of his long marvellous letters, but kept none.

Chorus from a Play

Doom is dark and deeper than any sea-dingle:
Upon what man it fall
In spring, day-wishing flowers appearing,
Avalanche sliding, white snow from rock-face,

That he should leave his house;
No cloud-soft hands can hold him, restraint by women,
But ever that man goes
By place-keepers, by forest trees,
A stranger to strangers over undried sea,
Houses for fishes, suffocating water;
Or lonely on fell as chat,
By pot-holed becks
A bird stone-haunting, an unquiet bird.

There head falls forward, fatigued at evening,
And dreams of home:
Waving from window, spread of welcome,
Kissing of wife under single sheet;
But waking sees
Bird-flocks nameless to him, through doorway voices
Of new men making another love.

Save him from hostile capture
From sudden tiger's spring at corner:
Protect his house,
His anxious house where days are counted
From thunderbolt protect,
From gradual ruin spreading like a stain:
Converting number from vague to certain
Bring joy, bring day of his returning,
Lucky with day approaching, with leaning dawn.

The Strings' Excitement

The strings' excitement, the applauding drum
Are but the initiating ceremony
That out of cloud the ancestral face may come.

And never hear their subaltern mockery,
Graphiti-writers, moss-grown with whimsies,
Loquacious when the watercourse is dry.

It is your face I see, and morning's praise
Of you is ghost's approval of the choice,
Filtered through roots of the effacing grass.

Fear, taking me aside, would give advice
"To conquer her, the visible enemy,
It is enough to turn away the eyes."

Yet there's no peace in this assaulted city
But speeches at the corners, hope for news,
Outside the watchfires of a stronger army.

And all emotions to expression came,
Recovering the archaic imagery:
This longing for assurance takes the form

Of a hawk's vertical stooping from the sky;
These tears, salt for a disobedient dream,
The lunatic agitation of the sea;

While this despair with hardened eyeballs cries
"A Golden Age, a Silver . . . rather this,
Massive and taciturn years, the Age of Ice."

This Lunar Beauty

This lunar beauty
Has no history
Is complete and early;
If beauty later
Bear any feature
It had a lover
And is another.

This like a dream
Keeps other time
And daytime is
The loss of this;
For time is inches
And the heart's changes
Where ghost has haunted
Lost and wanted.

But this was never
A ghost's endeavor
Nor finished this,
Was ghost at ease;
And till it pass
Love shall not near
The sweetness here
Nor sorrow take
His endless look.

Ballad

O what is that sound which so thrills the ear
  Down in the valley drumming, drumming?
Only the scarlet soldiers, dear,
  The soldiers coming.

O what is that light I see flashing so clear
  Over the distance brightly, brightly?
Only the sun on their weapons, dear,
  As they step lightly.

O what are they doing with all that gear;
  What are they doing this morning, this morning?
Only the usual maneuvers, dear,
  Or perhaps a warning.

O why have they left the road down there;
  Why are they suddenly wheeling, wheeling?
Perhaps a change in the orders, dear;
  Why are you kneeling?

O haven't they stopped for the doctor's care;
  Haven't they reined their horses, their horses?
Why, they are none of them wounded, dear,
  None of these forces.

O is it the parson they want, with white hair;
  Is it the parson, is it, is it?
No, they are passing his gateway, dear,
  Without a visit.

O it must be the farmer who lives so near,
  It must be the farmer, so cunning, cunning;
They have passed the farm already, dear,
  And now they are running.

O where are you going? stay with me here.
  Were the vows you swore me deceiving, deceiving?
No, I promised to love you, my dear,
  But I must be leaving.

O it's broken the lock and splintered the door,
  O it's the gate where they're turning, turning;
Their feet are heavy on the floor
  And their eyes are burning.

Villanelle

Time can say nothing but I told you so,
Time only knows the price we have to pay;
If I could tell you, I would let you know.

If we should weep when clowns put on their show,
If we should stumble when musicians play,
Time can say nothing but I told you so.

There are no fortunes to be told, although
Because I love you more than I can say,
If I could tell you, I would let you know.

The winds must come from somewhere when they blow,
There must be reasons why the leaves decay;
Time can say nothing but I told you so.

Perhaps the roses really want to grow,
The vision seriously intends to stay;
If I could tell you, I would let you know.

Suppose the lions all get up and go,
And all the brooks and soldiers run away?
Time can say nothing but I told you so;
If I could tell you, I would let you know.

"Look, Stranger"

Look, stranger, at this island now
The leaping light for your delight discovers,
Stand stable here
And silent be,
That through the channels of the ear
May wander like a river
The swaying sound of the sea.

Here at the small field's ending pause
Where the chalk wall falls to the foam, and its tall ledges
Oppose the pluck
And knock of the tide,
And the shingle scrambles after the sucking surf, and the gull
lodges
A moment on its sheer side.

Far off like floating seeds the ships
Diverge on urgent voluntary errands;
And the full view
Indeed may enter
And move in memory as now these clouds do,
That pass the harbor mirror
And all the summer through the water saunter.

Hearing of Harvests Rotting in the Valleys

Hearing of harvests rotting in the valleys,
Seeing at end of street the barren mountains,
Round corners coming suddenly on water,
Knowing them shipwrecked who were launched for islands,
We honor founders of these starving cities,
Whose honor is the image of our sorrow.

Which cannot see its likeness in their sorrow
That brought them desperate to the brink of valleys;
Dreaming of evening walks through learned cities,
They reined their violent horses on the mountains,
Those fields like ships to castaways on islands,
Visions of green to them that craved for water.

They built by rivers and at night the water
Running past windows comforted their sorrow;
Each in his little bed conceived of islands
Where every day was dancing in the valleys,
And all the year trees blossomed on the mountains,
Where love was innocent, being far from cities.

But dawn came back and they were still in cities;
No marvellous creature rose up from the water,
There was still gold and silver in the mountains,
And hunger was a more immediate sorrow;

Although to moping villagers in valleys
Some waving pilgrims were describing islands.

"The gods," they promised, "visit us from islands,
Are stalking head-up, lovely through the cities;
Now is the time to leave your wretched valleys
And sail with them across the lime-green water;
Sitting at their white sides, forget their sorrow,
The shadow cast across your lives by mountains."

So many, doubtful, perished in the mountains
Climbing up crags to get a view of islands;
So many, fearful, took with them their sorrow
Which stayed them when they reached unhappy cities;
So many, careless, dived and drowned in water;
So many, wretched, would not leave their valleys.

It is the sorrow; shall it melt? Ah, water
Would gush, flush, green these mountains and these valleys
And we rebuild our cities, not dream of islands.

Law, Say the Gardeners, Is the Sun

Law, say the gardeners, is the sun,
Law is the one
All gardeners obey
Tomorrow, yesterday, today.

Law is the wisdom of the old
The impotent grandfathers shrilly scold;
The grandchildren put out a treble tongue,
Law is the senses of the young.

Law, says the priest with a priestly look,
Expounding to an unpriestly people,
Law is the words in my priestly book,
Law is my pulpit and my steeple.

Law, says the judge as he looks down his nose,
Speaking clearly and most severely,
Law is as I've told you before,
Law is as you know I suppose,
Law is but let me explain it once more,
Law is The Law.

Yet law-abiding scholars write;
Law is neither wrong nor right,
Law is only crimes
Punished by places and by times,
Law is the clothes men wear
Anytime, anywhere,
Law is Good-morning and Good-night.

Others say, Law is our Fate;
Others say, Law is our State;
Others say, others say
Law is no more,
Law is gone away.

And always the loud angry crowd
Very angry and very loud
Law is We,
And always the soft idiot softly Me.

If we, dear, know we know no more
Than they about the law,
If I no more than you
Know what we should and should not do
Except that all agree
Gladly or miserably
That the law is
And that all know this,
If therefore thinking it absurd
To identify Law with some other word,
Unlike so many men
I cannot say Law is again,
No more than they can we suppress
The universal wish to guess
Or slip out of our own position
Into an unconcerned condition.

Although I can at least confine
Your vanity and mine
To stating timidly
A timid similarity,
We shall boast anyway:
Like love I say.

Like love we dont know where or why
Like love we cant compel or fly

Like love we often weep
Like love we seldom keep.

Lay Your Sleeping Head, My Love

Lay your sleeping head, my love,
Human on my faithless arm;
Time and fevers burn away
Individual beauty from
Thoughtful children, and the grave
Proves the child ephemeral:
But in my arms till break of day
Let the living creature lie,
Mortal, guilty, but to me
The entirely beautiful.

Soul and body have no bounds:
To lovers as they lie upon
Her tolerant enchanted slope
In their ordinary swoon,
Grave the vision Venus sends
Of supernatural sympathy,
Universal love and hope;
While an abstract insight wakes
Among the glaciers and the rocks
The hermit's sensual ecstasy.

Certainty, fidelity
On the stroke of midnight pass
Like vibrations of a bell,
And fashionable madmen raise
Their pedantic boring cry:
Every farthing of the cost,
All the dreaded cards foretell,
Shall be paid, but from this night
Not a whisper, not a thought,
Not a kiss nor look be lost.

Beauty, midnight, vision dies:
Let the winds of dawn that blow
Softly round your dreaming head
Such a day of sweetness show
Eye and knocking heart may bless,
Find the mortal world enough;

Noons of dryness see you fed
By the involuntary powers,
Nights of insult let you pass
Watched by every human love.

In Memory of W. B. Yeats

I

He disappeared in the dead of winter:
The brooks were frozen, the airports almost deserted,
And snow disfigured the public statues;
The mercury sank in the mouth of the dying day.
O all the instruments agree
The day of his death was a dark cold day.

Far from his illness
The wolves ran on through the evergreen forests,
The peasant river was untempted by the fashionable quays;
By mourning tongues
The death of the poet was kept from his poems.

But for him it was his last afternoon as himself,
An afternoon of nurses and rumors;
The provinces of his body revolted,
The squares of his mind were empty,
Silence invaded the suburbs,
The current of his feeling failed: he became his admirers.

Now he is scattered among a hundred cities
And wholly given over to unfamiliar affections;
To find his happiness in another kind of wood
And be punished under a foreign code of conscience.
The words of a dead man
Are modified in the guts of the living.

But in the importance and noise of tomorrow
When the brokers are roaring like beasts on the floor of the
Bourse,
And the poor have the sufferings to which they are fairly
accustomed,
And each in the cell of himself is almost convinced of his
freedom;
A few thousand will think of this day
As one thinks of a day when one did something slightly un-
usual.

O all the instruments agree
The day of his death was a dark cold day.

II

You were silly like us: your gift survived it all;
The parish of rich women, physical decay,
Yourself; mad Ireland hurt you into poetry.
Now Ireland has her madness and her weather still,
For poetry makes nothing happen: it survives
In the valley of its saying where executives
Would never want to tamper; it flows south
From ranches of isolation and the busy griefs,
Raw towns that we believe and die in; it survives,
A way of happening, a mouth.

III

Earth, receive an honored guest;
William Yeats is laid to rest:
Let the Irish vessel lie
Emptied of its poetry.

Time that is intolerant
Of the brave and innocent,
And indifferent in a week
To a beautiful physique,

Worships language and forgives
Everyone by whom it lives;
Pardons cowardice, conceit,
Lays its honors at their feet.

Time that with this strange excuse
Pardoned Kipling and his views,
And will pardon Paul Claudel,
Pardons him for writing well.

In the nightmare of the dark
All the dogs of Europe bark,
And the living nations wait,
Each sequestered in its hate;

Intellectual disgrace
Stares from every human face,
And the seas of pity lie
Locked and frozen in each eye.

Follow, poet, follow right
To the bottom of the night,
With your unconstraining voice
Still persuade us to rejoice;

With the farming of a verse
Make a vineyard of the curse,
Sing of human unsuccess
In a rapture of distress;

In the deserts of the heart
Let the healing fountain start,
In the prison of his days
Teach the free man how to praise.

September 1, 1939

I sit in one of the dives
On Fifty-Second Street
Uncertain and afraid
As the clever hopes expire
Of a low dishonest decade:
Waves of anger and fear
Circulate over the bright
And darkened lands of the earth,
Obsessing our private lives;
The unmentionable odour of death
Offends the September night.

Accurate scholarship can
Unearth the whole offence
From Luther until now
That has driven a culture mad,
Find what occurred at Linz,
What huge imago made
A psychopathic god:
I and the public know
What all schoolchildren learn,
Those to whom evil is done
Do evil in return.

Exiled Thucydides knew
All that a speech can say
About Democracy,

And what dictators do,
The elderly rubbish they talk
To an apathetic grave;
Analysed all in his book,
The enlightenment driven away,
The habit-forming pain,
Mismanagement and grief:
We must suffer them all again.

Into this neutral air
Where blind skyscrapers use
Their full height to proclaim
The strength of Collective Man,
Each language pours its vain
Competitive excuse:
But who can live for long
In an euphoric dream;
Out of the mirror they stare,
Imperialism's face
And the international wrong.

Faces along the bar
Cling to their average day:
The lights must never go out,
The music must always play,
All the conventions conspire
To make this fort assume
The furniture of home;
Lest we should see where we are,
Lost in a haunted wood,
Children afraid of the night
Who have never been happy or good.

The windiest militant trash
Important Persons shout
Is not so crude as our wish:
What mad Nijinsky wrote
About Diaghilev
Is true of the normal heart;
For the error bred in the bone
Of each woman and each man
Craves what it cannot have,
Not universal love
But to be loved alone.

From the conservative dark
Into the ethical life
The dense commuters come,
Repeating their morning vow;
"I *will* be true to the wife,
I'll concentrate more on my work,"
And helpless governors wake
To resume their compulsory game:
Who can release them now,
Who can reach the deaf,
Who can speak for the dumb?

All I have is a voice
To undo the folded lie,
The romantic lie in the brain
Of the sensual man-in-the-street
And the lie of Authority
Whose buildings grope the sky:
There is no such thing as the State
And no one exists alone;
Hunger allows no choice
To the citizen or the police;
We must love one another or die.

Defenceless under the night
Our world in stupor lies;
Yet, dotted everywhere,
Ironic points of light
Flash out wherever the Just
Exchange their messages:
May I, composed like them
Of Eros and of dust,
Beleaguered by the same
Negation and despair,
Show an affirming flame.

Mundus et Infans

Kicking his mother until she let go of his soul
Has given him a healthy appetite: clearly, her rôle
    In the New Order must be
To supply and deliver his raw materials free;
    Should there be any shortage

She will be held responsible; she also promises
To show him all such attentions as befit his age.
Having dictated peace,

With one fist clenched behind his head, heel drawn up to thigh,
The cocky little ogre dozes off, ready,
Though, to take on the rest
Of the world at the drop of a hat or the mildest
Nudge of the impossible,
Resolved, cost what it may, to seize supreme power, and
Sworn to resist tyranny to the death with all
Forces at his command.

A pantheist not a solipsist, he cooperates
With a universe of large and noisy feeling states,
Without troubling to place
Them anywhere special; for, to his eyes, Funny face
Or Elephant as yet
Mean nothing. His distinction between Me and Us
Is a matter of taste; his seasons are Dry and Wet;
He thinks as his mouth does.

Still, his loud iniquity is still what only the
Greatest of saints become—someone who does not lie:
He because he cannot
Stop the vivid present to think; they by having got
Past reflection into
A passionate obedience in time. We have our Boy-
Meets-Girl era of mirrors and muddle to work through
Without rest, without joy.

Therefore we love him because his judgments are so
Frankly subjective that his abuse carries no
Personal sting. We should
Never dare offer our helplessness as a good
Bargain, without at least
Promising to overcome a misfortune we blame
History or Banks or the Weather for; but this beast
Dares to exist without shame.

Let him praise his Creator with the top of his voice,
Then, and the motions of his bowels; let us rejoice
That he lets us hope, for
He may never become a fashionable or
Important personage.

However bad he may be, he has not yet gone mad;
Whoever we are now, we were no worse at his age:
So of course we ought to be glad

When he bawls the house down. Has he not a perfect right
To remind us at any moment how we quite
Rightly expect each other
To go upstairs or for a walk if we must cry over
Spilt milk, such as our wish
That since, apparently, we shall never be above
Either or both, we had never learned to distinguish
Between hunger and love?

Song: As I Walked Out One Evening

As I walked out one evening,
Walking down Bristol Street,
The crowds upon the pavement
Were fields of harvest wheat.

And down by the brimming river
I heard a lover sing
Under an arch of the railway:
"Love has no ending.

I'll love you, dear, I'll love you
Till China and Africa meet
And the river jumps over the mountain
And the salmon sing in the street.

I'll love you till the ocean
Is folded and hung up to dry
And the seven stars go squawking
Like geese about the sky.

The years shall run like rabbits
For in my arms I hold
The Flower of the Ages
And the first love of the world."

But all the clocks in the city
Began to whirr and chime:
"O let not Time deceive you,
You cannot conquer Time.

In the burrows of the Nightmare
  Where Justice naked is,
Time watches from the shadow
  And coughs when you would kiss.

In headaches and in worry
  Vaguely life leaks away,
And Time will have his fancy
  To-morrow or to-day.

Into many a green valley
  Drifts the appalling snow;
Time breaks the threaded dances
  And the diver's brilliant bow.

O plunge your hands in water,
  Plunge them in up to the wrist;
Stare, stare in the basin
  And wonder what you've missed.

The glacier knocks in the cupboard,
  The desert sighs in the bed,
And the crack in the tea-cup opens
  A lane to the land of the dead

Where the beggars raffle the banknotes
  And the Giant is enchanting to Jack,
And the Lily-white Boy is a Roarer
  And Jill goes down on her back.

O look, look in the mirror,
  O look in your distress;
Life remains a blessing
  Although you cannot bless.

O stand, stand at the window
  As the tears scald and start;
You shall love your crooked neighbour
  With your crooked heart."

It was late, late in the evening,
  The lovers they were gone;
The clocks had ceased their chiming
  And the deep river ran on.

Song: Fish in the Unruffled Lakes

Fish in the unruffled lakes
The swarming colors wear,
Swans in the winter air
A white perfection have,
And the great lion walks
Through his innocent grove;
Lion, fish, and swan
Act, and are gone
Upon Time's toppling wave.

We till shadowed days are done,
We must weep and sing
Duty's conscious wrong,
The Devil in the clock,
The Goodness carefully worn
For atonement or for luck;
We must lose our loves;
On each beast and bird that moves
Turn an envious look.

Sighs for folly said and done
Twist our narrow days;
But I must bless, I must praise
That you, my swan, who have
All gifts that to the swan
Impulsive Nature gave,
The majesty and pride,
Last night should add
Your voluntary love.

Under Which Lyre

A Reactionary Tract for the Times

Ares at last has quit the field,
The bloodstains on the bushes yield
To seeping showers.
And in their convalescent state
The fractured towns associate
With summer flowers.

Encamped upon the college plain
Raw veterans already train
        As freshman forces;
Instructors with sarcastic tongue
Shepherd the battle-weary young
        Through basic courses.

Among bewildering appliances
For mastering the arts and sciences
        They stroll or run,
And nerves that never flinched at slaughter
Are shot to pieces by the shorter
        Poems of Donne.

Professors back from secret missions
Resume their proper eruditions,
        Though some regret it;
They liked their dictaphones a lot,
They met some big wheels and do not
        Let you forget it.

But Zeus' inscrutable decree
Permits the will to disagree
        To be pandemic,
Ordains that vaudeville shall preach,
And every commencement speech
        Be a polemic.

Let Ares doze, that other war
Is instantly declared once more
        'Twixt those who follow
Precocious Hermes all the way
And those who without qualms obey
        Pompous Apollo.

Brutal like all Olympic games,
Though fought with smiles and Christian names
        And less dramatic,
This dialectic strife between
The civil gods is just as mean,
        And more fanatic.

What high immortals do in mirth
Is life and death on Middle Earth;
        Their a-historic

Antipathy forever gripes
All ages and somatic types:
The sophomoric

Who face the future's darkest hints
With giggles or with prairie squints
As stout as Cortez,
And those who like myself turn pale
As we approach with ragged sail
The fattening forties.

The sons of Hermes love to play,
And only do their best when they
Are told they oughtn't;
Apollo's children never shrink
From boring jobs but have to think
Their work important.

Related by antithesis,
A compromise between them is
Impossible;
Respect perhaps, but friendship never:
Falstaff the fool confronts forever
The prig Prince Hal.

So, standing here, surrounded by
The eyes of Miltons and the high
Foreheads of Shaws,
A Hermes man, I call on you,
Phi-Beta-Kappa brethren, to
Defend his cause.

If he would leave the self alone,
Apollo's welcome to the throne,
Fasces and falcons;
He loves to rule, has always done it:
The earth would soon, did Hermes run it,
Be like the Balkans.

But, jealous of our god of dreams,
His common sense in secret schemes
To rule the heart;
Unable to invent the lyre,
Creates with simulated fire
Official art.

And when he occupies a college,
Truth is replaced by Useful Knowledge;
He pays particular
Attention to Commercial Thought,
Public Relations, Hygiene, Sport,
In his curricula.

Athletic, extrovert and crude,
For him, to work in solitude
Is the offense,
The goal a populous Nirvana:
His shield bears this device: *Mens sana*
Qui mal y pense.

Today his arms, we must confess,
From Right to Left have met success,
His banners wave
From Yale to Princeton, and the news
From Broadway to the Book Reviews
Is very grave.

His radio Homers all day long
In over-Whitmanated song
That does not scan,
With adjectives laid end to end,
Extol the doughnut and commend
The Common Man.

His too each homely lyric thing
On sport or spousal love or spring
Or dogs or dusters,
Invented by some courthouse bard
For recitation by the yard
In filibusters.

To him ascend the prize orations
And sets of fugal variations
On some folk ballad,
While dietitians sacrifice
A glass of prune juice or a nice
Marshmallow salad.

Charged with his compound of sensational
Sex plus some undenominational
Religious matter,

Enormous novels by co-eds
Rain down on our defenseless heads
Till our teeth chatter.

In fake Hermetic uniforms
Behind our battle-line, in swarms
That keep alighting,
His existentialists declare
That they are in complete despair,
Yet go on writing.

No matter. He shall be defied.
We have the ladies on our side.
What though his threat
To organize us grow more critical?
Zeus willing, we, the unpolitical
Shall best him yet.

Lone scholars, sniping from the walls
Of learned periodicals,
Our facts defend,
Our intellectual marines,
Landing in Little Magazines,
Capture a trend.

By night our student Underground
At cocktail parties whisper round
From ear to ear;
Fat figures in the public eye
Collapse next morning, ambushed by
Some witty sneer.

In our morale must lie our strength:
So, that we may behold at length
Routed Apollo's
Battalions melt away like fog,
Keep well the Hermetic Decalogue,
Which runs as follows:

Thou shalt not do as the dean pleases,
Thou shalt not write thy doctor's thesis
On education,
Thou shalt not worship projects nor
Shalt thou or thine bow down before
Administration.

Thou shalt not answer questionnaires
Or quizzes upon World Affairs,
Nor with compliance
Take any test. Thou shalt not sit
With statisticians nor commit
A social science.

Thou shalt not be on friendly terms
With guys in advertising firms,
Nor speak with such
As read the Bible for its prose,
Nor, above all, make love to those
Who wash too much.

Thou shalt not live within thy means
Nor on plain water and raw greens.
If thou must choose
Between the chances, choose the odd;
Read the *New Yorker;* trust in God;
And take short views.

Musée des Beaux Arts

About suffering they were never wrong,
The Old Masters: how well they understood
Its human position; how it takes place
While someone else is eating or opening a window or just walking dully along;
How, when the aged are reverently, passionately waiting
For the miraculous birth, there always must be
Children who did not specially want it to happen, skating
On a pond at the edge of the wood:
They never forgot
That even the dreadful martyrdom must run its course
Anyhow in a corner, some untidy spot
Where the dogs go on with their doggy life and the torturer's horse
Scratches its innocent behind on a tree.

In Brueghel's *Icarus,* for instance: how everything turns away
Quite leisurely from the disaster; the ploughman may
Have heard the splash, the forsaken cry,
But for him it was not an important failure; the sun shone

As it had to on the white legs disappearing into the green
Water; and the expensive delicate ship that must have seen
Something amazing, a boy falling out of the sky,
Had somewhere to get to and sailed calmly on.

The Unknown Citizen

(To JS/07/M/378 This Marble Monument Is Erected
by the State)

He was found by the Bureau of Statistics to be
One against whom there was no official complaint,
And all the reports on his conduct agree
That, in the modern sense of an old-fashioned word, he was a saint,
For in everything he did he served the Greater Community.
Except for the War till the day he retired
He worked in a factory and never got fired,
But satisfied his employers, Fudge Motors Inc.
Yet he wasn't a scab or odd in his views,
For his Union reports that he paid his dues,
(Our report on his Union shows it was sound)
And our Social Psychology workers found
That he was popular with his mates and liked a drink.
The Press are convinced that he bought a paper every day
And that his reactions to advertisements were normal in every way.
Policies taken out in his name prove that he was fully insured,
And his Health-card shows he was once in hospital but left it cured.
Both Producers Research and High-Grade Living declare
He was fully sensible to the advantages of the Installment Plan
And had everything necessary to the Modern Man,
A phonograph, a radio, a car and a frigidaire.
Our researchers into Public Opinion are content
That he held the proper opinions for the time of year;
When there was peace, he was for peace; when there was war, he went.
He was married and added five children to the population,
Which our Eugenist says was the right number for a parent of his generation,
And our teachers report that he never interfered with their education.
Was he free? Was he happy? The question is absurd:
Had anything been wrong, we should certainly have heard.

After Christmas

(From "For the Time Being")

Well, so that is that. Now we must dismantle the tree,
Putting the decorations back into their cardboard boxes—
Some have got broken—and carrying them up to the attic.
The holly and the mistletoe must be taken down and burnt,
And the children got ready for school. There are enough
Left-overs to do, warmed-up, for the rest of the week—
Not that we have much appetite, having drunk such a lot,
Stayed up so late, attempted—quite unsuccessfully—
To love all of our relatives, and in general
Grossly overestimated our powers. Once again
As in previous years we have seen the actual Vision and failed
To do more than entertain it as an agreeable
Possibility, once again we have sent Him away,
Begging though to remain His disobedient servant,
The promising child who cannot keep His word for long.
The Christmas Feast is already a fading memory,
And already the mind begins to be vaguely aware
Of an unpleasant whiff of apprehension at the thought
Of Lent and Good Friday which cannot, after all, now
Be very far off. But, for the time being, here we all are,
Back in the moderate Aristotelian city
Of darning and the Eight-Fifteen, where Euclid's geometry
And Newton's mechanics would account for our experience,
And the kitchen table exists because I scrub it.
It seems to have shrunk during the holidays. The streets
Are much narrower than we remembered; we had forgotten
The office was as depressing as this. To those who have seen
The Child, however dimly, however incredulously,
The Time Being is, in a sense, the most trying time of all.
For the innocent children who whispered so excitedly
Outside the locked door where they knew the presents to be
Grew up when it opened. Now, recollecting that moment
We can repress the joy, but the guilt remains conscious;
Remembering the stable where for once in our lives
Everything became a You and nothing was an It.
And craving the sensation but ignoring the cause,
We look round for something, no matter what, to inhibit
Our self-reflection, and the obvious thing for that purpose
Would be some great suffering. So, once we have met the Son,
We are tempted ever after to pray to the Father;

"Lead us into temptation and evil for our sake."
They will come, all right, don't worry; probably in a form
That we do not expect, and certainly with a force
More dreadful than we can imagine. In the meantime
There are bills to be paid, machines to keep in repair,
Irregular verbs to learn, the Time Being to redeem
From insignificance. The happy morning is over,
The night of agony still to come; the time is noon:
When the Spirit must practise his scales of rejoicing
Without even a hostile audience, and the Soul endure
A silence that is neither for nor against her faith
That God's Will will be done, that, in spite of her prayers,
God will cheat no one, not even the world of its triumph.

In Praise of Limestone

If it form the one landscape that we the inconstant ones
    Are consistently homesick for, this is chiefly
Because it dissolves in water. Mark these rounded slopes
    With their surface fragrance of thyme and beneath
A secret system of caves and conduits; hear these springs
    That spurt out everywhere with a chuckle
Each filling a private pool for its fish and carving
    Its own little ravine whose cliffs entertain
The butterfly and the lizard; examine this region
    Of short distances and definite places:
What could be more like Mother or a fitter background
    For her son, for the nude young male who lounges
Against a rock displaying his dildo, never doubting
    That for all his faults he is loved, whose works are but
Extensions of his power to charm? From weathered outcrop
    To hill-top temple, from appearing waters to
Conspicuous fountains, from a wild to a formal vineyard,
    Are ingenious but short steps that a child's wish
To receive more attention than his brothers, whether
    By pleasing or teasing, can easily take.

Watch, then, the band of rivals as they climb up and down
    Their steep stone gennels in twos and threes, sometimes
Arm in arm, but never, thank God, in step; or engaged
    On the shady side of a square at midday in
Voluble discourse, knowing each other too well to think
    There are any important secrets, unable

To conceive a god whose temper-tantrums are moral
And not to be pacified by a clever line
Or a good lay: for, accustomed to a stone that responds,
They have never had to veil their faces in awe
Of a crater whose blazing fury could not be fixed;
Adjusted to the local needs of valleys
Where everything can be touched or reached by walking,
Their eyes have never looked into infinite space
Through the lattice-work of a nomad's comb; born lucky,
Their legs have never encountered the fungi
And insects of the jungle, the monstrous forms and lives
With which we have nothing, we like to hope, in common.
So, when one of them goes to the bad, the way his mind works
Remains comprehensible: to become a pimp
Or deal in fake jewelry or ruin a fine tenor voice
For effects that bring down the house could happen to all
But the best and the worst of us . . .
That is why, I suppose,
The best and worst never stayed here long but sought
Immoderate soils where the beauty was not so external,
The light less public and the meaning of life
Something more than a mad camp. "Come!" cried the granite wastes,
"How evasive is your humor, how accidental
Your kindest kiss, how permanent is death." (Saints-to-be
Slipped away sighing.) "Come!" purred the clays and gravels.
"On our plains there is room for armies to drill; rivers
Wait to be tamed and slaves to construct you a tomb
In the grand manner: soft as the earth is mankind and both
Need to be altered." (Intendant Caesars rose and
Left, slamming the door.) But the really reckless were fetched
By an older colder voice, the oceanic whisper:
"I am the solitude that asks and promises nothing;
That is how I shall set you free. There is no love;
There are only the various envies, all of them sad."

They were right, my dear, all those voices were right
And still are; this land is not the sweet home that it looks,
Nor its peace the historical calm of a site
Where something was settled once and for all: A backward
And dilapidated province, connected
To the big busy world by a tunnel, with a certain
Seedy appeal, is that all it is now? Not quite:

It has a worldly duty which in spite of itself
    It does not neglect, but calls into question
All the Great Powers assume; it disturbs our rights. The poet,
    Admired for his earnest habit of calling
The sun the sun, his mind Puzzle, is made uneasy
    By these solid statues which so obviously doubt
His antimythological myth; and these gamins,
    Pursuing the scientist down the tiled colonnade
With such lively offers, rebuke his concern for Nature's
    Remotest aspects: I, too, am reproached, for what
And how much you know. Not to lose time, not to get caught,
    Not to be left behind, not, please! to resemble
The beasts who repeat themselves, or a thing like water
    Or stone whose conduct can be predicted, these
Are our Common Prayer, whose greatest comfort is music
    Which can be made anywhere, is invisible,
And does not smell. In so far as we have to look forward
    To death as a fact, no doubt we are right: But if
Sins can be forgiven, if bodies rise from the dead,
    These modifications of matter into
Innocent athletes and gesticulating fountains,
    Made solely for pleasure, make a further point:
The blessed will not care what angle they are regarded from,
    Having nothing to hide. Dear, I know nothing of
Either, but when I try to imagine a faultless love
    Or the life to come, what I hear is the murmur
Of underground streams, what I see is a limestone landscape.

Kathleen Raine

1908-

Love Poem

Yours is the face that the earth turns to me,
Continuous beyond its human features lie
The mountain forms that rest against the sky.
With your eyes, the reflecting rainbow, the sun's light

Sees me; forest and flowers, bird and beast
Know and hold me forever in the world's thought,
Creation's deep untroubled retrospect.

When your hand touches mine, it is the earth
That takes me—the deep grass,
And rocks and rivers; the green graves,
And children still unborn, and ancestors,
In love passed down from hand to hand from God.
Your love comes from the creation of the world,
From those paternal fingers, streaming through the clouds
That break with light the surface of the sea.

Here, where I trace your body with my hand,
Love's presence has no end;
For these, your arms that hold me, are the world's.
In us, the continents, clouds and oceans meet
Our arbitrary selves, extensive with the night,
Lost, in the heart's worship, and the body's sleep.

The Still Pool

The still pool! Give here grace
Even of reflected trees, reflected stars, though these
That rest upon the water's quiet surface
Are not tangible leaves, are not uplifted skies.

Yet not unreal. Like painting and symphony
They draw their veil
Of true illusion, rainbow over the grey.

Quiet semblances. Real otherwise but not less than these
Sombre deep pools, where, like troubled thoughts
Inhabits the unsmiling water-life.

(Native to that state only—as to selves
Pains, lusts, pleasures, and desires—these die
Translated to the green earth and the open sky.)

Not to that under-world are the sky's stars native, nor its birds.
Nor the abundant trees, whose roots
Stir in the water's depths an impulse to ascend

Into those leaves and boughs, into those flowers
Out of an element whose nature is to fall
Yet, against nature, may in nature rise.

The pool holds their images; to weed and fish not real
They rest upon the surface, colour and form of things
True, though not here as they to themselves elsewhere are.

Air

Element that utters doves, angels and cleft flames,
The bees of Helicon and the cloudy houses,
Impulse of music and the world's equipoise,

Dancer that never wearies of the dance
That prints in the blown dust eternal wisdom
Or carves its abstract sculptures in the snow,
The wind unhindered passes beyond its trace.

But from a high fell on a summer day
Sometimes below you may see the air like water,
The dazzle of the light upon its waves,
The flow unbroken to the end of the world.

The bird of god descends between two moments
Like silence into music, opening a way through time.

Invocation of Death

Death, I repent
Of these hands and feet
That for forty years
Have been my own
And I repent
Of flesh and bone,
Of heart and liver,
Of hair and skin—
Rid me, death,
Of face and form,
Of all that I am.

And I repent
Of the forms of thought,

The habit of mind
And heart crippled
By long-spent pain,
The memory-traces
Faded and worn
Of vanished places
And human faces
Not rightly seen
Or understood,
Rid me, death,
Of the words I have used.

Not this or that
But all is amiss
That I have done,
And I have seen
Sin and sorrow
Befoul the world—
Release me, death,
Forgive, remove
From place and time
The trace of all
That I have been.

Stephen Spender

1909-

Farewell in a Dream

Now shout into my dream. These trumpets snored
Less golden by my side, when you were there . . .
It is no reason now to think me coward
That, being insulted by a gamekeeper,
I hung my head, or looked into the air:
Thrusting between the peaks without a word,
Buttressed against the winds, or like a sword,
Then you were undisputed conqueror.

But dragged into this nightmare symphony
Of drum and tempest surging in my head,
Faced by these symbols of reality
You showed as one most pitifully naked.
I hailed your earth. Salute my Hades too.
Since we must part, let's part as heroes do.

A Whim of Time

A whim of time, the general arbiter,
Proclaims the love instead of death of friends.
Under the domed sky and athletic sun
The three stand naked, the new, bronzed German,
The young communist and myself, being English.
Yet to unwind the traveled sphere ten years
And two take arms, spring to a ghostly posture:
Or else roll on the thing a further ten
And the poor clerk with world-offended eyes
Builds with red hands his heaven; makes our bones
A necessary scaffolding to peace.

Now I suppose that the once-envious dead
Have learnt a strict philosophy of clay
After these centuries, to haunt us no longer
In the churchyard, or at the end of the lane,
Or howling at the edge of the city
Beyond the last bean-rows, near the new factory.
Our fathers enemies, yet lives no feud
Of prompting Hamlet on the kitchen stair,
There falls no shade across our blank of peace
Being together struck across the path
Or taper finger threatening solitude.

Our father's misery, the dead man's mercy,
The cynic's mystery, weaves a philosophy—
That history of man traced purely from dust
Is lipping skulls on the revolving rim
Or posture of slavery with the granite head bowed:
These, risen a moment, joined or separate,
Fall heavily, then are always separate.
A stratum scarce reckoned by geologers,
Sod lifted, turned, slapped back again with spade.

What I Expected

What I expected was
Thunder, fighting,
Long struggles with men
And climbing.
After continual straining
I should grow strong;
Then the rocks would shake
And I should rest long.

What I had not foreseen
Was the gradual day
Weakening the will
Leaking the brightness away,
The lack of good to touch
The fading of body and soul
Like smoke before wind
Corrupt, unsubstantial.

The wearing of Time,
And the watching of cripples pass
With limbs shaped like questions
In their odd twist,
The pulverous grief
Melting the bones with pity,
The sick falling from earth–
These, I could not foresee.

For I had expected always
Some brightness to hold in trust,
Some final innocence
To save from dust;
That, hanging solid,
Would dangle through all
Like the created poem
Or the dazzling crystal.

The Prisoners

Far, far the least of all, in want,
Are these,
The prisoners
Turned massive with their vaults and dark with dark.

They raise no hands, which rest upon their knees,
But lean their solid eyes against the night,
Dimly they feel
Only the furniture they use in cells.

Their time is almost Death. The silted flow
Of years on years
Is marked by dawns
As faint as cracks on mud-flats of despair.

My pity moves amongst them like a breeze
On walls of stone
Fretting for summer leaves, or like a tune
On ears of stone.

Then, when I raise my hands to strike,
It is too late,
There are no chains that fall
Nor visionary liquid door
Melted with anger.

When have their lives been free from walls and dark
And airs that choke?
And where less prisoner to let my anger
Like a sun strike?

If I could follow them from room to womb
To plant some hope
Through the black silk of the big-bellied gown
There would I win.

No, no, no,
It is too late for anger,
Nothing prevails
But pity for the grief they cannot feel.

Winter Landscape

Come home with white gulls waving across gray
Fields. Evening. A daffodil West.
Somewhere in clefts of rock the birds hide, breast to breast.

I warm with fire. Curtain shrouds dying day.
Alone. By the glowing ember
I shut out the bleak-tombed evenings of November.

And breast to breast, those swans. Sheep huddle and press
Close. Each to each. Oh,
Is there no herd of men like beasts where man may go?

Come home at last; come, end of loneliness.
Sea. Evening. Daffodil West.
And our thin dying souls against Eternity pressed.

The Funeral

Death is another milestone on their way.
With laughter on their lips and with winds blowing round
them
They record simply
How this one excelled all others in making driving-belts.

This is festivity, it is the time of statistics
When they record what one unit contributed:
They are glad as they lay him back in the earth
And thank him for what he gave them.

They walk home remembering the straining red flags,
And with pennons of song still fluttering through their blood
They speak of the world-state
With its towns like brain-centers and its pulsing arteries.

They think how one life hums, revolves and toils,
One cog in a golden and singing hive:
Like spark from fire, its task happily achieved,
It falls away quietly.

No more are they haunted by the individual grief
Nor the crocodile tears of European genius,
The decline of a culture
Mourned by scholars who dream of the ghosts of Greek boys.

The Express

After the first powerful plain manifesto
The black statement of pistons, without more fuss
But gliding like a queen, she leaves the station.
Without bowing and with restrained unconcern
She passes the houses which humbly crowd outside,
The gasworks and at last the heavy page
Of death, printed by gravestones in the cemetery.
Beyond the town there lies the open country
Where, gathering speed, she acquires mystery,
The luminous self-possession of ships on ocean.
It is now she begins to sing—at first quite low
Then loud, and at last with a jazzy madness—
The song of her whistle screaming at curves,
Of deafening tunnels, brakes, innumerable bolts.
And always light, aerial, underneath
Goes the elate meter of her wheels.
Steaming through metal landscape on her lines
She plunges new eras of wild happiness
Where speed throws up strange shapes, broad curves
And parallels clean like the steel of guns.
At last, further than Edinburgh or Rome,
Beyond the crest of the world, she reaches night
Where only a low streamline brightness
Of phosphorus on the tossing hills is white.
Ah, like a comet through flames she moves entranced
Wrapt in her music no bird song, no, nor bough
Breaking with honey buds, shall ever equal.

The Landscape Near an Aerodrome

More beautiful and soft than any moth
With burring furred antennae feeling its huge path
Through dusk, the air-liner with shut-off engines
Glides over suburbs and the sleeves set trailing tall
To point the wind. Gently, broadly, she falls,
Scarcely disturbing charted currents of air.

Lulled by descent, the travelers across sea
And across feminine land indulging its easy limbs
In miles of softness, now let their eyes trained by watching
Penetrate through dusk the outskirts of this town
Here where industry shows a fraying edge.
Here they may see what is being done.

Beyond the winking masthead light
And the landing-ground, they observe the outposts
Of work: chimneys like lank black fingers
Or figures frightening and mad: and squat buildings
With their strange air behind trees, like women's faces
Shattered by grief. Here where few houses
Moan with faint light behind their blinds
They remark the unhomely sense of complaint, like a dog
Shut out and shivering at the foreign moon.

In the last sweep of love, they pass over fields
Behind the aerodrome, where boys play all day
Hacking dead grass: whose cries, like wild birds,
Settle upon the nearest roofs
But soon are hid under the loud city.

Then, as they land, they hear the tolling bell
Reaching across the landscape of hysteria
To where, larger than all the charcoaled batteries
And imaged towers against that dying sky,
Religion stands, the church blocking the sun.

An Elementary School Classroom in a Slum

Far far from gusty waves, these children's faces.
Like rootless weeds the torn hair round their paleness.
The tall girl with her weighed-down head. The paper-
seeming boy with rat's eyes. The stunted unlucky heir
Of twisted bones, reciting a father's gnarled disease,
His lesson from his desk. At back of the dim class
One unnoted, mild and young: his eyes live in a dream
Of squirrels' game, in tree room, other than this.

On sour cream walls, donations. Shakespeare's head
Cloudless at dawn, civilized dome riding all cities.
Belled, flowery, Tyrolese valley. Open-handed map
Awarding the world its world. And yet, for these

Children, these windows, not this world, are world,
Where all their future's painted with a fog,
A narrow street sealed in with a lead sky,
Far far from rivers, capes, and stars of words.

Surely Shakespeare is wicked, the map a bad example
With ships and sun and love tempting them to steal—
For lives that slyly turn in their cramped holes
From fog to endless night? On their slag heap, these children
Wear skins peeped through by bones, and spectacles of steel
With mended glass, like bottle bits in slag.
Tyrol is wicked; map's promising a fable:
All of their time and space are foggy slum,
So blot their maps with slums as big as doom.

Unless, governor, teacher, inspector, visitor,
This map becomes their window and these windows
That open on their lives like crouching tombs
Break, O break open, till they break the town
And show the children to the fields and all their world
Azure on their sands, to let their tongues
Run naked into books, the white and green leaves open
The history theirs whose language is the sun.

Mask

The face of the landscape is a mask
Of bone and iron lines where time
Has plowed its character.
I look and look to read a sign,
Through errors of light and eyes of water
Beneath the land's will, of a fear
And the memory of a struggle,
As man behind his mask still wears a child.

Not Palaces

Not palaces, an era's crown
Where the mind dreams, intrigues, rests;
The architectural gold-leaved flower
From people ordered like a single mind,
I build. This only what I tell:
It is too late for rare accumulation,

For family pride, for beauty's filtered dusts;
I say, stamping the words with emphasis,
Drink from here energy and only energy,
As from the electric charge of a battery,
To will this time's change.
Eye, gazelle, delicate wanderer,
Drinker of horizon's fluid line;
Ear that suspends on a chord
The spirit drinking timelessness;
Touch, love—all senses—
Leave your gardens, your singing feasts,
Your dreams of suns circling before our sun,
Of heaven after our world.
Instead, watch images of flashing brass
That strike the outward sense, the polished will,
Flag of our purpose which the wind engraves.
No spirit seek here rest. But this: No man
Shall hunger; Man shall spend equally.
Our goal which we compel: Man shall be man.

The program of the antique Satan
Bristling with guns on the indented page,
With battleship towering from hilly waves:
For what? Drive of a ruining purpose,
Destroying all but its age-long exploiters.
Our program like this, yet opposite:
Death to the killers, bringing light to life.

I Think Continually of Those

I think continually of those who were truly great.
Who, from the womb, remembered the soul's history
Through corridors of light where the hours are suns,
Endless and singing. Whose lovely ambition
Was that their lips, still touched with fire,
Should tell of the spirit clothed from head to foot in song.
And who hoarded from the spring branches
The desires falling across their bodies like blossoms.

What is precious is never to forget
The delight of the blood drawn from ageless springs
Breaking through rocks in worlds before our earth;
Never to deny its pleasure in the simple morning light,
Nor its grave evening demand for love;

Never to allow gradually the traffic to smother
With noise and fog the flowering of the spirit.

Near the snow, near the sun, in the highest fields
See how these names are fêted by the waving grass,
And by the streamers of white cloud,
And whispers of wind in the listening sky;
The names of those who in their lives fought for life,
Who wore at their hearts the fire's center.
Born of the sun they traveled a short while towards the sun,
And left the vivid air signed with their honor.

Sonnet: "You Were Born; Must Die"

You were born; must die; were loved; must love;
Born naked; were clothed; still naked walk
Under your clothes. Under your skin you move
Naked; naked under acts and talk.
  The miles and hours upon you feed.
They eat your eyes out with their distance
They eat your heart out with devouring need
They eat your death out with lost significance.
  There is one fate beneath those ignorances
Those flesh and bone parcels in which you're split
O thing of skin and words hanging on breath:
Harlequin skeleton, it
Strums on your gut such songs and merry dances
Of love, of loneliness, of life being death.

Judas Iscariot

The eyes of twenty centuries
Pursue me along corridors to where
I am painted at their ends on many walls.
  Ever-revolving futures recognize
This red hair and red beard, where I am seated
Within the dark cave of the feast of light.
  Out of my heart-shaped shadow I stretch my hand
Across the white table into the dish
But not to dip the bread. It is as though
The cloth on each side of one dove-bright face
Spread dazzling wings on which the apostles ride
Uplifting them into the vision

Where their eyes watch themselves enthroned.
  My russet hand across the dish
Plucks enviously against one feather
  —But still the rushing wings spurn me below!

  Saint Sebastian of wickedness
I stand: all eyes legitimate arrows piercing through
The darkness of my wickedness. They recognize
My halo hammered from thirty silver pieces
And the hemp rope around my neck
Soft as that spirit's hanging arms
When on my cheek he answered with the kiss
Which cuts for ever—
                My strange stigmata,
All love and hate, all fire and ice!

  But who betrayed whom? O you,
Whose light gaze forms the azure corridor
Through which those other pouring eyes
Arrow into me—answer! Who
Betrayed whom? Who had foreseen
All, from the first? Who read
In his mind's light from the first day
That the kingdom of heaven on earth must always
Reiterate the garden of Eden,
And each day's revolution be betrayed
Within man's heart each day?
                Who wrapped
The whispering serpent round the tree
And hung between the leaves the glittering purse
And trapped the fangs with God-appointed poison?
Who knew
I must betray the truth, and made the lie
Betray its truth in me?

  Those hypocrite eyes which aimed at you
Now aim at me. And yet, beyond this world
We are alone, eternal opposites,
Each turning on his pole of truth, your pole
Invisible light, and mine
Becoming what man is. We stare
Across two thousand years, and heaven, and hell,
Into each other's gaze.

Winter and Summer

Within my head, aches the perpetual winter
Of this violent time, where pleasures freeze.
My inner eye anticipates for ever
Looking through naked trees and running wheels
Onto a blank transparent sky
Leading to nothing; as though, through iron aims,
It was stared back at by the filmy surface
Of a lid covering its own despair.
Thus, when the summer breaks upon my face
With the outward shock of a green wave
Crested with leaves and creamy foam of flowers,
I think the luxurious lazy meadows
Are a deceiving canvas covering
With a balmy paint of leafy billows,
The furious volleys of charioteering power
Behind the sun, racing to destroy.
When under light lawns, heavy in their soil,
I hear the groaning of the wasted lives
Of those who revolve unreflecting wheels,
Alas, I prove that I am right,
For if my shadowed mind affirmed the light
It would return to those green, foolish years
When to live seemed to stand knee-deep in flowers:
There, winter was an indoor accident,
Where, with head pressed against the glass, I watched
The garden, falsified by snow,
Waiting to melt, and become real again.

Polar Exploration

Our single purpose was to walk through snow
With faces swung to their prodigious North
Like compass iron. As clerks in whited banks
With bird-claw pens column virgin paper,
To snow we added foot-prints.
Extensive whiteness drowned
All sense of space. We tramped through
Static, glaring days, Time's suspended blank.
That was in Spring and Autumn. Summer struck
Water over rocks, and half the world

Became a ship with a deep keel, the booming floes
And icebergs with their little birds:
Twittering Snow Bunting, Greenland Wheatear,
Red-throated Divers; imagine butterflies
Sulphurous cloudy yellow; glory of bees
That suck from saxifrage; crowberry,
Bilberry, cranberry, *Pyrola Uniflora.*
There followed Winter in a frozen hut
Warm enough at the kernel, but dare to sleep
With head against the wall—ice gummed my hair!
Hate Culver's loud breathing, despise Freeman's
Fidget for washing; love only the dogs
That whine for scraps, and scratch. Notice
How they run better (on short journeys) with a bitch.
In that, different from us.
Return, return, you warn. We do. There is
A network of railways, money, words, words, words.
Meals, papers, exchanges, debates,
Cinema, wireless: the worst is Marriage.
We cannot sleep. At night we watch
A speaking clearness through cloudy paranoia.
These questions are white rifts:—Was
Ice our anger transformed? The raw, the motionless
Skies, were these the Spirit's hunger?
The continual and hypnotized march through snow,
The dropping nights of precious extinction, were these
Only the wide inventions of the will,
The frozen will's evasion? If this exists
In us as madness here, as coldness
In these summer, civilized sheets: Is the North,
Over there, a tangible, real madness,
A glittering simpleton, one without towns,
Only with bears and fish, a staring eye,
A new and singular sex?

W. R. Rodgers

1909-

Neither Here nor There

In that land all Is and nothing's Ought;
No owners or notices, only birds;
No walls anywhere, only lean wire of words
Worming brokenly out from eaten thought;
No oats growing, only ankle-lace grass
Easing and not resenting the feet that pass;
No enormous beasts, only names of them;
No bones made, bans laid, or boons expected,
No contracts, entails, hereditaments,
Anything at all that might tie or hem.

In that land all's lackadaisical;
No lakes of coddled spawn, and no locked ponds
Of settled purpose, no netted fishes;
But only inkling streams and running fronds,
Fritillaried with dreams, weedy with wishes;
Nor arrogant talk is heard, haggling phrase,
But undertones, and hesitance, and haze;
On clear days mountains of meaning are seen
Humped high on the horizon; no one goes
To con their meaning, no one cares or knows.

In that land all's flat, indifferent; there
Is neither springing house nor hanging tent,
No aims are entertained, and nothing is meant,
For there are no ends and no trends, no roads,
Only follow your nose to anywhere.
No one is born there, no one stays or dies,
For it is a timeless land, it lies
Between the act and the attrition, it
Marks off bound from rebound, make from break, tit
From tat, also to-day from to-morrow.

No Cause there comes to term, but each departs
Elsewhere to whelp its deeds, expel its darts;
There are no homecomings, of course, no good-byes
In that land, neither yearning nor scorning,
Though at night there is the smell of morning.

Sing, Brothers, Sing!

In cinemas we sought
The syrupy event,
In morning paper bought
Our cosy sentiment.

We eyed shop-windows packed
With leisure gun and rod
For the fastidious act
Of poking fun like God.

Each evening to amuse,
The radio-cage unveiled,
To speak the shocking news
The parrot never failed,

Its insulated tones
Reporting perfectly
Alarming war-zones,
The usual perfidy.

The bright and mirror voice
Reviewed the scrimmages,
Deleting heat and noise
From all its images.

Each evening it drew
A round-robin applause,
For it confirmed anew
Our own and Nature's laws.

At our back-door we failed to hear
War's dust-bin chariot drawing near.

White Christmas

Punctually at Christmas the soft plush
Of sentiment snows down, embosoms all
The sharp and pointed shapes of venom, shawls
The hills and hides the shocking holes of this
Uneven world of want and wealth, cushions
With cosy wish like cotton-wool the cool
Arm's-length interstices of caste and class,
And into obese folds subtracts from sight
All truculent acts, bleeding the world white.

Punctually that glib pair, Peace and Goodwill,
Emerges royally to take the air,
Collect the bows, assimilate the smiles,
Of waiting men. It is a genial time;
Angels, like stalactites, descend from heaven;
Bishops distribute their own weight in words,
Congratulate the poor on Christlike lack;
And the member for the constituency
Feeds the five thousand, and has plenty back.

Punctually, to-night, in old stone circles
Of set reunion, families stiffly sit
And listen: this is the night and this the happy time
When the tinned milk of human kindness is
Upheld and holed by radio-appeal:
Hushed are hurrying heels on hard roads,
And every parlour's a pink pond of light
To the cold and travelling man going by
In the dark, without a bark or a bite.

But punctually to-morrow you will see
All this silent and dissembling world
Of stilted sentiment suddenly melt
Into mush and watery welter of words
Beneath the warm and moving traffic of
Feet and actual fact. Over the stark plain
The silted mill-chimneys once again spread
Their sackcloth and ashes, a flowing mane
Of repentance for the false day that's fled.

Christ Walking on the Water

Slowly, O so slowly, longing rose up
In the forenoon of his face, till only
A ringlet of fog lingered round his loins.
And fast he went down beaches all weeping
With weed, and waded out. Twelve tall waves,
Sequent and equated, hollowed and followed.
O what a cock-eyed sea he walked on,
What poke-end of foam, what elbowings
And lugubrious looks, what ebullient
And contumacious musics. Always there were
Hills and holes, pills and poles, a wavy wall
And bucking ribbon caterpillaring past
With glossy ease. And often, as he walked,
The slow curtains of swell swung open and showed,
Miles and smiles away, the bottle-boat
Flung on a wavering frond of froth that fell
Knee-deep and heaved thigh-high. In his forward face
No cave of afterthought opened; to his ear
No bottom clamour climbed up; nothing blinked.
For he was the horizon, he the hub,
Both bone and flesh, finger and ring of all
This clangorous sea. Docile, at his toe's touch
Each tottering dot stood roundaboutly calm
And jammed the following others fast as stone.
The ironical wave smoothed itself out
To meet him, and the mocking hollow
Hooped its back for his feet. A spine of light
Sniggered on the knobbly water, ahead.
But he like a lover, caught up,
Pushed past all wrigglings and remonstrances
And entered the rolling belly of the boat
That shuddered and lay still. And he lay there
Emptied of his errand, oozing still. Slowly
The misted mirror of his eyes grew clear
And cold, the bell of blood tolled lower,
And bright before his sight the ocean bared
And rolled its horrible bold eye-balls endlessly
In round rebuke. Looking over the edge
He shivered. Was this the way he had come?
Was that the one who came? The whole wieldy world
And all the welded welt that he had walked on

Burst like a plate into purposelessness.
All, all was gone, the fervour and the froth
Of confidence, and flat as water was
The sad and glassy round. Somewhere, then,
A tiny flute wriggled like a worm, O so lonely.
A ring of birds rose up and wound away
Into nothingness. Beyond himself he saw
The settled steeples, and breathing beaches
Running with people. But he,
He was custodian to nothing now,
And boneless as an empty sleeve hung down.
Down from crowned noon to cambered evening
He fell, fell, from white to amber, till night
Slid over him like an eyelid. And he,
His knees drawn up, his head dropped deep,
Curled like a question mark asleep.

George Barker

1913-

My Joy, My Jockey, My Gabriel

(First Cycle of Love Poems: V)

My joy, my jockey, my Gabriel
Who bares his horns above my sleep
Is sleeping now. And I shall keep him
In valley and on pinnacle
And marvellous in my tabernacle.

My peace is where his shoulder holds
My clouds among his skies of face;
His plenty is my peace, my peace:
And like a serpent by a boulder
His shade I rest in glory coiled.

Time will divide us and the sea
Wrings its sad hands all day between;

The autumn bring a change of scene.
But always and for ever he
At night will sleep and keep by me.

O Tender Under Her Right Breast

(Second Cycle of Love Poems: II)

O tender under her right breast
  Sleep at the waterfall
My daughter, my daughter, and be at rest
  As I at her left shall.

At night the pigeon in the eaves
  Leaves open its bright eye;
Nor will the Seven Sisters cease
  To watch you where you lie.

The pine like a father over your bed
  Will bend down from above
To lay in duty at your head
  The candles of its love.

And in their mothering embrace,
  Sleep on the Rockies' bosom;
The Okanogan Valley shall grace
  Canada round your cradle.

The silver spoon and the one-eyed man,
  The rabbit's foot and the clover,
Be at your bed from morning till
  As now, the day is over.

Shut the Seven Seas Against Us

(Third Cycle of Love Poems: II)

Shut the Seven Seas against us,
Close the five continents,
Set sepulchred the North Star
In a forsaken tense;
Lay every Sun and System
For ever away in bed,—
Nevertheless that day shall come
That resurrects the dead.

When sleepless the wakes, weeping,
Mourn life on every leaf,
And the Moon covers her eye over
Rather than see our grief;
When in their dreams the liars and
The loveless regret life,—
The dove that stirs in every storm
Shall arrive bright with olive.

Step, Primavera, from your bed,
Dazzling with existence;
Put the Sun and the Moon and the Systems right;
Hang heaven on circumstance:
Lean from all windows like waterfalls,
Look, Love, on us below:—
And so from their somnolence in sense
All things shall rise to you.

Satan Is on Your Tongue

(Secular Elegy: III)

Satan is on your tongue, sweet singer, with
Your eye on the income and the encomium,
Angels rhapsodize for and from their faith.
And in the studios of chromium
Lucifer seduces Orpheus with a myth.

But the principle of evil is not autonomous.
Like the liberty horse with a plume at a circus
Under the whipmaster it steps proud in its circles.
When I let slip an instant the whip of the will
All hell's scot-free with fire at the nostril.

Thus if the crux and judgment never is
Left to our own to do with as we will,
But the decision, like a master key, lies
Entirely in the higher hands that holds all—
How can we be as innocent as this?

Everything that is profound loves the mask,
Said the Dionysian who never wore one.
Thus our damnation and our condemnation,
Wiser than Nietzsche, never taking a risk,
Wears the face of a necessary satisfaction.

Not, Love, when we kiss do the archangels weep
For we are naked then wherever we are
Like tigers in the night. But in our sleep
The masks go down and the beast is bare:
It is not Love but double damnation there.

Marooned on the islands of pride, lonely
And mad on the pyramids of achievement,
Disillusioned in cathedrals of doxology,
The sad man senses this continual bereavement:
God has just died, and now there is only

Us. The gold bull with its horns of finances
Over the sensual mountains goes gallivanting
In glory: all night and all day it dances
Absurd and happy because nothing is wanting.
The sad man hides his grief in his five senses.

Boy with the marvellous silver fish at thigh,
Whom two hundred million could call Little Father
Spawning all Russia in a night, go gather
Kisses and rosebuds under the German sky:
Tomorrow they'll find the mess of blood and the feather.

O Golden Fleece

(Secular Elegy: VI)

O Golden Fleece she is where she lies tonight
Trammelled in her sheets like midsummer on a bed,
Kisses like moths flitter over her bright
Mouth, and as she turns her head,
All space moves over to give her beauty room.

Where her hand, like a bird on the branches of her arm,
Droops its wings over the bedside as she sleeps,
There the air perpetually stays warm
Since, nested, her hand rested there. And she keeps
Under her green thumb life like a growing poem.

My nine-tiered tigress in the cage of sex
I feed with meat that you tear from my side
Crowning your nine months with the paradox:
The love that kisses with a homicide
In robes of red generation resurrects.

The bride who rides the hymeneal waterfall
Spawning all possibles in her pools of surplus,
Whom the train rapes going into a tunnel,
The imperial multiplicator nothing can nonplus:
My mother Nature is the origin of it all.

At Pharaoh's Feast and in the family cupboard,
Gay corpse, bright skeleton, and the fly in amber,
She sits with her laws like antlers from her forehead
Enmeshing everyone, with flowers and thunder
Adorning the head that destiny never worried.

Verses for a First Birthday

Hang at my hand as I write now
My small one whom the dogs follow,
That, nuzzled in my stomach, dance
Like sea-lions with her innocence.

The roaring forties in the bed
Beat up disaster on her head,
And on the wall the calendar
Always enumerated War.

Thunder in the teacup and
Prognostications in the sand
Menaced her amusements with
The abracadabra of death.

She who kisses prettier than
Two breezes meeting round a fan
What shall she hold in her arms
But the catastrophes like lambs?

And when, among the temporal
Ruins of her landscape, shall
The giddygoat and Cupid chase
All but Disney from the place?

On the rag of a single summer
She dried all the tears of the future;
When the Winter made her grieve
The vernal equinox was up her sleeve.

Happily the unhappy shall lie down
By her, and bounty be her own
Bubble. The hitherto inconsolable
Find solace at her first syllable.

The dove, in its code of coos,
Will carry abroad her good news:
That it was Love, and not
Law kept the ark afloat.

For the desire, and the daughter,
And the dog chasing its tail,
Renew all things in Nature,
And Nature renews it all.

Sonnet to My Mother

Most near, most dear, most loved and most far,
Under the window where I often found her
Sitting as huge as Asia, seismic with laughter,
Gin and chicken helpless in her Irish hand,
Irresistible as Rabelais but most tender for
The lame dogs and hurt birds that surround her,—
She is a procession no one can follow after
But be like a little dog following a brass band.
She will not glance up at the bomber or condescend
To drop her gin and scuttle to a cellar,
But lean on the mahogany table like a mountain
Whom only faith can move, and so I send
O all my faith and all my love to tell her
That she will move from mourning into morning.

Dylan Thomas

1914-1953

When All My Five and Country Senses See

When all my five and country senses see,
The fingers will forget green thumbs and mark
How, through the halfmoon's vegetable eye,
Husk of young stars and handful zodiac,
Love in the frost is pared and wintered by,
The whispering ears will watch love drummed away
Down breeze and shell to a discordant beach,
And, lashed to syllables, the lynx tongue cry
That her fond wounds are mended bitterly.
My nostrils see her breath burn like a bush.

My one and noble heart has witnesses
In all love's countries, that will grope awake;
And when blind sleep drops on the spying senses,
The heart is sensual, though five eyes break.

Light Breaks Where No Sun Shines

Light breaks where no sun shines;
Where no sea runs, the waters of the heart
Push in their tides;
And, broken ghosts with glowworms in their heads,
The things of light
File through the flesh where no flesh decks the bones.

Dawn breaks behind the eyes;
From poles of skull and toe the windy blood
Slides like a sea;
Nor fenced, nor staked, the gushers of the sky
Spout to the rod
Divining in a smile the oil of tears.

Night in the sockets rounds,
Like some pitch moon, the limit of the globes;
Day lights the bone;
Where no cold is, the skinning gales unpin
The winter's robes;
The film of spring is hanging from the lids.

Light breaks on secret lots,
On tips of thought where thoughts smell in the rain;
When logics die,
The secret of the soil grows through the eye,
And blood jumps in the sun;
Above the waste allotments the dawn halts.

The Hand That Signed the Paper Felled a City

The hand that signed the paper felled a city;
Five sovereign fingers taxed the breath,
Doubled the globe of dead and halved a country;
These five kings did a king to death.

The mighty hand leads to a sloping shoulder,
The finger joints are cramped with chalk;
A goose's quill has put an end to murder
That put an end to talk.

The hand that signed the treaty bred a fever,
And famine grew, and locusts came;
Great is the hand that holds dominion over
Man by a scribbled name.

The five kings count the dead but do not soften
The crusted wound nor pat the brow;
A hand rules pity as a hand rules heaven;
Hands have no tears to flow.

The Force That Through the Green Fuse Drives

The force that through the green fuse drives the flower
Drives my green age; that blasts the roots of trees
Is my destroyer.
And I am dumb to tell the crooked rose
My youth is bent by the same wintry fever.

The force that drives the water through the rocks
Drives my red blood; that dries the mouthing streams
Turns mine to wax.
And I am dumb to mouth unto my veins
How at the mountain spring the same mouth sucks.

The hand that whirls the water in the pool
Stirs the quicksand; that ropes the blowing wind
Hauls my shroud sail.
And I am dumb to tell the hanging man
How of my clay is made the hangman's lime.

The lips of time leech to the fountain head;
Love drips and gathers, but the fallen blood
Shall calm her sores.
And I am dumb to tell a weather's wind
How time has ticked a heaven round the stars.

And I am dumb to tell the lover's tomb
How at my sheet goes the same crooked worm.

Two Sonnets

Altarwise by owl-light in the halfway-house
The gentleman lay graveward with his furies;
Abaddon in the hang-nail cracked from Adam,
And, from his fork, a dog among the fairies,
The atlas-eater with a jaw for news,
Bit out the mandrake with to-morrow's scream.
Then, penny-eyed, that gentleman of wounds,
Old cock from nowheres and the heaven's egg,
With bones unbuttoned to the halfway winds,
Hatched from the windy salvage on one leg,
Scraped at my cradle in a walking word
That night of time under the Christward shelter:
I am the long world's gentleman, he said,
And share my bed with Capricorn and Cancer.

Death is all metaphors, shape in one history;
The child that sucketh long is shooting up,
The planet-ducted pelican of circles
Weans on an artery the gender's strip;
Child of the short spark in a shapeless country
Soon sets alight a long stick from the cradle;

The horizontal cross-bones of Abaddon,
You by the cavern over the black stairs,
Rung bone and blade, the verticals of Adam,
And, manned by midnight, Jacob to the stars;
Hairs of your head, then said the hollow agent,
Are but the roots of nettles and of feathers
Over these groundworks thrusting through a pavement
And hemlock-headed in the wood of weathers.

The Hunchback in the Park

The hunchback in the park
A solitary mister
Propped between trees and water
From the opening of the garden lock
That let the trees and water enter
Until the Sunday sombre bell at dark,

Eating bread from a newspaper
Drinking water from the chained cup
That the children filled with gravel
In the fountain basin where I sailed my ship
Slept at night in a dog kennel
But nobody chained him up.

Like the park birds he came early
Like the water he sat down
And Mister they called hey Mister
The truant boys from the town
Running when he had heard them clearly
On out of sound

Past lake and rockery
Laughing when he shook his paper
Hunchbacked in mockery
Through the loud zoo of the willow groves
Dodging the park keeper
With his stick that picked up leaves.

And the old dog sleeper
Alone between nurses and swans
While the boys among willows
Made the tiger jump out of their eyes

To roar on the rockery stones
And the groves were blue with sailors

Made all day until bell time
A woman figure without fault
Straight as a young elm
Straight and tall from his crooked bones
That she might stand in the night
After the lock and chains

All night in the unmade park
After the railings and shrubberies
The birds the grass the trees the lake
Had followed the hunchback
And the wild boys innocent as strawberries
To his kennel in the dark.

And Death Shall Have No Dominion

And death shall have no dominion.
Dead men naked they shall be one
With the man in the wind and the west moon;
When their bones are picked clean and the clean bones gone,
They shall have stars at elbow and foot;
Though they go mad they shall be sane,
Though they sink through the sea they shall rise again;
Though lovers be lost love shall not;
And death shall have no dominion.

And death shall have no dominion.
Under the windings of the sea
They lying long shall not die windily;
Twisting on racks when sinews give way,
Strapped to a wheel, yet they shall not break;
Faith in their hands shall snap in two,
And the unicorn evils run them through;
Split all ends up they shan't crack;
And death shall have no dominion.

And death shall have no dominion.
No more may gulls cry at their ears
Or waves break loud on the seashores;
Where blew a flower may a flower no more

Lift its head to the blows of the rain;
Though they be mad and dead as nails,
Heads of the characters hammer through daisies;
Break in the sun till the sun breaks down,
And death shall have no dominion.

Especially When the October Wind

Especially when the October wind
With frosty fingers punishes my hair,
Caught by the crabbing sun I walk on fire
And cast a shadow crab upon the land,
By the sea's side, hearing the noise of birds,
Hearing the raven cough in winter sticks,
My busy heart who shudders as she talks
Sheds the syllabic blood and drains her words.

Shut, too, in a tower of words, I mark
On the horizon walking like the trees
The wordy shapes of women, and the rows
Of the star-gestured children in the park.
Some let me make you of the vowelled beeches,
Some of the oaken voices, from the roots
Of many a thorny shire tell you notes,
Some let me make you of the water's speeches.

Behind a pot of ferns the wagging clock
Tells me the hour's word, the neural meaning
Flies on the shafted disc, declaims the morning
And tells the windy weather in the cock.
Some let me make you of the meadow's signs;
The signal grass that tells me all I know
Breaks with the wormy winter through the eye.
Some let me tell you of the raven's sins.

Especially when the October wind
(Some let me make you of autumnal spells,
The spider-tongued, and the loud hill of Wales)
With fist of turnips punishes the land,
Some let me make you of the heartless words.
The heart is drained that, spelling in the scurry
Of chemic blood, warned of the coming fury.
By the sea's side hear the dark-vowelled birds.

After the Funeral (In Memory of Ann Jones)

After the funeral, mule praises, brays,
Windshake of sailshaped ears, muffle-toed tap
Tap happily of one peg in the thick
Grave's foot, blinds down the lids, the teeth in black,
The spittled eyes, the salt ponds in the sleeves,
Morning smack of the spade that wakes up sleep,
Shakes a desolate boy who slits his throat
In the dark of the coffin and sheds dry leaves,
That breaks one bone to light with a judgment clout,
After the feast of tear-stuffed time and thistles
In a room with a stuffed fox and a stale fern,
I stand, for this memorial's sake, alone
In the snivelling hours with dead, humped Ann
Whose hooded, fountain heart once fell in puddles
Round the parched worlds of Wales and drowned each sun
(Though this for her is a monstrous image blindly
Magnified out of praise; her death was a still drop;
She would not have me sinking in the holy
Flood of her heart's fame; she would lie dumb and deep
And need no druid of her broken body).
But I, Ann's bard on a raised hearth, call all
The seas to service that her wood-tongued virtue
Babble like a bellbuoy over the hymning heads,
Bow down the walls of the ferned and foxy woods
That her love sing and swing through a brown chapel,
Bless her bent spirit with four, crossing birds.
Her flesh was meek as milk, but this skyward statue
With the wild breast and blessed and giant skull
Is carved from her in a room with a wet window
In a fiercely mourning house in a crooked year.
I know her scrubbed and sour humble hands
Lie with religion in their cramp, her threadbare
Whisper in a damp word, her wits drilled hollow,
Her fist of a face died clenched on a round pain;
And sculptured Ann is seventy years of stone.
These cloud-sopped, marble hands, this monumental
Argument of the hewn voice, gesture and psalm
Storm me forever over her grave until
The stuffed lung of the fox twitch and cry Love
And the strutting fern lay seeds on the black sill.

Fern Hill

Now as I was young and easy under the apple boughs
About the lilting house and happy as the grass was green,
The night above the dingle starry,
Time let me hail and climb
Golden in the heydays of his eyes,
And honored among wagons I was prince of the apple towns
And once below a time I lordly had the trees and leaves
Trail with daisies and barley
Down the rivers of the windfall light.

And as I was green and carefree, famous among the barns
About the happy yard and singing as the farm was home,
In the sun that is young once only,
Time let me play and be
Golden in the mercy of his means,
And green and golden I was huntsman and herdsman, the calves
Sang to my horn, the foxes on the hills barked clear and cold,
And the sabbath rang slowly
In the pebbles of the holy streams.

All the sun long it was running, it was lovely, the hay-
Fields high as the house, the tunes from the chimneys, it was air
And playing, lovely and watery
And fire green as grass.
And nightly under the simple stars
As I rode to sleep the owls were bearing the farm away,
All the moon long I heard, blessed among stables, the nightjars
Flying with the ricks, and horses
Flashing into the dark.

And then to awake, and the farm, like a wanderer white
With the dew, come back, the cock on his shoulder: it was all
Shining, it was Adam and maiden,
The sky gathered again
And the sun grew round that very day.
So it must have been after the birth of the simple light
In the first, spinning place, the spellbound horses walking warm
Out of the whinnying green stable
On to the fields of praise.

And honored among foxes and pheasants by the gay house
Under the new made clouds and happy as the heart was long
In the sun born over and over,
I ran my heedless ways,
My wishes raced through the house-high hay
And nothing I cared, at my sky blue trades, that time allows
In all his tuneful turning so few and such morning songs
Before the children green and golden
Follow him out of grace.

Nothing I cared, in the lamb white days, that time would take
me
Up to the swallow-thronged loft by the shadow of my hand,
In the moon that is always rising,
Nor that riding to sleep
I should hear him fly with the high fields
And wake to the farm forever fled from the childless land.
Oh as I was young and easy in the mercy of his means,
Time held me green and dying
Though I sang in my chains like the sea.

A Refusal to Mourn the Death, by Fire, of a Child in London

Never until the mankind making
Bird beast and flower
Fathering and all humbling darkness
Tells with silence the last light breaking
And the still hour
Is come of the sea tumbling in harness

And I must enter again the round
Zion of the water bead
And the synagogue of the ear of corn
Shall I let pray the shadow of a sound
Or sow my salt seed
In the least valley of sackcloth to mourn

The majesty and burning of the child's death.
I shall not murder
The mankind of her going with a grave truth
Nor blaspheme down the stations of the breath
With any further
Elegy of innocence and youth.

Deep with the first dead lies London's daughter,
Robed in the long friends,
The grains beyond age, the dark veins of her mother,
Secret by the unmourning water
Of the riding Thames.
After the first death, there is no other.

Over Sir John's Hill

Over Sir John's hill,
The hawk on fire hangs still;
In a hoisted cloud, at drop of dusk, he pulls to his claws
And gallows, up the rays of his eyes the small birds of the bay
And the shrill child's play
Wars
Of the sparrows and such who swansing, dusk, in wrangling
hedges.
And blithely they squawk
To fiery tyburn over the wrestle of elms until
The flash the noosed hawk
Crashes, and slowly the fishing holy stalking heron
In the river Towy below bows his tilted headstone.

Flash, and the plumes crack,
And a black cap of jack-
Daws Sir John's just hill dons, and again the gulled birds hare
To the hawk on fire, the halter height, over Towy's fins,
In a whack of wind.
There
Where the elegiac fisherbird stabs and paddles
In the pebbly dab filled
Shallow and sedge, and "dilly dilly," calls the loft hawk,
"Come and be killed,"
I open the leaves of the water at a passage
Of psalms and shadows among the pincered sandcrabs prancing

And hear, in a shell,
Death clear as a buoy's bell:
All praise of the hawk on fire in hawk-eyed dusk be sung,
When his viperish fuse hangs looped with flames under the
brand
Wing, and blest shall
Young
Green chickens of the bay and bushes cluck, "dilly dilly,
Come let us die."

We grieve as the blithe birds, never again, leave shingle and elm,
The heron and I,
I young Aesop fabling to the near night by the dingle
Of eels, saint heron hymning in the shell-hung distant

Crystal harbour vale
Where the sea cobbles sail,
And wharves of water where the walls dance and the white cranes stilt.
It is the heron and I, under judging Sir John's elmed
Hill, tell-tale the knelled
Guilt
Of the led-astray birds whom God, for their breast of whistles,
Have mercy on,
God in his whirlwind silence save, who marks the sparrows hail,
For their souls' song.
Now the heron grieves in the weeded verge. Through windows
Of dusk and water I see the tilting whispering

Heron, mirrored, go,
As the snapt feathers snow,
Fishing in the tear of the Towy. Only a hoot owl
Hollows, a grassblade blown in cupped hands, in the looted elms
And no green cocks or hens
Shout
Now on Sir John's hill. The heron, ankling the scaly
Lowlands of the waves,
Makes all the music; and I who hear the tune of the slow,
Wear-willow river, grave,
Before the lunge of the night, the notes on this time-shaken
Stone for the sake of the souls of the slain birds sailing.

Twenty-Four Years

Twenty-four years remind the tears of my eyes.
(Bury the dead for fear that they walk to the grave in labour.)
In the groin of the natural doorway I crouched like a tailor
Sewing a shroud for a journey
By the light of the meat-eating sun.
Dressed to die, the sensual strut begun,
With my red veins full of money,
In the final direction of the elementary town
I advance for as long as forever is.

A Process in the Weather of the Heart

A process in the weather of the heart
Turns damp to dry; the golden shot
Storms in the freezing tomb.
A weather in the quarter of the veins
Turns night to day; blood in their suns
Lights up the living worm.

A process in the eye forewarns
The bones of blindness; and the womb
Drives in a death as life leaks out.

A darkness in the weather of the eye
Is half its light; the fathomed sea
Breaks on unangled land.
The seed that makes a forest of the loin
Forks half its fruit; and half drops down,
Slow in a sleeping wind.

A weather in the flesh and bone
Is damp and dry; the quick and dead
Move like two ghosts before the eye.

A process in the weather of the world
Turns ghost to ghost; each mothered child
Sits in their double shade.
A process blows the moon into the sun,
Pulls down the shabby curtains of the skin;
And the heart gives up its dead.

Do Not Go Gentle into That Good Night

Do not go gentle into that good night,
Old age should burn and rave at close of day;
Rage, rage against the dying of the light.

Though wise men at their end know dark is right,
Because their words had forked no lightning they
Do not go gentle into that good night.

Good men, the last wave by, crying how bright
Their frail deeds might have danced in a green bay,
Rage, rage against the dying of the light.

Wild men who caught and sang the sun in flight,
And learn, too late, they grieved it on its way,
Do not go gentle into that good night.

Grave men, near death, who see with blinding sight
Blind eyes could blaze like meteors and be gay,
Rage, rage against the dying of the light.

And you, my father, there on the sad height,
Curse, bless, me now with your fierce tears, I pray.
Do not go gentle into that good night.
Rage, rage against the dying of the light.

Henry Reed

1914-

Lessons of the War

NAMING OF PARTS

Today we have naming of parts. Yesterday,
We had daily cleaning. And tomorrow morning,
We shall have what to do after firing. But today,
Today we have naming of parts. Japonica
Glistens like coral in all of the neighbouring gardens,
And today we have naming of parts.

This is the lower sling swivel. And this
Is the upper sling swivel, whose use you will see,
When you are given your slings. And this is the piling swivel,
Which in your case you have not got. The branches
Hold in the gardens their silent, eloquent gestures,
Which in our case we have not got.

This is the safety-catch, which is always released
With an easy flick of the thumb. And please do not let me
See anyone using his finger. You can do it quite easy
If you have any strength in your thumb. The blossoms
Are fragile and motionless, never letting anyone see
 Any of them using their finger.

And this you can see is the bolt. The purpose of this
Is to open the breech, as you see. We can slide it
Rapidly backwards and forwards: we call this
Easing the spring. And rapidly backwards and forwards
The early bees are assaulting and fumbling the flowers:
 They call it easing the Spring.

They call it easing the Spring: it is perfectly easy
If you have any strength in your thumb: like the bolt,
And the breech, and the cocking-piece, and the point of balance,
Which in our case we have not got; and the almond-blossom
Silent in all of the gardens and the bees going backwards and forwards,
 For today we have naming of parts.

JUDGING DISTANCES

Not only how far away, but the way that you say it
Is very important. Perhaps you may never get
The knack of judging a distance, but at least you know
How to report on a landscape: the central sector,
The right of arc and that, which we had last Tuesday,
 And at least you know

That maps are of time, not place, so far as the army
Happens to be concerned—the reason being,
Is one which need not delay us. Again, you know
There are three kinds of tree, three only, the fir and the poplar,
And those which have bushy tops to; and lastly
 That things only seem to be things.

A barn is not called a barn, to put it more plainly,
Or a field in the distance, where sheep may be safely grazing.
You must never be over-sure. You must say, when reporting:
At five o'clock in the central sector is a dozen
Of what appear to be animals; whatever you do,
 Don't call the bleeders *sheep*.

I am sure that's quite clear; and suppose, for the sake of
example,
The one at the end, asleep, endeavors to tell us
What he sees over there to the west, and how far away,
After first having come to attention. There to the west,
On the fields of summer the sun and the shadows bestow
Vestments of purple and gold.

The still white dwellings are like a mirage in the heat,
And under the swaying elms a man and a woman
Lie gently together. Which is, perhaps, only to say
That there is a row of houses to the left of arc,
And that under some poplars a pair of what appear to be
humans
Appear to be loving.

Well that, for an answer, is what we might rightly call
Moderately satisfactory only, the reason being,
Is that two things have been omitted, and those are important.
The human beings, now: in what direction are they,
And how far away, would you say? And do not forget
There may be dead ground in between.

There may be dead ground in between; and I may not have got
The knack of judging a distance; I will only venture
A guess that perhaps between me and the apparent lovers,
(Who, incidentally, appear by now to have finished,)
At seven o'clock from the houses, is roughly a distance
Of about one year and a half.

Sailor's Harbor

My thoughts, like sailors becalmed in Cape Town harbor,
Await your return, like a favorable wind, or like
New tackle for the voyage, without which it is useless starting.
We watch the sea daily, finish our daily tasks
By ten in the morning, and with the day to waste,
Wander through the suburbs, with quiet thoughts of the
brothels,
And sometimes thoughts of the churches.

In the eating-houses we always contrive to get near to
The window, where we can keep an eye on the life-

Bearing sea. Suddenly a wind might blow, and we must not
miss
First sight of the waves as they darken with promise for us.
We have been here too long. We know the quays,
And the streets near the quays, more than should ever be
necessary.
When can we go on our way?

Certain we are of this, that when the wind comes,
It may be deceptive and sweet and finally blow
To shipwreck and ruin between here and the next port of call.
At all times we think of this. At last we have come to know
The marine charts can safely assure us of less and less
As we go farther south. So we cannot go out on the boulevards
Or climb Table Mountain,

Though if we had certainty, here there might be delight.
But all that is world in itself, the mountain, the streets,
The sand-dunes outside the town, we shyly and sadly return
from.
They are too much to bear. And our curiosity
Lies alone in the over-scrubbed decks and the polished brasses
(For we have to look trim in the port) and in
The high-piled ambiguous cargo.

Sidney Keyes

1922-1943

Greenwich Observatory

This onion-dome holds all intricacies
Of intellect and star-struck wisdom; so
Like Coleridge's head with multitudinous
Passages riddled, full of strange instruments
Unbalanced by a touch, this organism
From wires and dials spins introverted life.
It never looks, squat on its concrete shoulders,

Down at the river's swarming life, nor sees
Cranes' groping insect-like activity
Nor slow procession of funnels past the docks.
Turning its inner wheels, absorbed in problems
Of space and time, it never hears
Birds singing in the park or children's laughter.
Alive, but in another way, it broods
On this its Highgate, hypnotized
In lunar reverie and calculation.
Yet night awakes it; blind lids open
Leaden to look upon the moon:
A single goggling telescopic eye
Enfolds the spheric wonder of the sky.

The Gardener

If you will come on such a day
As this, between the pink and yellow lines
Of parrot-tulips, I will be your lover.
My boots flash as they beat the silly gravel.
O come, this is your day.

Were you to lay your hand like a veined leaf
Upon my square-cut hand, I would caress
The shape of it, and that would be enough.
I note the greenfly working on the rose.
Time slips between my fingers like a leaf.

Do you resemble the silent pale-eyed angels
That follow children? Is your face a flower?
The lovers and the beggars leave the park—
And still you will not come. The gates are closing.

O it is terrible to dream of angels.

Plowman

Time was I was a plowman driving
Hard furrows, never resting, under the moon
Or in the frostbound bright-eyed morning
Labouring still; my team sleek-hided
As mulberry leaves, my team my best delight
After the sidelong blade my hero.

My iron-shod horses, my heroic walkers.
Now all that's finished. Rain's fallen now
Smudging my furrows, the comfortable
Elms are windpicked and harbour now no singer
Or southward homing bird; my horses grazing
Impossible mountain-sides, long-frogged and lonely.
And I'm gone on the roads, a peevish man
Contending with the landscape, arguing
With shrike and shrewmouse and my face in puddles;
A tiresome man not listened to nor housed
By the wise housewife, not kissed nor handled
By any but wild weeds and summer winds.
Time was I was a fine strong fellow
Followed by girls. Now I keep company
Only with seasons and the cold crazy moon.

Rome Remember

The bright waves scour the wound of Carthage.
The shadows of gulls run spiderlike through Carthage.
The cohorts of the sand are wearing Carthage
Hollow and desolate as a turning wave;
But the bronze eagle has flown east from Rome.

Rome remember, remember the seafowls' sermon
That followed the beaked ships westward to their triumph.
O Rome, you city of soldiers, remember the singers
That cry with dead voices along the African shore.

Rome remember, the courts of learning are tiled
With figures from the east like running nooses.
The desolate bodies of boys in the blue glare
Of falling torches cannot stir your passion.
Remember the Greeks who measured out your doom.
Remember the soft funereal Etruscans.

O when the rain beats with a sound like bells
Upon your bronze-faced monuments, remember
This European fretful-fingered rain
Will turn to swords in the hand of Europe's anger.
Remember the Nordic snarl and the African sorrow.

The bronze wolf howls when the moon turns red.
The trolls are massing for their last assault.

Your dreams are full of claws and scaly faces
And the Gothic arrow is pointed at your heart.

Rome remember your birth in Trojan chaos.
O think how savage will be your last lamenters:
How alien the lovers of your ghost.

Neutrality

Here not the flags, the rhythmic
Feet of returning legions; nor at household shrines
The small tears' offering, the postcards
Treasured for years, nor the names cut in brass.
Here not the lowered voices.
Not the drum.

Only at suppertime, rain slanting
Among our orchards, printing its coded
But peaceful messages across our pavements.
Only the cryptic swift performing
His ordered evolutions through our sky.
Only the growing.

And in the night, the secret voices
Of summer, the progression
Of hours without suspense, without surprise.
Only the moon beholds us, even the hunting owl
May watch us without malice.
Without envy.

We are no cowards, we are pictures
Of ordinary people, as you once were.
Blame not nor pity us; we are the people
Who laugh in dreams before the ramping boar
Appears, before the loved one's death.
We are your hope.

INDEX OF TITLES AND AUTHORS

G 2
H 3
I 4
J 5
K 6
L 7
M 8
N 9
O 0
P 1